Annual Cookbook Has a Year's Worth Of Great Eating—504 Recipes in All!

YEAR AFTER YEAR, *Taste of Home* dishes out the best down-home food shared by wonderful cooks from around the country—that's what makes it America's No. 1 cooking magazine...and what makes our annual cookbooks a yearly "must-have" as well.

This *2005 Taste of Home Annual Recipes* cookbook contains every single delicious recipe published during 2004, plus 18 "bonus" recipes—504 recipes in all—so you have a year's worth of great eating in one convenient recipe collection!

Whether you're fixing dinner for your family, cooking for a holiday crowd or simply whipping up something for yourself, you'll have plenty of fitting recipes from which to choose. To get you started, take a peak at the winners of our six national recipe contests held last year.

• Christmas Cookies. The holidays wouldn't be complete without cookies, and everyone has tried-and-true favorites that have become Yuletide traditions. Almond Sugar Cookies (p. 100) stood out on our contest's cookie tray, winning the top prize. Peanut Butter Christmas Mice (p. 110) scampered away with second place.

• Cooking for Two. Good things come in small packages, as lovely Pineapple-Stuffed Cornish Hens (p. 182) and Rustic Fruit Tart (p. 183) deliciously prove! So treat yourself and a loved one to these perfect-for-a-pair dishes that won first- and second-place honors.

• Garden-Fresh Asparagus. Nothing says "spring" quite like the arrival of asparagus. From a crop of savory springtime fare, Asparagus Sausage Crepes (p. 87) was picked the best of the bunch, and Lime Shrimp with Asparagus (p. 69) came in a close second.

• Ice Cream Social. When you crave something sweet to beat the heat, dip into a cool dish of refreshing homemade ice cream. Contest-winner Strawberry Cheesecake Ice Cream (p. 151) would taste even more scrumptious topped with second-place finisher Rich Hot Fudge Sauce (p. 141).

• Savory Squash. When the gardening season's in bloom, squash is at a surplus, so it was no surprise a bounty of recipes came rolling in to our Test Kitchen. Butternut Cream Pie (p. 120) won our home economists' approval as well as the grand

prize. With zesty south-of-the-border taste, Spicy Zucchini Quesadillas (p. 79) placed second.

• The Best Beef. Beefed-up menus are especially welcome when cooler fall and winter months build up hearty appetites. Curried Beef with Dumplings (p. 74) was rounded up out of the herd of finalists, winning the blue ribbon. Second prize went to Colony Mountain Chili (p. 45), which warms you from the inside out.

With 504 recipes in this colorful big cookbook, you won't run out of choices any time soon. You're sure to find something for everyone and every occasion.

GRAB A SPOON! Strawberry Cheesecake Ice Cream (p. 151) won the grand prize and Rich Hot Fudge Sauce (p. 141) took second place in our national "Ice Cream Social" contest.

2005 Taste of Home Annual Recipes

Editor: Jean Steiner
Art Director: Lori Arndt
Food Editor: Janaan Cunningham
Associate Editors: Beth Wittlinger,
Heidi Reuter Lloyd
Associate Art Director: Nicholas Mork

Taste of Home®

Executive Editor: Kathy Pohl
Food Editor: Janaan Cunningham
Associate Food Editor: Diane Werner RD
Managing Editor: Ann Kaiser
Assistant Managing Editor: Barbara Schuetz
Art Director: Emma Acevedo
Copy Editor: S.K. Enk
Senior Recipe Editor: Sue A. Jurack
Test Kitchen Director: Karen Johnson
Senior Home Economist: Patricia Schmeling
Test Kitchen Home Economists: Tamra Duncan,
Sue Draheim, Mark Morgan RD, Karen Wright
Test Kitchen Assistants: Kris Lehman,
Megan Taylor
Editorial Assistants: Barb Czysz,
Mary Ann Koebernik
Food Stylists: Joylyn Trickel, Kristin Arnett
Food Photographers: Rob Hagen, Dan Roberts
Senior Food Photography Artist:
Stephanie Marchese
Food Photography Artist: Julie Ferron
Photo Studio Manager: Anne Schimmel
Graphic Art Associates: Ellen Lloyd,
Catherine Fletcher
Chairman and Founder: Roy Reiman
President: Barbara Newton

Taste of Home Books
©2004 Reiman Media Group, Inc.
5400 S. 60th St., Greendale WI 53129

International Standard Book Number:
0-89821-417-3
International Standard Serial Number:
1094-3463

PICTURED AT RIGHT. Clockwise from upper left: Pork Roast Supper (p. 85); Meringue Ice Cream Torte (p. 135); Cranberry Feta Pinwheels (p. 7); Asparagus Leek Chowder (p. 47); and Sausage Pasta Sauce, Fruited Floret Salad, Italian Sweet Bread and Chippy Blond Brownies (p. 166-167).

Taste of Home 2005
Annual Recipes

PICTURED ON FRONT COVER. From top: Chocolate Pecan Ice Cream Torte (p. 147), Golden Baked Chicken (p. 156) and Warm Asparagus Spinach Salad (p. 31).

PICTURED ON BACK COVER. From top: Ladyfinger Lemon Torte (p. 130), Lemon Cream Puffs (p. 143), Frozen Lemon Yogurt (p. 141) and Buttermilk Lemon Pie (p. 124).

FOR ADDITIONAL COPIES of this book, write *Taste of Home* Books, P.O.. Box 908, Greendale WI 53129.

To order by credit card, call toll-free 1-800/344-2560 or visit our Web site at www.reimanpub.com.

Snacks & Beverages

Whether you're having a get-together or simply hungry for an afternoon "nibble", these appealing snacks and beverages will satisfy appetites.

— 🍴🍴🍴 —

TASTY TIDBITS. Clockwise from upper left: Tomato Focaccia (p. 16), Trout-Stuffed Red Potatoes (p. 12), Shrimp Tartlets (p. 7), Sparkling Rhubarb Spritzer (p. 19) and Grilled Corn Salsa (p. 6).

Mushroom Puffs

(Pictured below)

You can make these attractive appetizers in a jiffy with refrigerated crescent roll dough. The tasty little spirals disappear fast at a holiday party!
—Marilin Rosborough, Altoona, Pennsylvania

☑ Uses less fat, sugar or salt. Includes Nutritional Analysis and Diabetic Exchanges.

- 4 ounces cream cheese, cubed
- 1 can (4 ounces) mushroom stems and pieces, drained
- 1 tablespoon chopped onion
- 1/8 teaspoon hot pepper sauce
- 1 tube (8 ounces) crescent roll dough

In a blender or food processor, combine cream cheese, mushrooms, onion and hot pepper sauce; cover and process until blended.

Unroll crescent dough; separate into four rectangles. Press perforations to seal. Spread mushroom mixture over dough. Roll up jelly-roll style, starting with a long side. Cut each roll into five slices; place on an ungreased baking sheet. Bake at 425° for 8-10 minutes or until puffed and golden brown. **Yield:** 20 appetizers.

Nutritional Analysis: One piece (prepared with reduced-fat cream cheese) equals 54 calories, 3 g fat (1 g saturated fat), 2 mg cholesterol, 132 mg sodium, 5 g carbohydrate, trace fiber, 2 g protein. **Diabetic Exchanges:** 1 vegetable, 1/2 fat.

Grilled Corn Salsa

(Pictured on page 4)

Lime juice lends a tartness to this colorful salsa—a zippy mixture of fresh corn, sweet red pepper, red onion and jalapeno peppers. With its great grilled flavor, this chunky dip is perfect for summer gatherings and backyard patio parties. *—Lorie Fiock, Warren, Indiana*

☑ Uses less fat, sugar or salt. Includes Nutritional Analysis and Diabetic Exchanges.

- 6 ears fresh corn
- 1 large sweet red pepper, quartered and seeded
- 3 teaspoons canola oil, *divided*
- 1/2 cup finely chopped red onion
- 2 medium jalapeno peppers, seeded and chopped*
- 1/4 cup lime juice
- 1/4 teaspoon salt

Baked tortilla chips

Brush corn and red pepper with 2 teaspoons oil. Coat grill rack with nonstick cooking spray before starting the grill. Prepare grill for indirect heat. Grill corn, covered, over indirect medium heat for 20-25 minutes or until tender, turning often. Grill red pepper over indirect medium heat for 5 minutes on each side. Cool.

Cut the corn from the cobs and dice the red pepper; place in a bowl. Add the onion, jalapeno peppers, lime juice, salt and the remaining oil and toss to coat. Serve with tortilla chips. **Yield:** 3 cups.

Nutritional Analysis: One 1/4-cup serving (calculated without tortilla chips) equals 61 calories, 2 g fat (trace saturated fat), 0 cholesterol, 56 mg sodium, 12 g carbohydrate, 2 g fiber, 2 g protein. **Diabetic Exchanges:** 1 vegetable, 1/2 starch.

***Editor's Note:** When cutting or seeding hot peppers, use rubber or plastic gloves to protect your hands. Avoid touching your face.

Sugar Spiced Almonds

These zippy almonds are spicy yet sweet, and once you start eating them, you can't stop. The recipe also works well with pecans and cashews with equally delicious results. *—Sherri Jackson Chillicothe, Ohio*

- 1/4 cup sugar
- 2 tablespoons vegetable oil
- 1 teaspoon cayenne pepper
- 1/2 teaspoon garlic salt

1/2 teaspoon chili powder
1/4 teaspoon crushed red pepper flakes
2 cups unblanched whole almonds

In a bowl, combine the first six ingredients. Add almonds; toss to coat. Spread into a greased 15-in. x 10-in. x 1-in. baking pan. Bake at 250° for 30 minutes or until lightly browned, stirring occasionally. Cool. Store in an airtight container. **Yield:** 2 cups.

Cranberry Feta Pinwheels

(Pictured at right)

These pretty pinwheels will disappear so fast, it will make your head spin! The dried cranberries and chopped green onions make these perfect for a Christmas buffet. —Joyce Benninger, Owen Sound, Ontario

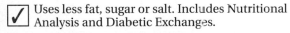 Uses less fat, sugar or salt. Includes Nutritional Analysis and Diabetic Exchanges.

1 carton (8 ounces) whipped cream cheese, softened
1 cup (8 ounces) crumbled feta cheese
1/4 cup chopped green onions
1 package (6 ounces) dried cranberries
4 flour tortillas (10 inches)

In a small bowl, combine the cream cheese, feta cheese and onions. Stir in cranberries. Spread about 1/2 cup mixture over each tortilla and roll up tightly. Wrap with plastic wrap and refrigerate for at least 1 hour. Cut each roll-up into 10 slices. **Yield:** 40 appetizers.

Nutritional Analysis: One serving (two pinwheels prepared with reduced-fat cream cheese) equals 97 calories, 4 g fat (2 g saturated fat), 12 mg cholesterol, 183 mg sodium, 13 g carbohydrate, 1 g fiber, 2 g protein. **Diabetic Exchanges:** 1 starch, 1/2 fat.

Shrimp Tartlets

(Pictured on page 4)

Here in the Southwest, anything with green chilies is sure to please. And these shrimp-and-cheese appetizers are no exception. You can alter the amount of chilies according to your taste. —Terry Thompson Albuquerque, New Mexico

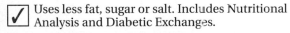 Uses less fat, sugar or salt. Includes Nutritional Analysis and Diabetic Exchanges.

18 slices white bread
Refrigerated butter-flavored spray

FILLING:
1 cup (4 ounces) shredded part-skim mozzarella cheese
1/4 cup canned chopped green chilies
1/4 cup diced cooked shrimp
1 green onion, thinly sliced
18 whole small cooked shrimp
Paprika

With a rolling pin, flatten bread to 1/8-in. thickness. Using a 2-1/2-in. biscuit cutter, cut out a circle from each slice. (Save scraps for another use.) Spritz both sides of circles with butter-flavored spray. Press into ungreased miniature muffin cups. Bake at 400° for 8-10 minutes or until lightly browned.

Combine the cheese, chilies, diced shrimp and onion; spoon into cups. Top with whole shrimp and paprika. Broil 5-6 in. from the heat for 2-4 minutes or until golden brown. Serve immediately. **Yield:** 1-1/2 dozen.

Nutritional Analysis: One tartlet equals 60 calories, 2 g fat (1 g saturated fat), 17 mg cholesterol, 168 mg sodium, 7 g carbohydrate, trace fiber, 4 g protein. **Diabetic Exchanges:** 1/2 starch, 1/2 meat.

Editor's Note: This recipe was tested with Pepperidge Farm bread and I Can't Believe It's Not Butter! spray.

Microwave the reserved syrup for 20 seconds or until melted. Cut the rounded ends from two candy canes (save rounded ends for another use). For runners, attach a whole candy cane and a straight candy cane piece with syrup to the bottom of each long side of sleigh.

For holly garnish, flatten gumdrops between waxed paper; cut each into three leaf shapes. Attach leaves and red-hot candies with syrup to each side. Fill sleigh with mint candies. **Yield:** 1 sleigh.

Editor's Note: We recommend that you test your candy thermometer before each use by bringing water to a boil; the thermometer should read 212°. Adjust your recipe temperature up or down based on your test.

Popcorn Sleigh

(Pictured above)

I am a candy maker who gets wrapped up in Christmas. For many years, I have given away my sweet treats in a popcorn sleigh. It's easy to do…and makes a fun, edible centerpiece, too. Just add a few candles and sprigs of pine to help set a festive scene.
—*Donna Torres, Grand Rapids, Minnesota*

      1/2 cup sugar
      1/2 cup light corn syrup
      1/4 cup water
         1 tablespoon butter
         4 drops green food coloring
         2 quarts popped popcorn
         4 candy canes
         2 large green gumdrops
         6 red-hot candies
  Assorted wrapped peppermint candies

In a large saucepan, combine the sugar, corn syrup and water. Bring to a boil; cook without stirring until a candy thermometer reaches 250° (firm-ball stage). Remove from the heat; add the butter and food coloring. Set aside 2 tablespoons. Place the popcorn in a large bowl; drizzle with remaining syrup. Stir until well coated.

For sleigh, press popcorn mixture onto the bottom and all the way up the sides of a greased 8-in. x 4-in. x 2-in. loaf pan, forming a 1-in.-thick shell. Beginning 3 in. from one corner, remove a small amount of popcorn mixture from a long side, so side tapers toward front end, as shown in photo above. Repeat on the other side. Remove from the pan. Curve the sleigh front toward the back.

Jalapeno Quail Appetizers

My husband quail-hunts every season, and this recipe has become our favorite way to serve the birds. The bacon keeps the meat from drying out, and the jalapeno lends a little zip.
—*Dianna Johnston*
Kingston, Oklahoma

      2 large jalapeno peppers, halved lengthwise and seeded*
     12 boneless quail breasts (about 1 pound)
     12 bacon strips
      1 bottle (16 ounces) Italian salad dressing

Cut each jalapeno half into three long strips. Place a strip widthwise in the center of each quail breast; roll up from a short side. Wrap each with a bacon strip and secure with toothpicks. Place in a large resealable plastic bag. Add salad dressing; seal bag and turn to coat. Refrigerate for 8 hours or overnight.

Drain and discard marinade. Grill appetizers, covered, over indirect medium heat for 16-20 minutes or until quail juices run clear and bacon is crisp, turning occasionally. **Yield:** 1 dozen.

*Editor's Note: When cutting or seeding hot peppers, use rubber or plastic gloves to protect your hands. Avoid touching your face.

Hot Cheese Dunk

This is a fun and economical fondue, made with dry milk powder, cheese, chicken bouillon and garlic. It's a great dipper for veggies, pretzels and crackers.
—*Sharon Mensing, Greenfield, Iowa*

1/2 cup nonfat dry milk powder
1-1/4 cups water
1/2 cup finely chopped onion
1 garlic clove, minced
3 tablespoons butter, cubed
3 tablespoons all-purpose flour
1 teaspoon chicken bouillon granules
1/8 teaspoon hot pepper sauce
1-1/2 cups (6 ounces) shredded Swiss *or* American cheese
1/3 cup grated Parmesan cheese
Assorted vegetables *or* bread cubes

In a bowl, combine the milk powder and water; set aside. In a skillet, saute the onion and garlic in butter until tender. Stir in flour and bouillon until blended. Add the pepper sauce and reserved milk; stir until thickened. Stir in cheeses until melted. Serve warm with vegetables or bread cubes. **Yield:** 2 cups.

Saucy Cherry Meatballs

Water chestnuts lend a crunch to these moist ground beef and pork sausage meatballs. The baked bites are glazed with a sweet sauce made with cherry pie filling. They're perfect for potlucks or parties.
—*Marina Castle-Henry, Burbank, California*

1/2 cup milk
1 tablespoon soy sauce
7 slices bread, crusts removed and cut into 1/2-inch cubes
1 teaspoon garlic salt
1/4 teaspoon onion powder
1/2 pound lean ground beef
1/2 pound bulk pork sausage
1 can (8 ounces) water chestnuts, drained and chopped
CHERRY SAUCE:
1 can (21 ounces) cherry pie filling
1/3 cup apple juice
1/4 cup cider vinegar
1/4 cup steak sauce
2 tablespoons brown sugar
2 tablespoons soy sauce

In a bowl, combine the milk, soy sauce, bread cubes, garlic salt and onion powder. Crumble beef and sausage over mixture and mix well. Stir in water chestnuts.

Shape into 1-in. balls. Line a 15-in. x 10-in. x 1-in. baking pan with foil; place meatballs in pan. Broil 4-6 in. from the heat for 10 minutes or until meat is no longer pink; drain.

In a large skillet, combine the sauce ingredients.

Bring to a boil. Reduce heat; simmer, uncovered, until thickened. Add meatballs; cook and stir until heated through. **Yield:** about 4 dozen.

Asparagus Ham Spirals
(Pictured below)

These appealing appetizers are sure to be a hit at your next party. People will think you really fussed with these yummy bites!
—*Linda Fischer*
Stuttgart, Arkansas

8 fresh asparagus spears, trimmed
1 tube (8 ounces) refrigerated crescent rolls
1 carton (8 ounces) spreadable chive-and-onion cream cheese
4 thin rectangular slices deli ham
2 tablespoons butter, melted
1/4 teaspoon garlic powder

Place asparagus in a skillet; add 1/2 in. of water. Bring to a boil. Reduce heat; cover and simmer for 3-5 minutes or until crisp-tender. Drain and set aside.

Separate crescent dough into four rectangles; seal perforations. Spread cream cheese over each rectangle to within 1/4 in. of edges. Top each with ham, leaving 1/4 in. uncovered on one long side. Place two asparagus spears along the long side with the ham; roll up and press seam to seal.

Cut each roll into seven pieces. Place cut side down 1 in. apart on greased baking sheets. Combine butter and garlic powder; brush over spirals. Bake at 375° for 10-12 minutes or until golden brown. **Yield:** 28 appetizers.

Taco Cheesecake

(Pictured below)

One taste of this eye-catching appetizer proves cheesecake isn't just for dessert. This savory variation is a crowd favorite at parties. —Judy Eckert
Fulton, New York

    3 teaspoons cornmeal
    3 packages (8 ounces *each*) cream cheese,
      softened
    1 envelope taco seasoning
1/2 cup sour cream
1/2 cup salsa
    2 eggs, lightly beaten
    1 cup (4 ounces) shredded pepper Jack
      cheese
    1 can (4 ounces) chopped green chilies,
      drained
1/2 cup chopped ripe olives
TOPPING:
    1 cup (8 ounces) sour cream
1/4 cup sliced ripe olives
1/4 cup sliced green onions
1/4 cup sliced cherry tomatoes
    1 jalapeno pepper, sliced*
Assorted crackers

Sprinkle bottom of greased 9-in. springform pan with cornmeal; set aside. In mixing bowl, beat cream cheese until smooth. Add the taco season-ing, sour cream and salsa. Stir in the eggs, pepper Jack cheese and chilies. Fold in olives. Pour over cornmeal. Place pan on a baking sheet.

Bake at 350° for 30-35 minutes or until center is almost set. Cool on a wire rack for 10 minutes. Carefully run a knife around edge of pan to loosen; cool for 1 hour. (Top of cheesecake may crack.) Refrigerate overnight.

Remove sides of pan. Spread sour cream over top and sides of cheesecake. Arrange olives, onions, tomato slices and jalapeno slices on top. Serve with crackers. **Yield:** 18-20 servings.

*Editor's Note: When cutting or seeding hot peppers, use rubber or plastic gloves to protect your hands. Avoid touching your face.

Sugared Curry Walnuts

(Pictured below)

To head off the hungries, call on this change-of-pace treatment for walnuts. —Ann Harris
Fresno, California

    1 tablespoon olive oil
    1 teaspoon ground ginger
    1 teaspoon curry powder
1/2 teaspoon cayenne pepper
1/4 cup sugar

TREAT guests to an array of festive appetizers (shown below, clockwise from top): Taco Cheesecake, Sugared Curry Walnuts and Nuggets with Chili Sauce.

2 tablespoons honey
3 cups walnut halves, toasted
1/2 teaspoon salt

In a large skillet, heat oil over medium heat. Stir in the ginger, curry powder and cayenne until smooth. Add sugar and honey; stir until blended. Stir in walnuts until well coated.

Spread onto a waxed paper-lined baking sheet. Sprinkle with salt. Cool and break apart. Store in an airtight container. **Yield:** 3 cups.

Nuggets with Chili Sauce

(Pictured below left)

Whenever I serve these crisp golden bites of chicken, my husband is all smiles. He prefers them to fast-food versions. —Diane Hixon, Niceville, Florida

1 cup chicken broth
2 cans (4 ounces *each*) chopped green
  chilies
2 medium onions, diced
3 tablespoons butter
1 tablespoon chili powder
2 teaspoons ground cumin
2 garlic cloves, minced
1/4 cup packed brown sugar
1/4 cup orange juice
1/4 cup ketchup
2 tablespoons lemon juice
CHICKEN NUGGETS:
1/2 cup cornmeal
1 tablespoon chili powder
2 teaspoons ground cumin
1/4 teaspoon salt
1-1/2 pounds boneless skinless chicken breasts,
  cut into 1-inch cubes
3 tablespoons vegetable oil

In blender or food processor, combine broth and chilies; cover and process until pureed. Set aside. In a large skillet, saute onions in butter until tender. Stir in the chili powder, cumin, garlic and pureed mixture. Bring to a boil. Reduce heat to low; simmer, uncovered, for 20 minutes, stirring occasionally.

Add the brown sugar, orange juice, ketchup and lemon juice. Cook and stir over low heat for 15 minutes or until thickened; keep warm.

For nuggets, combine the cornmeal, chili powder, cumin and salt in a large resealable plastic bag. Add chicken pieces, a few at a time, to bag; shake to coat. Heat oil in skillet; cook chicken for 6-8 minutes or until juices run clear, turning frequently. Serve with sauce. **Yield:** 4 servings.

Coconut Shrimp

(Pictured above)

Jumbo shrimp is big on flavor when I give it a tropical twist. Coconut offers subtle sweetness, and the salsa is delightful as a dip. —Marie Hattrup
The Dalles, Oregon

18 uncooked jumbo shrimp (about 1 pound)
1/3 cup cornstarch
3/4 teaspoon salt
1/2 teaspoon cayenne pepper
3 egg whites
2 cups flaked coconut
Vegetable oil for deep-fat frying
APRICOT-PINEAPPLE SALSA:
1 cup diced pineapple
1/2 cup finely chopped red onion
1/2 cup apricot preserves
1/4 cup minced fresh cilantro
2 tablespoons lime juice
1 jalapeno pepper, seeded and chopped
Salt and pepper to taste

Peel and devein shrimp, leaving tails intact. Make a slit down inner curve of each shrimp, starting at the tail; press lightly to flatten. In a shallow dish, combine the cornstarch, salt and cayenne; set aside. In a mixing bowl, beat egg whites until stiff peaks form. Place the coconut in another shallow dish. Coat shrimp with cornstarch mixture; dip into egg whites, then coat with coconut.

In an electric skillet or deep-fat fryer, heat oil to 375°. Fry shrimp, a few at a time, for 1 to 1-1/2 minutes on each side or until golden brown. Drain on paper towels.

In a bowl, combine salsa ingredients. Serve with shrimp. **Yield:** 6 servings.

Garlic Cucumber Dip

Creamy and full of fresh cucumber flavor, this classic Greek dip is a great appetizer served with pita bread, crackers or vegetables. This dip is also a must-have accompaniment to marinated lamb chunks cooked on a skewer.
—Lisa Stavropoulos
Stouffville, Ontario

✓ Uses less fat, sugar or salt. Includes Nutritional Analysis and Diabetic Exchanges.

    1 **large cucumber**
  3/4 **cup plain yogurt**
  3/4 **cup sour cream**
    3 **tablespoons olive oil**
4-1/2 **teaspoons minced fresh dill**
4-1/2 **teaspoons red wine vinegar**
    3 **garlic cloves, minced**
  1/4 **teaspoon salt**
Additional minced fresh dill
Pita bread wedges

Peel cucumber; cut in half lengthwise and scoop out seeds. Grate cucumber; squeeze between paper towels several times to remove excess moisture. Place cucumber in a small bowl; stir in the yogurt, sour cream, oil, dill, vinegar, garlic and salt. Refrigerate until chilled. Sprinkle with additional dill. Serve with pita wedges. **Yield:** 2 cups.

Nutritional Analysis: One 1/4-cup serving (prepared with fat-free yogurt and reduced-fat sour cream; calculated without pita bread) equals 94 calories, 7 g fat (2 g saturated fat), 8 mg cholesterol, 108 mg sodium, 5 g carbohydrate, trace fiber, 3 g protein. **Diabetic Exchanges:** 1-1/2 fat, 1 vegetable.

Artichoke Nibbles

(Pictured above)

My mother-in-law gave me the recipe for these cheesy appetizers when I married her son, and I've been making them for special occasions ever since.
—Karen Brown, Trenton, Michigan

1 **small onion, chopped**
1 **garlic clove, minced**
1 **teaspoon vegetable oil**
2 **jars (6-1/2 ounces *each*) marinated artichoke hearts, drained and chopped**
4 **eggs**
2 **tablespoons minced fresh parsley**
1/4 **teaspoon salt**
1/8 **teaspoon pepper**
1/8 **teaspoon dried oregano**
1/8 **teaspoon hot pepper sauce**
2 **cups (8 ounces) shredded cheddar cheese**
1/3 **cup crushed saltines (about 10 crackers)**

In a small skillet, saute onion and garlic in oil until tender. Stir in artichokes. Remove from the heat; set aside. In a large bowl, whisk the eggs, parsley, salt, pepper, oregano and hot pepper sauce. Stir in the cheese, cracker crumbs and artichoke mixture.

Pour into a greased 11-in. x 7-in. x 2-in. baking dish. Bake, uncovered, at 325° for 25-30 minutes or until a knife inserted near the center comes out clean. Cool for 10-15 minutes before cutting into 1-in. squares. Serve warm. **Yield:** about 6 dozen.

Trout-Stuffed Red Potatoes

(Pictured on page 4)

Hollowed-out small red potatoes serve as "cups" to hold a creamy trout filling, seasoned with lemon, dill and a dash of hot pepper sauce. My husband, who's a chef, prepared these for the State of Colorado Potato Commissioners and they were a hit. He smokes the trout, but you could also substitute baked trout or salmon in this recipe.
—Bonnie Gomez, Rio Rancho, New Mexico

✓ Uses less fat, sugar or salt. Includes Nutritional Analysis and Diabetic Exchanges.

12 **tiny red potatoes (about 1-1/2-inch diameter)**
1/4 **cup mayonnaise**
1/4 **cup sour cream**
2 **tablespoons finely chopped green onion**
1 **teaspoon snipped fresh dill**

1/4 teaspoon lemon juice
1/8 teaspoon salt
1/8 teaspoon pepper
Dash hot pepper sauce, optional
1 cup flaked smoked trout
Fresh dill sprigs

Place potatoes in a saucepan and cover with water. Bring to a boil. Reduce heat; cover and cook for 10-15 minutes or until tender. Drain. Cut potatoes in half horizontally. Cut a thin slice from the bottom of each potato to level if necessary. Scoop out the pulp with a melon baller, leaving a thick shell.

In a bowl, mash the pulp. Stir in the mayonnaise, sour cream, onion, dill, lemon juice, salt, pepper and hot pepper sauce if desired. Fold in trout. Pipe into potato shells. Garnish with dill sprigs. **Yield:** 2 dozen.

Nutritional Analysis: Two appetizers (prepared with fat-free mayonnaise and reduced-fat sour cream) equal 78 calories, 2 g fat (1 g saturated fat), 18 mg cholesterol, 448 mg sodium, 8 g carbohydrate, 1 g fiber, 6 g protein. **Diabetic Exchanges:** 1 lean meat, 1/2 starch.

Creamy Onion Spread

My daughter came across this recipe a few years ago, and I have adapted it to our family's tastes. They request it at every gathering. It's rich and creamy and gets a little kick from cayenne pepper. —*Janet Joecks Menomonee Falls, Wisconsin*

1 large sweet onion, finely chopped
1 garlic clove, minced
1 tablespoon olive oil
1/4 cup sliced green onions
3/4 teaspoon salt
1/2 teaspoon pepper
1/8 to 1/4 teaspoon cayenne pepper
3/4 cup sour cream
3/4 cup mayonnaise
1/2 cup whipped cream cheese
Additional sliced green onions
Breadsticks and sweet red and yellow pepper strips

In a skillet, saute onion and garlic in oil for 1 minute. Reduce heat to medium-low. Cover and cook for 8 minutes or until onion begins to turn golden brown. Add the green onions, salt, pepper and cayenne. Cook and stir for 2 minutes. Remove from the heat; cool to room temperature, about 15 minutes.

Meanwhile, in a small mixing bowl, combine the sour cream, mayonnaise and cream cheese until smooth. Stir in onion mixture. Garnish with additional green onions. Cover and refrigerate for at least 1 hour. Serve with breadsticks and peppers. **Yield:** about 2 cups.

Tomato Leek Tarts

(Pictured below)

This appetizer recipe yields two attractive tarts. The crisp pastry crust cuts easily into wedges.
—*Kathleen Tribble, Santa Ynez, California*

1 package (15 ounces) refrigerated pie pastry
1 cup (4 ounces) shredded provolone cheese
1 pound leeks (white portion only), sliced
6 medium plum tomatoes, thinly sliced
1/4 cup grated Parmesan cheese
1-1/2 teaspoons garlic powder
1/8 teaspoon pepper
1 cup (8 ounces) shredded mozzarella cheese

Place both pastry sheets on greased baking sheets. Sprinkle each with provolone cheese, leaving 1 in. around edges. Arrange leeks and tomato slices over provolone cheese. Sprinkle with Parmesan cheese, garlic powder and pepper. Top with mozzarella cheese. Fold edges over filling.

Bake at 425° for 18-22 minutes or until crusts are lightly browned. Cut into wedges. Serve warm. **Yield:** 2 tarts.

Cheese Balls Shape Up for the Season

WHEN we bounced the idea of doing a cheese ball feature off of our readers, they threw in some delectable ideas! Here are several of the popular appetizers they shape and serve to appreciative guests.

Smoky Sesame Cheese Log

(Pictured below)

We love the bacon flavor in this cheesy mixture. Served with wheat or sesame crackers, it's yummy!
—Katie Sloan, Charlotte, North Carolina

2 packages (8 ounces *each*) cream cheese, softened

FAN FARE. Crab Football Spread makes a great game-time snack, while Holiday Cheese Ball and Smoky Sesame Cheese Log bring their own flavors to the party table (shown below, clockwise from bottom).

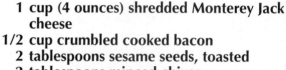

1 cup (4 ounces) shredded Monterey Jack cheese
1/2 cup crumbled cooked bacon
2 tablespoons sesame seeds, toasted
2 tablespoons minced chives
2 tablespoons Worcestershire sauce
1 teaspoon Liquid Smoke
TOPPING:
1/2 cup crumbled cooked bacon
1/2 cup sesame seeds, toasted
1 tablespoon minced chives
Assorted fresh vegetables *or* crackers

In a mixing bowl, combine the first seven ingredients; mix well. Shape mixture into a log. Cover and refrigerate for 8 hours or overnight. For topping, combine the bacon, sesame seeds and chives; roll cheese log in topping. Serve with vegetables or crackers. **Yield:** 1 cheese log (2-1/2 cups).

Crab Football Spread

(Pictured at left)

Fans keep coming back for more after tasting this delicious cheese ball. I don't make this spread just on football Sundays. You can be creative about molding the mixture into different shapes.
—Kathy Kittell, Lenexa, Kansas

1 package (8 ounces) cream cheese, softened
2 cups (8 ounces) shredded cheddar cheese
1 cup (4 ounces) shredded provolone cheese
1 cup canned crabmeat
1 cup (8 ounces) small-curd cottage cheese
2 teaspoons seafood seasoning
2 teaspoons Worcestershire sauce
1 teaspoon prepared mustard
Pretzel sticks
Assorted crackers *and/or* fresh vegetables

In large mixing bowl, beat cream cheese until smooth. Add cheddar cheese, provolone cheese, crab, cottage cheese, seafood seasoning, Worcestershire sauce and mustard; mix

well. Cover and refrigerate overnight.

Form mixture into a football shape. Arrange pretzels over top for laces. Serve with crackers and/or vegetables. **Yield:** 1 cheese ball (4 cups).

Holiday Cheese Ball

(Pictured below left)

With its colorful flecks of green onion and pimiento, this cheese ball is great as a Christmas or New Year's appetizer. It can be made with fat-free cheeses without sacrificing the zesty Italian taste.
—Andrea Bolden, Unionville, Tennessee

    1 package (8 ounces) cream cheese, softened
    1 cup (4 ounces) shredded mozzarella
      cheese
  1/2 cup chopped green onions
    1 jar (2 ounces) diced pimientos, drained
    1 teaspoon Italian seasoning
  1/2 teaspoon dried parsley flakes
  1/8 teaspoon cayenne pepper
    1 cup finely chopped walnuts
Assorted crackers, breadsticks *and/or* fresh
  vegetables

In a small mixing bowl, combine the first seven ingredients; mix well.

Cover and refrigerate for 30 minutes. Shape into a ball; roll in walnuts. Cover and refrigerate overnight. Serve with crackers, breadsticks and/or vegetables. **Yield:** 1 cheese ball (1-1/2 cups).

Snowman Cheese Ball

(Pictured above right)

This frosty fellow is always welcome at a winter gathering. He's very tasty, too—and gets a little zip from horseradish and garlic. —*Susan Seymour*
Valatie, New York

    2 packages (8 ounces each) cream cheese,
      softened
    1 package (4-1/2 ounces) dried beef,
      chopped
  1/2 cup finely chopped green onions
    1 teaspoon prepared horseradish
  1/2 teaspoon garlic powder
  1/2 cup dried parsley flakes
    2 cartons (4 ounces *each*) spreadable cream
      cheese
    5 dried cranberries
    1 baby carrot

    2 pretzel sticks
    1 large round cracker
    4 round butter-flavored crackers
Assorted crackers

In a large mixing bowl, combine the first five ingredients until blended. Shape into two balls, one slightly larger than the other. Roll each in parsley. Cover and refrigerate for 8 hours or overnight.

On a serving plate, place the smaller cheese ball on top of larger cheese ball, forming a snowman. Set aside 1 teaspoon spreadable cream cheese. Carefully cover snowman with remaining spreadable cream cheese.

Arrange cranberries for eyes and buttons. Insert carrot for nose and pretzel sticks for arms.

Place a small dab of reserved cream cheese on top of large cracker. Top with a butter-flavored cracker. Repeat with three remaining butter-flavored crackers. Place on top of snowman. Serve with crackers. **Yield:** 1 snowman (2-1/2 cups).

✓ *Cheese Ball Basics*

To keep your hands and the countertop clean when shaping a cheese ball, spoon the cheese mixture onto a piece of plastic wrap. Working from the underside of the wrap, pat the mixture into a ball. Complete the recipe as directed.

Allow cheese balls, dips and spreads that contain cream cheese to stand at room temperature for 15 minutes before serving for easier spreading and more flavor.

1 teaspoon sugar
3 teaspoons active dry yeast
1 cup warm water (110° to 115°)
1 tablespoon olive oil
TOPPING:
   1 tablespoon olive oil
   2 tablespoons grated Parmesan cheese
   1 tablespoon minced fresh rosemary
   2 garlic cloves, minced
1/4 teaspoon salt
   1 small red onion, thinly sliced and
      separated into rings
   3 to 4 medium plum tomatoes, thinly sliced

In a large mixing bowl, combine 2-1/2 cups flour, salt and sugar. Dissolve yeast in warm water; stir in oil. Add to the dry ingredients; beat until smooth. Stir in enough remaining flour to form a soft dough.

Turn dough onto a floured surface; knead until smooth and elastic, about 6-8 minutes. Place in a greased bowl, turning once to grease top. Cover and let rise in a warm place until doubled, about 30 minutes.

Punch dough down. On a lightly floured surface, roll dough into a 12-in. circle. Place on a greased 12-in. pizza pan. Brush with oil. Combine the Parmesan cheese, rosemary, garlic and salt; sprinkle over dough. Arrange onion rings and tomatoes over top, pressing down lightly. Bake at 400° for 15-20 minutes or until crust is golden brown. Cut into wedges. **Yield:** 10 servings.

Harvest Pumpkin Dip

(Pictured above)

After trying to make my own pies and failing miserably with the crust, I decided to try something new with the same great pumpkin pie taste. This creamy dip is the result. —Christy Johnson, Columbus, Ohio

   1 package (8 ounces) cream cheese,
      softened
   2 cups confectioners' sugar
   1 can (15 ounces) solid-pack pumpkin
   3 teaspoons pumpkin pie spice
   1 teaspoon vanilla extract
1/2 teaspoon ground ginger
Apple and pear slices

In a large mixing bowl, beat the cream cheese and confectioners' sugar. Gradually add the pumpkin, pie spice, vanilla and ginger; beat until smooth. Serve with fruit. Refrigerate leftovers. **Yield:** 3-1/2 cups.

Tomato Focaccia

(Pictured on page 4)

I like to serve these savory yeast bread appetizers topped with tomato, onion and Parmesan cheese. —Mary Lou Wayman, Salt Lake City, Utah

2-1/2 to 3 cups all-purpose flour
   1 teaspoon salt

Sausage-Stuffed Jalapenos

If you like appetizers with a little kick, you'll savor these zippy cream cheese- and sausage-filled jalapenos. —Rachel Oswald, Greenville, Michigan

   1 pound bulk pork sausage
   1 package (8 ounces) cream cheese,
      softened
   1 cup (4 ounces) shredded Parmesan cheese
  22 large jalapeno peppers, halved lengthwise
      and seeded*
Ranch salad dressing, optional

In a large skillet, cook the sausage over medium heat until no longer pink; drain. In a small mixing bowl, combine the cream cheese and Parmesan cheese; fold in sausage.

Spoon about 1 tablespoonful into each jalapeno half. Place in two ungreased 13-in. x 9-in. x 2-in. baking dishes. Bake, uncovered, at 425° for 15-20 minutes or until filling is lightly browned and bubbly. Serve with ranch dressing if desired. **Yield:** 44 appetizers.

*Editor's Note: When cutting or seeding hot peppers, use rubber or plastic gloves to protect your hands. Avoid touching your face.

Lemon Mint Cooler

This fizzy beverage blends sherbet and ginger ale with tangy ice cubes made with lemon juice and chopped mint. —Chava Karlovich, Monroe, Connecticut

2-1/4 cups water
  1/2 cup coarsely chopped fresh mint
  1/2 cup lemon juice
    2 medium lemons, sliced
  1/2 cup lemon sherbet, softened
    1 liter ginger ale, chilled

For mint ice cubes, combine the water, mint and lemon juice; pour into two ice cube trays. Freeze until set. In a pitcher, combine the lemons and sherbet; slowly stir in ginger ale. Add the mint ice cubes. **Yield:** about 5 cups.

Creamy Cantaloupe Pops

I make these delicious pops when the melons are ripening quickly in our cantaloupe patch. —Deanna Richter, Elmore, Minnesota

1-1/2 cups cubed cantaloupe
    1 cup heavy whipping cream
  1/2 cup sugar
    8 Popsicle molds *or* plastic cups (3 ounces)
    8 Popsicle sticks

Place cantaloupe in a blender. Cover and process until smooth; set aside. In a small saucepan, combine the cream and sugar. Cook and stir over low heat until sugar is dissolved. Remove from the heat. Stir in pureed cantaloupe. Pour 1/4 cup into each mold; insert the Popsicle sticks. Freeze until firm. **Yield:** 8 servings.

Sweet Onion Turnovers

(Pictured at right)

Making these delightful turnovers is my favorite way to use onions. They're lovely as a snack. The pastry dough for the rich tender crust is easy to work with, and the filling is so good. —Doris Crouse, Sheridan, Wyoming

    2 cups all-purpose flour
    1 tablespoon sugar
  3/4 teaspoon salt
  3/4 cup plus 3 tablespoons cold butter, *divided*
  1/3 to 1/2 cup cold water
    6 cups thinly sliced sweet onions
1-1/2 teaspoons minced fresh rosemary
1-1/2 teaspoons minced fresh thyme
  1/2 cup chicken broth
  1/8 teaspoon coarsely ground pepper
    2 eggs
  1/4 cup heavy whipping cream
    1 tablespoon Dijon mustard
  1/2 cup soft bread crumbs
  1/4 cup grated Parmesan cheese

In a bowl, combine the flour, sugar and salt; cut in 3/4 cup butter until mixture resembles coarse crumbs. Gradually add water, tossing with a fork until mixture forms a ball. Shape into a flattened ball; wrap in plastic wrap and refrigerate.

In a large skillet, cook the onions, rosemary and thyme in remaining butter over medium-low heat until onions begin to turn golden brown. Add broth and pepper; cook over high heat until liquid is absorbed. Cool slightly. In a bowl, beat eggs; set aside 2 tablespoons. Stir cream and mustard into remaining beaten eggs. Stir in bread crumbs, Parmesan cheese and onion mixture.

Divide dough into six portions. On a lightly floured surface, roll each portion into a 6-in. circle. Place on two greased baking sheets. Spoon about 1/2 cup onion mixture on one side of each. Fold dough over filling; press edges with a fork to seal.

Brush with reserved beaten egg. Bake at 400° for 20-25 minutes or until filling reaches 160° and crust is golden brown. **Yield:** 6 servings.

Roasted Eggplant Dip

(Pictured below)

Here's a fun way to use some of your garden-fresh eggplant crop. This chunky guacamole-like dip—seasoned with lemon juice, onions and chives—goes great with pita wedges or melba toast. —Nina Hall
Citrus Heights, California

✓ Uses less fat, sugar or salt. Includes Nutritional Analysis and Diabetic Exchanges.

   1 **medium eggplant (about 1 pound)**
   9 **green onions (white portion only)**
   3 **tablespoons reduced-fat plain yogurt**
   1 **tablespoon lemon juice**
   1 **tablespoon olive oil**
1/2 **teaspoon salt**
1/4 **teaspoon pepper**
   3 **tablespoons minced chives,** *divided*
Pita breads (6 inches), cut into 6 wedges
Carrot sticks, optional

Pierce eggplant several times with a fork. Place eggplant and onions in a shallow foil-lined baking pan. Bake at 400° for 25-30 minutes or until tender. Cool. Peel and cube the eggplant.

In a blender or food processor, combine the yogurt, lemon juice, oil, salt, pepper, eggplant and onions. Cover and process until almost smooth. Add 2 tablespoons chives; cover and process until blended. Transfer to a serving bowl; sprinkle with remaining chives. Serve with pita wedges and carrots if desired. **Yield:** 1-1/2 cups.

Nutritional Analysis: One serving (1/4 cup dip with 6 pita wedges) equals 158 calories, 3 g fat (trace saturated fat), trace cholesterol, 421 mg sodium, 28 g carbohydrate, 3 g fiber, 5 g protein. **Diabetic Exchanges:** 1-1/2 starch, 1 vegetable, 1/2 fat.

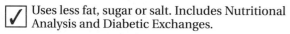

Perky Penguins

My children and I needed something to perk up our spirits during the cold month of January, so we decided to celebrate Penguin Awareness Month with these cute critters. —Julie Lavender
Silverdale, Washington

1/2 **cup milk chocolate chips**
1-1/2 **teaspoons shortening**
 12 **large marshmallows**
  2 **packages (2-1/4 ounces** *each***) Tootsie Rolls**
 12 **miniature chocolate chips**
 18 **pieces candy corn**
  6 **cream-filled chocolate sandwich cookies**

In a microwave-safe bowl, combine the milk chocolate chips and shortening. Microwave, uncovered, at 50% power for 1 to 1-1/2 minutes or until chips are melted, stirring every 30 seconds. Cool slightly. Place a small amount of chocolate mixture on top of six marshmallows; top with remaining marshmallows. Let stand for 1 hour or until set.

Warm chocolate mixture. For penguin bodies, carefully dip sides of the marshmallows in chocolate mixture so three-fourths of marshmallows are covered, leaving about a 3/4-in. vertical strip of white. Let stand on waxed paper until set, about 1 hour.

For penguin heads, cut Tootsie Rolls into two-piece sections. Place on a microwave-safe plate; microwave at 10% power for 10-15 seconds or until slightly warmed. Carefully roll each into a ball.

With a toothpick, position chocolate chips for eyes. For beaks, cut off yellow end of six candy corn pieces; flatten remaining candy slightly. Press gently into chocolate balls. Reheat chocolate mixture. Dab a small amount onto bottom of each ball; position on penguin bodies. Let stand until set, about 45 minutes.

Separate cream-filled cookies; remove and discard cream filling. For wings, cut six cookies in half. Rewarm the chocolate mixture. Spread a small amount on each cookie half; attach to penguins with cut edge facing forward.

For bases, attach penguins to remaining cookies using melted chocolate. For feet, remove white ends of remaining candy corn pieces and discard; flatten candy. Attach two candies to each cookie base. Let stand for 45 minutes or until set. **Yield:** 6 penguins.

Sparkling Rhubarb Spritzer

(Pictured on page 4)

Folks with a rhubarb plant or two will love this recipe. We enjoy it all summer long. —Sue Rebers
Campbellsport, Wisconsin

12 cups chopped fresh *or* frozen rhubarb
4 cups water
2-1/2 to 3 cups sugar
1 cup pineapple juice
2 liters lemon-lime soda, chilled

In a Dutch oven, bring rhubarb and water to a boil. Boil for 15 minutes. Cool for 10 minutes; strain and reserve juice. Discard pulp. Add sugar and pineapple juice to reserved juice; stir until sugar is dissolved. Chill thoroughly. Just before serving, add soda and ice cubes. **Yield:** 3-1/2 quarts.

Grilled Asparagus Pizzas

Tired of pepperoni pizza? When we have the grill going, we like to make this recipe. —M. Woods
Springfield, Missouri

1-3/4 to 2-1/2 cups all-purpose flour
1 package (1/4 ounce) quick-rise yeast
1 tablespoon minced fresh thyme
1 teaspoon salt
1/2 teaspoon sugar
3/4 cup warm water (120° to 130°)
24 asparagus spears, trimmed
1 tablespoon olive oil
1/8 teaspoon garlic salt
1/8 teaspoon pepper
1 cup pizza sauce
3 ounces thinly sliced deli ham, chopped
2 cups (8 ounces) shredded mozzarella cheese

In a large mixing bowl, combine 1 cup flour, yeast, thyme, salt and sugar. Add water; beat until blended. Stir in enough remaining flour to form a soft dough. Turn onto a floured surface; knead until smooth and elastic, about 6-8 minutes. Place in a greased bowl, turning once to grease top. Cover and let rise in warm place until doubled, about 1 hour.

Brush asparagus with oil; sprinkle with garlic salt and pepper. Grill asparagus, uncovered, over medium heat for 6-8 minutes or until tender, turning every 2 minutes. Cut into 1-in. pieces.

Punch the dough down. Turn onto a floured surface; divide into eight portions. Roll each portion into a 6-in. circle. Place dough directly on grill. Grill, uncovered, over medium heat for 1-2 min-

utes or until bubbles form on top. Place toasted side up on two ungreased baking sheets. Top with pizza sauce, asparagus, ham and cheese. Cover and grill 2-3 minutes longer or until bottom of crust is golden brown. **Yield:** 8 servings.

Potato Nachos

(Pictured above)

Cheese, jalapeno pepper, sour cream and green onions top these pretty potato slices, seasoned with dry ranch dressing mix. —Tony Horton
Van Buren, Arkansas

8 medium red potatoes
1 envelope ranch salad dressing mix
1 jar (12 ounces) pickled jalapeno pepper slices, drained
2 cups (8 ounces) shredded cheddar cheese
2 cups (8 ounces) shredded Monterey Jack cheese
2 cups (16 ounces) sour cream
6 to 8 green onions, chopped

Place potatoes in a saucepan and cover with water. Bring to a boil. Reduce heat; cover and cook for 15-20 minutes or just until tender. Drain; cool slightly.

Cut potatoes into 1/4-in.-thick slices. Place in a single layer in three greased 15-in. x 10-in. x 1-in. baking pans. Top each with salad dressing mix, a jalapeno slice, cheddar cheese and Monterey Jack cheese. Bake, uncovered, at 350° for 10-12 minutes or until cheese is melted. Top with sour cream and green onions. **Yield:** 12 servings.

form a soft dough. Turn onto a floured surface; knead until smooth and elastic, about 6-8 minutes. Place in a greased bowl, turning once to grease top. Cover; let rise in a warm place until doubled, about 1 hour.

Punch dough down. Turn onto a lightly floured surface; roll into a 14-in. x 12-in. rectangle. Sprinkle pepperoni, 1/4 cup cheddar cheese, Parmesan cheese, 2 tablespoons mozzarella cheese, onion, olives and mushrooms to within 1/2 in. of edges. Roll up jelly-roll style, starting with a long side; pinch seam to seal and tuck ends under. Place seam side down on a greased baking sheet. Cover and let rise for 45 minutes.

Sprinkle with remaining cheeses. Bake at 350° for 25-30 minutes or until a toothpick comes out clean. Remove from pan to a wire rack. Serve warm. Refrigerate leftovers. **Yield:** 1 loaf.

Ham 'n' Asparagus Roll-Ups

These light refreshers go together in a jiffy, so they're perfect when unexpected guests drop by.
—*Mary Steiner, West Bend, Wisconsin*

 16 **fresh asparagus spears (about 1 pound), trimmed**
 1 **tablespoon water**
 16 **thin slices fully cooked ham (about 3/4 pound)**
DILL SAUCE:
 1 **cup (8 ounces) plain yogurt**
 1/2 **cup diced seeded and peeled cucumber**
 1 **teaspoon dill weed**
 1 **teaspoon lemon juice**

Place asparagus and water in a microwave-safe 11-in. x 7-in. x 2-in. dish. Cover and cook on high for 2-3 minutes or until crisp-tender. Immediately place asparagus in ice water; drain and pat dry. Wrap each asparagus spear with a slice of ham. Just before serving, combine sauce ingredients. Serve with roll-ups. **Yield:** 8 servings.

Editor's Note: This recipe was tested in a 1,100-watt microwave.

Spiced Tea Mix

Perfect for a gift or to keep on hand when friends stop by, this versatile mix can be served hot or cold. This was my grandma's favorite tea mixture. The blend of ingredients makes it one of a kind!
—*Julie Dvornicky, Broadview Heights, Ohio*

Pizza Stromboli

(Pictured above)

I used to own a bakery, and this bread was one of our customers' favorites. Once they smelled the aroma of pizza and sampled these tempting spiral slices, they just couldn't resist taking some home.
—*John Morcom, Oxford, Michigan*

 1 **package (1/4 ounce) active dry yeast**
 3/4 **cup warm water (110° to 115°)**
 4-1/2 **teaspoons honey**
 1 **tablespoon nonfat dry milk powder**
 2 **cups bread flour**
 1/2 **cup whole wheat flour**
 2 **teaspoons Italian seasoning**
 1 **teaspoon salt**
 4-1/2 **teaspoons pizza sauce**
 3/4 **cup chopped pepperoni**
 1/2 **cup shredded cheddar cheese,** *divided*
 1/4 **cup shredded Parmesan cheese**
 1/4 **cup shredded mozzarella cheese,** *divided*
 2 **tablespoons finely chopped onion**
 1 **tablespoon** *each* **chopped ripe olives, chopped stuffed olives and chopped canned mushrooms**

In a large mixing bowl, dissolve the yeast in warm water. Stir in honey and milk powder until well blended. In a small bowl, combine 1 cup bread flour, whole wheat flour and seasonings. Add to yeast mixture; beat until smooth. Stir in pizza sauce. Stir in enough remaining bread flour to

8 cups sweetened lemonade mix
1 cup orange breakfast drink mix
3/4 cup sugar
1/2 cup unsweetened instant tea
1 teaspoon ground nutmeg
1/2 teaspoon ground cinnamon
1/4 teaspoon ground cloves

In a large bowl, combine all ingredients; mix well. Store in an airtight container in a cool dry place for up to 6 months. **Yield:** about 9 cups total.

To prepare 1 gallon iced tea: Dissolve 2 cups of tea mix in 1 gallon of water; stir well. Serve over ice. **Yield:** 16 servings.

To prepare 1 cup hot tea: Dissolve 2 tablespoons of tea mix in 1 cup of boiling water; stir well. **Yield:** 1 serving.

Grilled Seasoned Shrimp

A marinade using balsamic vinegar, lemon juice and Italian dressing boosts the flavor of these tender shrimp. I serve the delightful bites chilled.
—*Diane Harrison*
Mechanicsburg, Pennsylvania

✓ Uses less fat, sugar or salt. Includes Nutritional Analysis and Diabetic Exchanges.

1-1/2 pounds uncooked large shrimp
1 small red onion, sliced and separated into rings
1/4 cup prepared Italian salad dressing
2 green onions, chopped
2 tablespoons lemon juice
2 tablespoons balsamic vinegar
2 tablespoons olive oil
3 garlic cloves, minced
Salt and coarsely ground pepper to taste, optional

Peel and devein shrimp, leaving tails intact if desired. Coat a grill rack with nonstick cooking spray before starting the grill. Grill shrimp, covered, over indirect medium heat for 2-3 minutes on each side or until shrimp turn pink. Refrigerate until chilled.

In a large resealable plastic bag, combine the remaining ingredients; add shrimp. Seal bag and turn to coat; refrigerate for at least 2 hours. Serve with a slotted spoon. **Yield:** 4 servings.

Nutritional Analysis: One serving (3 large shrimp, prepared with fat-free salad dressing and without salt) equals 267 calories, 10 g fat (2 g saturated fat), 259 mg cholesterol, 470 mg sodium, 7 g carbohydrate, 1 g fiber, 35 g protein. **Diabetic Exchanges:** 4 very lean meat, 2 fat, 1/2 fruit.

Asparagus Salsa

(Pictured below)

Jalapeno pepper and cilantro spice up this refreshing salsa that's made with tomatoes, onion and fresh asparagus. Served chilled with tortilla chips, it won't last long.   —*Emma Thomas, Rome, Georgia*

✓ Uses less fat, sugar or salt. Includes Nutritional Analysis and Diabetic Exchanges.

1 pound fresh asparagus, trimmed and cut into 1/2-inch pieces
1 cup chopped seeded tomatoes
1/2 cup finely chopped onion
1 small jalapeno pepper, seeded and finely chopped*
1 tablespoon minced fresh cilantro
1 garlic clove, minced
1 teaspoon cider vinegar
1/4 teaspoon salt
Tortilla chips

Place asparagus in a large saucepan; add 1/2 in. of water. Bring to a boil. Reduce heat; cover and simmer for 2 minutes. Drain and rinse in cold water.

In a bowl, combine the asparagus, tomatoes, onion, jalapeno, cilantro, garlic, vinegar and salt. Cover and refrigerate for at least 4 hours, stirring several times. Serve with tortilla chips. **Yield:** 3 cups.

Nutritional Analysis: One 1/4-cup serving (calculated without chips) equals 15 calories, trace fat (trace saturated fat), 0 cholesterol, 52 mg sodium, 3 g carbohydrate, 1 g fiber, 1 g protein. **Diabetic Exchange:** Free food.

*****Editor's Note:** When cutting or seeding hot peppers, use rubber or plastic gloves to protect your hands. Avoid touching your face.

Barbecue Chicken Wings

(Pictured below)

Make sure everyone has extra napkins…these wings are messy to eat but oh, so good! —Jean Ann Herritt
Canton, Ohio

   3 pounds whole chicken wings*
   2 cups ketchup
1/2 cup honey
   2 tablespoons lemon juice
   2 tablespoons vegetable oil
   2 tablespoons soy sauce
   2 tablespoons Worcestershire sauce
   1 tablespoon paprika
   4 garlic cloves, minced
1-1/2 teaspoons curry powder
1/2 teaspoon pepper
1/8 teaspoon hot pepper sauce

Cut chicken wings into three sections; discard wing tips. Place wings in a greased 15-in. x 10-in. x 1-in. baking pan. Bake at 350° for 35-40 minutes or until juices run clear. In a bowl, combine the remaining ingredients.

Pour 1/2 cup into a 3-qt. slow cooker. Drain chicken wings; add to slow cooker. Drizzle with remaining sauce. Cover and cook on low for 1 hour, basting occasionally. **Yield:** 10 servings.

   *Editor's Note: 3 pounds of uncooked chicken wing sections (wingettes) may be substituted for the whole chicken wings. Omit the first step.

Trail Mix

(Pictured below)

Prepackaged trail mix doesn't compare to this fun homemade variety of dried fruit, nuts, cereal and chocolate chips. —Michael Vyskocil
Glen Rock, Pennsylvania

1/2 cup unblanched whole almonds
1/2 cup coarsely chopped walnuts
1/2 cup golden raisins
1/2 cup chopped dates
1/2 cup dried apple slices, chopped

FUN FINGER FOODS like Peanutty Pops, Trail Mix and Barbecue Chicken Wings (shown below, clockwise from bottom) add appeal to casual get-togethers.

1/2 cup dried apricots, chopped
1/2 cup semisweet chocolate chips
1/2 cup Honey Nut Cheerios

In a large bowl, combine all ingredients. Store in an airtight container. **Yield:** 4 cups.

Peanutty Pops

(Pictured below left)

When my sons were young, these pops were a favorite treat, and they still enjoy them. For variety, add mini chocolate chips, mini marshmallows or chopped banana. —*Lynn Lehman, Superior, Wisconsin*

✓ Uses less fat, sugar or salt. Includes Nutritional Analysis and Diabetic Exchanges.

  1 envelope unflavored gelatin
  1 cup cold water
1/2 cup sugar
  1 cup creamy peanut butter
  1 cup chocolate milk
 10 disposable plastic cups (3 ounces *each*)
 10 Popsicle sticks

In a small saucepan, sprinkle gelatin over cold water; let stand for 1 minute. Stir in sugar. Cook and stir over medium heat until gelatin and sugar are dissolved. Transfer to a mixing bowl; beat in peanut butter and milk. Pour into cups.

Cover each cup with heavy-duty foil; insert sticks through foil. Place in a 9-in. square pan. Freeze until firm. Remove foil and cups before serving. **Yield:** 10 ice pops.

Nutritional Analysis: One ice pop (prepared with reduced-fat peanut butter and 2% chocolate milk) equals 187 calories, 9 g fat (2 g saturated fat), 1 mg cholesterol, 159 mg sodium, 21 g carbohydrate, 2 g fiber, 8 g protein. **Diabetic Exchanges:** 1 milk, 1/2 starch.

Crispy Oven-Fried Oysters

(Pictured above right)

I created these flavorful breaded and baked oysters, served with a zippy jalapeno mayonnaise. I entered the recipe in a seafood contest and took first place in the hors d'oeuvres category. —*Marie Rizzio*
Traverse City, Michigan

3/4 cup all-purpose flour
1/8 teaspoon salt
1/8 teaspoon pepper

  2 eggs
  1 cup dry bread crumbs
2/3 cup grated Romano cheese
1/4 cup minced fresh parsley
1/2 teaspoon garlic salt
  1 pint shucked oysters *or* 2 cans (8 ounces *each*) whole oysters, drained
  2 tablespoons olive oil
JALAPENO MAYONNAISE:
1/4 cup mayonnaise
1/4 cup sour cream
  2 medium jalapeno peppers, seeded and finely chopped*
  2 tablespoons milk
  1 teaspoon lemon juice
1/4 teaspoon grated lemon peel
1/8 teaspoon salt
1/8 teaspoon pepper

In a shallow bowl, combine the flour, salt and pepper. In another shallow bowl, beat eggs. In a third bowl, combine the bread crumbs, Romano cheese, parsley and garlic salt.

Coat oysters with flour mixture; dip in eggs, then coat with crumb mixture. Place in a greased 15-in. x 10-in. x 1-in. baking pan; drizzle with oil.

Bake at 400° for 15 minutes or until golden brown. Meanwhile, in a small bowl, whisk the jalapeno mayonnaise ingredients. Serve with oysters. **Yield:** about 2-1/2 dozen (about 2/3 cup jalapeno mayonnaise).

*Editor's Note: When cutting or seeding hot peppers, use rubber or plastic gloves to protect your hands. Avoid touching your face.

Place onion and butter in a microwave-safe dish. Cover; microwave on high until onion is tender. Add egg, zucchini and carrot. In a bowl, combine flour, cheese, cornmeal, salt and pepper; stir in vegetable mixture just until combined.

In a skillet or deep-fat fryer, heat 2 in. of oil to 375°. Drop rounded tablespoonfuls of batter into oil. Fry for 1-2 minutes until deep golden brown, turning once. Drain on paper towels. **Yield:** 1-1/2 dozen fritters, 2/3 cup basil sauce and 1-1/2 cups horseradish sauce.

Brie in Puff Pastry

This rich stylish appetizer adds an elegant touch to any get-together. —Marion Lowery, Medford, Oregon

> 1 sheet frozen puff pastry, thawed
> 1/4 cup apricot jam
> 1 round (13.2 ounces) Brie cheese
> 1 egg
> 1 tablespoon water
Apple slices

Roll puff pastry into a 14-in. square. Spread jam into a 4-1/2-in. circle in center of pastry; place cheese over jam. Fold pastry around cheese; trim excess dough. Pinch edges to seal. Place seam side down on ungreased baking sheet. Beat egg and water; brush over pastry.

If desired, cut the trimmed pastry pieces into decorative shapes and place on top; brush with egg mixture. Bake at 400° for 20-25 minutes or until puffed and golden brown. Serve warm with apple slices. **Yield:** 8-10 servings.

Carrot Zucchini Fritters

(Pictured above)

I'm always looking for flavorful recipes that increase my veggie intake. This one fills the bill. The crispy fritters are delicious with or without the dipping sauces.
—Laura Mize, Waco, Kentucky

DIPPING SAUCES:
> 2/3 cup plus 1/2 cup sour cream, *divided*
> 2/3 cup lightly packed fresh basil leaves
> 1 teaspoon lemon juice
Salt and pepper to taste
> 1/2 cup mayonnaise
> 1/2 cup horseradish sauce
FRITTERS:
> 2 tablespoons finely chopped onion
> 1 tablespoon butter
> 1 egg, lightly beaten
> 2 medium zucchini, shredded and squeezed
>   dry (about 1-1/2 cups)
> 1 large carrot, shredded
> 1/3 cup all-purpose flour
> 1/3 cup grated Parmesan cheese
> 1 tablespoon cornmeal
> 1/2 teaspoon salt
> 1/8 teaspoon pepper
Oil for deep-fat frying

In a blender or food processor, place 2/3 cup sour cream, basil, lemon juice, salt and pepper; cover and process until blended. Transfer to a small bowl. In another bowl, combine the mayonnaise, horseradish and remaining sour cream. Cover and refrigerate both sauces.

Chewy Granola Bars

This chewy treat is full of goodies like marshmallows, raisins, chocolate chips and sunflower kernels.
—Alice McVey, Evansville, Indiana

> 1 package (10-1/2 ounces) large
>   marshmallows
> 2/3 cup chunky peanut butter*
> 1/2 cup butter, cubed
> 1/4 cup corn syrup
> 2 teaspoons vanilla extract
> 4 cups quick-cooking oats
> 1 cup crisp rice cereal
> 1 cup miniature semisweet chocolate chips
> 1/2 cup flaked coconut
> 1/2 cup sunflower kernels

1/2 cup chopped peanuts
1/2 cup raisins
2 tablespoons toasted wheat germ
2 tablespoons sesame seeds

In a large microwave-safe bowl, combine the marshmallows, peanut butter, butter, corn syrup and vanilla. Microwave, uncovered, at 70% power for 2-3 minutes, stirring often until blended. Stir in the remaining ingredients.

Spread into a greased 13-in. x 9-in. x 2-in. baking pan. Bake at 350° for 15-20 minutes or until set. Cool on a wire rack. Cut into bars. **Yield:** 2 dozen.

*Editor's Note: Reduced-fat or generic brands of peanut butter are not recommended for this recipe.

Zesty Salsa

This chunky and colorful salsa is the ideal companion for crispy tortilla chips and goes together in a jiffy.
—Susan Causey, Columbia, Louisiana

2 large tomatoes, diced
6 green onions, chopped
1 cup (4 ounces) finely shredded Monterey Jack cheese
1 can (4 ounces) chopped green chilies
1 can (2-1/4 ounces) sliced ripe olives, drained
1/4 cup prepared zesty Italian salad dressing
Tortilla chips

In a bowl, combine the first six ingredients; mix well. Cover and refrigerate for at least 1 hour. Serve with tortilla chips. **Yield:** 4 cups.

Asparagus Ham Tartlets

(Pictured at right)

We have our own asparagus patch, and each spring I look forward to making treats like these tartlets.
—Elaine Anderson, Aliquippa, Pennsylvania

1 package (3 ounces) cream cheese, softened
1/4 cup butter, softened
3/4 cup plus 1 tablespoon all-purpose flour, *divided*
1/4 cup cornmeal
1 egg
1/3 cup heavy whipping cream
3/4 cup shredded Swiss cheese
1/2 cup diced fully cooked ham
18 fresh asparagus tips (1-inch pieces)

In a small mixing bowl, beat cream cheese and butter until smooth. Add 3/4 cup flour and cornmeal; mix well. Cover and refrigerate for 1 hour.

Shape dough into 18 balls. Press onto the bottom and up the sides of greased miniature muffin cups. In a bowl, whisk egg and cream. Stir in remaining flour until smooth. Add cheese and ham; mix well. Spoon about 1 tablespoon into each cup. Bake at 425° for 7 minutes.

Reduce heat to 325°. Top each tart with an asparagus tip. Cover loosely with foil. Bake 17-20 minutes longer or until a knife inserted near the center comes out clean. **Yield:** 1-1/2 dozen.

Homemade Lemonade

Chilled club soda adds fizz to this refreshing sweet-tart beverage. *—Becky Baird, Salt Lake City, Utah*

3 cups sugar
2 cups water
1 cup lemon peel strips (about 6 lemons)
3 cups lemon juice (about 14 lemons)
1 bottle (1 liter) club soda, chilled

In a large saucepan, cook and stir sugar and water over medium heat until sugar is dissolved. Stir in lemon strips. Bring to a boil. Reduce heat; simmer, uncovered, for 5 minutes.

Remove from the heat. Cool slightly. Stir in lemon juice; cover and refrigerate until chilled. Discard lemon strips. Pour mixture into a pitcher; gradually stir in club soda. **Yield:** 10 cups.

Tangy Marinated Shrimp

I like the fact that I can make this colorful, unusual appetizer ahead of time. I'm always on the lookout for new and different appetizers, and this one is simply delicious. —Pat Waymire, Yellow Springs, Ohio

   1 **pound medium uncooked shrimp, peeled and deveined**
   3/4 **cup white vinegar**
   1/2 **cup lemon juice**
   1/2 **cup olive oil**
   1/4 **cup honey**
Hot pepper sauce, salt and pepper to taste
   2 **medium onions, thinly sliced and separated into rings**
   1 **jar (5-3/4 ounces) stuffed olives, undrained**

Place shrimp in a steamer basket. Place in a saucepan over 1 in. of water; bring to a boil. Cover and steam for 3-5 minutes or until shrimp turn pink. Cool.

In a large bowl, whisk vinegar, lemon juice, oil, honey, pepper sauce, salt and pepper until blended. Stir in onions, olives with juice and shrimp. Cover and refrigerate for 4 hours or overnight. Serve with a slotted spoon. **Yield:** 4-6 servings.

Easter Bunnies 'n' Chicks

(Pictured below)

These hard-cooked eggs are quick to make and fun to serve at Easter. —Lois Jacobson, Dallas, Wisconsin

Egg dyes
Hard-cooked eggs, peeled
Whole cloves
   1 **small carrot, peeled**

Prepare egg dyes according to package directions. Place peeled hard-cooked eggs in egg dyes. Let stand for 3-5 minutes or until tinted to desired shades. Remove to paper towels to dry.

For bunny: With a sharp knife, cut a thin slice of egg white from one side of egg to level. From removed slice, cut two ears and a tail. Make two deep small slits in top of egg; insert the ears. Position tail. Insert cloves for eyes and nose.

For chick: With a sharp knife, cut a thin piece of egg white from one side of the egg to level. Insert cloves for eyes. Cut carrot lengthwise into thin strips (about 1/16 in. thick). Cut a small triangle for the beak and two larger triangles for wings. Make two small shallow slits in the sides of the egg; insert wings. Gently press beak into front of egg.

Pepper Jack Cheese Sticks

If you see a group of people huddled around an appetizer table, it's probably because they're feasting on these fun snacks. —Darlene Brenden Salem, Oregon

   1 **pound pepper Jack cheese**
   3 **cups all-purpose flour**
   3 **eggs, beaten**
   3 **cups crushed cornflakes**
Oil for deep-fat frying
Salsa and guacamole

Cut cheese into 2-3/4-in. x 1/2-in. sticks. Place the flour, eggs and cornflakes in three separate shallow bowls. Coat cheese sticks with flour; dip in egg, then roll in cornflakes until well coated. Let stand for 5 minutes.

In an electric skillet or deep-fat fryer, heat oil to 375°. Cook cheese sticks in batches for 30 seconds or until golden brown. Drain on paper towels. Let stand for 3-5 minutes. Serve with salsa and guacamole. **Yield:** 2-1/2 dozen.

Zesty Snack Mix

Pep up a party with this crunchy well-seasoned blend of cereal, pretzels and cheese crackers. You can alter it by adding mixed nuts. —Codie Ray Tallulah, Louisiana

   4 **cups Corn Chex cereal**
   4 **cups Cheerios**
   4 **cups pretzel sticks**
   4 **cups cheese-flavored snack crackers**

1 cup butter, melted
1/2 cup vegetable oil
3 tablespoons Worcestershire sauce
1 tablespoon garlic powder
1 tablespoon seasoned salt
1 tablespoon chili powder
1 teaspoon cayenne pepper

In a large bowl, combine the cereals, pretzels and crackers. Spread onto two ungreased 15-in. x 10-in. x 1-in. baking pans. Combine the remaining ingredients; pour over the cereal mixture and toss to coat. Bake at 225° for 2 to 2-1/2 hours, stirring every 30 minutes. Store in airtight containers. **Yield:** 16 cups.

Minty Mango Salsa

My husband likes to smoke a whole turkey, and I make this colorful salsa with fresh mint to accompany it. It's always a hit with our guests, especially when served as an appetizer with tortilla chips.
—Diane Thompson, Nutrioso, Arizona

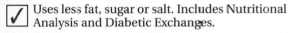 Uses less fat, sugar or salt. Includes Nutritional Analysis and Diabetic Exchanges.

1 large ripe mango, peeled and diced
1 medium sweet red pepper, diced
1 can (4 ounces) chopped green chilies
1/4 cup chopped green onions
1 tablespoon lime juice
2 teaspoons minced fresh mint
1/4 teaspoon ground ginger
Tortilla chips

In a bowl, combine the first seven ingredients. Cover and refrigerate for at least 8 hours. Serve with tortilla chips. **Yield:** about 2-1/2 cups.

Nutritional Analysis: One 1/4-cup serving (calculated without tortilla chips) equals 20 calories, trace fat (trace saturated fat), 0 cholesterol, 43 mg sodium, 5 g carbohydrate, 1 g fiber, trace protein. **Diabetic Exchange:** Free food.

Jack's Stuffed Mushrooms

(Pictured above right)

Since my son loves stuffed mushrooms, we came up with this wild-game appetizer. We enjoy it before the big meal is served. —*Jack D. Hunter II, Harlingen, Texas*

12 large fresh mushrooms
3 to 4 whole dove *or* quail, cooked and deboned

1 cup (4 ounces) shredded cheddar cheese
1 serrano *or* jalapeno pepper, seeded*
Salt and pepper to taste
2 bacon strips, cooked and crumbled

Remove stems from mushrooms; set caps aside. (Discard stems or save for another use.) In a food processor, combine the dove, cheese, serrano, salt and pepper. Cover and pulse until finely chopped. Stuff mushroom caps with meat mixture. Sprinkle with bacon. Place on a baking sheet. Bake at 400° for 10-15 minutes or until cheese is melted. **Yield:** 1 dozen.

Editor's Note: When cutting or seeding hot peppers, use rubber or plastic gloves to protect your hands. Avoid touching your face.

A Mint Refresher

Mint is a really large family of more than 30 varieties. The most common are peppermint and spearmint. In general, spearmint is used for beverages, peppermint flavors desserts, and garden mint is the choice for general cooking.

Fresh is best, right from the garden or grocery store. Keep mint in the refrigerator, wrapped in paper towels and enclosed in a plastic bag. Dried mint is also available and should be stored away from heat, light and moisture.

Salads & Dressings

Served as a well-dressed side or as the main course, these sensational salads are sure to make a fresh impression on family and friends.

REFRESHING FARE. Clockwise from upper left: Marshmallow Fruit Salad (p. 31), Tomato Onion Salad (p. 30), Frosted Fruit Gelatin (p. 33), Mostaccioli Veggie Salad (p. 34) and Roasted Potato Salad (p. 34).

starch and mustard. Stir in cream, egg and vinegar until smooth. Cook and stir over medium heat until mixture coats the back of a metal spoon. Cook and stir 1-2 minutes longer or until thickened.

Remove from the heat; let stand for 20 minutes. Whisk in mayonnaise and butter until smooth. Cool slightly. Pour over potato mixture; mix well. Cover and refrigerate for at least 6 hours. **Yield:** 10-12 servings.

Raspberry Vinaigrette

Raspberries give this fruity salad dressing a beautiful red color. A hint of Dijon mustard gives it just the right touch of tartness. —Dorothy Smith
El Dorado, Arkansas

☑ Uses less fat, sugar or salt. Includes Nutritional Analysis and Diabetic Exchanges.

1-1/3 **cups fresh *or* frozen unsweetened raspberries**
  1/3 **cup reduced-sodium chicken broth**
    2 **tablespoons sugar**
    1 **tablespoon cider vinegar**
2-1/2 **teaspoons olive *or* canola oil**
    2 **teaspoons Dijon mustard**
Mixed salad greens

Press raspberries through a sieve, reserving juice; discard seeds. In a jar with tight-fitting lid, combine the broth, sugar, vinegar, oil, mustard and reserved juice. Refrigerate. Shake before serving over salad greens. **Yield:** 1 cup.

Nutritional Analysis: One serving (2 tablespoons salad dressing) equals 37 calories, 2 g fat (trace saturated fat), 0 cholesterol, 57 mg sodium, 6 g carbohydrate, 1 g fiber, trace protein. **Diabetic Exchange:** 1/2 fruit.

Celery Seed Potato Salad

(Pictured above)

This is a fresh-tasting potato salad seasoned with onion and celery seed. The mayonnaise dressing gets its sweetness from sugar and whipping cream, and its tang from mustard and vinegar. —Grace Yaskovic
Branchville, New Jersey

    6 **medium red potatoes**
    4 **hard-cooked eggs, diced**
    2 **celery ribs, finely chopped**
    1 **small onion, finely chopped**
    1 **teaspoon salt**
    1 **teaspoon celery seed**
    6 **tablespoons sugar**
  1/2 **teaspoon cornstarch**
  1/2 **teaspoon ground mustard**
  1/4 **cup heavy whipping cream**
    1 **egg, beaten**
    2 **tablespoons white vinegar**
  1/2 **cup mayonnaise**
4-1/2 **teaspoons butter**

Place potatoes in a Dutch oven and cover with water. Bring to a boil. Reduce heat; cover and simmer for 20-25 minutes or until tender. Drain. When cool enough to handle, peel and cube potatoes. Place in a large bowl. Add the hard-cooked eggs, celery, onion, salt and celery seed; set aside.

In a small saucepan, combine the sugar, corn-

Tomato Onion Salad

(Pictured on page 29)

I worked as a summer cook at a Wyoming ranch for more than 20 years, and I made this marinated salad often. It was obviously a favorite because there were never any leftovers. —Nell Cruse, Ontario, Oregon

☑ Uses less fat, sugar or salt. Includes Nutritional Analysis and Diabetic Exchanges.

    4 **large tomatoes, sliced**
    2 **medium sweet onions, thinly sliced and separated into rings**
  1/4 **cup olive oil**

2 tablespoons red wine vinegar
2 tablespoons minced fresh parsley
1 teaspoon salt
1 teaspoon Italian seasoning
1 teaspoon finely chopped onion
1/2 teaspoon sugar
1/4 teaspoon garlic powder
1/4 teaspoon pepper

Layer tomatoes and onions in a shallow serving dish. In a jar with a tight-fitting lid, combine the remaining ingredients; shake well. Drizzle over salad. Cover and refrigerate for at least 2 hours before serving. **Yield:** 6 servings.

Nutritional Analysis: One serving (3/4 cup) equals 119 calories, 9 g fat (1 g saturated fat), 0 cholesterol, 406 mg sodium, 9 g carbohydrate, 2 g fiber, 1 g protein. **Diabetic Exchanges:** 2 vegetable, 1-1/2 fat.

Marshmallow Fruit Salad

(Pictured on page 28)

The cooked custard dressing for this salad is uniquely delicious. Mixing in marshmallow halves with the fruit makes each serving light, fluffy and fun!
—*Beverly Wade, Park Forest, Illinois*

1 package (16 ounces) large marshmallows, halved
3 egg yolks, beaten
1/2 cup milk
1/8 teaspoon ground mustard
1 cup heavy whipping cream
2 teaspoons confectioners' sugar
1 teaspoon vanilla extract
1 can (20 ounces) pineapple chunks, drained
1 can (15 ounces) mandarin oranges, drained
3 cups sliced fresh strawberries
1 cup fresh blueberries
1/2 cup chopped pecans

Place marshmallows in a large bowl; set aside. In a saucepan, whisk the egg yolks, milk and mustard. Cook and stir over medium heat until mixture reaches 160° and coats the back of a metal spoon. Cool for 5 minutes. Stir into marshmallows.

In a mixing bowl, beat the cream, confectioners' sugar and vanilla on medium speed until soft peaks form. Fold into marshmallow mixture. Add fruit; gently toss to coat. Cover and refrigerate for at least 3 hours. Just before serving, stir in pecans. **Yield:** 18 servings.

Warm Asparagus Spinach Salad

(Pictured below and on cover)

Spinach, cashews and pasta are mixed with roasted asparagus in this delightful spring salad. The mixture is topped with a light vinaigrette, seasoned with soy sauce and sprinkled with Parmesan cheese. I've used this recipe many times.
—*Kathleen Lucas, Trumbull, Connecticut*

1-1/2 pounds fresh asparagus, trimmed and cut into 1-inch pieces
2 tablespoons plus 1/2 cup olive oil, *divided*
1/4 teaspoon salt
1-1/2 pounds uncooked penne *or* medium tube pasta
3/4 cup chopped green onions
6 tablespoons white wine vinegar
2 tablespoons soy sauce
1 package (6 ounces) fresh baby spinach
1 cup coarsely chopped cashews
1/2 cup shredded Parmesan cheese

Place asparagus in a 13-in. x 9-in. x 2-in. baking dish. Drizzle with 2 tablespoons oil; sprinkle with salt. Bake, uncovered, at 400° for 20-25 minutes or until crisp-tender, stirring every 10 minutes. Meanwhile, cook pasta according to package directions; drain.

For dressing, combine the onions, vinegar and soy sauce in a blender; cover and process. While processing, gradually add the remaining oil in a steady stream.

In a large salad bowl, combine pasta, spinach and asparagus. Drizzle with dressing; toss to coat. Sprinkle with cashews and Parmesan cheese. Serve immediately. **Yield:** 14-16 servings.

Grilled Steak Caesar Salad

A tangy anchovy dressing coats this hearty Caesar salad. It's my version of a delicious dish offered at one of our finer restaurants. My quilting group really enjoys this salad served with hard rolls.
—*Eleanor Froehlich, Rochester Hills, Michigan*

- 4 hard-cooked egg yolks
- 4 anchovy fillets *or* 2 tablespoons anchovy paste
- 4 garlic cloves, minced
- 3 tablespoons Dijon mustard
- 2 tablespoons red wine vinegar
- 2 tablespoons lemon juice
- 1 tablespoon Worcestershire sauce
- 1 tablespoon ground mustard
- 2 teaspoons coarsely ground pepper
- 1 teaspoon sugar
- 1 cup olive oil

- 1 boneless beef sirloin steak (1-1/4 pounds)
- 1 large bunch romaine, torn
- 2/3 cup shredded Parmesan cheese, *divided*
- 2 medium tomatoes, cut into wedges
- 2 cups Caesar salad croutons

In a blender or food processor, combine the first 10 ingredients; cover and process until blended. While processing, gradually add oil in a steady stream. Cover and refrigerate.

Grill steak, covered, over medium heat for 5-7 minutes on each side or until meat reaches desired doneness (for rare, a meat thermometer should read 140; medium, 160°; well-done, 170°).

In a large bowl, toss the romaine, 1/3 cup Parmesan cheese and salad dressing. Divide among salad plates. Slice the steak; arrange steak and tomatoes on salads. Top with croutons and remaining Parmesan cheese. **Yield:** 6 servings.

'I'd Like That Restaurant Recipe'

a little taste, so a dining area was built."

Now operated by Susan and her husband, Dudley, the restaurant offers indoor and outdoor seating for 300 people on a 4-1/2-acre site with giant oak trees and a spring.

Located at Highway 46 and I-35 (Exit 189), New Braunfels Smokehouse is open daily from 7:30 a.m. to 9 p.m. For more information, call 1-830/625-2416 or visit *www.nbsmokehouse.com.*

Cranberry Relish Mold

(Pictured at left)

- 1 teaspoon unflavored gelatin
- 1 tablespoon cold water
- 2 packages (3 ounces *each*) cherry gelatin
- 2 cups boiling water
- 1 can (16 ounces) whole-berry cranberry sauce
- 1 can (8 ounces) crushed pineapple, drained
- 1/4 cup chopped celery

"WHILE shopping in New Braunfels, Texas, I had lunch at New Braunfels Smokehouse," recalls Wanna Wade from San Angelo. "The chicken and dumplings, one of their specialties, was served with a wonderful Cranberry Relish Mold that I enjoyed. Could *Taste of Home* get that salad recipe?"

Susan Dunbar Snyder was happy to share it. "This cranberry salad was a recipe from my mother's family, and we have served it at New Braunfels Smokehouse for as long as any of us can remember," she says.

"My parents owned a locker plant and in 1951 built a 'tasting room' and retail shop—my mother's pet project—to let customers sample our hickory-smoked meats. Soon people wanted more than just

In a bowl, combine unflavored gelatin and cold water; let stand for 1 minute. Add cherry gelatin and boiling water; stir until dissolved. Stir in the cranberry sauce, pineapple and celery.

Pour into a 6-cup mold coated with nonstick cooking spray. Refrigerate until set. Unmold onto a serving plate. **Yield:** 12 servings.

Raisin-Walnut Waldorf Salad

(Pictured at right)

I enjoy playing around with recipes, trying to create tastes that I like without sacrificing my diabetic diet. A creamy pudding-and-yogurt dressing drapes this healthy salad. —Jean Mabis, Shumway, Illinois

✓ Uses less fat, sugar or salt. Includes Nutritional Analysis and Diabetic Exchanges.

    1/2 cup raisins
      1 cup boiling water
      4 cups chopped unpeeled red apples
      2 celery ribs, thinly sliced
      2 tablespoons lemon juice
      1 cup (8 ounces) fat-free plain yogurt
      2 tablespoons sugar-free instant vanilla
         pudding mix
Sugar substitute* equivalent to 2 tablespoons
      sugar, optional
    1/2 cup chopped walnuts

In a bowl, combine raisins and boiling water. Let stand for 5 minutes; drain. Combine raisins, apples, celery and lemon juice; toss. Combine yogurt, pudding mix and sweetener if desired. Pour over apple mixture; toss to coat. Cover and refrigerate for 1 hour. Just before serving, stir in walnuts. **Yield:** 6 servings.

Nutritional Analysis: One serving (3/4 cup) equals 181 calories, 7 g fat (1 g saturated fat), 1 mg cholesterol, 232 mg sodium, 30 g carbohydrate, 3 g fiber, 4 g protein. **Diabetic Exchanges:** 2 fruit, 1 fat.

*Editor's Note: This recipe was tested with Splenda No Calorie Sweetener. Look for it in the baking aisle of your grocery store.

Three-Bean Salad

This three-bean salad bursts with the flavor of savory. Honey gives a pleasant sweetness to the vinaigrette that coats the blend of green beans, kidney beans and lima beans. —Amy Short, Lesage, West Virginia

    1/3 cup cider vinegar
    1/3 cup vegetable oil
    1/3 cup honey
      2 tablespoons minced fresh savory *or* 2
         teaspoons dried savory
    1/4 teaspoon salt
      2 cups frozen cut green beans, thawed
      1 can (16 ounces) kidney beans, rinsed and
         drained
      1 can (15 ounces) lima beans, rinsed and
         drained
      1 medium onion, chopped
      1 medium green pepper, chopped

In a large bowl, whisk the vinegar, oil, honey, savory and salt until blended. Add the beans, onion and green pepper; stir to coat. Cover and refrigerate until chilled. Serve with a slotted spoon. **Yield:** 8 servings.

Frosted Fruit Gelatin

(Pictured on page 28)

I like to serve this combination of fruit, gelatin and cream cheese as a salad with a main dish or as a light, refreshing dessert. My close friend, Joanie, shared the recipe after I raved about it. —Sonja Blow
Reeds Spring, Missouri

      2 packages (3 ounces *each*) raspberry gelatin
      2 cups boiling water
      1 can (8 ounces) crushed pineapple
1-1/2 cups fresh blueberries
      3 to 4 medium firm bananas, sliced
      1 package (8 ounces) cream cheese, softened
      1 cup (8 ounces) sour cream
    1/2 cup sugar
    1/2 cup chopped walnuts

In a large bowl, dissolve gelatin in boiling water. Drain pineapple, reserving juice in a measuring cup. Add enough water to the juice to measure 1 cup; stir into gelatin mixture. Stir in pineapple and blueberries. Place bananas in a 13-in. x 9-in. x 2-in. dish. Pour gelatin mixture over bananas. Cover and refrigerate until firm.

In a small mixing bowl, beat cream cheese, sour cream and sugar until smooth. Spread over gelatin. Cover and refrigerate until serving. Sprinkle with walnuts. **Yield:** 8 servings.

Watermelon Basket

(Pictured above)

I cut a watermelon into a basket shape, then fill it with melon balls to serve with a creamy dip.
—Christine Johnson, Ricetown, Kentucky

   1 large watermelon (about 10 pounds)
   1 medium honeydew, cut into balls
   3 cups white cranberry juice
   1 cup light corn syrup
   2 tablespoons lime juice
FRUIT DIP:
   1 package (8 ounces) cream cheese, softened
1/4 cup milk
   3 tablespoons sugar
   3 tablespoons lemon juice
3/4 teaspoon ground cardamom

Cut a thin slice from the bottom of watermelon with a sharp knife so it sits flat. Mark a horizontal cutting line 2 in. above center and around the melon.

For handle, score a 1-1/2-in.-wide strip across the top of melon, connecting both sides to the horizontal line. With a long sharp knife, cut all the way through the rind above the cutting line in a zigzag pattern.

Carefully lift off side pieces. Remove fruit from both sections and cut into balls. Refrigerate basket.

In a large bowl, combine watermelon and honeydew balls. In another bowl, whisk cranberry juice, corn syrup and lime juice until blended; pour over melon balls. Cover and chill for 3 hours.

Drain; spoon melon into watermelon basket. In a small mixing bowl, beat the cream cheese and milk until smooth. Beat in the sugar, lemon juice and cardamom; serve with melon. **Yield:** 32 servings.

Mostaccioli Veggie Salad

(Pictured on page 29)

This mix of pasta, zucchini, summer squash, cucumber, sweet peppers and black olives is coated with a light vinaigrette. —Julie Sterchi, Harrisburg, Illinois

   3 cups uncooked mostaccioli *or* large tube pasta
   1 medium cucumber, thinly sliced
   1 small yellow summer squash, quartered and sliced
   1 small zucchini, halved and sliced
1/2 cup diced sweet red pepper
1/2 cup diced green pepper
1/2 cup sliced ripe olives
   3 to 4 green onions, chopped
DRESSING:
1/3 cup sugar
1/3 cup white wine vinegar
1/3 cup vegetable oil
1-1/2 teaspoons prepared mustard
3/4 teaspoon dried minced onion
3/4 teaspoon garlic powder
3/4 teaspoon salt
1/2 teaspoon pepper

Cook pasta according to package directions. Drain and rinse in cold water. Place in a large bowl; add the cucumber, summer squash, zucchini, peppers, olives and onions.

In a jar with a tight-fitting lid, combine dressing ingredients; shake well. Pour over pasta mixture; toss to coat. Cover; refrigerate 8 hours or overnight. Toss before serving. **Yield:** 10 servings.

Roasted Potato Salad

(Pictured on page 28)

I pack this potato salad in a cooler to dish up cold at picnics or transfer it to a slow cooker to serve it warm for potlucks. —Terri Adams, Shawnee, Kansas

☑ Uses less fat, sugar or salt. Includes Nutritional Analysis and Diabetic Exchanges.

1/2 pound fresh green beans, cut into 1-1/2-inch pieces
   1 large whole garlic bulb
   2 pounds small red potatoes, quartered
   2 medium sweet red peppers, cut into large chunks
   2 green onions, sliced
1/4 cup chicken broth
1/4 cup balsamic vinegar
   2 tablespoons olive oil

2 teaspoons sugar
1 teaspoon minced fresh rosemary *or* 1/4
    teaspoon dried rosemary, crushed
1/2 teaspoon salt

In a large saucepan, bring 6 cups water to a boil. Add beans; bring to a boil. Cover and cook for 3 minutes. Drain and immediately place beans in ice water; drain and pat dry.

Remove papery outer skin from garlic (do not peel or separate cloves). Cut top off garlic bulb. Place cut side up in a greased 15-in. x 10-in. x 1-in. baking pan. Add the potatoes, red peppers, onions and beans; drizzle with broth. Bake, uncovered, at 400° for 30-40 minutes or until garlic is softened.

Remove garlic; set aside. Bake vegetables 30-35 minutes longer or until tender. Cool for 10-15 minutes. Squeeze softened garlic into a large bowl. Stir in the vinegar, oil, sugar, rosemary and salt. Add vegetables; toss to coat. **Yield:** 9 servings.

Nutritional Analysis: One serving (3/4 cup) equals 124 calories, 3 g fat (trace saturated fat), 0 cholesterol, 167 mg sodium, 22 g carbohydrate, 3 g fiber, 3 g protein. **Diabetic Exchanges:** 1 starch, 1 vegetable, 1/2 fat.

Chinese Turkey Pasta Salad

This colorful, palate-pleasing salad is ideal for weddings, luncheons and birthday parties.
        —*Nancy Bergeland, Madison, Minnesota*

2 cups uncooked spiral pasta
2 cups cubed cooked turkey
1-1/2 cups fresh *or* frozen snow peas, thawed
1/2 cup chopped sweet red pepper
1/2 cup chopped green pepper
1/4 cup thinly sliced green onions
1/4 cup diced celery
1 can (8 ounces) sliced water chestnuts, drained
1 jar (2 ounces) diced pimientos, drained
1 cup mayonnaise
2 tablespoons soy sauce
1 teaspoon sugar
1 teaspoon ground ginger
1/4 to 1/2 teaspoon hot pepper sauce
1 cup salted cashew halves, *divided*

Cook pasta according to package directions; drain and rinse in cold water. Place in a large bowl; add the next eight ingredients.

In a small bowl, combine mayonnaise, soy sauce, sugar, ginger and hot pepper sauce. Stir in 1/2 cup cashews. Pour over pasta mixture; toss to coat. Cov-er; refrigerate for 1 hour before serving. Sprinkle with remaining cashews. **Yield:** 4-6 servings.

Fruit 'n' Rice Salad

(Pictured below)

This colorful combination of strawberries, pear, peach, pineapple and banana is tossed with yogurt and rice for a delightful side dish that really says summer.
        —*Violet Beard, Marshall, Illinois*

✓ Uses less fat, sugar or salt. Includes Nutritional Analysis and Diabetic Exchanges.

1 can (8 ounces) unsweetened pineapple chunks
2 cups cooked rice
1/2 cup quartered strawberries
1/2 cup sliced ripe pear
1/2 cup sliced ripe peach
1/2 cup sliced firm banana
2 tablespoons fat-free plain yogurt
1 tablespoon honey
4 cups baby spinach

Drain pineapple, reserving 1/4 cup juice. In a large bowl, combine the pineapple, rice, strawberries, pear, peach and banana. In a small bowl, combine the yogurt, honey and reserved pineapple juice. Pour over fruit mixture and stir to coat. Line salad plates with spinach; top with fruit mixture. **Yield:** 8 servings.

Nutritional Analysis: One serving (3/4 cup fruit mixture with 1/2 cup spinach) equals 159 calories, 1 g fat (trace saturated fat), trace cholesterol, 24 mg sodium, 37 g carbohydrate, 2 g fiber, 3 g protein. **Diabetic Exchanges:** 1-1/2 fruit, 1 starch.

Cinnamon-Basil Fruit Salad

It's easy to vary the flavors in this salad by using different fruits, but the herb syrup always makes it taste special. —Sue Gronholz, Beaver Dam, Wisconsin

- 2 cups sugar
- 1 cup water
- 1 cup packed fresh basil leaves
- 3 sprigs fresh spearmint *or* mint
- 1 cinnamon stick (3 inches)
- 2 cups fresh raspberries *or* blackberries
- 1 cup cubed cantaloupe
- 1 cup cubed honeydew
- 1 cup fresh blueberries
- 1 medium apple, sliced

In a small saucepan, bring the sugar and water to a boil. Remove from the heat. Stir in the basil, spearmint and cinnamon stick. Cover and refrigerate overnight.

Discard the herbs and cinnamon stick from syrup. In a serving bowl, combine the fruit. Drizzle with syrup; gently toss to coat. Cover and refrigerate until chilled. Serve with a slotted spoon. **Yield:** 8-10 servings.

Onion Cucumber Salad

(Pictured below)

This crisp refreshing salad is flavored with green pepper and a sprinkling of celery seed, then drizzled with a slightly sweet vinegar dressing. I love using this recipe over and over.

—Mildred Mann
Jeffersonville, Kentucky

- 7 medium cucumbers, sliced
- 1 small onion, sliced
- 1 small green pepper, cut into thin rings
- 2 tablespoons salt
- 1 tablespoon celery seed
- 2 cups sugar
- 1 cup white vinegar

In a large serving bowl, combine cucumbers, onion and green pepper. Sprinkle with salt and celery seed. Combine sugar and vinegar; pour over cucumber mixture. Cover; refrigerate for at least 8 hours. Serve with a slotted spoon. **Yield:** 14 servings.

Warm Pecan Cabbage Slaw

I give a new twist to this slaw by serving it warm. The mild mustard flavor and pleasing blend of crisp-tender vegetables and toasted pecans nicely complement fish or ham. —Marie Hattrup, The Dalles, Oregon

☑ Uses less fat, sugar or salt. Includes Nutritional Analysis and Diabetic Exchanges.

- 4 cups coarsely shredded cabbage
- 1/2 cup shredded carrot
- 1/4 cup sliced green onions
- 2 tablespoons water

1/2 teaspoon salt
1/4 teaspoon pepper
1 tablespoon butter, melted
1 teaspoon Dijon mustard
1/4 cup chopped pecans, toasted

In a large saucepan, combine the cabbage, carrot, green onions, water, salt and pepper. Cover and cook over medium heat for 5-7 minutes or until cabbage is crisp-tender. Combine butter and mustard; pour over cabbage mixture; toss to coat. Stir in pecans. **Yield:** 6 servings.

Nutritional Analysis: One serving (1/2 cup) equals 109 calories, 8 g fat (2 g saturated fat), 8 mg cholesterol, 376 mg sodium, 8 g carbohydrate, 3 g fiber, 2 g protein. **Diabetic Exchanges:** 1-1/2 fat, 1 vegetable.

Fruited Carrot Salad

Full of fruity sweetness, this fresh-tasting salad tosses together grated carrot with mandarin oranges, apple, celery and raisins—all coated with tangy lemon yogurt. —Shirley Glaab
Hattiesburg, Mississippi

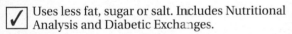
Uses less fat, sugar or salt. Includes Nutritional Analysis and Diabetic Exchanges.

2 cans (11 ounces _each_) mandarin
   oranges, drained
2 medium carrots, grated
1 medium apple, chopped
1/4 cup thinly sliced celery
1/4 cup golden raisins
3 tablespoons reduced-fat lemon yogurt

In a bowl, combine the oranges, carrots, apple, celery and raisins. Add yogurt; stir to coat. Cover and refrigerate until chilled. **Yield:** 4 servings.

Nutritional Analysis: One serving (3/4 cup) equals 112 calories, trace fat (trace saturated fat), 1 mg cholesterol, 34 mg sodium, 27 g carbohydrate, 4 g fiber, 2 g protein. **Diabetic Exchanges:** 1-1/2 fruit, 1 vegetable.

Grilled Chicken Caesar Salad

(Pictured above right)

Whenever we're invited to potlucks, I'm always asked to bring a salad because people know it's one of my specialties. This dish is especially good on summer days when it's too hot to cook on the stove.
—Deb Weisberger, Mullett Lake, Michigan

1/2 cup red wine vinegar
1/2 cup soy sauce
1/2 cup olive oil
1 tablespoon dried parsley flakes
1 teaspoon dried basil
1 teaspoon dried oregano
1/2 teaspoon garlic powder
1/2 teaspoon pepper
6 boneless skinless chicken breast halves
1 large bunch romaine, torn (12 cups)
1-1/2 cups Caesar salad croutons
1 cup halved cherry tomatoes
2/3 cup creamy Caesar salad dressing

In a large resealable plastic bag, combine the first eight ingredients; add the chicken. Seal bag and turn to coat; refrigerate for at least 4 hours.

Drain and discard marinade. Grill chicken, uncovered, over medium-low heat for 12-15 minutes or until juices run clear, turning several times.

Meanwhile, in a bowl, combine the romaine, croutons and tomatoes; add dressing and toss to coat. Divide among six salad plates. Slice chicken; arrange on salads. **Yield:** 6 servings.

Soups & Sandwiches

Score points with your family by serving a heaping bowlful of hot homemade soup and a piled-high sandwich for a winning meal.

WINNING TEAM. Clockwise from upper left: Chunky Taco Soup (p. 40), Crunchy Veggie Sandwiches (p. 40), Creamy Red Pepper Soup (p. 44) and Shredded Venison Sandwiches (p. 44).

350° for 22-26 minutes or until meat juices run clear. Serve on rolls with cheese and tomato if desired. **Yield:** 8 servings.

Chunky Taco Soup

(Pictured on page 38)

I've gotten great response at our church dinners and senior groups whenever I bring this thick, easy-to-fix soup. I usually take home an empty pot.
—Evelyn Buford, Belton, Missouri

1-1/2 **pounds boneless beef sirloin *or* round steak, cut into 3/4-inch cubes**
  1 **medium onion, chopped**
  1 **tablespoon olive oil**
  2 **cans (15 ounces *each*) pinto beans, rinsed and drained**
  2 **cans (14-1/2 ounces *each*) diced tomatoes with green chilies, undrained**
  2 **cups water**
  1 **can (15 ounces) black beans, rinsed and drained**
  1 **can (14-3/4 ounces) cream-style corn**
  1 **envelope ranch salad dressing mix**
  1 **envelope taco seasoning**
1/4 **cup minced fresh cilantro**

In a large kettle or Dutch oven, brown beef and onion in oil. Add the pinto beans, tomatoes, water, black beans, corn, salad dressing mix and taco seasoning. Bring to a boil. Reduce heat; cover and simmer for 20-30 minutes or until meat is tender. Sprinkle with cilantro. **Yield:** 12 servings (about 3 quarts).

Baked Venison Burgers

(Pictured above)

Since my husband is an avid hunter, we have an abundance of venison each winter. I adapted a meat loaf recipe to make these baked burgers, and we haven't eaten plain burgers since! —Teresa Bowen
Choudrant, Louisiana

3/4 **cup quick-cooking oats**
3/4 **cup milk**
1/4 **cup chopped onion**
  1 **egg, beaten**
1/2 **to 1 teaspoon seasoned salt**
  1 **pound ground venison**
  1 **pound ground beef**
1/3 **cup ketchup**
  1 **tablespoon brown sugar**
  1 **tablespoon Worcestershire sauce**
  1 **tablespoon prepared mustard**
  8 **sandwich rolls, split**
Swiss cheese and tomato slices, optional

In a large bowl, combine the oats, milk, onion, egg and seasoned salt. Crumble venison and beef over mixture; mix well. Shape into eight patties; place in a greased 15-in. x 10-in. x 1-in. baking pan.

In a small bowl, whisk the ketchup, brown sugar, Worcestershire sauce and mustard until blended. Spoon over patties. Bake, uncovered, at

Crunchy Veggie Sandwiches

(Pictured on page 39)

These sandwiches are a creative way to get kids to eat veggies. I've been making them for about 25 years. They're a great picnic food. —Bridget Ward
Roeland Park, Kansas

✓ Uses less fat, sugar or salt. Includes Nutritional Analysis and Diabetic Exchanges.

  1 **cup chopped green pepper**
  1 **cup chopped seeded cucumber**
  1 **cup chopped celery**
  1 **cup chopped seeded tomato**
  2 **tablespoons chopped onion**

2 tablespoons minced fresh parsley
2 tablespoons chopped dill pickle
1/3 cup fat-free sour cream
1/4 cup reduced-fat mayonnaise
1/4 teaspoon salt
Lettuce leaves
6 sandwich rolls, split

In a bowl, combine the first seven ingredients. In a small bowl, whisk the sour cream, mayonnaise and salt until blended. Stir into vegetable mixture. Cover and refrigerate for 1-2 hours. Serve on lettuce-lined rolls. **Yield:** 6 servings.

Nutritional Analysis: One serving equals 162 calories, 3 g fat (1 g saturated fat), 1 mg cholesterol, 519 mg sodium, 30 g carbohydrate, 2 g fiber, 5 g protein. **Diabetic Exchange:** 2 starch.

Sweet Potato Kale Soup

If you're looking for a healthier dish with a difference, try this recipe. Cannellini beans, sweet potatoes, kale and plenty of garlic flavor this brothy blend. It's the perfect winter soup and has soothed me through many a cold. —Tamara Holmes
San Diego, California

✓ Uses less fat, sugar or salt. Includes Nutritional Analysis and Diabetic Exchanges.

4 ounces fresh kale
1 large onion, chopped
3-1/2 teaspoons Italian seasoning
2 teaspoons olive oil
3 cans (14-1/2 ounces *each*) vegetable broth
2 cans (15 ounces *each*) white kidney *or* cannellini beans, rinsed and drained
1 pound sweet potatoes, peeled and cubed
12 garlic cloves, minced
1/2 teaspoon salt
1/4 teaspoon pepper

Cut out and discard the thick vein from each kale leaf. Coarsely chop kale; set aside. In a large saucepan or Dutch oven, saute onion and Italian seasoning in oil until onion is tender.

Stir in the broth, beans, sweet potatoes and kale. Bring to a boil. Reduce heat; simmer, uncovered, for 10 minutes. Stir in the garlic, salt and pepper. Simmer 10-15 minutes longer or until potatoes are tender. **Yield:** 8 servings (2 quarts).

Nutritional Analysis: One serving (1 cup) equals 150 calories, 2 g fat (trace saturated fat), 0 cholesterol, 836 mg sodium, 28 g carbohydrate, 5 g fiber, 6 g protein. **Diabetic Exchange:** 2 starch.

Mountain Man Soup

(Pictured below)

This stew-like soup is sure to satisfy your hearty hunter's appetite. It's chock-full of tender buffalo meat, tomatoes, and chunks of carrot and potato, lightly seasoned with bay leaf and clove. —Cordella Campbell
Rapid City, South Dakota

1 pound buffalo stew meat
2 tablespoons vegetable oil
2 cups chopped celery
2/3 cup chopped onion
1/4 cup chopped green pepper
2 cans (14-1/2 ounces *each*) beef broth
1 can (28 ounces) diced tomatoes, undrained
1 large potato, peeled and cubed
1 large carrot, sliced
2 teaspoons garlic salt
1 whole clove
1 bay leaf
1/4 cup minced fresh parsley

In a Dutch oven, brown meat in oil; drain. Add the celery, onion and green pepper; saute for 5 minutes or until tender. Stir in the broth, tomatoes, potato, carrot, garlic salt, clove and bay leaf. Bring to a boil. Reduce heat; simmer, uncovered, for 1 hour or until meat is tender. Discard clove and bay leaf. Stir in parsley. **Yield:** 6 servings.

Spicy Chuck-Wagon Soup
(Pictured below)

This thick and hearty beef soup is full of rich, spicy flavor. —Kelly Thornberry, La Porte, Indiana

2 tablespoons all-purpose flour
1 tablespoon paprika

1 teaspoon plus 1 tablespoon chili powder, *divided*
2 teaspoons salt
1 teaspoon garlic powder
1 boneless beef chuck roast (3 pounds), cut into 1-inch pieces
1/4 cup vegetable oil

LADLE OUT satisfying servings of Spicy Chuck-Wagon Soup, Hearty Garlic Potato Soup or Chicken Vegetable Soup (shown below, from top). Who wouldn't welcome some on a chilly day?

2 medium onions, chopped
1 can (28 ounces) stewed tomatoes, undrained
1 can (10-1/2 ounces) condensed beef broth, undiluted
1 bay leaf
1/4 to 1/2 teaspoon cayenne pepper
5 medium red potatoes, cubed
4 medium carrots, sliced
1 can (11 ounces) whole kernel corn, drained

In a large resealable plastic bag, combine the flour, paprika, 1 teaspoon chili powder, salt and garlic powder. Add beef, a few pieces at a time, and shake to coat. In a large soup kettle, brown beef in oil in batches. Stir in the onions, tomatoes, broth, bay leaf, cayenne and remaining chili powder. Bring to a boil. Reduce heat; cover and simmer for 30 minutes, stirring occasionally.

Add potatoes and carrots. Cover and simmer 35-40 minutes longer or until meat and vegetables are tender. Add corn and heat through. Discard the bay leaf before serving. **Yield:** 10 servings (4 quarts).

Hearty Garlic Potato Soup

(Pictured at left)

I started with a basic potato soup and added my own touches to come up with this comforting recipe. The addition of garlic is wonderful. —Beth Allard
Belmont, New Hampshire

8 medium potatoes, peeled and cut into 1/2-inch cubes
1 large carrot, peeled and chopped
2 garlic cloves, peeled
1/2 pound bulk Italian sausage
1 small onion, chopped
1/4 cup butter
1/4 cup all-purpose flour
8 cups milk
2 teaspoons minced fresh parsley
1-1/2 teaspoons salt
1 teaspoon chicken bouillon granules
1/2 teaspoon seasoned salt
1/4 teaspoon pepper

Place potatoes, carrot and garlic in a Dutch oven and cover with water. Bring to a boil. Reduce heat; cover and simmer for 15-20 minutes or until tender. Drain. Place 3 cups potato mixture in a bowl and mash. Set aside mashed potatoes and remaining potato mixture.

In a skillet, cook sausage and onion over medium

heat until meat is no longer pink; drain and set aside. In a soup kettle, melt butter. Stir in flour until smooth; gradually add the milk. Bring to a boil; cook and stir for 2 minutes or until soup is thickened.

Add the parsley, salt, bouillon, seasoned salt and pepper; mix well. Add the mashed potato mixture; cook and stir until heated through. Add the reserved potato and sausage mixtures. Heat through. **Yield:** 12 servings (about 3 quarts).

Chicken Vegetable Soup

(Pictured at left)

I'm always looking for recipes that are low in fat but don't taste like it. Even my picky son likes this vegetable-packed soup!
—Anna Overton
Lakewood, California

1 pound boneless skinless chicken breasts, cut into cubes
2 cups chicken broth, *divided*
1 teaspoon Italian seasoning
1 garlic clove, minced
1/4 teaspoon paprika
4 small red potatoes, cut into 1-inch pieces
3 small carrots, cut into 1/2-inch pieces
5 celery ribs, cut into 1/2-inch pieces
1 medium onion, cut into wedges
2 tablespoons chopped celery leaves
2 tablespoons all-purpose flour
2 tablespoons minced fresh parsley
1-1/2 teaspoons lemon juice

In a large saucepan, combine chicken, 1-3/4 cups broth, Italian seasoning, garlic and paprika. Bring to a boil. Reduce heat; cover and simmer for 10 minutes. Add potatoes, carrots, celery, onion and celery leaves. Bring to a boil. Reduce heat; cover and simmer for 20-25 minutes or until vegetables are tender.

In a small bowl, combine flour and remaining broth until smooth; add to pan. Bring to a boil; cook and stir for 2 minutes or until thickened. Stir in parsley and lemon juice. **Yield:** 4 servings.

Take Stock in Veggies

After buying fresh carrots, celery and onions, chop them up, use what you need and then freeze the rest in small amounts. That way, you'll always have vegetables on hand to make soups, stews and casseroles.

Squeeze softened garlic into a small bowl; mash with a fork. Stir into squash mixture. Cool slightly. Puree squash mixture in batches in a blender; return to pan. Stir in 1/2 cup cream, salt and pepper; heat through. Garnish with remaining cream and sage. **Yield:** 9 servings (3 quarts).

Creamy Red Pepper Soup

(Pictured on page 39)

Everyone loves this soup's taste, but no one guesses that pears are the secret ingredient. —Connie Summers
Augusta, Michigan

   2 large onions, chopped
   4 garlic cloves, minced
 1/4 cup butter
   2 large potatoes, peeled and diced
   2 jars (7 ounces *each*) roasted red
      peppers, drained, patted dry and chopped
   5 cups chicken broth
   2 cans (15 ounces *each*) pears in juice
 1/8 teaspoon cayenne pepper
 1/8 teaspoon black pepper

In a Dutch oven, saute onions and garlic in butter until tender. Add potatoes, red peppers and broth. Bring to a boil. Reduce heat; cover and simmer for 15-20 minutes or until vegetables are tender. Remove from the heat. Add pears; let cool.

In a blender, cover and puree in batches. Return to the pan. Stir in cayenne and black pepper. Heat through. **Yield:** 12 servings (3 quarts).

Garlic Butternut Bisque

(Pictured above)

With its pleasant squash and garlic flavor and golden-orange color, this rich and creamy soup is sure to be a hit whether you serve it for an everyday meal or a holiday dinner. —Della Clarke, Vista, California

   2 whole garlic bulbs
   1 teaspoon olive oil
   3 large onions, chopped
 3/4 cup chopped carrots
 1/2 cup chopped celery
 1/4 cup butter
   4 pounds butternut squash, peeled, seeded
      and cubed (about 8 cups)
   6 cups chicken broth
   3 tablespoons chopped fresh sage, *divided*
 1/2 cup plus 1 tablespoon heavy whipping
      cream, *divided*
1-1/2 teaspoons salt
 1/4 teaspoon pepper

Remove papery outer skin from garlic (do not peel or separate cloves). Cut tops off bulbs; brush with oil. Wrap each in heavy-duty foil.

Bake at 425° for 30-35 minutes or until softened. Cool 10-15 minutes. Meanwhile, in a Dutch oven, saute the onions, carrots and celery in butter until tender. Add the squash, broth and 2 tablespoons sage. Bring to a boil. Reduce heat; simmer, uncovered, for 25-30 minutes or until squash is tender.

Shredded Venison Sandwiches

(Pictured on page 38)

My husband hunts for deer every November, so I'm always looking for new recipes for venison. The whole family loves these slow cooker sandwiches.
—Ruth Setterlund, Fryeburg, Maine

   1 boneless venison roast (4 pounds)
1-1/2 cups ketchup
   3 tablespoons brown sugar
   1 tablespoon ground mustard
   1 tablespoon lemon juice
   1 tablespoon soy sauce
   1 tablespoon Liquid Smoke, optional
   2 teaspoons celery salt
   2 teaspoons pepper
   2 teaspoons Worcestershire sauce

  1 teaspoon onion powder
  1 teaspoon garlic powder
  1/8 teaspoon ground nutmeg
  3 drops hot pepper sauce
  14 to 18 hamburger buns, split

Cut venison roast in half; place in a 5-qt. slow cooker. In a large bowl, combine the ketchup, brown sugar, mustard, lemon juice, soy sauce, Liquid Smoke if desired and seasonings. Pour over venison. Cover and cook on high for 4-1/2 to 5 hours or until meat is tender.

Remove the roast; set aside to cool. Strain sauce and return to slow cooker. Shred meat, using two forks; stir into sauce and heat through. Using a slotted spoon, spoon meat mixture onto each bun. **Yield:** 14-18 servings.

Colony Mountain Chili

My husband created this chili for a local cooking contest, and it won the People's Choice award. It's loaded with beef, Italian sausage, tomatoes and beans.
—Marjorie O'Dell, Bow, Washington

  1 pound boneless beef sirloin steak, cut
    into 3/4-inch cubes
  4 Italian sausage links, casings removed and
    cut into 3/4-inch slices
  2 tablespoons olive oil, *divided*
  1 medium onion, chopped
  3 garlic cloves, minced
  2 green onions, thinly sliced
  2 teaspoons beef bouillon granules
  1 cup boiling water
  1 can (6 ounces) tomato paste
  3 tablespoons chili powder
  2 tablespoons brown sugar
  2 tablespoons Worcestershire sauce
  2 teaspoons ground cumin
  1 to 2 teaspoons crushed red pepper flakes
  1 teaspoon salt
  1/2 teaspoon pepper
  3 cans (14-1/2 ounces *each*) stewed
    tomatoes, cut up
  2 cans (15 ounces *each*) pinto beans, rinsed
    and drained
Shredded cheddar cheese, optional

In a large skillet, brown beef and sausage in 1 tablespoon oil; drain. Transfer meat to a 5-qt. slow cooker. In the same skillet, saute the onion, garlic and green onions in remaining oil until tender. Transfer to slow cooker.

In a small bowl, dissolve bouillon in water. Stir in the tomato paste, chili powder, brown sugar, Worces-

tershire sauce and seasonings until blended; add to slow cooker. Stir in tomatoes and beans. Cover and cook on high for 6-8 hours or until meat is tender. Serve with cheese if desired. **Yield:** 10 servings.

Waldorf Turkey Sandwiches

(Pictured below)

Whether we eat these sandwiches indoors or outside at a picnic, they are always popular. Children especially enjoy the touch of sweetness from apples and raisins.
—Lillian Julow, Gainesville, Florida

  1 cup diced cooked turkey
  2/3 cup chopped peeled apple
  1 celery rib, finely chopped
  1/2 cup chopped walnuts, toasted
  1/4 cup golden raisins
  1/3 cup vanilla yogurt
  1/3 cup mayonnaise
  1 teaspoon minced fresh tarragon *or* 1/2
    teaspoon dried tarragon
  1/2 to 1 teaspoon grated orange peel
  1/8 teaspoon salt
Dash pepper
  4 sandwich rolls, split

In a bowl, combine the turkey, apple, celery, walnuts and raisins. Combine the yogurt, mayonnaise, tarragon, orange peel, salt and pepper; pour over turkey mixture and stir to coat. Spoon 1/2 cup onto each roll. **Yield:** 4 servings.

Grilled Sub Sandwich

(Pictured below)

After a long hard day at band camp, my daughter comes home with a huge appetite. This sandwich not only satisfies my hungry marcher, it is also fast and easy to prepare.
— Char Shanahan
Schererville, Indiana

  1 large green pepper, thinly sliced
  1 small onion, thinly sliced and separated into rings
1/2 teaspoon olive oil
  1 loaf (1 pound) unsliced Italian bread
1/3 cup prepared Italian salad dressing, *divided*
  2 ounces sliced deli turkey
  4 slices Swiss cheese
  2 ounces sliced deli ham
  3 slices cheddar cheese
  2 ounces sliced deli pastrami
1/2 cup sliced dill pickles
  1 large tomato, thinly sliced
Additional olive oil

In a bowl, toss green pepper and onion with oil. Place on a double thickness of heavy-duty foil (about 12 in. square). Fold foil around vegetables and seal tightly. Grill, covered, over medium-hot heat for 12-15 minutes or until tender; set aside.

Cut loaf in half horizontally; remove bread from top piece, leaving a 1/2-in. shell. Brush cut sides of loaf with salad dressing; place cut side down on grill. Grill, uncovered, over medium heat for 3-5 minutes or until golden brown.

Place bottom of loaf on a double thickness of heavy-duty foil (about 18 in. x 12 in.). Layer with turkey, two Swiss cheese slices, ham, cheddar cheese, pastrami and remaining Swiss cheese. Top with green pepper mixture, pickles and tomato.

Drizzle remaining dressing over cut side of bread top; place over filling. Brush bread with additional oil. Fold foil around sandwich and seal tightly. Grill, covered, over medium heat for 4-8 minutes or until cheese is melted. Cut into slices with a serrated knife. **Yield:** 4 servings.

Turkey Barley Soup

My husband and I enjoy soup anytime. This light and satisfying soup has an interesting blend of flavors...and it's good for you, too. It's a great way to use up leftover holiday turkey.
— Betty Kleberger
Florissant, Missouri

✓ Uses less fat, sugar or salt. Includes Nutritional Analysis and Diabetic Exchanges.

  1 medium green pepper, chopped
  1 celery rib, chopped
  3 garlic cloves, minced
  2 cans (one 40-1/2 ounces, one 14-1/2 ounces) chicken broth
  4 cups cubed cooked turkey
  2 medium carrots, halved and thinly sliced
  1 large potato, peeled and cubed
  2 cups frozen cut green beans
1/2 cup uncooked medium pearl barley
  2 bay leaves
  1 teaspoon dried thyme
  1 teaspoon rubbed sage
1/2 teaspoon salt

In a Dutch oven or soup kettle, combine all of the ingredients. Bring to a boil. Reduce heat; simmer, uncovered, for 45-55 minutes or until barley and vegetables are tender. Discard bay leaves. **Yield:** 10 servings (3 quarts).

Nutritional Analysis: One serving (prepared with reduced-sodium broth) equals 183 calories, 2 g fat (1 g saturated fat), 39 mg cholesterol, 566 mg sodium, 20 g carbohydrate, 4 g fiber, 21 g protein. **Diabetic Exchanges:** 2 lean meat, 1 starch, 1 vegetable.

Corny Chicken Wraps

I'm a clinical dietitian, so I like to prepare foods that are both healthy and low-fat. This zippy Tex-Mex wrap is a quick alternative to a taco or sandwich for our

on-the-go family. To increase the spicy flavor, I suggest using a medium or hot salsa.
—Susan Alverson, Chester, South Dakota

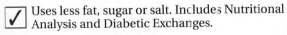 Uses less fat, sugar or salt. Includes Nutritional Analysis and Diabetic Exchanges.

  1 **pound boneless skinless chicken breasts, cut into strips**
1/2 **cup chopped green pepper**
1/4 **cup chopped green onions**
  2 **teaspoons canola** *or* **vegetable oil**
1-1/2 **cups frozen whole kernel corn, thawed**
1-1/2 **cups salsa**
1/4 **cup sliced ripe olives**
1/2 **teaspoon chili powder**
  6 **flour tortillas (8 inches), warmed**
  1 **cup (4 ounces) shredded reduced-fat cheddar cheese**

In a nonstick skillet, saute the chicken, green pepper and onions in oil for 3-4 minutes or until chicken juices run clear; drain. Stir in the corn, salsa, olives and chili powder. Cook and stir over medium heat for 3-4 minutes or until heated through. Spoon about 1/2 cup chicken mixture over one side of each tortilla. Sprinkle with cheese; roll up and secure with toothpicks. **Yield:** 6 servings.

   Nutritional Analysis: One filled tortilla equals 368 calories, 11 g fat (4 g saturated fat), 58 mg cholesterol, 632 mg sodium, 40 g carbohydrate, 3 g fiber, 29 g protein. **Diabetic Exchanges:** 3 lean meat, 2-1/2 starch.

Asparagus Leek Chowder

(Pictured above right)

To us, asparagus is the taste of spring, so we enjoy it in as many meals as we can. When this thick and creamy chowder is on the table, we know spring has arrived.
—Elisabeth Harders, West Allis, Wisconsin

  1 **pound fresh asparagus, trimmed and cut into 1-inch pieces**
  3 **cups sliced fresh mushrooms**
  3 **large leeks (white portion only), sliced**
  6 **tablespoons butter**
1/4 **cup all-purpose flour**
1/2 **teaspoon salt**
Dash pepper
  2 **cups chicken broth**
  2 **cups half-and-half cream**
  1 **can (11 ounces) whole kernel corn, drained**
  1 **tablespoon chopped pimientos**

In a large saucepan, saute the asparagus, mushrooms and leeks in butter for 10 minutes or until tender. Stir in the flour, salt and pepper until blended.

   Gradually stir in broth and cream. Bring to a boil. Reduce heat; cook and stir for 2 minutes or until thickened. Stir in corn and pimientos; heat through. **Yield:** 7 servings.

♪ Soup Suggestions

If you can, make soups a day ahead and refrigerate them overnight. The extra time allows the flavors to meld and heighten. Refrigerating soups before serving also allows any fat to float to the surface and solidify, making it easy to lift off before the soup is reheated.

To freeze soup, place a heavy-duty resealable plastic bag inside a bowl, pour the soup into the bag, then freeze. When solid, lift the plastic bag out of the bowl, seal it and return it to the freezer for up to 3 months.

Side Dishes & Condiments

Turn to this chapter for all sorts of complementary side dishes and condiments to serve alongside or to top off main courses.

APPEALING PARTNERS. Clockwise from upper left: Vegetable Stuffing Bake (p. 50), Mint Jelly (p. 52), Roasted Squash Medley (p. 54), Asparagus with Mustard Sauce (p. 54) and Cranberry Tomato Chutney (p. 56).

Glazed Winter Vegetables

(Pictured below)

A buttery sweet sauce seasoned with cinnamon coats the russets, sweet potatoes, squash and carrots in this delicious side dish. It goes well with beef, pork, poultry, sausage—just about anything. —Pam Holloway
Marion, Louisiana

4 large sweet potatoes, peeled, halved lengthwise and cut into 1/2-inch slices
2 medium acorn squash, peeled, seeded and cubed
2 large russet potatoes, peeled, halved lengthwise and cut into 1/2-inch slices
1 pound baby carrots
1 cup packed brown sugar
1/2 cup water
1/2 cup butter, melted
1/2 cup molasses
2 teaspoons ground cinnamon
2 teaspoons vanilla extract
1 teaspoon salt

Divide sweet potatoes, squash, potatoes and carrots among four greased 13-in. x 9-in. x 2-in. baking pans. In a bowl, combine the brown sugar, water, butter, molasses, cinnamon, vanilla and salt. Drizzle over vegetables; toss to coat.

Cover and bake at 425° for 30 minutes. Stir vegetables. Bake, uncovered, for 15-20 minutes longer or until vegetables are tender. **Yield:** 24 servings (3/4 cup each).

Dilly Pickled Asparagus

These dilled spears are really popular with my family. My granddaughter always says, "Oh, Grammy, these are soooo good!" They're easy to prepare and turn out perfect every time. My husband loves it when I add a dried hot red pepper to each jar. —Annie Merrell
Fenelon Falls, Ontario

6 pounds fresh asparagus
3 large garlic cloves, halved
6 teaspoons dill seed
6 teaspoons mustard seed
36 whole peppercorns
2 quarts water
2-1/2 cups white vinegar
1/2 cup sugar
3 tablespoons canning salt

Wash, drain and trim asparagus; cut into 4-1/2-in. spears. Discard ends or save for another use. Place asparagus in a large container; cover with ice water. In each of six 1-pint jars, place half of a garlic clove, 1 teaspoon dill seed, 1 teaspoon mustard seed and six whole peppercorns.

In a Dutch oven, bring the water, vinegar, sugar and salt to a boil. Drain asparagus; pack in jars to within 1/2 in. of top. Ladle boiling liquid over asparagus, leaving 1/4-in. headspace. Adjust caps. Process for 20 minutes in a boiling-water bath. Remove jars to wire racks to cool completely. **Yield:** 6 pints.

Vegetable Stuffing Bake

(Pictured on page 48)

This vegetable medley has become a family tradition for Thanksgiving and Christmas. Even though our three children are now married, when we get together for the holidays this dish is always on the menu. It's as important to them as the turkey! —Becky Kusmaul, Ankeny, Iowa

1 medium onion, chopped
1 tablespoon vegetable oil

2 cans (10-3/4 ounces *each*) condensed cream of mushroom soup, undiluted
1 cup process cheese sauce
1 package (16 ounces) frozen broccoli florets, thawed
1 package (16 ounces) frozen cauliflower, thawed
1 package (16 ounces) frozen corn, thawed
1 package (16 ounces) frozen brussels sprouts, thawed and halved
1 package (6 ounces) corn bread stuffing mix, *divided*

In a large skillet, saute the onion in oil until tender. Stir in the soup and cheese sauce until blended; heat through. In a large bowl, combine vegetables and 1 cup stuffing mix. Add soup mixture and mix well.

Transfer to two greased shallow 2-qt. baking dishes. Sprinkle with remaining stuffing mix. Bake, uncovered, at 350° for 30-35 minutes or until vegetables are tender and edges are bubbly. **Yield:** 2 casseroles (6-8 servings each).

Noodle Kugel

(Pictured above right)

I'm what you'd call a "ballabusta" in the Jewish culture—a woman who is a good homemaker. I make this traditional side dish along with other Jewish specialties for an annual Hanukkah/Christmas party with our friends.
—Lauren Kargen
Williamsville, New York

1 package (1 pound) egg noodles
1/2 cup butter, melted
8 eggs
2 cups sugar
2 cups (16 ounces) sour cream
2 cups (16 ounces) small-curd cottage cheese
TOPPING:
9 whole cinnamon graham crackers, crushed
3 tablespoons butter, melted

Cook noodles according to package directions; drain. Toss with butter; set aside. In a large mixing bowl, beat the eggs, sugar, sour cream and cottage cheese until well blended. Stir in the noodles.

Transfer to a greased 13-in. x 9-in. x 2-in. baking dish. Combine the cracker crumbs and butter; sprinkle over the top.

Bake, uncovered, at 350° for 50-55 minutes or until a thermometer reads 160°. Let stand for 10 minutes before cutting. Serve warm or cold. **Yield:** 12-15 servings.

Selecting Side Dishes

A main dish and side dishes should complement one another. If your entree has intense flavor, pair it with more mild-flavored side dishes and vice versa. If your entree has lots of garlic, onion or nuts, stay away from a side dish that's loaded with any of those same ingredients.

For ease of preparation, look for an oven-baked side dish that cooks at the same temperature as your main dish.

If your oven will be full with the entree and other side dishes, choose another side that can be prepared on the stovetop or in a slow cooker. Or for a refreshing break from the hot foods, turn to an assortment of fresh fruit or a relish tray.

Recipes that can be prepared ahead (like gelatin salads and overnight casseroles) are a real boon to busy cooks.

and dill; toss to coat. Grill, covered, over indirect medium heat for 20-25 minutes or until vegetables are crisp-tender, stirring occasionally. **Yield:** 8 servings.

Nutritional Analysis: One serving (3/4 cup) equals 78 calories, 5 g fat (1 g saturated fat), 0 cholesterol, 241 mg sodium, 8 g carbohydrate, 2 g fiber, 3 g protein. **Diabetic Exchanges:** 1 vegetable, 1 fat.

Mint Jelly

(Pictured on page 48)

This festive-looking jelly can be served with lamb or used as a dessert topping. With its bright-green color, the jelly makes a great gift, too.
—*Naomi Giddis, Two Buttes, Colorado*

    4-1/2 cups water
        3 cups packed fresh mint, crushed
        7 cups sugar
      1/4 cup lemon juice
        2 to 4 drops green food coloring
        2 pouches (3 ounces *each*) liquid pectin

In a large saucepan, bring water and mint to a boil. Remove from the heat; cover and let stand for 15 minutes. Strain, reserving 3-1/3 cups liquid (discard remaining liquid).

In a Dutch oven, combine the sugar, lemon juice, food coloring and reserved liquid. Bring to a boil; cook and stir for 1 minute. Add pectin; return to a boil. Cook and stir for 1 minute. Remove from the heat; let stand for 5 minutes.

Skim off foam. Pour hot liquid into hot sterilized jars, leaving 1/4-in. headspace. Adjust caps. Process for 10 minutes in a boiling-water bath. **Yield:** 11 half-pints.

Grilled Asparagus Medley

(Pictured above)

This colorful veggie recipe happened by accident. One evening, I didn't have room on the grill for all the things I wanted to prepare, so I threw two of the dishes together and came up with this medley. It goes great with any grilled meat. —*Pam Gaspers Hastings, Nebraska*

✓ Uses less fat, sugar or salt. Includes Nutritional Analysis and Diabetic Exchanges.

      1 **pound fresh asparagus, trimmed**
      1 *each* **sweet red, yellow and green pepper, julienned**
      1 **cup sliced fresh mushrooms**
      1 **medium tomato, chopped**
      1 **medium onion, sliced**
      1 **can (2-1/4 ounces) sliced ripe olives, drained**
      2 **garlic cloves, minced**
      2 **tablespoons olive oil**
      1 **teaspoon minced fresh parsley**
    1/2 **teaspoon salt**
    1/2 **teaspoon pepper**
    1/4 **teaspoon lemon-pepper seasoning**
    1/4 **teaspoon dill weed**

In a disposable foil pan, combine the vegetables, olives and garlic; drizzle with oil and toss to coat. Sprinkle with parsley, salt, pepper, lemon-pepper

Grilled Corn with Dill

I like to peel the husks back and rub ears of sweet corn with delicious dill butter before putting them on the grill. The butter melts over the golden kernels as the corn steams inside the husk. —*Jeannie Klugh Lancaster, Pennsylvania*

    10 **medium ears sweet corn in husks**
      1 **cup butter, softened**
      2 **tablespoons minced chives**
      2 **tablespoons minced fresh dill *or* 2 teaspoons dill weed**

1 teaspoon lemon juice
1 teaspoon Worcestershire sauce
1/2 teaspoon garlic salt
1/4 teaspoon pepper

Soak the corn in cold water for 1 hour. Meanwhile, in a small mixing bowl, beat the butter, chives, dill, lemon juice, Worcestershire sauce, garlic salt and pepper; set aside.

Carefully peel back husks from corn to within 1 in. of bottom; remove silk. Spread each ear of corn with butter mixture. Rewrap corn husks and secure with kitchen string.

Coat grill rack with nonstick cooking spray before starting the grill. Grill corn, covered, over medium heat for 25-30 minutes or until tender, turning occasionally. **Yield:** 10 servings.

Apple-Cranberry Wild Rice

Dried apples, cranberries and savory nicely complement the wild rice and leek in this delicious recipe.
—Marion Karlin, Waterloo, Iowa

☑ Uses less fat, sugar or salt. Includes Nutritional Analysis and Diabetic Exchanges.

2-3/4 cups water
1/4 teaspoon salt
2/3 cup wild rice
1 teaspoon dried savory
1 small leek (white portion only), coarsely chopped
1 teaspoon olive oil
1/3 cup dried cranberries
1/4 cup chopped dried apples
6 tablespoons chicken broth, *divided*
1/2 teaspoon onion salt
1/2 teaspoon lemon-pepper seasoning

In a large saucepan, bring water and salt to a boil. Stir in the rice. Reduce heat; cover and simmer for 1 hour or until rice is tender. Drain. Stir in savory; set aside.

In a nonstick skillet, saute leek in oil for 1 minute. Stir in cranberries, apples and 3 tablespoons broth. Cover and simmer for 6-8 minutes or until the fruit is tender, stirring occasionally.

Add rice, onion salt, lemon-pepper and remaining broth. Cook and stir for 1-2 minutes or until liquid is absorbed. **Yield:** 6 servings.

Nutritional Analysis: One 1/2-cup serving (prepared with reduced-sodium broth) equals 124 calories, 1 g fat (trace saturated fat), trace cholesterol, 359 mg sodium, 26 g carbohy-

drate, 2 g fiber, 3 g protein. **Diabetic Exchanges:** 1 starch, 1/2 fruit.

So-Sweet Squash Pickles
(Pictured below)

These crisp crunchy slices, seasoned with celery seed and mustard seed, have a sweet-sour taste that everyone is sure to relish! The colorful blend of yellow squash, sweet red pepper and chopped onion makes a beautiful presentation.
—Eleanor Sundman
Farmington, Connecticut

3 small yellow summer squash, thinly sliced
1 medium onion, chopped
1 large sweet red pepper, cut into 1/4-inch strips
1 tablespoon salt
1 cup sugar
3/4 cup white vinegar
3/4 teaspoon mustard seed
3/4 teaspoon celery seed
1/4 teaspoon ground mustard

In a large bowl, combine the squash, onion, red pepper and salt. Cover and refrigerate for 1 hour; drain. In a large saucepan, combine the remaining ingredients. Bring to a boil. Add squash mixture; return to a boil. Remove from the heat; cool.

Store in an airtight container in the refrigerator for at least 4 days before serving. May be stored in the refrigerator for up to 3 weeks. **Yield:** 4 cups.

Summer Garden Pasta

(Pictured below)

This fresh-tasting side dish pairs pasta with an array of nutritious veggies, including zucchini, bell peppers and tomato. —*April Johnson, Tonasket, Washington*

☑ Uses less fat, sugar or salt. Includes Nutritional Analysis and Diabetic Exchanges.

    1 package (1 pound) small shell pasta
    1 cup sliced yellow summer squash
    1 cup sliced zucchini
    1 cup julienned sweet red pepper
    1 cup julienned green pepper
    1 cup sliced green onions
    6 garlic cloves, peeled and thinly sliced
  1/4 cup butter
1-1/2 cups reduced-sodium chicken broth
    1 small tomato, chopped
  1/2 cup grated Parmesan cheese
    1 tablespoon minced fresh parsley
    2 teaspoons garlic pepper
    1 teaspoon salt

Cook pasta according to package directions. Meanwhile, in a large skillet, saute the yellow squash, zucchini, peppers, onions and garlic in butter until crisp-tender. Add broth and tomato; bring to a boil. Cook and stir until liquid is reduced by half.

Drain pasta; stir into vegetable mixture. Cook 1 minute longer or until heated through. Transfer to a large bowl. Sprinkle with Parmesan cheese, parsley, garlic pepper and salt; toss to coat. Serve immediately. **Yield:** 9 servings.

Nutritional Analysis: One serving (1 cup) equals 277 calories, 8 g fat (5 g saturated fat), 16 mg cholesterol, 487 mg sodium, 42 g carbohydrate, 3 g fiber, 11 g protein. **Diabetic Exchanges:** 2 starch, 2 vegetable, 1-1/2 fat.

Asparagus with Mustard Sauce

(Pictured on page 49)

Here in Iowa, asparagus patches grow wild along the roads. My husband and I often go asparagus picking on Saturday and Sunday mornings. A tangy mustard sauce complements the fresh asparagus in this easy recipe. —*Nancy Hasbrouck, Ida Grove, Iowa*

    2 pounds fresh asparagus, trimmed
    3 tablespoons butter, cubed
Salt and pepper to taste
    1 cup (8 ounces) sour cream
  1/4 cup Dijon mustard
    2 tablespoons red wine vinegar
    2 teaspoons sugar
  1/8 teaspoon crushed red pepper flakes

Place asparagus in a shallow baking dish; dot with butter. Sprinkle with salt and pepper. Cover and bake at 400° for 25-30 minutes or until tender. In a microwave-safe bowl, combine the remaining ingredients. Cover and microwave on high for 1 to 1-1/4 minutes or until heated through. Serve over asparagus. **Yield:** 6-8 servings.

Editor's Note: This recipe was tested in a 1,100-watt microwave.

Roasted Squash Medley

(Pictured on page 49)

I concocted this recipe as a way to use up some vegetables before they went bad. Everyone loved this lively blend of roasted veggies, especially the acorn and butternut squash. It goes particularly well with pork roast, pork loin or pork chops. —*Elaine Wier, Guilford, Connecticut*

    1 large acorn squash, peeled and cubed
    1 small butternut squash, peeled and cubed
    2 large white potatoes, cubed
    2 large red potatoes, cubed
    1 medium green pepper, julienned
    1 medium sweet red pepper, julienned

1 small onion, quartered
12 whole garlic cloves, peeled
1 teaspoon salt
1 teaspoon garlic powder
1/2 teaspoon pepper
1/2 cup olive oil

In a large bowl, toss all ingredients until well coated. Arrange mixture in a single layer in two greased 15-in. x 10-in. x 1-in. baking pans. Bake, uncovered, at 425° for 20-30 minutes or until vegetables are tender, stirring occasionally. **Yield:** 6 servings.

Salsa Red Beans 'n' Rice

I stir up this quick side dish using canned kidney beans, brown rice and salsa. It's an ideal accompaniment to Mexican-style entrees but can also be served as a meatless main dish for a light meal. This is a family favorite.
—Diane Harrison, Mechanicsburg, Pennsylvania

☑ Uses less fat, sugar or salt. Includes Nutritional Analysis and Diabetic Exchanges.

1 medium green pepper, chopped
1/4 cup chopped red onion
3 green onions, finely chopped
4 garlic cloves, minced
1 tablespoon olive oil
5 cups cooked brown rice
1-1/4 cups salsa
1 can (16 ounces) kidney beans, rinsed and drained
1/2 teaspoon salt

In a large nonstick skillet, saute the green pepper, onions and garlic in oil until tender. Stir in the rice, salsa, beans and salt. Bring to a boil. Reduce heat; simmer, uncovered, for 2-3 minutes or until heated through. **Yield:** 8 servings.
Nutritional Analysis: One serving (3/4 cup) equals 215 calories, 3 g fat (trace saturated fat), 0 cholesterol, 401 mg sodium, 41 g carbohydrate, 6 g fiber, 6 g protein. **Diabetic Exchanges:** 2 starch, 1 vegetable, 1/2 fat.

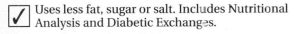

Watermelon Salsa

(Pictured above right)

This salsa is so good, I could just eat it with a spoon! It's wonderful over fish or chicken. —*Pat Bremson Kansas City, Missouri*

☑ Uses less fat, sugar or salt. Includes Nutritional Analysis and Diabetic Exchanges.

4 cups chopped seeded watermelon
2 tablespoons lime juice
1 tablespoon finely chopped red onion
1 tablespoon minced fresh cilantro
2 teaspoons finely chopped jalapeno pepper*
1/8 teaspoon salt

In a large bowl, combine all ingredients. Cover and refrigerate for at least 1 hour before serving. Serve with a slotted spoon. **Yield:** 4 cups.
Nutritional Analysis: One serving (1/2 cup) equals 26 calories, trace fat (trace saturated fat), 0 cholesterol, 39 mg sodium, 6 g carbohydrate, trace fiber, 1 g protein. **Diabetic Exchange:** 1/2 fruit.
***Editor's Note:** When cutting or seeding hot peppers, use rubber or plastic gloves to protect your hands. Avoid touching your face.

Pasta Pointers

Cooking twice as much pasta at a time gives you a head start on another night's meal. Thoroughly drain the portion you're not using, then put it in a bowl of ice water to stop the cooking. Drain again, then toss with 1 to 2 teaspoons oil. Cover and refrigerate for up to 3 days. You can use it in a salad, add it to soup or toss it with your favorite sauce.

Pickled Green Beans

You'll never be in a pickle to come up with a delicious condiment if you keep this recipe on hand! The green beans are crisp but delightfully tangy.
— *Tiffany Mitchell, Susanville, California*

 8 garlic cloves, peeled
 2-1/2 pounds fresh green beans, trimmed
 2 teaspoons mustard seed
 2 teaspoons dill seed
 1 teaspoon crushed red pepper flakes
 5 cups water
 3-1/2 cups cider vinegar
 1/4 cup canning salt

Place two garlic cloves in each of four 1-pint jars. Pack beans into jars to within 1/2 in. of top. Add 1/2 teaspoon mustard seed, 1/2 teaspoon dill seed and 1/4 teaspoon pepper flakes to each jar.

In a Dutch oven, bring the water, vinegar and canning salt to a boil. Ladle boiling liquid over beans, leaving 1/4-in. headspace. Adjust caps. Process for 10 minutes in a boiling-water bath. **Yield:** 4 pints.

Cranberry Tomato Chutney

(Pictured on page 48)

The unique flavor of this chutney goes well with turkey, pork and duck. At holiday time I make a big batch so I have some to serve, some to share and some to freeze.
— *Kathy Garnes, Laurel, Maryland*

 5 cups fresh *or* frozen cranberries
 1 can (28 ounces) crushed tomatoes
 1 cup golden raisins
 3/4 cup sugar
 1 teaspoon salt
 3/4 teaspoon ground ginger

In a large saucepan, combine all ingredients. Bring to a boil. Reduce heat; cover and simmer for 20-25 minutes or until cranberries and raisins are tender, stirring occasionally. Cool. Cover and refrigerate for 2-3 days before serving. **Yield:** 6 cups.

Creole Corn

Colorful veggies combine in this Southern-style skillet dish enhanced by bay leaf, bacon and zippy Creole seasoning. — *Joyce Turley, Slaughters, Kentucky*

 4 bacon strips, diced
 1 small onion, thinly sliced

Orange-Glazed Acorn Squash

(Pictured above)

This savory side dish gets its lovely flavor from orange juice, orange zest and nutmeg. The smooth syrupy sauce is a great complement to the squash. I serve this on Christmas Eve, and everyone loves it!
— *Joyce Moynihan, Lakeville, Minnesota*

 4 small acorn squash
 2 tablespoons butter
 1 cup sugar
 1 cup orange juice
 1/3 cup orange juice concentrate
 1/4 teaspoon salt
 1/4 teaspoon ground nutmeg
 1/4 teaspoon grated orange peel
 1/8 teaspoon pepper

Cut squash in half; discard seeds. Place squash cut side down in a 15-in. x 10-in. x 1-in. baking pan; add 1/2 in. of hot water. Bake, uncovered, at 350° for 30 minutes.

Meanwhile, in a saucepan, melt butter over medium heat. Stir in the remaining ingredients. Bring to a boil. Reduce heat to medium-low; cook, uncovered, for 30 minutes or until syrupy, stirring occasionally.

Drain water from baking pan; turn squash cut side up. Pour about 2 tablespoons orange glaze into each squash half. Bake 25-30 minutes longer or until squash is tender. **Yield:** 8 servings.

1/4 cup chopped green pepper
1/4 cup chopped sweet red pepper
  2 cups chopped seeded tomatoes
  1 to 2 bay leaves
  2 cups fresh *or* frozen corn, thawed
  2 teaspoons Creole seasoning
1/4 teaspoon pepper

In a large skillet, cook bacon over medium heat until crisp. Remove with a slotted spoon to paper towels; drain, reserving drippings. Saute onion and peppers in the drippings until tender. Add tomatoes and bay leaves. Cook, uncovered, over medium-low heat for 10 minutes.

Add corn; simmer, uncovered, for 10 minutes or until corn is tender. Discard bay leaves. Stir in Creole seasoning and pepper. Sprinkle with bacon. **Yield:** 4-6 servings.

Golden Baked Onions
(Pictured below)

I love to invent new dishes, but I also enjoy making tried-and-true recipes, like my mom's baked onions.

The onions are a rich and satisfying side dish with poultry and beef, but they can also be a meal all by themselves! —Chris Gaskill, Knoxville, Tennessee

  6 large sweet onions, thinly sliced
1/4 cup butter
  1 can (10-3/4 ounces) condensed cream of chicken soup, undiluted
1/2 cup milk
1/8 teaspoon pepper
  3 cups (12 ounces) shredded Swiss cheese, **divided**
  6 slices French bread (3/4 inch thick)
  2 tablespoons butter, melted

In a large skillet, saute the onions in butter until tender, about 12 minutes. In a bowl, combine the soup, milk, pepper and 2 cups of cheese. Stir in the onions.

Transfer to a greased 2-qt. baking dish. Sprinkle with remaining cheese. Brush bread slices with melted butter on one side. Arrange buttered side up over cheese.

Bake, uncovered, at 350° for 25-30 minutes or until bubbly. If desired, broil 4-6 in. from heat until bread is golden brown. Let stand for 5 minutes before serving. **Yield:** 6-8 servings.

Main Dishes

You're sure to attract attention from family and friends by making any selection from this hearty chapter the star of your next meal.

DOWN-HOME DINING. Clockwise from upper left: Fried Bluegill Fillets (p. 62), Baked Pork Chimichangas (p. 70), Chicken Patties (p. 80), Lime Shrimp with Asparagus (p. 69) and Spicy Beef Brisket (p. 73).

Broiled Orange Roughy

(Pictured below)

I'm constantly searching for new ways to prepare healthy meals. This fish dish has long been a favorite at my house—it is so simple to prepare and yet so tasty. Try the same recipe using cod or sole, too.
—Dorothy Swanson, Affton, Missouri

☑ Uses less fat, sugar or salt. Includes Nutritional Analysis and Diabetic Exchanges.

    6 orange roughy fillets (about 7 ounces
      each)
    1 tablespoon olive *or* canola oil
    1 tablespoon lemon juice
    1 teaspoon salt-free seasoning blend
ITALIAN SALSA:
    2 cups chopped plum tomatoes
    1 can (2-1/4 ounces) sliced ripe olives,
      drained
    2 tablespoons lemon juice
    2 tablespoons minced fresh parsley
    1 teaspoon salt-free seasoning blend
    1 teaspoon Italian seasoning

Place fish on a broiler pan. In a small bowl, combine the oil, lemon juice and seasoning blend; spoon over fish. Broil 4-5 in. from the heat for 10-15 minutes or until fish flakes easily with a fork. In a small bowl, combine the salsa ingredients; serve with fish. **Yield:** 6 servings.

Nutritional Analysis: One serving (1 fillet with 1/3 cup salsa) equals 181 calories, 5 g fat (1 g saturated fat), 40 mg cholesterol, 222 mg sodium, 4 g carbohydrate, 1 g fiber, 30 g protein. **Diabetic Exchanges:** 4 lean meat, 1 vegetable.

Turkey Spaghetti Pie

This pretty spaghetti pie blends well-seasoned ground turkey, cheese, veggies and tomato sauce in a crust formed from spaghetti. It's tasty comfort food your family will request again and again.
—Elnora Johnson, Union City, Tennessee

☑ Uses less fat, sugar or salt. Includes Nutritional Analysis and Diabetic Exchanges.

    1 pound ground turkey breast
    1 cup chopped green pepper
  1/2 cup chopped onion
  1/2 cup tomato sauce
  1/2 teaspoon dried basil
  1/2 teaspoon fennel seed, crushed
  1/8 teaspoon pepper
    6 ounces spaghetti
  1/4 cup egg substitute
    1 tablespoon reduced-fat stick margarine,
      melted
    1 tablespoon grated Parmesan cheese
    1 teaspoon dried parsley flakes
  1/2 cup part-skim shredded mozzarella
      cheese, *divided*

In a large skillet, cook the turkey, green pepper and onion over medium heat until meat is no longer pink; drain. Stir in the tomato sauce, basil, fennel seed and pepper. Bring to a boil. Reduce heat; simmer, uncovered, for 20-30 minutes.

Meanwhile, cook the spaghetti according to package directions; drain. In a bowl, combine the spaghetti, egg substitute, margarine, Parmesan cheese and parsley flakes. Form a crust in a 9-in. pie plate coated with nonstick cooking spray.

Stir 1/4 cup mozzarella cheese into the turkey mixture; spoon into spaghetti crust. Cover and bake at 350° for 30 minutes. Uncover and sprinkle with remaining mozzarella cheese. Bake 15 minutes longer or until cheese is melted. Let stand for 10 minutes before cutting into wedges. **Yield:** 6 servings.

Nutritional Analysis: One serving equals 213 calories, 9 g fat (3 g saturated fat), 66 mg cholesterol, 296 mg sodium, 13 g carbohydrate, 2 g fiber, 19 g protein. **Diabetic Exchanges:** 2 lean meat, 1 starch, 1 fat.

Steaks with Cucumber Sauce

This recipe combines some of my family's favorite flavors. The tender steaks, marinated with teriyaki sauce, are accompanied by a creamy cucumber sauce seasoned with dill and chives.
—Erika Aylward, Clinton, Michigan

4 boneless beef New York strip steaks (8
  to 10 ounces *each*)
3/4 cup teriyaki sauce
1/2 cup chopped seeded peeled cucumber
1/2 cup sour cream
1/2 cup mayonnaise
  1 tablespoon minced chives
1/2 to 1 teaspoon dill weed
1/4 teaspoon salt

Place steaks in a large resealable plastic bag; add teriyaki sauce. Seal bag and turn to coat; refrigerate overnight. In a bowl, combine the cucumber, sour cream, mayonnaise, chives, dill and salt. Cover and refrigerate.

Drain and discard marinade. Grill steaks, uncovered, over medium-hot heat for 4-5 minutes on each side or until meat reaches desired doneness (for rare, a meat thermometer should read 140°; medium, 160°; well-done, 170°). Serve with cucumber sauce. **Yield:** 4 servings.

Venison Tenderloins

Venison is not typically the best meat for grilling, but with this marinade, the steaks come out tender, juicy and delicious. They're so tasty, in fact, that leftovers taste great cold—right from the fridge!
—Brenda Koehmstedt, Rugby, North Dakota

✓ Uses less fat, sugar or salt. Includes Nutritional Analysis and Diabetic Exchanges.

3/4 cup soy sauce
1/2 cup red wine vinegar
1/2 cup vegetable oil
1/3 cup lemon juice
1/4 cup Worcestershire sauce
  2 tablespoons ground mustard
  1 tablespoon coarsely ground pepper
1-1/2 teaspoons dried parsley flakes
  2 garlic cloves, minced
  8 venison tenderloin fillets (4 ounces *each*)

In a large resealable plastic bag, combine the first nine ingredients; add fillets. Seal bag and turn to coat; refrigerate for 8 hours or overnight.

Drain and discard the marinade. Grill the fillets, uncovered, over medium-hot heat for 4 minutes on each side or until a meat thermometer reads 160° for medium or 170° for well-done. **Yield:** 8 servings.

Nutritional Analysis: One serving (prepared with reduced-sodium soy sauce) equals 179 calories, 6 g fat (1 g saturated fat), 96 mg cholesterol, 483 mg sodium, 2 g carbohydrate, trace fiber, 27 g protein. **Diabetic Exchange:** 3 lean meat.

Slow Cooker Cranberry Pork

(Pictured above)

You can put this roast in the slow cooker and then forget about it, knowing it will be moist and tender when you get home after a day of work or Christmas shopping. The fruity sauce complements the meat so well.
—Joyce Turley, Slaughters, Kentucky

  1 boneless rolled pork loin roast (3 to 4
    pounds), halved
  2 tablespoons vegetable oil
  1 can (16 ounces) whole-berry cranberry
    sauce
3/4 cup sugar
3/4 cup cranberry juice
  1 teaspoon ground mustard
  1 teaspoon pepper
1/4 teaspoon ground cloves
1/4 cup cornstarch
1/4 cup cold water
Salt to taste

In a Dutch oven, brown roast in oil on all sides over medium-high heat. Transfer to a 5-qt. slow cooker. Combine the cranberry sauce, sugar, cranberry juice, mustard, pepper and cloves; pour over roast. Cover and cook on low for 6-8 hours or until a meat thermometer reads 160°. Remove roast and keep warm.

In a saucepan, combine cornstarch, water and salt until smooth; stir in cooking juices. Bring to a boil; cook and stir for 2 minutes or until thickened. Serve with roast. **Yield:** 9-12 servings.

til thickened. Drain tortellini; add to the sausage mixture. Stir in the Parmesan cheese and Worcestershire sauce. **Yield:** 2 servings.

Corned Beef Potato Dinner

For St. Patrick's Day, I usually prepare this dish instead of the traditional corned beef dinner. This takes less time because it makes good use of the microwave, and it's very tasty. —*Brooke Staley, Mary Esther, Florida*

 1 **pound red potatoes, cut into small wedges**
1-1/2 **cups water**
 1 **large onion, thinly sliced and separated into rings**
 4 **cups coleslaw mix**
 8 **ounces thinly sliced deli corned beef, cut into 1/4-inch strips**
 1 **tablespoon vegetable oil**
1/3 **cup red wine vinegar**
 4 **teaspoons spicy brown *or* horseradish mustard**
 1 **teaspoon sugar**
 1 **teaspoon caraway seeds**
1/2 **teaspoon garlic powder**
1/2 **teaspoon salt**
1/2 **teaspoon pepper**

Place potatoes and water in a 3-qt. microwave-safe bowl. Cover; microwave on high for 6-8 minutes. Add the onion; cover and cook for 4 minutes. Stir in the coleslaw mix. Cover and cook for 3-4 minutes or until potatoes are tender; drain.

In a large skillet, saute the corned beef in oil for 3-4 minutes; stir in the remaining ingredients. Cook and stir for 1 minute or until heated through. Add to the potato mixture; toss to combine. Cover and microwave for 2-3 minutes or until heated through. Serve immediately. **Yield:** 4 servings.

Editor's Note: This recipe was tested in a 1,100-watt microwave.

Fried Bluegill Fillets

(Pictured on page 58)

This recipe is one I enjoy making each year (especially with fish caught in our pond) when our family gets together. The secret to the recipe is double-dipping the fish fillets. We like to serve them with coleslaw and hush puppies. —*Doug Wright, Maize, Kansas*

 1 **cup seasoned bread crumbs**
 1 **cup grated Parmesan cheese**

Tortellini Sausage Alfredo

(Pictured above)

I invented this dish for my kids when they were young using all the things they liked—sausage, mushrooms, onions, green pepper and pasta. It's still a favorite with them today. —*Nelson Wandrey Glendale, Arizona*

 1 **package (9 ounces) refrigerated cheese *or* spinach tortellini**
 1 **teaspoon olive oil**
1/4 **teaspoon salt**
1/4 **teaspoon white pepper**
1/8 **teaspoon garlic powder**
Dash ground nutmeg
1/4 **pound bulk Italian sausage**
1/2 **cup chopped onion**
1/4 **cup chopped green pepper**
1/4 **cup chopped fresh mushrooms**
 2 **tablespoons all-purpose flour**
1-1/4 **cups milk**
1/4 **cup grated Parmesan cheese**
1/8 **teaspoon Worcestershire sauce**

In a large saucepan, bring 2 qts. water to a boil. Add the tortellini, oil, salt, pepper, garlic powder and nutmeg. Cook according to package directions until pasta is tender.

Meanwhile, in a large skillet, cook sausage, onion, green pepper and mushrooms over medium heat until meat is no longer pink; drain. Stir in flour until blended. Gradually add milk.

Bring to a boil; cook and stir for 2 minutes or un-

1/2 teaspoon salt
1/2 teaspoon lemon-pepper seasoning
1/4 teaspoon pepper
   6 eggs
1-1/2 pounds bluegill fillets *or* crappie fillets
1/2 cup vegetable oil, *divided*

In a shallow bowl, combine the first five ingredients. In another bowl, whisk the eggs. Dip fillets in eggs, then coat with crumb mixture. Dip again in eggs and crumb mixture.

In a large skillet over medium-high heat, cook fillets in batches in 2 tablespoons oil for 2-3 minutes on each side or until fish flakes easily with a fork, adding oil as needed. **Yield:** 6 servings.

Linguine in Clam Sauce

I make this for my daughter's birthday celebration each year at her request. The zucchini adds such a nice touch to this traditional dish. —Ken Vouk, Willowick, Ohio

1 package (1 pound) linguine
1 large onion, finely chopped
1 garlic clove, minced
2 tablespoons olive oil
1 medium zucchini, diced
3 cans (6-1/2 ounces *each*) chopped clams
1/2 pound sliced fresh mushrooms
2 teaspoons chicken bouillon granules
1 teaspoon minced fresh basil
1/8 teaspoon pepper
Shredded Parmesan cheese

Cook linguine according to package directions. Meanwhile, in a large skillet, saute onion and garlic in oil until tender. Add zucchini; cook for 2 minutes.

Drain clams, reserving 1/2 cup juice. Add clams, mushrooms, bouillon, basil, pepper and reserved juice to the skillet. Bring to a boil. Reduce heat; simmer, uncovered for 5 minutes or until vegetables are tender. Drain linguine; top with clam mixture. Sprinkle with Parmesan cheese. **Yield:** 4-6 servings.

Barbecue Turkey Wings

(Pictured at right)

These moist turkey wings are marinated in a barbecue sauce with garlic, paprika, green onions and soy sauce. I never use recipes, so I came up with this zesty combination myself. —Francis Mitchell Brooklyn, New York

3 pounds turkey wings
1-1/4 cups barbecue sauce
2 green onions, sliced
1 teaspoon paprika
1/2 teaspoon garlic powder
1/2 teaspoon salt
1/2 teaspoon pepper
1/4 teaspoon soy sauce

Cut turkey wings into sections; discard wing tips. In a large resealable plastic bag, combine the remaining ingredients; add wing sections. Seal bag and turn to coat; refrigerate overnight.

Drain and discard marinade. Place wings in a greased 15-in. x 10-in. x 1-in. baking pan. Bake, uncovered, at 350° for 50-60 minutes or until a meat thermometer reads 180° and turkey is tender. **Yield:** 6 servings.

Fish Facts

Look for fish fillets and steaks that have a fresh odor, firm texture and moist appearance.

To test fish for doneness, poke it with a fork at its thickest point. Properly cooked fish is opaque, has milky white juices and flakes easily with a fork. Undercooked fish is still translucent and the juices are clear and watery.

If there's a fishy odor left in the pan after washing, fill the pan half full with a mixture of vinegar and water. Bring to a boil, cook for 5 minutes, then cool in the pan. Wash again with hot soapy water.

Steak Is a Cut Above

IF YOU PREFER beef for a holiday dinner or want something special for New Year's Eve, steak's a great choice. Try one of these mouth-watering versions.

Santa Fe Strip Steaks

(Pictured below)

We love Southwestern flavor, and this recipe certainly provides it. —Joan Hallford
North Richland Hills, Texas

1/2 cup chopped onion
1 tablespoon olive oil
2 cans (4 ounces *each*) chopped green chilies
1/2 cup fresh cilantro leaves
1 jalapeno pepper, seeded
2 teaspoons red currant jelly
1 teaspoon chicken bouillon granules
1 teaspoon Worcestershire sauce
1 garlic clove, peeled
1/2 teaspoon seasoned salt
1/4 teaspoon dried oregano
4 New York strip steaks (about 1 inch thick and 7 ounces *each*)
Salt and pepper to taste
1/2 cup shredded Monterey Jack cheese

In a small saucepan, saute onion in oil until tender. Transfer to a blender or food processor. Add green chilies, cilantro, jalapeno, jelly, bouillon, Worces-

EXCEPTIONAL ENTREES. Flavorful and tender Santa Fe Strip Steaks, Festive Beef Tenderloin and Vegetable Steak Kabobs (shown below, from top) are well suited to special occasions.

tershire sauce, garlic, seasoned salt and oregano. Cover and process until smooth. Return mixture to saucepan. Bring to a boil. Reduce heat and simmer, uncovered, for 10 minutes. Set aside and keep warm.

Sprinkle steaks with salt and pepper. Grill steaks, uncovered, over medium heat or broil 4-6 in. from heat for 4-8 minutes on each side or until meat reaches desired doneness (for rare, a meat thermometer should read 140°; medium, 160°; well-done, 170°).

Serve steaks with green chili sauce and sprinkle with cheese. **Yield:** 4 servings.

Editor's Note: When cutting or seeding hot peppers, use plastic gloves to protect your hands. Avoid touching your face. Steak may be known as strip steak, Kansas City steak, New York strip steak, Ambassador steak or boneless club steak.

Festive Beef Tenderloin

(Pictured at left)

Dressing up a tenderloin steak is quick and easy when you add a cracker crumb/herb topping.
—*Leann Meeds, Klamath Falls, Oregon*

  4 beef tenderloin steaks (about 1-1/2 inches thick)
1/4 cup crushed saltines
1/4 cup mayonnaise
  2 tablespoons minced fresh parsley
  2 teaspoons prepared horseradish
1/4 teaspoon pepper

Place steaks on a greased broiler pan. Broil 3-4 in. from the heat for 8 minutes on each side.

Combine cracker crumbs, mayonnaise, parsley, horseradish and pepper. Spread over steaks. Broil 2-6 minutes longer or until meat reaches desired doneness (for rare, a meat thermometer should read 140°; medium, 160°; well-done, 170°). **Yield:** 4 servings.

Vegetable Steak Kabobs

(Pictured at left)

The marinade for this steak-and-vegetable skewer is the best one I've ever found. —*Norma Harder*
Melfort, Saskatchewan

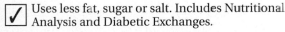

✓ Uses less fat, sugar or salt. Includes Nutritional Analysis and Diabetic Exchanges.

1/2 cup vegetable *or* canola oil
1/3 cup red wine vinegar
  2 tablespoons ketchup
  2 to 3 garlic cloves, minced
  1 teaspoon Worcestershire sauce
1/2 teaspoon *each* dried marjoram, basil and oregano
1/2 teaspoon dried rosemary, crushed
1-1/2 pounds boneless beef sirloin steak
1-1/2 cups cherry tomatoes
1/2 pound whole fresh mushrooms
  2 medium onions, cut into wedges
  2 small green peppers, cut into 1-inch pieces

In a large resealable plastic bag, combine the oil, vinegar, ketchup, garlic, Worcestershire sauce and seasonings; set aside. Trim steak if necessary and cut into 1-in. cubes. Add the meat and vegetables to marinade. Seal bag and turn to coat; refrigerate overnight.

Drain and discard the marinade. Alternately thread beef and vegetables onto six metal or soaked wooden skewers. Grill, covered, over medium-hot heat or broil 4-6 in. from heat for 6-8 minutes. Turn kabobs; cook 4-6 minutes longer or until beef reaches desired doneness. **Yield:** 6 servings.

Nutritional Analysis: One kabob equals 234 calories, 10 g fat (2 g saturated fat), 69 mg cholesterol, 99 mg sodium, 10 g carbohydrate, 2 g fiber, 26 g protein. **Diabetic Exchanges:** 3 lean meat, 2 vegetable.

Steak and...Snowmen?

Add to ever-popular steak and potatoes with this clever presentation from Miriam Nachbar of Manheim, Pennsylvania.

"I fixed these snowman potato servings (below) for a church carry-in," says Miriam. "My grandson was going with us, and he loves mashed potatoes. But bringing a bowl of plain mashed didn't sound like a good idea.

"So I put the potatoes into a pastry bag and swirled them out into individual servings. Then I added peas for eyes, a baby carrot for the nose and half a black olive for the smiley mouth. The snowmen were a big hit at the gathering."

for 7 minutes. Add mushrooms; stir-fry 6-8 minutes longer or until vegetables are crisp-tender.

Stir broth mixture and add to the pan. Bring to a boil; cook and stir for 2 minutes or until thickened. Reduce heat; add beef and peanut butter. Cook and stir over medium heat until peanut butter is blended. Serve over spaghetti. Sprinkle with peanuts. **Yield:** 6 servings.

Beefy Corn Bread Casserole

To stretch our grocery budget, we eat a lot of soups and pots o' beans. This satisfying Mexican corn bread always livens up the meal. Like many of my recipes, this one came from a church cookbook.
—Patty Boling, Seymour, Tennessee

  1 **pound ground beef**
  1 **small onion, chopped**
  2 **to 3 jalapeno peppers, seeded and chopped***
  2 **packages (8-1/2 ounce *each*) corn bread/muffin mix**
3/4 **teaspoon salt**
1/2 **teaspoon baking soda**
  1 **can (14-3/4 ounces) cream-style corn**
  1 **cup milk**
1/2 **cup vegetable oil**
  2 **eggs, beaten**
  3 **cups (12 ounces) shredded cheddar cheese, *divided***

In a large skillet, cook beef, onion, and peppers over medium heat until meat is no longer pink; drain and set aside. In a small bowl, combine corn bread mix, salt, baking soda, corn, milk, oil and eggs.

Pour half in a greased 13-in. x 9-in. x 2-in. baking dish. Layer with half of the cheese and all of the beef mixture. Top with remaining cheese. Carefully spread remaining batter over top. Bake, uncovered, at 350° for 40-45 minutes or until a toothpick inserted near the center comes out clean. **Yield:** 8-12 servings.

*Editor's Note: When cutting or seeding hot peppers, use rubber or plastic gloves to protect your hands. Avoid touching your face.

Thai Beef Stir-Fry

(Pictured above)

A distinctive peanut sauce complements this colorful combination of tender sirloin strips, cauliflower, carrots, broccoli and mushrooms. I dish it up over spaghetti, but you could also use fried noodles.
—Janice Fehr, Austin, Manitoba

  1/2 **cup packed brown sugar**
    2 **tablespoons cornstarch**
    2 **cups beef broth**
  1/3 **cup soy sauce**
    1 **teaspoon onion powder**
    1 **teaspoon garlic powder**
    1 **teaspoon ground ginger**
  1/4 **teaspoon hot pepper sauce**
    2 **pounds boneless beef sirloin steak, cut into thin strips**
    6 **tablespoons olive oil, *divided***
    2 **cups fresh cauliflowerets**
1-1/2 **cups julienned carrots**
    4 **cups fresh broccoli florets**
    2 **cups sliced fresh mushrooms**
  1/4 **cup peanut butter**
Hot cooked spaghetti
  1/2 **cup chopped peanuts**

In a bowl, combine the first eight ingredients until smooth; set aside. In a large skillet or wok, stir-fry beef in 3 tablespoons oil until meat is no longer pink. Remove and keep warm.

In the same skillet, stir-fry cauliflower and carrots in remaining oil for 5 minutes. Add broccoli; stir-fry

Sausage Marinara over Pasta

My husband and I enjoy pasta, so after I discovered low-fat Italian turkey sausage at the supermarket, I came up with this chunky sauce. *—Shirley Meletes*
Lehigh Acres, Florida

1 pound turkey Italian sausage links
4 cups uncooked spiral pasta
1/2 pound fresh mushrooms, sliced
1 large onion, chopped
1 medium sweet red pepper, chopped
1 medium green pepper, chopped
3 large garlic cloves, minced
1 tablespoon olive *or* canola oil
1 jar (26 ounces) meatless spaghetti sauce
1 tablespoon dried basil
1 tablespoon dried oregano
1 teaspoon pepper
1/3 cup crumbled feta cheese

Place sausages in a large nonstick skillet coated with nonstick cooking spray. Cover and cook over medium heat for 12-14 minutes or until browned, turning twice. Cool; slice sausages and set aside. Prepare pasta according to package directions.

In same skillet, saute mushrooms, onion, peppers and garlic in oil until tender. Stir in spaghetti sauce, basil, oregano, pepper and reserved sausage. Bring to a boil. Reduce heat; simmer, uncovered, for 5 minutes, stirring occasionally. Drain pasta. Serve sauce over pasta. Sprinkle with feta cheese. **Yield:** 6 servings.

Nutritional Analysis: One serving (1 cup meat sauce with 2/3 cup cooked pasta) equals 372 calories, 12 g fat (4 g saturated fat), 48 mg cholesterol, 1,106 mg sodium, 45 g carbohydrate, 6 g fiber, 22 g protein. **Diabetic Exchanges:** 2-1/2 starch, 2 lean meat, 1 vegetable, 1 fat.

Country-Style Grilled Ribs

A sweet and tangy barbecue sauce, sprinkled with celery seed, coats these tender ribs. Chili powder and hot pepper sauce contribute to the zesty flavor of this recipe. —Marilyn Beerman, Worthington, Ohio

3 pounds boneless country-style pork ribs
1 cup water
1 cup ketchup
1/4 cup packed brown sugar
1/4 cup cider vinegar
1/4 cup Worcestershire sauce
1 tablespoon celery seed
1 teaspoon chili powder
1/8 teaspoon hot pepper sauce
Dash pepper

Place ribs in a shallow roasting pan. Cover and bake at 325° for 1-1/4 hours or until a meat thermometer reads 160°. Meanwhile, in a small saucepan, combine the remaining ingredients. Bring to a boil. Reduce heat; simmer, uncovered, for 5 minutes, stirring occasionally. Pour 1 cup sauce over ribs; turn to coat. Let stand for 15 minutes.

Grill ribs, uncovered, over medium heat for 10-12 minutes, basting with 1 cup sauce and turning occasionally. Serve with remaining sauce. **Yield:** 4 servings.

Baked Trout Fillets

(Pictured below)

Moist tender trout is draped in a creamy Parmesan cheese coating that makes this dish elegant enough to serve company. I picked up this recipe at the campground where we were staying. I also use the delicious sour cream mixture on salmon. —Mary Zimmerman Spring Lake, Michigan

1 pound trout fillets
1 cup (8 ounces) sour cream
1/4 cup grated Parmesan cheese
1 tablespoon lemon juice
1 tablespoon finely chopped onion
1/2 teaspoon salt
Paprika

Place fish in a greased shallow 3-qt. baking dish. In a small bowl, combine the sour cream, Parmesan cheese, lemon juice, onion and salt; spread over fish. Sprinkle with paprika. Bake, uncovered, at 350° for 20-25 minutes or until fish flakes easily with a fork. **Yield:** 4 servings.

Overnight Asparagus Strata

(Pictured below)

I've made this tasty egg dish for breakfast, brunch and even as a Christmas dinner side dish. With its English muffin "crust", this is not your run-of-the-mill strata. —Lynn Licata, Sylvania, Ohio

   1 **pound fresh asparagus, trimmed and cut into 1-inch pieces**
   4 **English muffins, split and toasted**
   2 **cups (8 ounces) shredded Colby-Monterey Jack cheese, *divided***
   1 **cup diced fully cooked ham**
1/2 **cup chopped sweet red pepper**
   8 **eggs**
   2 **cups milk**
   1 **teaspoon salt**
   1 **teaspoon ground mustard**
1/4 **teaspoon pepper**

In a large saucepan, bring 8 cups water to a boil. Add asparagus; cover and cook for 3 minutes. Drain and immediately place asparagus in ice water. Drain and pat dry.

Arrange six English muffin halves, cut side up, in a greased 13-in. x 9-in. x 2-in. baking dish. Fill in spaces with remaining muffin halves. Sprinkle with 1 cup cheese, asparagus, ham and red pepper. In a bowl, whisk the eggs, milk, salt, mustard and pepper; pour over muffins. Cover and refrigerate overnight.

Remove from the refrigerator 30 minutes before baking. Sprinkle with remaining cheese. Bake, uncovered, at 375° for 40-45 minutes or until a knife inserted near the edge comes out clean. Let stand for 5 minutes before cutting. **Yield:** 6-8 servings.

Spinach-Filled Turkey Roll

This attractive ground turkey loaf is something special, but you won't have to fuss a lot. The tasty entree features a swirl of spinach filling. —Louise Tomb
Harrison Valley, Pennsylvania

✓ Uses less fat, sugar or salt. Includes Nutritional Analysis and Diabetic Exchanges.

3/4 **pound fresh mushrooms, sliced**
1/2 **cup chopped green onions**
1/3 **cup finely chopped celery**
   2 **tablespoons butter**
   2 **packages (10 ounces *each*) frozen chopped spinach, drained and squeezed dry**
1/8 **teaspoon salt**
   2 **eggs, beaten**
   4 **slices day-old whole wheat bread, crumbled**
   2 **tablespoons dried minced onion**
   4 **teaspoons herb and garlic onion soup mix**
1/4 **teaspoon pepper**
   2 **pounds lean ground turkey**

In a large skillet, saute the mushrooms, green onions and celery in butter until tender. Stir in spinach and salt; heat through. Remove from the heat; cool. In a large bowl, combine the eggs, bread, minced onion, soup mix and pepper. Crumble turkey over mixture; mix well.

On a large piece of heavy-duty foil, pat turkey mixture into a 16-in. x 10-in. rectangle. Spread spinach mixture to within 1 in. of edges. Roll up, starting with a short side; seal seam and ends.

Place seam side down in a 13-in. x 9-in. x 2-in. baking dish coated with nonstick cooking spray. Cover and bake at 350° for 50 minutes. Uncover; bake 10 minutes longer or until a meat thermometer reads 165°. Let stand for 5 minutes before cutting. **Yield:** 8 servings.

Nutritional Analysis: One serving equals 297 calories, 15 g fat (5 g saturated fat), 150 mg cholesterol, 470 mg sodium, 16 g carbohydrate, 4 g fiber, 26 g protein. **Diabetic Exchanges:** 3 lean meat, 1 starch, 1 fat.

Breaded Orange Roughy

My family loves fish, so I serve it often. Seasoned pepper really adds to the flavor of these tender fillets. —Joann Frazier Hensley, McGaheysville, Virginia

✓ Uses less fat, sugar or salt. Includes Nutritional Analysis and Diabetic Exchanges.

   1 **cup crushed cornflakes**
   2 **teaspoons seasoned pepper**

1/4 teaspoon salt
  4 egg whites
1/4 cup water
  6 orange roughy fillets (4 ounces *each*)
1/4 cup all-purpose flour

In a shallow dish, combine the cornflakes, seasoned pepper and salt. In another shallow dish, beat egg whites and water. Sprinkle fish with flour; dip in egg white mixture, then coat with cornflake mixture.

Place on a baking sheet coated with nonstick cooking spray. Bake at 425° for 9-11 minutes or until fish flakes easily with a fork. **Yield:** 6 servings.

Nutritional Analysis: One serving equals 158 calories, 1 g fat (trace saturated fat), 23 mg cholesterol, 400 mg sodium, 16 g carbohydrate, trace fiber, 20 g protein. **Diabetic Exchanges:** 3 very lean meat, 1 starch.

Lime Shrimp with Asparagus

(Pictured on page 58)

For this colorful main dish, I combine shrimp, asparagus and sweet red pepper and flavor them with lime juice, lime peel, garlic and soy sauce.
    —Peggy Davies, Canon City, Colorado

3/4 pound fresh asparagus, trimmed and cut into 2-inch pieces
  1 garlic clove, minced
  2 tablespoons water
3/4 pound uncooked medium shrimp, peeled and deveined
  1 medium sweet red pepper, thinly sliced
  1 jalapeno pepper, seeded and finely chopped
  1 teaspoon cornstarch
  2 tablespoons soy sauce
  1 tablespoon lime juice
1/2 teaspoon grated lime peel
Hot cooked rice

Place the asparagus, garlic and water in a 1-1/2-qt. microwave-safe dish. Cover and microwave on high for 3-4 minutes or until asparagus is crisp-tender. Remove with a slotted spoon; keep warm.

Add shrimp, red pepper and jalapeno to dish. Cover and cook on high for 3 minutes or until shrimp turn pink. Remove with a slotted spoon; keep warm.

In a small bowl, whisk the cornstarch, soy sauce, lime juice and lime peel until blended; stir into the cooking juices. Microwave, uncovered, on high for 1 minute or until sauce is thickened and bubbly.

Stir in shrimp and asparagus mixtures. Cook, uncovered, on high for 30-60 seconds or until heated through. Serve with rice. **Yield:** 4 servings.

Editor's Note: This recipe was tested in a 1,100-watt microwave. When cutting or seeding hot peppers, use rubber or plastic gloves to protect your hands. Avoid touching your face.

Crab Rockefeller

(Pictured above)

When you're entertaining seafood lovers, you can't go wrong with this delightful main course. It has such rich flavor! The spinach and golden crumb topping make the casserole look very attractive.
    —Cheryl Maczko, Arthurdale, West Virginia

    4 tablespoons butter, *divided*
    2 tablespoons all-purpose flour
1-1/3 cups milk
  1/2 cup grated Parmesan cheese
    1 package (10 ounces) frozen chopped spinach, thawed and squeezed dry
    1 can (6 ounces) crabmeat, drained, flaked and cartilage removed
  1/2 cup dry bread crumbs

In a saucepan, melt 2 tablespoons butter. Stir in flour until smooth; gradually add the milk. Bring to a boil; cook and stir for 2 minutes or until thickened. Reduce heat; stir in the cheese until smooth. Add the spinach and crab.

Transfer to a greased shallow 1-qt. baking dish. Melt the remaining butter; toss with bread crumbs. Sprinkle over the top. Bake, uncovered, at 375° for 15-20 minutes or until bubbly. **Yield:** 3-4 servings.

Baked Pork Chimichangas

(Pictured on page 58)

Lean shredded pork and pinto beans combine with south-of-the-border ingredients like green chilies and picante sauce in these from-scratch chimichangas.
—LaDonna Reed
Ponca City, Oklahoma

✓ Uses less fat, sugar or salt. Includes Nutritional Analysis and Diabetic Exchanges.

  1 pound dried pinto beans
  1 boneless pork loin roast (3 pounds), trimmed
  3 cans (4 ounces *each*) chopped green chilies
  1 large onion, chopped
1/3 cup chili powder
1/2 cup reduced-sodium chicken broth
 30 flour tortillas (6 inches)
  4 cups (16 ounces) reduced-fat shredded cheddar cheese
  2 cups picante sauce
  1 egg white
  2 teaspoons water

Place beans in a soup kettle; add water to cover by 2 in. Bring to a boil; boil for 2 minutes. Remove from the heat; cover and let stand for 1 hour. Drain and rinse beans, discarding liquid.

Place roast in a Dutch oven. In a bowl, combine chilies, onion, chili powder and beans. Spoon over roast. Cover and bake at 325° for 1-1/2 hours. Stir in broth; cover and bake 30-45 minutes longer or until a meat thermometer reads 160°. Increase oven temperature to 350°.

Remove meat and shred with two forks; set aside. Mash bean mixture; stir in shredded pork. Spoon 1/3 cup mixture down the center of each tortilla; top with 2 tablespoons cheese and 1 tablespoon picante sauce. Fold sides and ends over filling and roll up. Place seam side down on two 15-in. x 10-in. x 1-in. baking pans coated with nonstick cooking spray.

In a bowl, whisk egg white and water; brush over top. Bake, uncovered, at 350° for 25-30 minutes or until heated through. Serve immediately or cool, wrap and freeze for up to 3 months. **Yield:** 2-1/2 dozen.

To use frozen chimichangas: Place chimichangas on a baking sheet coated with nonstick cooking spray. Bake at 400° for 10-15 minutes or until heated through.

Nutritional Analysis: One chimichanga equals 276 calories, 8 g fat (4 g saturated fat), 36 mg cholesterol, 475 mg sodium, 30 g carbohydrate, 6 g fiber, 20 g protein. **Diabetic Exchanges:** 2 starch, 2 lean meat.

Turkey with Cherry Stuffing

(Pictured above)

Since our state is a big cherry producer, I use cherries in many recipes. They add lots of flavor to stuffing.
—Kathy Lee, Elk Rapids, Michigan

   8 bacon strips, diced
1-1/2 cups chopped celery
 3/4 cup chopped onion
   7 ounces unseasoned stuffing cubes
1-3/4 cups chicken broth
1-1/2 teaspoons rubbed sage
   1 teaspoon dried thyme
1/2 teaspoon pepper
1/4 teaspoon salt
1/2 cup dried cherries
   1 turkey (12 to 14 pounds)
Melted butter

In a skillet, cook bacon over medium heat until crisp. Remove with a slotted spoon to paper towels; drain, reserving 2 tablespoons drippings. Saute celery and onion in drippings until tender. In a bowl, combine stuffing cubes, broth, sage, thyme, pepper and salt. Stir in bacon, celery mixture and cherries.

Just before baking, loosely stuff turkey. Skewer turkey openings; tie drumsticks together. Place breast side up on a rack in a roasting pan. Brush with butter. Bake, uncovered, at 325° for 3-1/2 to 4-1/2 hours or until a meat thermometer reads 180° for the turkey and 165° for the stuffing, basting occasionally with pan drippings (cover loosely with foil if turkey browns too quickly).

Cover turkey and let stand for 20 minutes before removing stuffing and carving turkey. If desired, thicken pan drippings for gravy. **Yield:** 10-12 servings.

Spinach Venison Lasagna

Two different sauces—red and white—give this hearty lasagna personality. My husband is an avid hunter, so I always have plenty of wild meat on hand. I often use elk for this dish, but you could also use venison or ground beef.
—Jo Mitchell
Mountain View, Wyoming

    1/4 cup chopped onion
      2 tablespoons butter
      2 cans (8 ounces *each*) tomato sauce
    1/2 cup water
      1 tablespoon barbecue sauce
      1 teaspoon Worcestershire sauce
      1 teaspoon dried basil
      1 bay leaf
    1/4 teaspoon *each* garlic powder, ground
         cloves, ground allspice and dried oregano
WHITE SAUCE:
      1 can (4 ounces) mushroom stems and
         pieces, drained
    1/4 cup chopped onion
    1/4 cup butter
    1/3 cup all-purpose flour
      2 cups milk
     12 lasagna noodles, cooked and drained
      2 packages (10 ounces *each*) frozen
         chopped spinach, thawed and squeezed
         dry
      1 cup (8 ounces) cottage cheese
      3 cups (12 ounces) shredded mozzarella
         cheese
      2 pounds ground venison, cooked and
         drained
      1 cup (4 ounces) shredded cheddar cheese

In a large skillet, saute the onion in butter until tender. Stir in tomato sauce, water, barbecue sauce, Worcestershire sauce and seasonings. Bring to a boil. Reduce the heat; cover and simmer for 30 minutes.

Meanwhile, in a saucepan, saute the mushrooms and onion in butter until tender. Stir in the flour. Gradually whisk in milk until blended. Bring to a boil; cook and stir for 2 minutes or until thickened.

Discard bay leaf from tomato sauce. Spread 1/2 cup into a greased 13-in. x 9-in. x 2-in. baking dish; top with four noodles. Layer with 1 cup spinach, 1/2 cup cottage cheese, half of the white sauce, 1 cup mozzarella cheese, half of the venison and 1/2 cup cheddar cheese. Repeat layers once. Top with remaining noodles, tomato sauce and mozzarella cheese.

Cover and bake at 350° for 35 minutes. Uncover; bake 10-15 minutes longer or until cheese is lightly browned. Let stand for 10 minutes before cutting. **Yield:** 8 servings.

Rigatoni Florentine

(Pictured below)

I replaced the ham in the original recipe for this skillet dinner with turkey ham and used less olive oil and more veggies. The result is an appealing entree without the feel of a heavy pasta meal.
—Lynda McClellan, West Melbourne, Florida

☑ Uses less fat, sugar or salt. Includes Nutritional Analysis and Diabetic Exchanges.

     12 ounces uncooked rigatoni *or* large tube
         pasta
  1-1/2 cups diced fully cooked turkey ham
      1 cup sliced fresh mushrooms
      1 medium sweet red pepper, julienned
      1 medium sweet yellow pepper, julienned
      2 garlic cloves, minced
      2 tablespoons olive oil
    3/4 cup reduced-sodium chicken broth
    1/4 teaspoon pepper
  1-3/4 cups fresh baby spinach
    1/2 cup grated Parmesan cheese

Cook pasta according to package directions. Meanwhile, in a large skillet, saute the ham, mushrooms, peppers and garlic in oil until vegetables are tender. Stir in the broth and pepper. Bring to a boil. Reduce heat; simmer for 3 minutes. Drain pasta. Add pasta and spinach to ham mixture; toss to coat. Sprinkle with Parmesan cheese. **Yield:** 6 servings.

Nutritional Analysis: One serving (1-1/2 cups) equals 319 calories, 9 g fat (2 g saturated fat), 31 mg cholesterol, 562 mg sodium, 45 g carbohydrate, 3 g fiber, 17 g protein. **Diabetic Exchanges:** 2-1/2 starch, 2 lean meat, 1 vegetable.

Let Them Eat Lamb

WHEN it comes to planning springtime meals, tender lamb can add variety, interest and unmatched flavor. Three readers share their favorite recipes here.

Lamb with Raspberry Sauce

(Pictured below)

I like to dress up lamb chops with a wonderful fruity sauce. —Scott Beatrice, Lakeland, Florida

2 cups fresh *or* frozen unsweetened raspberries

3/4 cup finely chopped seeded peeled cucumber
1/2 cup finely chopped peeled tart apple
2 tablespoons white grape juice
1 to 2 tablespoons sugar
4 garlic cloves, minced
3 tablespoons olive oil
8 lamb loin chops (1 to 1-1/2 inches thick)

Place raspberries in a blender or food processor; cover and process until pureed. Strain and discard seeds; transfer puree to a small saucepan. Stir in the cucumber, apple, grape juice and sugar. Bring to a boil. Reduce heat; simmer, uncovered, for 5-7

SAVOR Traditional Lamb Stew, Breaded Rack of Lamb and Lamb with Raspberry Sauce (shown below, from top) this spring.

minutes or until cucumber and apple are tender.

Meanwhile, in a large skillet, saute garlic in oil until tender. Add lamb chops. Cook, uncovered, for 7-10 minutes on each side or until meat reaches desired doneness (160° for medium-well; 170° for well-done). Serve with sauce. **Yield:** 4 servings.

Breaded Rack of Lamb

(Pictured below left)

*This recipe is so easy and quick to prepare. We have lamb often on Saturday nights for dinner along with double-baked potatoes, tossed salad and a vegetable.
—Lorene Whittingham, Denver, Colorado*

    1 rack of lamb (1 to 1-1/2 pounds), trimmed
    3 to 4 garlic cloves, minced
  1/8 teaspoon salt
  1/8 teaspoon pepper
  1/2 cup dry bread crumbs
    3 tablespoons butter, melted
    1 tablespoon dried parsley flakes
  1/4 teaspoon dried thyme

Place the lamb on a greased rack in a greased roasting pan; rub with garlic, salt and pepper. Bake, uncovered, at 375° for 20 minutes.

In a bowl, combine crumbs, butter, parsley and thyme. Press onto meat. Bake 20-30 minutes longer or until meat reaches desired doneness (for rare, a meat thermometer should read 140°; medium, 160°; well-done, 170°). **Yield:** 2-3 servings.

Traditional Lamb Stew

(Pictured at left)

This is a delicious and nourishing dish. The flavor improves if you make the stew the day before you serve it. —Margery Richmond, Fort Collins, Colorado

1-1/2 pounds lamb stew meat
    2 tablespoons olive oil, *divided*
    3 large onions, quartered
    3 medium carrots, cut into 1-inch pieces
    4 small potatoes, peeled and cubed
    1 can (14-1/2 ounces) beef broth
    1 teaspoon salt
  1/4 teaspoon pepper
    1 tablespoon butter
    1 tablespoon all-purpose flour
1-1/2 teaspoons minced fresh parsley
1-1/2 teaspoons minced chives
  1/2 teaspoon minced fresh thyme

In a Dutch oven, brown meat in 1 tablespoon oil over medium heat. Remove with a slotted spoon; set aside. Add onions, carrots and remaining oil to pan. Cook for 5 minutes or until onions are tender, stirring occasionally. Add potatoes, broth, salt, pepper and lamb. Bring to a boil. Remove from the heat. Cover and bake at 350° for 50-60 minutes or until meat and vegetables are tender.

With a slotted spoon, remove meat and vegetables to a large bowl; keep warm. Pour pan juices into another bowl; set aside. In the Dutch oven, melt butter over medium heat. Stir in flour until smooth. Gradually whisk in pan juices. Bring to a boil; cook and stir for 2 minutes or until thickened. Stir in the parsley, chives, thyme, and meat and vegetables; heat through. **Yield:** 4 servings.

Spicy Beef Brisket

(Pictured on page 58)

This fork-tender brisket is just as good when cooked a day ahead, refrigerated and reheated. I like to serve it with mashed potatoes, rice or noodles to take advantage of the flavorful sauce. —Wendy Kiehn, Sebring, Florida

    1 fresh beef brisket (3 pounds)*
  1/2 teaspoon seasoned salt
  1/4 teaspoon pepper
    2 tablespoons olive oil
    2 large onions, sliced
    3 garlic cloves, minced
    1 cup beef broth
    1 cup chili sauce
  1/3 cup packed brown sugar
  1/3 cup cider vinegar
    2 to 3 tablespoons chili powder
    2 bay leaves
    3 tablespoons all-purpose flour
  1/4 cup cold water

Sprinkle beef with seasoned salt and pepper. In a Dutch oven, brown beef in oil on both sides. Remove and set aside. In the drippings, saute onions and garlic until tender. Return beef to pan. Combine the broth, chili sauce, brown sugar, vinegar, chili powder and bay leaves; pour over beef. Bring to a boil. Reduce heat; cover and simmer for 2-1/2 to 3 hours or until meat is tender.

Discard bay leaves. Remove beef to a cutting board; slice across the grain. Combine flour and cold water until smooth; stir into cooking juices. Bring to a boil; cook and stir for 2 minutes or until thickened. Serve with sliced beef. **Yield:** 10-12 servings.

*Editor's Note: This is a fresh beef brisket, not corned beef.

with egg substitute and using nonstick cooking spray instead of oil) equals 213 calories, 6 g fat (1 g saturated fat), 115 mg cholesterol, 568 mg sodium, 8 g carbohydrate, trace fiber, 29 g protein. **Diabetic Exchanges:** 3 lean meat, 1/2 starch.

Pasta Pizza Venison Bake

Venison gives a pleasant change-of-pace flavor to this quick-to-fix pasta casserole. Since my husband is an avid hunter, I'm always trying to find new ways to prepare ground venison. Even those who usually don't care for the meat will like this hearty one-dish meal.
—*Donna Thomas, Bark River, Michigan*

   8 ounces uncooked elbow macaroni
   1 pound ground venison
1/2 teaspoon salt
1/4 teaspoon pepper
   1 can (16 ounces) pizza sauce
   1 can (4 ounces) mushroom stems and pieces, drained
   2 cups (8 ounces) shredded mozzarella cheese

Cook macaroni according to package directions. Meanwhile, in a large skillet, cook the venison, salt and pepper over medium heat until meat is no longer pink; drain if necessary.

Drain the macaroni; place half in a greased 2-qt. baking dish. Top with half of the venison, pizza sauce, mushrooms and cheese. Repeat layers. Cover and bake at 350° for 15 minutes. Uncover; bake 10 minutes longer or until heated through and cheese is melted. **Yield:** 6 servings.

Curried Beef with Dumplings

I like making this hearty pot roast in winter and serving leftovers the next day. It's not only easy to prepare, but the aroma is wonderful while it's cooking.
—*Janell Schmidt, Athelstane, Wisconsin*

   1 boneless beef rump roast (3 pounds)
   2 tablespoons olive oil
   6 medium carrots, cut into chunks
   1 can (14-1/2 ounces) diced tomatoes, undrained
   1 medium onion, sliced
   2 teaspoons curry powder
   1 teaspoon sugar
   2 teaspoons salt, *divided*
   1 teaspoon Worcestershire sauce
   1 cup hot water

Bob's Crab Cakes

(Pictured above)

When I had my first crab cake, I was hooked from the first bite. I tried many recipes, adding and taking out ingredients until I found what I was looking for. I've used this recipe for more than 30 years.
—*Bob Kolwyck, Germantown, Tennessee*

☑ Uses less fat, sugar or salt. Includes Nutritional Analysis and Diabetic Exchanges.

   2 slices day-old bread, cut into 1/4-inch cubes
   1 egg, lightly beaten
   1 tablespoon dried parsley flakes
   1 tablespoon lemon juice
   1 tablespoon mayonnaise
   2 teaspoons Worcestershire sauce
   1 teaspoon ground mustard
1/2 teaspoon pepper
   3 cans (6 ounces *each*) crabmeat, drained, flaked and cartilage removed
   2 tablespoons vegetable oil

In a large bowl, combine the first eight ingredients; mix well. Add crab; mix gently. Form mixture into eight balls; flatten slightly. In a large nonstick skillet, cook crab cakes in oil for 4-5 minutes on each side or until browned. **Yield:** 8 crab cakes.

Nutritional Analysis: Two crab cakes (prepared

1-2/3 cups all-purpose flour
3 teaspoons baking powder
2 tablespoons cold butter
3/4 cup milk
2 tablespoons minced fresh parsley
2 tablespoons chopped pimientos

In a Dutch oven, brown roast in oil on all sides; drain. Combine the carrots, tomatoes, onion, curry powder, sugar, 1 teaspoon salt and Worcestershire sauce; pour over roast. Bring to a boil. Reduce heat to low; cover and cook for 2-1/2 hours or until meat and carrots are tender.

Remove roast and carrots; keep warm. Add hot water to pan; bring to a boil. For dumplings, combine the flour, baking powder and remaining salt in a large bowl. Cut in butter until mixture resembles fine crumbs. Stir in the milk, parsley and pimientos just until moistened.

Drop by tablespoonfuls onto simmering liquid. Cover and cook for 15 minutes or until a toothpick inserted in a dumpling comes out clean (do not lift the cover while simmering). Remove dumplings. Strain cooking juices; serve with roast, dumplings and carrots. **Yield:** 8 servings.

Beef 'n' Eggplant Pie

Everyone likes eggplant when they taste it in this savory pie. If you have eggplant in the garden or can get it at the market, I'd recommend this recipe. If the eggplant is large and the skin seems tough, it's a good idea to peel it first. —Audrey Nemeth, Chesterville, Maine

2 cups cubed eggplant
1/4 cup butter
3/4 pound ground beef
1/2 cup finely chopped onion
1 celery rib with leaves, chopped
1 garlic clove, minced
1 can (8 ounces) tomato sauce
1 tablespoon minced fresh parsley
1 tablespoon dried oregano
1 teaspoon salt
1/8 teaspoon pepper
1 unbaked pastry shell (9 inches)
1/2 to 1 cup shredded mozzarella cheese

In a small skillet, saute eggplant in butter until tender, about 5 minutes. In a large skillet, cook the beef, onion, celery and garlic over medium heat until meat is no longer pink; drain. Add the eggplant, tomato sauce, parsley, oregano, salt and pepper; bring to a boil. Remove from the heat.

Prick pastry shell with a fork. Add beef mixture. Bake at 375° for 20-25 minutes. Sprinkle with

cheese. Bake 5-10 minutes longer or until cheese is melted. Let stand for 10 minutes before cutting. **Yield:** 4-6 servings.

Marinated Chicken Breasts

(Pictured below)

I've tried other marinades for chicken, but this one is the best. It makes the meat so tender, and the flavor is great! —Nonie Covey, Omaha, Texas

✓ Uses less fat, sugar or salt. Includes Nutritional Analysis and Diabetic Exchanges.

2 cups lemon-lime soda
1 cup soy sauce
1/2 cup olive oil
1/2 teaspoon garlic powder
1/2 teaspoon prepared horseradish
6 boneless skinless chicken breast halves (6 ounces *each*)

In a large resealable plastic bag, combine the soda, soy sauce, oil, garlic powder and horseradish; add chicken. Seal the bag and turn to coat. Refrigerate overnight.

Drain and discard marinade. Grill chicken, uncovered, over medium heat for 6-7 minutes on each side or until juices run clear. **Yield:** 6 servings.

Nutritional Analysis: One serving (prepared with diet soda and reduced-sodium soy sauce) equals 234 calories, 7 g fat (1 g saturated fat), 99 mg cholesterol, 517 mg sodium, 1 g carbohydrate, trace fiber, 40 g protein. **Diabetic Exchanges:** 5 very lean meat, 1 fat.

Salsa Chicken Skillet

(Pictured below)

Diced chicken and veggies are stirred with spicy salsa to create this satisfying skillet dish. —LaDonna Reed
Ponca City, Oklahoma

✓ Uses less fat, sugar or salt. Includes Nutritional Analysis and Diabetic Exchanges.

  1 pound boneless skinless chicken breasts, cut into 1/2-inch pieces
  2 teaspoons canola oil
1/2 pound fresh mushrooms, sliced
  1 medium green pepper, chopped
3/4 cup chopped onion
1/2 cup chopped celery
1/2 cup frozen corn, thawed
  1 garlic clove, minced
  2 cups salsa
  2 cups hot cooked rice
1/4 cup shredded reduced-fat cheddar cheese
1/2 cup reduced-fat sour cream

In a large skillet, saute chicken in oil until no longer pink; drain and set aside. Coat skillet with nonstick cooking spray. Saute mushrooms, green pepper, onion, celery, corn and garlic for 6-8 minutes or until vegetables are tender. Add salsa and reserved chicken; heat through. Serve over rice. Top with cheese and sour cream. **Yield:** 4 servings.
    Nutritional Analysis: One serving (1-1/4 cups chicken mixture over 1/2 cup cooked rice with 1 tablespoon cheese and 2 tablespoons sour cream) equals 379 calories, 9 g fat (4 g saturated fat), 81 mg cholesterol, 736 mg sodium, 40 g carbohydrate, 5 g fiber, 36 g protein. **Diabetic Exchanges:** 3 lean meat, 2 starch, 2 vegetable.

Family-Style Turkey Potpie

Despite our last name, we like spicy, flavorful foods like this hearty potpie seasoned with green chilies and zesty cheese. —Karen Ann Bland, Gove, Kansas

  3 cups all-purpose flour
  1 teaspoon baking powder
1/2 teaspoon salt
1/2 cup cold butter
3/4 to 1 cup cold water
  4 cups cubed cooked turkey
  2 cups (8 ounces) shredded Monterey Jack cheese
  1 can (10-3/4 ounces) condensed cream of chicken soup, undiluted
  1 cup (8 ounces) sour cream
  1 small onion, finely chopped
  1 can (4 ounces) chopped green chilies, drained
  2 green onions, sliced

In a large bowl, combine the flour, baking powder and salt. Cut in butter until crumbly. Gradually add water, tossing with a fork until dough forms a ball. Turn onto a lightly floured surface; knead 10-12 times or until smooth. Set aside a third of the dough. Roll remaining dough into a 15-in. x 11-in. rectangle. Transfer to an ungreased 11-in. x 7-in. x 2-in. baking dish.
    In a bowl, combine the turkey, cheese, soup, sour cream, onion, chilies and greens onions. Spoon into crust. Roll out reserved dough; make a lattice crust. Place over filling; trim and flute edges. Bake at 400° for 45-50 minutes or until crust is golden brown and filling is bubbly. **Yield:** 6 servings.

Italian Pepper Steak

Thin tender strips of sirloin steak are served with sauteed sweet peppers and onion in this entree.
—Nancy Saffield, Pasadena, Maryland

✓ Uses less fat, sugar or salt. Includes Nutritional Analysis and Diabetic Exchanges.

  1 teaspoon Italian seasoning, *divided*
1/2 teaspoon salt, *divided*
1/2 teaspoon pepper, *divided*
  1 pound boneless beef sirloin steak, trimmed
  1 medium sweet red pepper, julienned
  1 medium sweet yellow pepper, julienned
  1 medium onion, julienned
  6 garlic cloves, peeled and thinly sliced
  1 tablespoon olive oil

1 can (14-1/2 ounces) diced tomatoes, drained
1 teaspoon balsamic vinegar

In a small bowl, combine 1/2 teaspoon Italian seasoning, 1/4 teaspoon salt and 1/4 teaspoon pepper. Rub mixture over both sides of steak; set aside.

In a large nonstick skillet, saute the peppers, onion and garlic in oil until vegetables are crisp-tender. Stir in the tomatoes and remaining Italian seasoning, salt and pepper. Reduce heat; cover and simmer for 5 minutes. Remove from the heat. Stir in vinegar; keep warm.

Place steak on a broiler pan coated with nonstick cooking spray. Broil 4-6 in. from the heat for 4-8 minutes on each side or until the meat reaches desired doneness (for rare, a meat thermometer should read 140°; medium, 160°; well-done, 170°). Let stand for 5 minutes before slicing; serve with vegetable mixture. **Yield:** 4 servings.

Nutritional Analysis: One serving (3 ounces cooked beef with 1/2 cup vegetables) equals 244 calories, 10 g fat (3 g saturated fat), 67 mg cholesterol, 500 mg sodium, 12 g carbohydrate, 3 g fiber, 26 g protein. **Diabetic Exchanges:** 3 lean meat, 2 vegetable, 1 fat.

until smooth; stir into pan juices. Bring to a boil; cook and stir for 2 minutes or until thickened. Serve with rabbit. **Yield:** 4 servings.

Braised Rabbit

My husband and I do a lot of hunting and eat more wild game than domestic meat. I came up with this recipe for wild rabbit, and the meat cooks up tender and tangy. —Dawn Bryant, North Platte, Nebraska

1 dressed rabbit (about 2-1/2 pounds), cut into serving-size pieces
1/4 cup olive oil
1 large onion, halved and thinly sliced
4 garlic cloves, minced
2 cups chicken broth
1-1/2 teaspoons dried thyme
1/4 teaspoon pepper
1 bay leaf
1/4 cup all-purpose flour
1/4 cup lemon juice
5 tablespoons cold water

In a large skillet over medium heat, cook rabbit in oil until lightly browned; remove and keep warm. In the same skillet, saute onion and garlic until tender. Stir in the broth, thyme, pepper and bay leaf. Return rabbit to pan. Bring to a boil. Reduce heat; cover and simmer for 30-45 minutes or until meat is tender and a meat thermometer reads 160°.

Remove rabbit to a serving platter. Discard bay leaf. Combine the flour, lemon juice and water

Thyme Lemon Sirloins

(Pictured above)

We love to serve steaks when friends drop by...and have found that the tangy lemon herb rub in this recipe really livens up the taste buds.
—Suzanne Whitaker, Knoxville, Tennessee

2 teaspoons grated lemon peel
2 garlic cloves, minced
1 teaspoon dried thyme
1/4 teaspoon salt
1/4 teaspoon pepper
2 tablespoons butter
1 tablespoon lemon juice
4 boneless beef sirloin steaks (about 2 pounds and 1 inch thick)

In a small bowl, combine lemon peel, garlic, thyme, salt and pepper. Set aside 1 tablespoon seasoning mixture for steaks. In a small saucepan, melt butter; stir in lemon juice and remaining seasoning mixture. Set aside and keep warm.

Rub steaks with reserved seasoning mixture. Grill steaks, uncovered, over medium heat for 8-12 minutes on each side or until meat reaches desired doneness (for rare, a meat thermometer should read 140°; medium, 160°; well-done, 170°). Serve with reserved butter sauce. **Yield:** 4 servings.

TRY three different types of quesadillas: Bean 'n' Beef, Rio Grande and Shrimp (shown above, top to bottom).

Wrap Up Supper Swiftly...

...with quesadillas! They're fast, fun and versatile, so everyone's tastes can be satisfied.

Bean 'n' Beef Quesadillas

(Pictured above)

Either leftover roast beef or deli beef works well in this recipe. To complement the hearty quesadillas, I dress up purchased salsa. —Marion Platt, Sequim, Washington

1-1/2 cups chunky salsa
  1/4 cup minced fresh cilantro
    3 tablespoons lime juice
    1 cup canned black beans, rinsed, drained
  1/2 cup frozen corn, thawed
    2 cups julienned cooked roast beef
    2 cups (12 ounces) shredded Monterey Jack cheese
    8 flour tortillas (10 inches)
    1 to 2 tablespoons vegetable oil

In a small bowl, combine the salsa, cilantro and lime juice. In another bowl, combine the beans, corn and 1/2 cup salsa mixture. Set remaining salsa mixture aside.

Place beef, cheese and bean mixture on half of each tortilla; fold over. In a skillet over medium heat, cook quesadillas in 1 tablespoon oil for 1-2 minutes on each side or until cheese is melted, using additional oil as needed. Cut into wedges. Serve with reserved salsa. **Yield:** 4-6 servings.

Rio Grande Quesadillas

(Pictured above)

A well-seasoned filling of chicken and refried beans makes this quick Southwestern specialty a popular choice.   *—Shawn Nelson, Evansville, Indiana*

    2 cups shredded cooked chicken
3/4 cup water

1 envelope taco seasoning
1 cup refried beans
6 flour tortillas (7 inches)
1 jar (2 ounces) diced pimientos, drained
1/4 cup chopped green onions
1/4 cup minced fresh cilantro
1-1/2 cups (6 ounces) shredded Monterey Jack cheese
1 to 2 tablespoons vegetable oil

In a saucepan, bring the chicken, water and taco seasoning to a boil. Reduce heat; simmer, uncovered, for 10 minutes. Stir in the beans.

Spoon 1/3 cup mixture over half of each tortilla; top with pimientos, onions, cilantro and cheese. Fold over. In a skillet over medium heat, cook quesadillas in 1 tablespoon oil for 1-2 minutes on each side or until cheese is melted, using additional oil as needed. Cut into wedges. **Yield:** 3-6 servings.

Shrimp Quesadillas

(Pictured at left)

For variety, substitute cooked chicken or ground beef for the shrimp in these easy quesadillas.
—Joan Schroeder, Pinedale, Wyoming

1 can (28 ounces) diced tomatoes, drained
1/2 cup chopped green onions
1 can (4 ounces) chopped green chilies
3 jalapeno peppers, seeded and chopped*
1 garlic clove, minced
1 tablespoon minced fresh cilantro
1 teaspoon salt
1/2 teaspoon dried oregano
1/2 teaspoon ground cumin
QUESADILLAS:
1-1/3 cups shredded Mexican cheese blend
1 can (4 ounces) chopped green chilies, drained
1/2 cup chopped seeded tomato
3 tablespoons sliced green onions
1 package (8 ounces) frozen cooked salad shrimp, thawed
4 flour tortillas (10 inches)
1 tablespoon butter

For salsa, place the first nine ingredients in a blender or food processor; cover and process until finely chopped. Transfer to a bowl; set aside.

Sprinkle cheese, chilies, tomato, onions and shrimp over half of each tortilla; fold over. In a skillet over medium heat, cook quesadillas in butter for 1-2 minutes on each side or until cheese is melted. Cut into wedges. Serve with salsa. Refrigerate leftover salsa. **Yield:** 2-4 servings (2-1/2 cups salsa).

*Editor's Note: When cutting or seeding hot peppers, use rubber or plastic gloves to protect your hands. Avoid touching your face.

Spicy Zucchini Quesadillas

(Pictured below)

My family loves Mexican food, so I created this easy recipe one summer when our garden was bursting with zucchini. —Linda Taylor, Lenexa, Kansas

1 large onion, chopped
1/2 cup chopped sweet red pepper
1 teaspoon plus 2 tablespoons butter, softened, *divided*
2 cups shredded zucchini
2 tablespoons taco seasoning
8 flour tortillas (7 inches)
8 ounces pepper Jack cheese, shredded
Salsa, sour cream and pickled jalapeno pepper slices

In a skillet, saute onion and red pepper in 1 teaspoon butter for 3 minutes. Stir in zucchini and taco seasoning; saute 3-4 minutes longer or until vegetables are tender. Remove from the heat.

Spread remaining butter over one side of each tortilla. Place tortillas butter side down on a griddle. Sprinkle about 1/4 cup cheese and 1/4 cup zucchini mixture over half of each tortilla; fold over.

Cook over low heat for 1-2 minutes on each side or until cheese is melted. Serve with salsa, sour cream and jalapenos. **Yield:** 4 servings.

Oriental Pot Roast

(Pictured below)

I love Oriental food, so this pot roast satisfies my cravings. The original recipe called for spinach, but I use sugar snap peas and carrots instead.
— *Donna Staley, Randleman, North Carolina*

    1 boneless beef rump roast (3 pounds)
    1 tablespoon vegetable oil
    1 large onion, chopped
    1 can (20 ounces) pineapple chunks
    3 tablespoons soy sauce
    1 garlic clove, minced
    1 teaspoon ground ginger
    3 celery ribs, sliced
    2 medium carrots, sliced
    1 cup fresh sugar snap peas
    1 cup sliced fresh mushrooms
    1 to 2 tablespoons cornstarch
  1/4 cup cold water

In a Dutch oven over medium heat, brown roast in oil on all sides; drain. Add onion. Drain pineapple, reserving juice; set pineapple aside. In a small bowl, combine the pineapple juice, soy sauce, garlic and ginger. Pour over roast. Bring to a boil. Reduce heat; cover and simmer for 2 hours or until meat is almost tender.

Add celery and carrots. Cover and simmer for 20 minutes or until vegetables are crisp-tender. Add the peas, mushrooms and reserved pineapple. Cover and simmer 15 minutes longer or until vegetables and meat are tender.

Remove roast, vegetables and pineapple; keep warm. Skim fat from pan drippings. Combine cornstarch and cold water until smooth; gradually stir into the drippings. Bring to a boil; cook and stir for 2 minutes or until thickened. Slice roast across the grain. Serve meat and vegetables with gravy. **Yield:** 6 servings.

Chicken Patties

(Pictured on page 58)

This recipe is a great way to use up leftover chicken. I've even used canned chicken, as long as it's drained well. I usually serve the patties with flavored rice, a vegetable and salad. — *Larry Laatsch, Saginaw, Michigan*

    2 cups shredded cooked chicken
  1/2 cup crushed saltines (about 15 crackers)
  1/3 cup mayonnaise
    4 green onions, finely chopped
    2 tablespoons lemon juice
  1/8 teaspoon pepper
    2 tablespoons vegetable oil

In a bowl, combine the chicken, cracker crumbs, mayonnaise, onions, lemon juice and pepper. Shape into six patties. Heat oil in a large skillet; fry patties over medium heat for 2-3 minutes on each side or until golden brown and heated through. **Yield:** 6 servings.

Mushroom Quiche

Savory, onion and sweet red pepper perk up the mushroom and cheese flavors in this pretty deep-dish pie...and add a little color, too.
— *Ruth Andrewson, Leavenworth, Washington*

    1 unbaked deep-dish pastry shell (9 inches)
    4 cups sliced fresh mushrooms
  1/2 cup diced onion
  1/4 cup diced sweet red pepper
    1 tablespoon butter
    1 cup (4 ounces) shredded cheddar cheese
    2 tablespoons all-purpose flour
1-1/4 cups milk
    4 eggs, lightly beaten
    1 to 2 tablespoons minced fresh savory *or* 1 to 2 teaspoons dried savory
    1 teaspoon salt
  1/2 teaspoon cayenne pepper

Line unpricked pastry shell with a double thickness of heavy-duty foil. Bake at 450° for 8 minutes. Remove foil; bake 5 minutes longer. Cool on a wire rack. Reduce heat to 350°.

In a skillet, saute mushrooms, onion and red pepper in butter until mushrooms are tender. Drain

and set aside. In a bowl, combine cheese and flour. Stir in milk, eggs, savory, salt and cayenne until blended. Stir in mushroom mixture. Pour into crust.

Bake for 40-50 minutes or until a knife inserted near the center comes out clean (cover edges loosely with foil if needed to prevent overbrowning). Let stand for 10 minutes before cutting. **Yield:** 4-6 servings.

Braised Short Ribs

These delicious ribs are often on the menu when my husband and I have company for dinner. The allspice and bay leaf come through nicely, and the meat is very tender. —Mary Gill, Florence, Oregon

    3 pounds beef short ribs
1-1/2 teaspoons butter
1-1/2 teaspoons vegetable oil
    1 large onion, thinly sliced
    1 cup water
1-1/4 teaspoons salt
    1 teaspoon sugar
  1/4 teaspoon coarsely ground pepper
    2 bay leaves
    1 teaspoon whole allspice
    1 tablespoon all-purpose flour
  1/4 cup cold water

In a Dutch oven, brown ribs in butter and oil for about 3 minutes on each side; drain. Remove and keep warm. In the same pan, cook and stir the onion for 2 minutes. Add water, salt, sugar and pepper, stirring to loosen browned bits from pan.

Place bay leaves and allspice on a double thickness of cheesecloth; bring up corners of cloth and tie with kitchen string to form a bag. Place in pan. Return ribs to pan. Bring to a boil. Reduce heat; cover and simmer for 1-1/2 to 1-3/4 hours or until meat is tender.

Remove ribs and keep warm. Discard the spice bag. Skim fat from pan drippings. Combine flour and cold water until smooth; gradually stir into drippings. Bring to a boil; cook and stir for 2 minutes or until thickened. Serve with ribs. **Yield:** 4 servings.

Chili Stew

(Pictured above right)

This thick zippy stew is loaded with familiar ingredients, such as ground beef, tomatoes, kidney beans and chili beans. Chili powder and green chilies season it just right. —Amy Short, Lesage, West Virginia

✓ Uses less fat, sugar or salt. Includes Nutritional Analysis and Diabetic Exchanges.

    1 **pound ground beef**
    1 **medium onion, chopped**
    1 **small green pepper, chopped**
    2 **cans (15-1/2 ounces *each*) hot chili beans**
    1 **can (16 ounces) kidney beans, rinsed and drained**
    1 **can (15-1/4 ounces) whole kernel corn, drained**
    1 **can (14-1/2 ounces) diced tomatoes with garlic and onion**
    1 **can (8 ounces) tomato sauce**
    1 **can (4 ounces) chopped green chilies**
    2 **tablespoons chili powder**
  1/2 **teaspoon salt**

In a Dutch oven or large saucepan, cook the beef, onion and green pepper over medium heat until meat is no longer pink; drain. Stir in remaining ingredients. Bring to a boil. Reduce heat; simmer, uncovered, for 15 minutes, stirring occasionally. **Yield:** 10 servings (2-1/2 quarts).

Nutritional Analysis: One 1-cup serving (recipe prepared with lean ground beef and 1-1/2 cups frozen corn) equals 263 calories, 5 g fat (2 g saturated fat), 17 mg cholesterol, 812 mg sodium, 36 g carbohydrate, 10 g fiber, 19 g protein. **Diabetic Exchanges:** 2 starch, 1-1/2 lean meat, 1 vegetable.

RACK UP compliments when you serve tender and flavorful Best Baby-Back Ribs, Herbed Spareribs or Barbecued Beef Short Ribs (shown above, top to bottom).

Succulent Ribs Are Standouts

RIBS sizzling on the grill or baking to tender perfection in the oven—just the thought is enough to make your mouth water!

Best Baby-Back Ribs

(Pictured above)

I first marinate the racks of ribs, then add a zesty rub before grilling them. They turn out moist and flavorful.
—*Iola Egle, Bella Vista, Arkansas*

3/4 cup chicken broth
3/4 cup soy sauce
1/2 cup sugar
  6 tablespoons cider vinegar
  6 tablespoons olive oil
  3 garlic cloves, minced
  2 racks pork baby-back ribs (about 4-1/2 pounds)
SEASONING RUB:
1/2 cup sugar
  1 tablespoon salt
  1 tablespoon paprika
1/2 teaspoon chili powder

1/2 teaspoon pepper
1/4 teaspoon garlic powder
Dash cayenne pepper

In a bowl, combine first six ingredients. Pour two-thirds of marinade into a 2-gal. resealable plastic bag; add ribs. Seal bag; turn to coat. Refrigerate overnight. Cover and refrigerate remaining marinade.

Drain and discard marinade from ribs. In a bowl, combine rub ingredients; rub over both sides of ribs.

Coat grill rack with nonstick cooking spray before starting grill. Grill ribs, covered, over medium heat for 20 minutes. Turn and grill 20 minutes longer.

Baste with reserved marinade. Cook 20-40 minutes longer or until a meat thermometer reads 160° and pork is tender, turning and basting occasionally. **Yield:** 4 servings.

Herbed Spareribs

(Pictured at left)

I often make these delicious ribs in the summer when we're at our lake cottage. I serve them with couscous, Caesar salad and garlic toast. —Norma Harder
Melfort, Saskatchewan

    4 pounds pork spareribs, cut into serving-size
      pieces
1/4 cup olive oil
    2 tablespoons lemon juice
    3 garlic cloves, minced
    1 teaspoon salt
    1 teaspoon dried rosemary, crushed
    1 teaspoon paprika
1/2 teaspoon dried oregano
1/2 teaspoon dried marjoram

Place ribs in two ungreased 13-in. x 9-in. x 2-in. baking pans. Cover and bake at 350° for 45-55 minutes or until juices run clear and meat is tender.

In a small bowl, combine the remaining ingredients. Brush over ribs. Grill, uncovered, over medium-hot heat for 6-8 minutes on each side or until lightly browned, brushing occasionally with herb mixture. **Yield:** 4-5 servings.

Barbecued Beef Short Ribs

(Pictured above left)

These sweet-spicy barbecue ribs are always a hit. The sauce is also very good on pork ribs. —Paula Zsiray
Logan, Utah

    1 cup sugar
1/2 cup packed brown sugar
    2 tablespoons salt
    2 tablespoons garlic powder
    2 tablespoons paprika
    2 teaspoons pepper
1/4 teaspoon cayenne pepper
    7 pounds beef short ribs, trimmed
SAUCE:
    1 small onion, finely chopped
    2 teaspoons vegetable oil
1-1/2 cups water
    1 cup ketchup
    1 can (6 ounces) tomato paste
    2 tablespoons brown sugar
Pepper to taste

In a bowl, combine the first seven ingredients; rub over ribs. Place in two large resealable plastic bags; seal and refrigerate overnight.

Line two 15-in. x 10-in. x 1-in. baking pans with foil; grease foil. Place ribs in prepared pans. Bake, uncovered, at 325° for 2 hours or until tender.

Meanwhile, in a large saucepan, saute onion in oil until tender. Stir in the water, ketchup, tomato paste, brown sugar and pepper. Bring to a boil. Reduce heat; cover and simmer for 1 hour.

Remove ribs from oven. Grill, covered, over indirect medium heat for 20 minutes, turning and basting frequently with sauce. **Yield:** 14 servings.

Plum-Glazed Country Ribs

When planning to make ribs one day, I remembered that a friend had given me homemade plum jelly. I stirred some into the sauce for a pleasant fruity accent.
—Ila Mae Alderman, Galax, Virginia

    4 to 4-1/2 pounds bone-in pork
      country-style spareribs
    1 bottle (12 ounces) chili sauce
    1 jar (12 ounces) plum preserves
1/4 cup soy sauce
1/4 teaspoon hot pepper sauce

Place ribs in two ungreased 13-in. x 9-in. x 2-in. baking dishes. Bake, uncovered, at 350° for 45 minutes; drain. In a small saucepan, combine the remaining ingredients. Bring to a boil, stirring occasionally. Remove from the heat. Set aside 3/4 cup sauce for serving.

Brush ribs with some of the remaining sauce. Bake, uncovered, for 30-45 minutes or until ribs are tender, turning and basting frequently with remaining sauce. Serve with the reserved sauce. **Yield:** 8 servings.

Chicken Pesto Pizza

(Pictured below)

My wife and I love this pizza! The crisp crust, made from frozen bread dough, is topped with a tasty mixture of sauteed onion, sweet pepper and chicken as well as tomato slices and mozzarella cheese.
—Paul Piantek, Middletown, Connecticut

- 1 loaf (1 pound) frozen bread dough, thawed
- 1 egg, beaten
- 1/2 pound boneless skinless chicken breasts, cut into 1/2-inch pieces
- 1 small onion, sliced
- 1 small sweet yellow pepper, julienned
- 1/4 teaspoon lemon-pepper seasoning
- 1 tablespoon olive oil
- 1/4 cup prepared pesto sauce
- 3 plum tomatoes, thinly sliced
- 1 cup (4 ounces) shredded mozzarella cheese

With greased fingers, pat dough into an ungreased 12-in. pizza pan. Prick dough thoroughly with a fork. Brush with egg. Bake at 400° for 12-15 minutes or until lightly browned.

In a large skillet, saute the chicken, onion, yellow pepper and lemon-pepper in oil until chicken is no longer pink; drain.

Spread the pesto sauce over the crust. Top with chicken mixture, tomatoes and cheese. Bake for 12-15 minutes or until lightly browned. **Yield:** 6 slices.

Herbed Shepherd's Pie

This one-dish meal pleases the meat-and-potato lovers in my family...and they also get their veggies. The hearty casserole is seasoned with bay leaves, cloves and thyme. —Margaret Wagner Allen, Abingdon, Virginia

- 1 pound ground beef
- 1 can (14-1/2 ounces) beef broth, *divided*
- 3 to 4 bay leaves
- 2 whole cloves
- 1/2 teaspoon pepper
- 1/8 teaspoon dried thyme
- 1 pound potatoes, peeled and cubed
- 1/4 to 1/2 cup milk
- 2 tablespoons butter
- 1 tablespoon minced chives
- 1 teaspoon salt, *divided*
- 1 cup (4 ounces) shredded mozzarella cheese
- 2 medium onions, sliced
- 2 celery ribs, diced
- 1 large carrot, sliced
- 1 cup frozen corn, thawed
- 2 tablespoons all-purpose flour

In a large skillet, cook beef over medium heat until no longer pink; drain. Stir in 1 cup broth, bay leaves, cloves, pepper and thyme. Bring to a boil. Reduce heat; cover and simmer for 30 minutes.

Meanwhile, place potatoes in a large saucepan and cover with water. Bring to a boil. Reduce heat; cover and cook for 15-20 minutes or until tender. Drain. Mash potatoes with milk, butter, chives and 1/2 teaspoon salt. Stir in cheese; keep warm.

Add the onions, celery, carrot, corn and remaining salt to the beef mixture. Cover and simmer for 10 minutes. In a small bowl, whisk the flour and remaining broth until smooth. Gradually stir into beef mixture. Bring to a boil; cook and stir for 1-2 minutes or until thickened. Remove from the heat. Discard bay leaves and cloves.

Transfer beef mixture to a greased 11-in. x 7-in. x 2-in. baking dish. Top with mashed potatoes. Bake, uncovered, at 375° for 10 minutes or until heated through. **Yield:** 4-6 servings.

Hanukkah Brisket

I serve this flavorful baked beef brisket along with potato latkes (potato pancakes) during our celebration of Hanukkah. The recipe has been passed down in my family and is very easy to prepare. —Paula Levine
Lake Worth, Florida

- 1 flat cut beef brisket* (3 to 4 pounds)
- 1 can (28 ounces) stewed tomatoes
- 1 envelope onion soup mix

Place beef in a greased roasting pan. Combine tomatoes and soup mix; pour over beef. Cover and bake at 350° for 2-1/2 to 3 hours or until a meat thermometer reads 160° and meat is tender. **Yield:** 8-10 servings.

*Editor's Note: This is a fresh beef brisket, not corned beef. The meat comes from the first cut of the brisket.

Caramelized-Onion Pork

We live in a farming community, and onions are one of our main crops. When I competed in a cooking contest at the Idaho-Eastern Oregon Onion Festival, I was flabbergasted when I won the top three prizes. This was the first-place recipe.
—Nell Cruse
Ontario, Oregon

 Uses less fat, sugar or salt. Includes Nutritional Analysis and Diabetic Exchanges.

- **1 large sweet onion, thinly sliced**
- **1 teaspoon sugar**
- **2 teaspoons olive oil**
- **1 pork tenderloin (1 pound)**
- **1/4 teaspoon salt**
- **1/8 teaspoon pepper**

In a large skillet, cook onion and sugar in oil over medium-low heat until onion is tender and golden brown, about 30 minutes, stirring occasionally.

Place the pork in a 13-in. x 9-in. x 2-in. baking dish coated with nonstick cooking spray. Sprinkle with salt and pepper. Top with onion mixture. Bake, uncovered, at 350° for 40-45 minutes or until a meat thermometer reads 160°. Let stand for 5 minutes before slicing. **Yield:** 4 servings.

Nutritional Analysis: One serving (3 ounces cooked pork with about 2 tablespoons onions) equals 191 calories, 6 g fat (2 g saturated fat), 74 mg cholesterol, 207 mg sodium, 8 g carbohydrate, 1 g fiber, 25 g protein. **Diabetic Exchanges:** 3 lean meat, 1 vegetable.

Pork Roast Supper

(Pictured above right)

Featuring moist tender meat, savory veggies and a flavorful sauce, this supper is among my specialties. My wife and I love hosting dinner parties, and it's one of the dishes we often serve to guests.
—Garnett Brown Jr., Lexington, Kentucky

- **1 teaspoon *each* minced fresh tarragon, thyme and rosemary**

- **1/2 teaspoon salt**
- **1/2 teaspoon garlic powder**
- **1/2 teaspoon curry powder**
- **1/2 teaspoon pepper**
- **1 boneless pork loin roast (4 pounds), trimmed**
- **1 cup barbecue sauce**
- **1-1/2 teaspoons prepared mustard**
- **2 tablespoons brown sugar**
- **3 small onions, cut into chunks**
- **3 celery ribs, cut into chunks**
- **3 medium carrots, cut into chunks**
- **6 medium red potatoes, cut into chunks**
- **1/3 cup vegetable oil**
- **1/2 cup chicken broth**

In a small bowl, combine herbs, salt, garlic powder, curry powder and pepper; set aside 1 tablespoon. Rub remaining mixture over roast; place in a greased shallow roasting pan. Combine barbecue sauce and mustard; spread over roast. Sprinkle with brown sugar.

In a resealable plastic bag, combine onions, celery, carrots, potatoes, oil and reserved herb mixture; toss well. Arrange vegetables around roast. Pour broth into pan. Bake, uncovered, at 350° for 2 hours or until a meat thermometer reads 160°. Let stand for 10 minutes before slicing. **Yield:** 8 servings.

over beef. Bring to a boil. Reduce heat; cover and simmer for 60-75 minutes or until beef is tender. Serve over pasta. **Yield:** 6 servings.

Marinated Rosemary Chicken

This moist chicken is partially cooked in the microwave just before grilling to speed up cooking. The rosemary marinade enhances the meat flavor, and there's enough sauce to set aside for basting.
—*Wendy Molzahn, Beaumont, Alberta*

✓ Uses less fat, sugar or salt. Includes Nutritional Analysis and Diabetic Exchanges.

    1/3 cup reduced-sodium soy sauce
    1/4 cup lemon juice
      2 tablespoons olive oil
      4 garlic cloves, minced
      4 tablespoons minced fresh rosemary
         or 4 teaspoons dried rosemary, crushed
      1 broiler/fryer chicken (3 pounds), cut
         up and skin removed

In a measuring cup, combine the soy sauce, lemon juice, oil, garlic and rosemary. Pour 1/2 cup into a large resealable plastic bag; add chicken. Seal bag and turn to coat; refrigerate for 8 hours or overnight. Cover and refrigerate remaining marinade for basting.

Coat grill rack with nonstick cooking spray before starting the grill. Prepare grill for indirect heat. Drain and discard marinade from chicken.

Place chicken in an ungreased 13-in. x 9-in. x 2-in. microwave-safe dish. Cover loosely and microwave on high for 6 minutes, rotating once.

Immediately grill chicken, covered, over indirect medium heat for 5 minutes. Turn; grill 8-10 minutes longer or until juices run clear, basting occasionally with reserved marinade. **Yield:** 6 servings.

Nutritional Analysis: One serving (3 ounces cooked chicken) equals 175 calories, 8 g fat (2 g saturated fat), 66 mg cholesterol, 312 mg sodium, 2 g carbohydrate, trace fiber, 23 g protein. **Diabetic Exchange:** 3 lean meat.

Editor's Note: This recipe was tested in a 1,100-watt microwave.

Ribs 'n' Stuffed Cabbage

This recipe is one that I remember my Grandma Olah making often. She usually served it with sour cream on the side and fresh seeded rye bread.
—*Paul Joseph Yuhas, Denver, Colorado*

Indiana Swiss Steak

(Pictured above)

I entered the Indiana State Beef Contest and won first place with this recipe. A mixture of picante sauce, ketchup, vinegar and veggies enhances the tender slices of steak that are served over pasta. I use bow-tie pasta, but you could substitute rice. —*Ann Dixon*
North Vernon, Indiana

      1/4 cup all-purpose flour
        1 teaspoon salt
      1/2 teaspoon pepper
    1-1/2 pounds boneless beef top round steak, cut
           into serving-size pieces
        1 tablespoon vegetable oil
        1 medium onion, chopped
      3/4 cup grated carrot
      3/4 cup water
      1/2 cup chopped celery
      1/2 cup chopped green pepper
      1/2 cup ketchup
      1/4 cup picante sauce
        1 tablespoon cider vinegar
    Hot cooked pasta

In a large resealable plastic bag, combine the flour, salt and pepper. Add beef, a few pieces at a time, and shake to coat. In a large skillet, brown the beef in oil.

Combine the onion, carrot, water, celery, green pepper, ketchup, picante sauce and vinegar; pour

3 pounds pork spareribs
1 large head cabbage (3-1/4 pounds)
1-1/4 pounds uncooked ground beef
1 pound uncooked ground pork
2 large onions, finely chopped
1 cup cooked rice
4 garlic cloves, minced
1 teaspoon salt
1/2 teaspoon pepper
1 can (29 ounces) tomato puree
1 package (32 ounces) sauerkraut, rinsed
and drained

Place ribs in two 13-in. x 9-in. x 2-in. baking pans. Cover and bake at 325° for 30 minutes. Meanwhile, remove core from cabbage. In a large kettle, cook cabbage in boiling water just until leaves fall of head. Set aside 12 large leaves for rolls. (Refrigerate remaining cabbage for another use.)

Cut out the center vein from the bottom of each reserved leaf, making a V-shaped cut. In a bowl, combine the beef, pork, onions, rice, garlic, salt and pepper; mix well. Place about 1/2 cup on each cabbage leaf. Fold in sides; roll up, starting at an unfolded edge.

Drain ribs. Spread 1/4 cup tomato puree and 1 cup sauerkraut in a Dutch oven. Layer with ribs, 1 cup sauerkraut, cabbage rolls, remaining sauerkraut and remaining puree. Bring to a boil. Reduce heat; cover and cook over medium-low heat for 45-55 minutes or until ribs are tender and a meat thermometer inserted into cabbage rolls reads 160°. Serve with a slotted spoon or thicken juices if desired. **Yield:** 12 servings.

Asparagus Sausage Crepes

(Pictured at right)

This was my favorite recipe when I was growing up in western Michigan, where asparagus is a big spring crop. With its sausage-and-cheese filling, tender asparagus and rich sour cream topping, this pretty dish will impress guests.
—Lisa Hanson, Glenview, Illinois

1 pound bulk pork sausage
1 small onion, chopped
1 package (3 ounces) cream cheese, cubed
1/2 cup shredded Monterey Jack cheese
1/4 teaspoon dried marjoram
1 cup all-purpose flour
1/2 teaspoon salt
1 cup milk
3 eggs

1 tablespoon vegetable oil
32 fresh asparagus spears (about 1 pound), trimmed
TOPPING:
1/4 cup butter, softened
1/2 cup sour cream

In a large skillet, cook sausage and onion over medium heat until sausage is no longer pink; drain. Stir in the cream cheese, Monterey Jack cheese and marjoram; set aside.

In a mixing bowl, combine the flour and salt. Add milk, eggs and oil; mix well. Heat a lightly greased 8-in. nonstick skillet; pour 2 tablespoons batter into the center of skillet. Lift and tilt pan to evenly coat bottom. Cook until top appears dry; turn and cook for 15-20 seconds. Remove to a wire rack.

Repeat with remaining batter, adding oil to skillet as needed. When cool, stack crepes with waxed paper or paper towels in between.

Spoon 2 tablespoons of the sausage mixture onto the center of each crepe. Top with two asparagus spears. Roll up; place in two greased 13-in. x 9-in. x 2-in. baking dishes. Cover and bake at 375° for 15 minutes. Combine the butter and sour cream; spoon over crepes. Bake 5 minutes longer or until heated through. **Yield:** 8 servings.

Cube Steaks Parmigiana

(Pictured below)

Tired of chicken-fried steak? This recipe dresses up cube steaks Italian-style with cheese, tomatoes, basil and oregano. —Sarah Befort, Hays, Kansas

> 3 tablespoons all-purpose flour
> 1/2 teaspoon salt
> 1/4 teaspoon pepper
> 2 eggs
> 3 tablespoons water
> 1/3 cup finely crushed saltines (about 10 crackers)
> 1/3 cup grated Parmesan cheese
> 1/2 teaspoon dried basil
> 4 beef cube steaks (1 pound)
> 3 tablespoons vegetable oil
> 1-1/4 cups tomato sauce
> 2-1/4 teaspoons sugar
> 1/2 teaspoon dried oregano, *divided*
> 1/4 teaspoon garlic powder
> 4 slices mozzarella cheese
> 1/3 cup shredded Parmesan cheese

In a shallow bowl, combine the flour, salt and pepper. In another bowl, beat eggs and water. Place cracker crumbs, grated Parmesan cheese and basil in a third bowl. Coat steaks with flour mixture, then dip in egg mixture and coat with crumb mixture. In a large skillet, brown steaks in oil for 2-3 minutes on each side or until golden brown.

Arrange steaks in a greased 13-in. x 9-in. x 2-in. baking dish. Bake, uncovered, at 375° for 25 minutes. Combine the tomato sauce, sugar, 1/4 teaspoon oregano and garlic powder; spoon over steaks. Bake 10 minutes longer. Top each steak with mozzarella cheese; sprinkle with shredded Parmesan cheese and remaining oregano. Bake 2-3 minutes longer or until cheese is melted. **Yield:** 4 servings.

Tenderloin in Puff Pastry

I came up with this dish after combining several different recipes. I wrap up each beef tenderloin, topped with a tasty mushroom mixture, in a sheet of puff pastry. It sounds like a lot of work, but it isn't...and it's so elegant. —Julie Mahoney, St. Edward, Nebraska

> 4 beef tenderloin fillets (1-3/4 inches thick and about 5 ounces *each*)
> 1 tablespoon vegetable oil
> 1/2 pound sliced fresh mushrooms
> 4 green onions, chopped
> 1/4 cup butter
> 1/2 teaspoon salt
> 1/4 teaspoon pepper
> 1 sheet frozen puff pastry, thawed
> 1 egg
> 1 tablespoon water

In a large skillet, brown fillets in oil on both sides. Place a wire rack on a baking sheet. Transfer fillets to wire rack; refrigerate for 1 hour. In the same skillet, saute mushrooms and onions in butter until tender; drain. Stir in salt and pepper.

On a lightly floured surface, roll pastry into a 13-in. square. Cut into four squares. Place one fillet in the center of each square; top with mushroom mixture. Combine egg and water; brush over pastry. Bring up corners to center and tuck in edges; press to seal. Place on a parchment paper-lined baking sheet. Cover and refrigerate for 1 hour or overnight.

Bake, uncovered, at 400° for 20-25 minutes or until pastry is golden brown and meat reaches desired doneness (for rare, a meat thermometer should read 140°; medium, 160°; well-done, 170°). **Yield:** 4 servings.

Asparagus Pasta Primavera

There's plenty of fresh herb flavor in this delicious pasta meal that blends asparagus, ham, mushrooms and plum tomatoes. Sometimes I like to use spinach linguine or fettuccine.
—William Anatooskin, Burnaby, British Columbia

> 6 tablespoons butter, cubed
> 3 tablespoons olive oil
> 8 garlic cloves, minced
> 1-1/2 pounds fresh asparagus, trimmed and cut into 1-inch pieces
> 1-1/2 cups sliced fresh mushrooms
> 1/2 cup chopped fully cooked ham
> 2 tablespoons *each* chopped fresh basil, oregano and rosemary
> 4 large plum tomatoes, chopped

1 teaspoon salt
1/4 teaspoon pepper
12 ounces uncooked linguine
1/2 cup shredded Parmesan cheese

In a large skillet, melt butter with oil over medium heat. Add garlic; cook and stir for 3 minutes. Stir in the asparagus. Cover and cook for 1 minute. Add the mushrooms, ham, basil, oregano and rosemary. Cover and cook for 5 minutes or until asparagus is crisp-tender, stirring occasionally.

Stir in the tomatoes, salt and pepper. Cook 3 minutes longer or until heated through. Meanwhile, cook linguine according to package directions; drain and place in a large bowl. Add asparagus mixture and toss. Sprinkle with Parmesan cheese. **Yield:** 6-8 servings.

Zucchini Bacon Quiche

I look forward to midsummer, when the zucchini is ready and I can prepare this yummy quiche. The crust is made with convenient refrigerated crescent rolls. My family has been enjoying this quiche for years.
—Sheri Krueger, Black Creek, Wisconsin

1 tube (8 ounces) refrigerated crescent rolls
2 teaspoons prepared mustard
6 bacon strips, diced
3 cups thinly sliced zucchini (about 1-1/4 pounds)
1 medium onion, chopped
2 eggs, beaten
2 cups (8 ounces) shredded mozzarella cheese
2 tablespoons dried parsley flakes
1/2 teaspoon pepper
1/4 teaspoon garlic powder
1/4 teaspoon dried oregano
1/4 teaspoon dried basil

Separate crescent dough into eight triangles; place in a greased 10-in. pie plate with points toward the center. Press dough onto the bottom and up the sides of plate to form a crust; seal perforations. Spread with mustard.

In a skillet, cook bacon over medium heat until crisp. Remove to paper towels; drain, reserving 2 tablespoons drippings. Saute zucchini and onion in drippings until tender. In a large bowl, combine eggs, cheese, seasonings, bacon and zucchini mixture. Pour into crust.

Bake at 375° for 25-30 minutes or until a knife inserted near the center comes out clean. Cover edges loosely with foil if pastry browns too quickly. **Yield:** 6-8 servings.

Venison Fajitas

(Pictured above)

Use either venison or elk in this recipe, and you'll be pleased with the results! My husband asks for these fajitas frequently. He enjoys big-game hunting and usually comes home with an elk. To finish off the meal, we add some Mexican rice and corn bread.
—Daniell Rissinger, Dauphin, Pennsylvania

1/2 cup orange juice
1/4 cup white vinegar
1 tablespoon seasoned salt
1/4 teaspoon pepper
1/4 teaspoon cayenne pepper
1-1/2 pounds venison *or* elk flank steak, cut into thin strips
1 medium green pepper, julienned
1 medium sweet red pepper, julienned
1 medium onion, halved and sliced
2 tablespoons vegetable oil, *divided*
8 flour tortillas (8 inches)
2 cups (8 ounces) shredded Mexican cheese blend *or* cheddar cheese
Sour cream and salsa

In a large resealable plastic bag, combine the first five ingredients. Add meat. Seal bag and turn to coat; refrigerate for 2 hours.

Drain and discard marinade. In a large skillet, saute peppers and onion in 1 tablespoon oil until crisp-tender; remove and set aside. Heat remaining oil; stir-fry meat for 3-5 minutes or until no longer pink. Return vegetables to pan; heat through. Spoon over tortillas; top with cheese, sour cream and salsa; fold in sides. **Yield:** 4 servings.

Breads, Rolls & Muffins

*When you're in "knead"
of fresh new ideas, let this
basketful of bread, roll and
muffin recipes inspire you!*

FRESH FROM THE OVEN. Clockwise from upper left: Big Batch Bismarks (p. 96), Irish Freckle Bread (p. 94), Peachy Cheese Danish (p. 92) and Garlic Onion Focaccia (p. 94).

Eggnog French Toast

(Pictured below)

There's no last-minute fussing with this breakfast or brunch favorite. Slices of French bread soak up the egg-cream mixture overnight. A little nutmeg and rum extract give the dish its sweet eggnog-like taste.
—*Barbara Nowakowski*
North Tonawanda, New York

   24 slices French bread (3/4 inch thick)
    9 eggs
    3 cups half-and-half cream
  1/3 cup sugar
    2 teaspoons vanilla extract
1-1/2 teaspoons rum extract
  1/2 teaspoon ground nutmeg
Confectioners' sugar

Arrange the bread slices in two well-greased 15-in. x 10-in. x 1-in. baking pans. In a large bowl, beat the eggs, cream, sugar, extracts and nutmeg until blended; pour over bread. Turn bread to coat. Cover and refrigerate overnight.

Remove from the refrigerator 30 minutes before baking. Bake, uncovered, at 500° for 12-15 minutes or until lightly browned, turning bread once. Dust with confectioners' sugar. **Yield:** 12 servings.

Cranberry Orange Bread

I found this recipe in a children's storybook and it has become a family favorite. The festive quick bread is chock-full of flavor from cranberries, raisins, grated orange peel and orange juice.
—*Marsha Ransom*
South Haven, Michigan

✓ Uses less fat, sugar or salt. Includes Nutritional Analysis and Diabetic Exchanges.

1/4 cup butter, softened
  1 cup sugar
  1 egg
  1 teaspoon grated orange peel
  2 cups all-purpose flour
  1 teaspoon baking powder
  1 teaspoon salt
1/2 teaspoon baking soda
3/4 cup orange juice
  1 cup chopped fresh *or* frozen cranberries
  1 cup golden raisins

In a large mixing bowl, cream butter and sugar. Beat in egg and orange peel. Combine the dry ingredients; add to creamed mixture alternately with orange juice. Fold in cranberries and raisins. Pour into a greased 9-in. x 5-in. x 3-in. loaf pan.

Bake at 350° for 60-65 minutes or until a toothpick inserted near the center comes out clean. Cool for 10 minutes before removing from pan to a wire rack to cool completely. **Yield:** 1 loaf (16 slices).

Nutritional Analysis: One slice equals 164 calories, 3 g fat (2 g saturated fat), 21 mg cholesterol, 243 mg sodium, 32 g carbohydrate, 1 g fiber, 2 g protein. **Diabetic Exchange:** 2 starch.

Peachy Cheese Danish

(Pictured on page 91)

I've prepared these rich, sweet rolls for late-night snacks and for breakfast when we have guests, but they're a hit anytime. —*Carolyn Kyzer, Alexander, Arkansas*

  1 tube (8 ounces) refrigerated crescent rolls
  4 ounces cream cheese, softened
1/4 cup sugar
  2 tablespoons lemon juice
  8 teaspoons peach preserves *or* flavor of your choice
GLAZE:
1/4 cup confectioners' sugar
1/2 teaspoon vanilla extract
  1 to 2 teaspoons milk

Separate dough into four rectangles; seal perforations. On a lightly floured surface, roll each into a

7-in. x 3-1/2-in. rectangle. In a small mixing bowl, combine cream cheese, sugar and lemon juice until smooth; spread over rectangles. Roll up from a long side; pinch edges to seal. Holding one end, loosely coil each.

Place on an ungreased baking sheet. Top each coil with 2 teaspoons preserves. Bake at 350° for 15-20 minutes or until golden brown.

For glaze, in a bowl, combine confectioners' sugar, vanilla and enough milk to achieve desired consistency. Drizzle over top. **Yield:** 4 servings.

Cherry Kolaches
(Pictured at right)

I am of Czechoslovakian descent, and baking kolaches is my specialty. These sweet yeast buns with fruit or poppy seed filling are a true Czech tradition. Cherry is my filling of preference. —Evelyn Nesiba
Ravenna, Nebraska

    2 packages (1/4 ounce *each*) active dry
      yeast
  1/2 cup warm water (110° to 115°)
2-1/2 cups warm milk (110° to 115°)
  3/4 cup sugar
  3/4 cup butter, softened
    2 teaspoons salt
    4 eggs
   11 to 11-1/2 cups all-purpose flour
FILLING:
    2 cans (21 ounces *each*) cherry pie filling
  1/2 cup sugar
    2 tablespoons cornstarch
    2 tablespoons cold water
TOPPING:
    1 package (8 ounces) cream cheese,
      softened
  2/3 cup sugar
    1 egg yolk
Melted butter

In a large mixing bowl, dissolve yeast in warm water. Add the milk, sugar, butter, salt, eggs and 5 cups flour; beat until smooth. Stir in enough remaining flour to form a very soft dough. Do not knead. Cover and let rise in a warm place until doubled, about 75 minutes.

Turn onto a well-floured surface. Shape into 1-1/2-in. balls. Place 2 in. apart on greased baking sheets. Cover and let rise until doubled, about 40 minutes. Meanwhile, in a saucepan, combine pie filling and sugar. Combine cornstarch and cold water until smooth; stir into filling. Bring to a boil over medium heat. Cook and stir for 1 minute or until slightly thickened; set aside.

In a mixing bowl, beat cream cheese, sugar and egg yolk until smooth. Using the end of a wooden spoon handle, make an indentation in the center of each dough ball; fill with 2 rounded teaspoons of filling.

Make a small indentation in center of filling; add 1 teaspoon topping. Bake at 400° for 10-15 minutes or until lightly browned. Brush melted butter over rolls. Remove from pans to wire racks to cool. Refrigerate leftovers. **Yield:** about 6 dozen.

Bread-Baking Tidbits

Bread machines have made bread baking easier and faster...and you can bake bread year-round without heating up the kitchen. For the best bread, follow these tips:

Always use fresh ingredients. Check the yeast's expiration date for freshness.

Measure dry and liquid ingredients accurately. Measuring flour is especially critical. First, stir the flour, then spoon into a measuring cup and level off the top.

When using a time-delay feature, never use perishable ingredients, such as eggs, milk, cheese or meat, because they may spoil.

inserted near the center comes out clean. Cool for 10 minutes before removing from pan to a wire rack to cool completely. **Yield:** 12-14 servings.

Irish Freckle Bread

(Pictured on page 91)

This bread has been a favorite at family gatherings, either formal or casual, for years. It's tender and slightly sweet, with a light texture and attractive shape. Sometimes I change the "freckles", using dried cranberries, currants or chocolate chips instead of the raisins.
—*Mary Elizabeth Relyea, Canastota, New York*

    1 **package (1/4 ounce) active dry yeast**
    8 **tablespoons sugar,** *divided*
    1 **cup warm water (110° to 115°)**
1/2 **cup butter, melted**
    2 **eggs**
1/4 **cup warm mashed potatoes (without added milk** *or* **butter)**
1/2 **teaspoon salt**
3-1/4 **to 4 cups all-purpose flour**
    1 **cup raisins**

In a mixing bowl, dissolve yeast and 1 tablespoon sugar in warm water. Add the butter, eggs, potatoes, salt, remaining sugar and 2 cups flour; beat until smooth. Stir in raisins and enough remaining flour to form a soft dough.

Turn onto a floured surface; knead until smooth and elastic, about 6-8 minutes. Place in a greased bowl, turning once to grease top. Cover and let rise in a warm place until doubled, about 1 hour.

Punch dough down. Turn onto a lightly floured surface; divide into eight portions. Shape each into a ball. Place dough balls in a greased 10-in. springform pan. Cover and let rise until doubled, about 30 minutes.

Place on a baking sheet. Bake at 350° for 25-30 minutes or until golden brown. Remove sides of pan. Place on a wire rack to cool. **Yield:** 1 loaf.

Garlic Onion Focaccia

(Pictured on page 90)

I use my bread machine to prepare the dough for this Italian flat bread. It's a great addition to any meal. At times, I make it for myself as a main-dish pizza.
—*Cindy Cameron, Omaha, Nebraska*

Streusel Nut Coffee Cake

(Pictured above)

Wherever I take this delicious coffee cake, everyone loves it. I've been making it for about 30 years. I work as a cook at a county jail and enjoy preparing food for a lot of people.
—*Carol Roth*
Uhrichsville, Ohio

    1 **cup butter, softened**
2-1/2 **cups sugar,** *divided*
    4 **eggs**
    2 **teaspoons vanilla extract**
    2 **teaspoons almond extract**
    4 **cups all-purpose flour**
    1 **teaspoon baking soda**
    2 **cups (16 ounces) sour cream**
1/2 **cup chopped walnuts**
    3 **teaspoons instant chocolate drink mix**
    2 **teaspoons ground cinnamon**

In a large mixing bowl, cream butter and 2 cups sugar. Add eggs, one at a time, beating well after each addition. Beat in extracts. Combine flour and baking soda. Add to the creamed mixture alternately with sour cream. Spoon half into a greased 10-in. tube pan.

In a bowl, combine the walnuts, drink mix, cinnamon and remaining sugar. Sprinkle half over batter. Top with remaining batter and nut mixture. Bake at 350° for 60-70 minutes or until a toothpick

☑ Uses less fat, sugar or salt. Includes Nutritional Analysis and Diabetic Exchanges.

1 cup water (70° to 80°)
2 tablespoons olive *or* canola oil
1 tablespoon sugar
1 teaspoon salt
3 cups bread flour
1-1/2 teaspoons active dry yeast
2 large onions, thinly sliced
2 garlic cloves, minced
3 tablespoons butter
1 cup (4 ounces) shredded mozzarella cheese
2 tablespoons grated Parmesan cheese

In bread machine pan, place the first six ingredients in order suggested by manufacturer. Select dough setting (check dough after 5 minutes of mixing; add 1 to 2 tablespoons of water or flour if needed). When cycle is completed, turn dough onto floured surface. Roll into 12-in. circle. Transfer to a 14-in. pizza pan coated with nonstick cooking spray. Cover; let rise in a warm place until doubled, about 30 minutes.

In a large skillet, cook onions and garlic in butter over medium heat for 15-20 minutes or until onions are golden brown, stirring frequently.

With the end of a wooden spoon handle, make indentations in dough at 1-in. intervals. Top with onion mixture and sprinkle with mozzarella and Parmesan cheeses. Bake at 400° for 15-20 minutes or until golden brown. Remove to a wire rack. Cut into wedges and serve warm. **Yield:** 12 servings.

Nutritional Analysis: One slice (prepared with part-skim mozzarella cheese) equals 186 calories, 7 g fat (3 g saturated fat), 14 mg cholesterol, 270 mg sodium, 25 g carbohydrate, 1 g fiber, 7 g protein. **Diabetic Exchanges:** 1-1/2 starch, 1-1/2 fat.

Cran-Orange Bran Muffins

(Pictured at right)

With their pleasant orange-and-cranberry flavor, these moist muffins make a great lunch-box stuffer or after-school snack. —Kera Bredin
Vancouver, British Columbia

☑ Uses less fat, sugar or salt. Includes Nutritional Analysis and Diabetic Exchanges.

1-1/3 cups fat-free plain yogurt
1-1/4 cups 100% bran cereal
1 cup all-purpose flour
1 cup whole wheat flour
2 teaspoons baking powder
1/2 teaspoon baking soda
1/2 teaspoon salt
1/2 cup orange juice
1/2 cup honey
1/4 cup butter, melted
1 egg, beaten
1 tablespoon grated orange peel
1 cup dried cranberries

In a bowl, combine yogurt and cereal; let stand for 5 minutes. In a large bowl, combine flours, baking powder, baking soda and salt. Stir the orange juice, honey, butter, egg and orange peel into yogurt mixture. Stir into dry ingredients just until moistened. Fold in cranberries.

Coat muffin cups with nonstick cooking spray; fill three-fourths full. Bake at 375° for 18-22 minutes or until a toothpick comes out clean. Cool for 5 minutes before removing from the pans to wire racks. **Yield:** 17 muffins.

Nutritional Analysis: One muffin equals 161 calories, 3 g fat (2 g saturated fat), 20 mg cholesterol, 195 mg sodium, 32 g carbohydrate, 3 g fiber, 4 g protein. **Diabetic Exchanges:** 1 starch, 1 fruit, 1/2 fat.

Spiced Squash Muffins

(Pictured below)

When I created these moist muffins one day with our garden-fresh squash, my son kept asking for more. That batch disappeared quickly...and so did the second one! We especially like the topping of brown sugar and cinnamon, which adds a sweet crunch.
—*TaeRee Glover, Nelson, Nebraska*

    2 cups all-purpose flour
    1/3 cup packed brown sugar
    2 teaspoons baking powder
    1 teaspoon ground cinnamon
    1/2 teaspoon salt
    1/4 teaspoon ground ginger
    1/4 teaspoon ground nutmeg
    2 eggs, beaten
    3/4 cup mashed cooked butternut squash
    3/4 cup light corn syrup
    1/4 cup butter, melted
    1/4 cup vegetable oil
    1 teaspoon vanilla extract
TOPPING:
    1/2 cup packed brown sugar
    1 teaspoon ground cinnamon
    4 teaspoons cold butter

In a large bowl, combine the first seven ingredients. In another bowl, combine the eggs, squash, corn syrup, butter, oil and vanilla; stir into dry ingredients just until moistened. Fill greased or paper-lined muffin cups three-fourths full.

In a small bowl, combine brown sugar and cinnamon; cut in butter until crumbly. Sprinkle over batter. Bake at 400° for 15-20 minutes or until a toothpick comes out clean. Cool for 5 minutes before removing from pan to a wire rack. Serve warm. **Yield:** 1 dozen.

Chili Cheddar Biscuits

Chili powder lends a little kick to these flaky, buttery biscuits. I like to serve them with steaming bowls of chili or hearty beef soup. —*Kim Marie Van Rheenen Mendota, Illinois*

1-1/3 cups all-purpose flour
    3 teaspoons baking powder
    3 teaspoons dried parsley flakes
    1 teaspoon chili powder
    1/4 teaspoon salt
    1/2 cup cold butter
    1/2 cup milk
    1 egg, beaten
1-1/2 cups (6 ounces) shredded sharp cheddar cheese

In a large bowl, combine the first five ingredients. Cut in butter until mixture resembles coarse crumbs. Stir in milk and egg just until moistened. Add cheese; mix well. Turn onto a lightly floured surface. Roll to 1/2-in. thickness; cut with a 2-1/2-in. biscuit cutter. Place 1 in. apart on an ungreased baking sheet. Bake at 450° for 8-10 minutes or until golden brown. Serve warm. **Yield:** 15 biscuits.

Big Batch Bismarks

(Pictured on page 90)

These delicious jelly-filled doughnuts will disappear before your eyes—especially when there are youngsters around. It's a good thing the recipe makes a big batch! —*Araminta Adams Soldiers Grove, Wisconsin*

    2 tablespoons active dry yeast
    4 teaspoons plus 1 cup sugar, *divided*
    1/2 cup warm water (110° to 115°)
    4 cups warm milk (110° to 115°)
    2 eggs
    1 tablespoon vegetable oil
1-1/2 teaspoons salt
    11 to 12 cups all-purpose flour

Additional oil for deep-fat frying
Strawberry jelly
Frosting and sprinkles, optional

In a large mixing bowl, dissolve yeast and 4 teaspoons sugar in warm water. Add the milk, eggs, oil, salt, remaining sugar and 8 cups flour until blended. Stir in enough remaining flour to form a soft dough. Divide dough in half.

Turn onto a floured surface; knead until smooth and elastic, about 6-8 minutes. Place in two greased bowls, turning once to grease tops. Cover and let rise in a warm place until doubled, about 1 hour.

Punch dough down. Turn onto a floured surface; roll out to 1/2-in. thickness. Cut with a floured 3-in. biscuit cutter. Place on greased baking sheets. Cover and let rise until doubled, about 30 minutes.

In an electric skillet or deep-fat fryer, heat oil to 375°. Fry bismarcks a few at a time for 1 minute on each side or until golden brown. Drain on paper towels. Cool for 2-3 minutes. Cut a small slit with a sharp knife in one side of each bismarck; fill with about 1 teaspoon jelly. Decorate with frosting and sprinkles if desired. **Yield:** about 5 dozen.

Creamy Peach Coffee Cake

(Pictured above right)

Here is an awesome coffee cake worth splurging on. You can use any kind of preserves in this recipe, but my personal favorite is peach. —Jody Saulnier
North Woodstock, New Hampshire

2-1/4 cups all-purpose flour
  3/4 cup sugar
  3/4 cup cold butter
  3/4 cup sour cream
  1/2 teaspoon baking powder
  1/2 teaspoon baking soda
    1 egg
    1 teaspoon almond extract
FILLING:
    1 package (8 ounces) cream cheese,
      softened
  1/4 cup sugar
    1 egg
  3/4 cup peach preserves
  1/2 cup sliced almonds

In a mixing bowl, combine the flour and sugar; cut in butter until mixture resembles coarse crumbs. Set aside 1 cup for topping. To the remaining crumb mixture, add the sour cream, baking powder, baking soda, egg and extract; beat until blended. Press onto the bottom and 2 in. up the sides of a greased 9-in. springform pan.

In a small mixing bowl, combine the cream cheese, sugar and egg. Spoon into prepared crust. Top with preserves. Sprinkle with reserved crumb mixture; top with almonds.

Place pan on a baking sheet. Bake at 350° for 45-50 minutes or until filling is set and crust is golden brown. Cool on a wire rack for 15 minutes. Carefully run a knife around edge of pan to loosen; remove sides of pan. Cool for 1-1/2 hours before slicing. Store in refrigerator. **Yield:** 12-14 servings.

Muffin Magic

When making muffins, mix the dry ingredients and liquids just until the dry ingredients are moistened. A lumpy batter will yield tender muffins.

If you don't have enough batter to fill all of the muffin cups, put some water in the empty cups so the muffins will bake evenly.

Muffins are best served warm from the oven. Reheat muffins, loosely wrapped in foil, at 325° for about 10 minutes.

Cookies & Bars

*Bake sales, special
gatherings...any occasion
is a good reason to keep cookies
and bars on hand, even just to
satisfy your own sweet tooth!*

MMM...MORSELS. Clockwise from upper left: Pinwheels and Checkerboards (p. 110), Jeweled Coconut Drops (p. 102), Aniseed Biscotti (p. 109), Valentine Cookie Bouquet (p. 102) and Coconut Pecan Cookies (p. 104).

cookies with prepared glass, dipping glass in sugar again as needed. Bake at 400° for 7-9 minutes or until edges are lightly browned. Cool for 1 minute before removing to wire racks.

In a small bowl, whisk together the confectioners' sugar, almond extract and enough water to achieve glaze consistency. Tint with food coloring if desired; drizzle over cookies. Sprinkle with almonds. **Yield:** about 4-1/2 dozen.

Candy-Topped Bars

These yummy colorful bars have a nutty shortbread crust, a sweet cream cheese filling and a fun crumb and candy topping. They won't last long!
—Renee Anderson, Franklin, Tennessee

      1 cup all-purpose flour
  1/3 cup packed brown sugar
  1/2 cup cold butter
  1/2 cup chopped pecans
      1 package (8 ounces) cream cheese, softened
  1/4 cup sugar
      1 egg
      2 tablespoons milk
      1 tablespoon lemon juice
  1/2 teaspoon vanilla extract
  1/2 to 1 cup M&M miniature baking bits

In a large bowl, combine flour and brown sugar. Cut in butter until mixture resembles coarse crumbs. Stir in pecans. Set aside 1/2 cup for topping. Press remaining crumb mixture into a greased 9-in. square baking pan. Bake at 350° for 12-15 minutes or until edges are lightly browned.

In a small mixing bowl, beat cream cheese and sugar. Add the egg, milk, lemon juice and vanilla; mix well. Pour over warm crust. Sprinkle with reserved crumb mixture. Bake for 25-30 minutes or until set. Immediately sprinkle with baking bits. Cool on a wire rack. Cut into bars. Refrigerate leftovers. **Yield:** 16 servings.

Almond Sugar Cookies

(Pictured above)

It's a tradition in our home to start baking Christmas cookies early in the season and try some new recipes every year. This nutty, glazed melt-in-your-mouth cookie is one of my favorites.
—Lisa Hummell
Phillipsburg, New Jersey

      1 cup butter, softened
  3/4 cup sugar
      1 teaspoon almond extract
      2 cups all-purpose flour
  1/2 teaspoon baking powder
  1/4 teaspoon salt
Additional sugar
GLAZE:
      1 cup confectioners' sugar
  1-1/2 teaspoons almond extract
      2 to 3 teaspoons water
Green food coloring, optional
Sliced almonds, toasted

In a large mixing bowl, cream butter and sugar. Beat in almond extract. Combine flour, baking powder and salt; gradually add to creamed mixture.

Roll into 1-in. balls. Place 2 in. apart on ungreased baking sheets. Coat bottom of a glass with nonstick cooking spray; dip in sugar. Flatten

Oatmeal S'more Cookies

I can't count how many times I have made these cookies—we adore them. I love to bake all kinds of goodies with my two daughters, and my husband loves to sample the treats.
—Carmen Rae
New Haven, Indiana

  1/2 cup butter, softened
  1/2 cup shortening

1 cup packed brown sugar
1/2 cup sugar
2 eggs
1-1/2 teaspoons vanilla extract
2-1/4 cups all-purpose flour
1 teaspoon baking soda
1/4 teaspoon salt
1 cup old-fashioned oats
1 cup (6 ounces) semisweet chocolate chips
1 cup miniature marshmallows

In a large mixing bowl, cream the butter, shortening and sugars. Add eggs, one at a time, beating well after each addition. Beat in vanilla. Combine the flour, baking soda and salt; gradually add to creamed mixture. Stir in the oats, chocolate chips and marshmallows.

Drop by heaping teaspoonfuls 2 in. apart onto greased baking sheets. Bake at 350° for 11-13 minutes or until golden brown. Cool for 1-2 minutes before removing from pans to wire racks to cool completely. **Yield:** about 6 dozen.

Chocolate Mint Dreams

Since chocolate-mint is my favorite flavor combination, I sometimes eat these dainty treats by the dozen. But I manage to save some for guests because they make my cookie trays look so elegant. —*Anne Revers Omaha, Nebraska*

3/4 cup butter, softened
1 cup confectioners' sugar
2 squares (1 ounce *each*) unsweetened chocolate, melted and cooled
1/4 teaspoon peppermint extract
1-1/2 cups all-purpose flour
1 cup miniature semisweet chocolate chips
ICING:
2 tablespoons butter, softened
1 cup confectioners' sugar
1 to 2 tablespoons milk
1/4 teaspoon peppermint extract
1 to 2 drops green food coloring
DRIZZLE:
1/2 cup semisweet chocolate chips
1/2 teaspoon shortening

In a large mixing bowl, cream butter and confectioners' sugar. Beat in chocolate and mint extract. Gradually add flour. Stir in chocolate chips. (Dough will be soft.)

Drop by tablespoonfuls 2 in. apart on ungreased baking sheets. Bake at 375° for 6-8 minutes or until firm. Cool for 2 minutes before removing to wire racks to cool completely.

Meanwhile, combine icing ingredients; spread over cooled cookies. Let set. In a microwave, melt chocolate chips and shortening; stir until smooth. Drizzle over cookies. **Yield:** 4 dozen.

Candy Cane Snowballs

(Pictured below)

I bake dozens of different kinds of Christmas cookies to give to family and friends. I came up with this recipe when I had leftover candy canes I wanted to use up. The snowballs are dipped in a white candy coating, then into crushed peppermint candy.
—*Debby Anderson, Stockbridge, Georgia*

2 cups butter, softened
1 cup confectioners' sugar
1 teaspoon vanilla extract
3-1/2 cups all-purpose flour
1 cup chopped pecans
8 ounces white candy coating
1/3 to 1/2 cup crushed peppermint candy

In a large mixing bowl, cream butter and confectioners' sugar. Stir in vanilla. Gradually add flour. Stir in pecans. Refrigerate for 3-4 hours or until easy to handle.

Roll into 1-in. balls. Place 2 in. apart on ungreased baking sheets. Bake at 350° for 18-20 minutes or until lightly browned. Remove to wire racks to cool. In a microwave-safe bowl, melt candy coating; stir until smooth. Dip the top of each cookie into the candy coating, then into the peppermint candy. **Yield:** 5 dozen.

Jumbo Chocolate Chip Cookies

(Pictured below)

These gourmet cookies are my most asked for recipe. Chock-full of coconut and chocolate chips and dipped in white candy coating, they are truly a chocolate-lover's delight.
—*Jackie Ruckwardt*
Cottage Grove, Oregon

1 cup butter, softened
1 cup sugar
1 cup packed brown sugar
2 eggs
2 teaspoons vanilla extract
2-1/2 cups all-purpose flour
1 teaspoon baking soda
1 teaspoon baking powder
1 teaspoon salt
2-2/3 cups flaked coconut
1 cup (6 ounces) semisweet chocolate chips
1/2 cup milk chocolate chips
5 ounces white candy coating, chopped, optional

In a large mixing bowl, cream butter and sugars. Add eggs, one at a time, beating well after each addition. Beat in vanilla. Combine the flour, baking soda, baking powder and salt; gradually add to the creamed mixture. Stir in the coconut and chips.

Shape 3 tablespoonfuls of dough into a ball; repeat with remaining dough. Place balls 3 in. apart on ungreased baking sheets. Bake at 350° for 12-18 minutes or until lightly browned. Remove to wire racks to cool.

In a microwave-safe bowl, melt candy coating if desired. Dip one end of cooled cookies in candy coating. Allow excess to drip off. Place on waxed paper; let stand until set. **Yield:** about 2 dozen.

Jeweled Coconut Drops

(Pictured on page 98)

Red raspberry preserves add a festive flair to these tender coconut cookies. Perfect for potlucks and cookie exchanges, these shaped cookies never last long when I make them for my husband and two sons.
—*Ellen Marie Byler, Munfordville, Kentucky*

1/3 cup butter, softened
1 package (3 ounces) cream cheese, softened
3/4 cup sugar
1 egg yolk
2 teaspoons orange juice
1 teaspoon almond extract
1-1/4 cups all-purpose flour
1-1/2 teaspoons baking powder
1/4 teaspoon salt
3-3/4 cups flaked coconut, *divided*
1 cup seedless raspberry preserves, warmed

In a large mixing bowl, cream the butter, cream cheese and sugar. Beat in egg yolk, orange juice and almond extract. Combine the flour, baking powder and salt; gradually add to the creamed mixture. Stir in 3 cups of coconut. Refrigerate for 30 minutes or until easy to handle.

Shape dough into 2-in. balls; roll in remaining coconut. Place 2 in. apart on ungreased baking sheets. Using the end of a wooden spoon handle, make an indentation in the center of each ball. Bake at 350° for 8-10 minutes or until lightly browned. Remove to wire racks to cool. Fill each cookie with preserves. **Yield:** about 3-1/2 dozen.

Valentine Cookie Bouquet

(Pictured on page 99)

I always try to do something special with my fair entries. This cookie bouquet was a blue-ribbon winner. It is a great gift for a loved one or makes a nice Valentine's Day centerpiece. —*Marlene Gates*
Sun City, Arizona

1 cup butter, softened
1 cup sugar
1/4 cup milk

1 egg
1 teaspoon vanilla extract
2-3/4 cups all-purpose flour
1/2 cup baking cocoa
3/4 teaspoon baking powder
1/4 teaspoon baking soda
24 long wooden skewers
FROSTING:
1/2 cup butter, softened
2 cups confectioners' sugar
2 to 3 tablespoons maraschino cherry juice

In a large mixing bowl, cream butter and sugar. Beat in the milk, egg and vanilla. Combine the flour, cocoa, baking powder and baking soda; add to creamed mixture and mix well. Cover and refrigerate for 1 hour or until easy to handle.

On a lightly floured surface, roll out half of the dough to 1/8-in. thickness. Cut out with a floured 3-in. heart-shaped cookie cutter. Place 1 in. apart on ungreased baking sheets.

Place skewers on top of each cookie, with one end of each skewer about 1 in. from top of each heart. Gently press into the dough. Place a little extra dough over each skewer; press into cookie to secure. Bake at 350° for 8-10 minutes or until firm. Let stand for 2 minutes before removing to wire racks to cool.

Roll out remaining dough on a lightly floured surface. Cut out with a floured 3-in. heart-shaped cookie cutter. Cut out centers with a 1-in. heart-shaped cutter. Bake at 350° for 8-10 minutes or until firm. Let stand for 2 minutes before removing to wire racks to cool.

In a mixing bowl, combine butter, confectioners' sugar and enough cherry juice to achieve spreading consistency. Gently spread frosting over cookies with skewers; top with cookies with cutout centers. **Yield:** 2 dozen.

Lemon Tea Cookies

(Pictured above right)

These sandwich cookies taste rich and buttery and have a lovely lemon filling. The recipe has been in our family since the 1950s, when my mother got it from a French friend in her club. Mom always made them at Christmas, and now my sister and I do the same.
—Phyllis Dietz, Westland, Michigan

3/4 cup butter, softened
1/2 cup sugar
1 egg yolk
1/2 teaspoon vanilla extract
2 cups all-purpose flour
1/4 cup finely chopped walnuts
FILLING:
3 tablespoons butter, softened
4-1/2 teaspoons lemon juice
3/4 teaspoon grated orange peel
1-1/2 cups confectioners' sugar
2 drops yellow food coloring, optional

In a mixing bowl, cream butter and sugar. Beat in the egg yolk and vanilla. Gradually add flour. Shape into two 14-in. rolls; reshape each roll into a 14-in. x 1-1/8-in. x 1-1/8-in. block. Wrap each in plastic wrap. Refrigerate overnight.

Unwrap and cut into 1/4-in. slices. Place 2 in. apart on ungreased baking sheets. Sprinkle half of the cookies with nuts, gently pressing into dough. Bake at 400° for 8-10 minutes or until golden brown around the edges. Remove to wire racks to cool.

In a small mixing bowl, cream butter, lemon juice and orange peel. Gradually add confectioners' sugar. Tint yellow if desired. Spread about 1 teaspoon on bottom of the plain cookies; place nut-topped cookies over filling. **Yield:** about 4-1/2 dozen.

la chips and remaining shortening at 70% power; stir until smooth. Dip half of the cookies halfway in semisweet mixture; allow excess to drip off. Place on waxed paper to harden.

Dip remaining cookies halfway in vanilla mixture; allow excess to drip off. Place on waxed paper and sprinkle coated area with colored sprinkles. Let harden. **Yield:** 12-1/2 dozen.

Coconut Pecan Cookies

(Pictured on page 98)

These golden brown cookies will remind you of German chocolate cake, with chocolate chips and coconut in the batter and a yummy pecan-coconut frosting. A drizzle of chocolate tops them off in a festive way.
—Diane Selich, Vassar, Michigan

    1 egg, lightly beaten
    1 can (5 ounces) evaporated milk
  2/3 cup sugar
  1/4 cup butter, cubed
1-1/3 cups flaked coconut
  1/2 cup chopped pecans
COOKIE DOUGH:
    1 cup butter, softened
  3/4 cup sugar
  3/4 cup packed brown sugar
    2 eggs
    1 teaspoon vanilla extract
2-1/4 cups all-purpose flour
    1 teaspoon baking soda
    1 teaspoon salt
    4 cups (24 ounces) semisweet chocolate chips, *divided*
  1/4 cup flaked coconut

For frosting, in a saucepan, combine the egg, milk, sugar and butter. Cook and stir over medium-low heat for 10-12 minutes or until slightly thickened and mixture reaches 160°. Stir in coconut and pecans. Set aside.

In a mixing bowl, cream butter and sugars. Add eggs, one at a time, beating well after each addition. Beat in vanilla. Combine the flour, baking soda and salt; gradually add to creamed mixture. Stir in 2 cups chips and coconut.

Drop by tablespoonfuls 2 in. apart onto ungreased baking sheets. Bake at 350° for 8-10 minutes or until lightly browned. Cool for 10 minutes before removing to wire racks to cool completely.

In a microwave, melt the remaining chocolate chips; stir until smooth. Frost cooled cookies, then drizzle with melted chocolate. **Yield:** 6-1/2 dozen.

Dipped Pecan Spritz

(Pictured above)

With their pretty shapes, these treats look lovely at the center of the cookie plates I arrange for all our Christmas gatherings…and they are always the first to disappear. This is my husband's favorite Christmas cookie.
—Sylvia Neudorf, Abbotsford, British Columbia

1-1/2 cups butter, softened
    1 cup sugar
    1 egg
    1 teaspoon vanilla extract
  1/2 teaspoon almond extract
    3 cups all-purpose flour
    1 cup finely ground pecans
    1 teaspoon baking powder
  3/4 cup semisweet chocolate chips
1-1/2 teaspoons shortening, *divided*
  3/4 cup vanilla *or* white chips
Colored sprinkles

In a mixing bowl, cream butter and sugar; beat in egg and extracts. Combine the flour, pecans and baking powder; gradually add to creamed mixture.

Using a cookie press fitted with disk of your choice, press dough 2 in. apart onto ungreased baking sheets. Bake at 375° for 5-7 minutes or until set (do not brown). Remove to wire racks to cool.

In a microwave, melt chocolate chips and 3/4 teaspoon shortening; stir until smooth. Melt vanil-

Meringue Fudge Drops

Almond-flavored meringue, a fudgy filling and a sprinkling of pistachio nuts make these bite-size morsels a special addition to any holiday dessert tray. —Charlotte Elliott, Neenah, Wisconsin

        2 egg whites
    1/4 teaspoon almond extract
    1/8 teaspoon cream of tartar
    1/8 teaspoon salt
    1/2 cup sugar
FUDGE TOPPING:
    1/2 cup semisweet chocolate chips
        3 to 4 tablespoons butter
        2 egg yolks, lightly beaten
        2 tablespoons confectioners' sugar
        2 tablespoons chopped pistachio nuts

In a mixing bowl, beat egg whites, almond extract, cream of tartar and salt on medium speed until soft peaks form. Add sugar, 1 tablespoon at a time, beating on high until stiff peaks form and sugar is dissolved.

Line baking sheets with parchment paper. Drop meringue mixture by teaspoonfuls onto prepared sheets. With a small spoon, make a small indentation in the center of each. Bake at 250° for 30-35 minutes or until dry to the touch.

For topping, combine chocolate chips and butter in a small saucepan. Cook and stir over medium-low heat until chips are melted and mixture is smooth. Combine egg yolks and confectioners' sugar. Reduce heat to low. Gradually whisk into chocolate mixture. Cook and stir for 1 minute longer or until mixture reaches 160°. Cool to room temperature, whisking several times. Spoon into center of meringues. Sprinkle with pistachios. **Yield:** 4-1/2 dozen.

Sour Cream Cranberry Bars

(Pictured below)

A cranberry filling is layered between a buttery crust and a crumb topping in these bars.
—Barbara Nowakowski, Mesa, Arizona

        1 cup butter, softened
        1 cup packed brown sugar
        2 cups quick-cooking oats
1-1/2 cups plus 2 tablespoons all-purpose flour, _divided_
        2 cups dried cranberries
        1 cup (8 ounces) sour cream
    3/4 cup sugar
        1 egg, lightly beaten
        1 tablespoon grated lemon peel
        1 teaspoon vanilla extract

In a mixing bowl, cream butter and brown sugar. Combine oats and 1-1/2 cups flour; add to creamed mixture until blended. Set aside 1-1/2 cups for topping. Press remaining crumb mixture into an ungreased 13-in. x 9-in. x 2-in. baking pan. Bake at 350° for 10-12 minutes or until lightly browned.

Meanwhile, in a large bowl, combine the cranberries, sour cream, sugar, egg, lemon peel, vanilla and remaining flour. Spread evenly over crust. Sprinkle with reserved crumb mixture. Bake for 20-25 minutes or until lightly browned. Cool on a wire rack. Refrigerate leftovers. **Yield:** about 3 dozen.

Peanut Butter Bears

(Pictured below)

My granddaughter enjoys making cookies with me. Since she likes bears, this is one of her favorite recipes.
—Rose Reiser, Greenfield, Indiana

    1 cup butter, softened
    1 cup creamy peanut butter*
    1 cup packed brown sugar
2/3 cup light corn syrup
    2 eggs
    4 cups all-purpose flour
    3 teaspoons baking powder
1/4 teaspoon salt
Decorating gel *or* frosting, colors of your choice

In a large mixing bowl, cream the butter, peanut butter and brown sugar. Beat in the corn syrup and eggs. Combine the flour, baking powder and salt; gradually add to the creamed mixture. Cover and refrigerate for 2 hours or until easy to handle.

On a lightly floured surface, roll out to 1/8-in. thickness. Cut with a floured 4-in. bear-shaped cookie cutter. Place 2 in. apart on ungreased baking sheets. Roll leftover dough into small balls; press gently into each cookie, forming the bear's muzzle, nose and eyes.

Bake at 350° for 10-12 minutes or until set. Remove to wire racks to cool. Using gel or frosting, decorate each bear's face, paws and ears and form bow tie. **Yield:** about 3 dozen.

***Editor's Note:** Reduced-fat or generic brands of peanut butter are not recommended for this recipe.

Pumpkin Drop Cookies

With just a hint of pumpkin flavor and a buttery cinnamon frosting, these cake-like drop cookies are sure to be a hit at a fall gathering.
—Denise Smith
Lusk, Wyoming

1/2 cup butter-flavored shortening
    3 cups sugar
    1 can (15 ounces) solid-pack pumpkin
    2 eggs
1/2 cup milk
    6 cups all-purpose flour
    2 teaspoons baking soda
    2 teaspoons ground cinnamon
    1 teaspoon salt
    1 teaspoon ground allspice
1/2 teaspoon ground cloves
CINNAMON FROSTING:
1/2 cup butter, softened
2-1/2 cups confectioners' sugar
    2 tablespoons milk
    1 teaspoon ground cinnamon
    1 teaspoon vanilla extract

In a large mixing bowl, cream shortening and sugar. Beat in the pumpkin, eggs and milk. Combine the flour, baking soda, cinnamon, salt, allspice and cloves; gradually add to creamed mixture.

Drop by tablespoonfuls 2 in. apart onto greased baking sheets. Bake at 375° for 10-13 minutes or until lightly browned. Remove to wire racks to cool completely.

In a small mixing bowl, combine frosting ingredients; beat until smooth. Frost cookies. Store in the refrigerator. **Yield:** 11 dozen.

Vanilla-Glazed Apple Cookies

This delicious fruit- and nut-packed cookie recipe was my mother's, and it has been one of my favorites for many years.
—Sharon Crider
St. Robert, Missouri

1/2 cup shortening
1-1/3 cups packed brown sugar
1 egg
1/4 cup milk
2 cups all-purpose flour
1 teaspoon baking soda
1 teaspoon ground nutmeg
1 teaspoon ground cinnamon
1/2 teaspoon ground cloves
1 cup chopped walnuts
1 cup finely diced peeled apple
1 cup raisins
VANILLA GLAZE:
1-1/2 cups confectioners' sugar
1 tablespoon butter, melted
1/2 teaspoon vanilla extract
1/8 teaspoon salt
2 to 4 tablespoons milk

In a large mixing bowl, cream shortening and brown sugar. Beat in egg and milk. Combine the flour, baking soda, nutmeg, cinnamon and cloves; gradually add to the creamed mixture. Stir in walnuts, apple and raisins.

Drop by rounded tablespoonfuls 2 in. apart onto ungreased baking sheets. Bake at 400° for 8-10 minutes or until edges begin to brown. Remove to wire racks.

In a small bowl, combine the confectioners' sugar, butter, vanilla, salt and enough milk to achieve drizzling consistency. Drizzle over warm cookies. **Yield:** about 4 dozen.

Butterscotch Eggnog Stars

(Pictured above right)

These yellow star-shaped cookies with a "stained-glass" center are almost too pretty to eat! But they have a rich eggnog flavor that is irresistible.
—*Cheryl Hemmer, Swansea, Illinois*

2/3 cup butter, softened
1 cup sugar
1/4 cup eggnog*
1 egg
2 cups all-purpose flour
3/4 teaspoon baking powder
1/4 teaspoon salt
1/4 teaspoon ground nutmeg
1/2 cup crushed hard butterscotch candies
OPTIONAL ICING:
1-1/2 cups confectioners' sugar
1/4 teaspoon rum extract
2 to 3 tablespoons eggnog
Yellow colored sugar, optional

In a mixing bowl, cream butter and sugar; beat in eggnog and egg. Combine flour, baking powder, salt and nutmeg; gradually add to creamed mixture. Divide into three portions; chill overnight.

On a lightly floured surface, roll out one portion at a time to 1/4-in. thickness. Cut with a floured 3-1/2-in. star cutter. Cut out centers with a 1-1/2-in. star cutter. Line baking sheets with foil; grease foil. Place large star cutouts on prepared baking sheets. Sprinkle 1 teaspoon candy in center of each. Repeat with remaining dough; reroll small cutouts if desired. Bake at 375° for 6-8 minutes or until edges are golden. Cool on baking sheets for 5 minutes. Carefully slide foil and cookies from baking sheets onto wire racks to cool.

For icing, beat confectioners' sugar, rum extract and enough eggnog to achieve drizzling consistency. Drizzle over cooled cookies if desired. Sprinkle with colored sugar if desired. Let stand until hardened. **Yield:** about 3 dozen.

*Editor's Note: This recipe was tested with commercially prepared eggnog.

♪ In a Cookie Dough-lemma?

Avoid the holiday crunch by preparing cookie dough ahead. Tightly wrap the dough in plastic wrap and place in heavy-duty freezer bags. Freeze for up to 1 month. Thaw the dough in the refrigerator for 24-48 hours before baking.

until smooth. Spread over cooled cookies. Store in the refrigerator. **Yield:** about 5 dozen.

Acorn Cookies

Perfect for an autumn party, these cute cookies are my specialty. —Virginia Kroon
Roanoke Rapids, North Carolina

  1 **cup butter, softened**
  1 **cup sugar**
  1 **egg**
 1/2 **cup milk**
  1 **teaspoon almond extract**
  1 **teaspoon vanilla extract**
3-1/2 **cups all-purpose flour**
  1 **teaspoon baking powder**
 1/2 **teaspoon salt**
  2 **cups (12 ounces) semisweet chocolate chips**
  1 **cup ground pecans**

In a large mixing bowl, cream butter and sugar. Beat in the egg, milk and extracts. Combine the flour, baking powder and salt; gradually add to creamed mixture. Cover and refrigerate for 4 hours or until easy to handle.

Divide dough in half. On a lightly floured surface, roll out each portion to 1/4-in. thickness. Cut with 2-1/2-in. acorn cookie cutter. Place 1 in. apart on ungreased baking sheets. Bake at 375° for 8-10 minutes or until edges are firm. Remove to wire racks to cool completely.

In a microwave-safe bowl, melt chocolate chips; stir until smooth. Spread chocolate over the stem and cap of the acorn, leaving about a 1/4-in. border. Sprinkle with pecans. Pipe remaining chocolate in a crisscross pattern over acorn. Let stand until firm. **Yield:** about 3 dozen.

Peanut Butter Cookies

When you bite into one of these yummy cookies, you'll never guess it's low in fat. —Maria Regakis
Somerville, Massachusetts

✓ Uses less fat, sugar or salt. Includes Nutritional Analysis and Diabetic Exchanges.

  3 **tablespoons butter**
  2 **tablespoons reduced-fat peanut butter**
 1/2 **cup packed brown sugar**
 1/4 **cup sugar**
  1 **egg white**

Frosted Rhubarb Cookies

(Pictured above)

Since these cookies freeze well, I make a lot of them during rhubarb season. They are best when you use young tender stalks. —Ann Marie Moch
Kintyre, North Dakota

  1 **cup shortening**
1-1/2 **cups packed brown sugar**
  2 **eggs**
  3 **cups all-purpose flour**
  1 **teaspoon baking soda**
 1/2 **teaspoon salt**
1-1/2 **cups diced fresh rhubarb**
 3/4 **cup flaked coconut**
CREAM CHEESE FROSTING:
  1 **package (3 ounces) cream cheese, softened**
  1 **tablespoon butter, softened**
  3 **teaspoons vanilla extract**
1-1/2 **cups confectioners' sugar**

In a large mixing bowl, cream shortening and brown sugar. Beat in eggs. Combine the flour, baking soda and salt; gradually add to creamed mixture.

Stir in rhubarb and coconut. Drop by tablespoonfuls 2 in. apart onto greased baking sheets. Bake at 350° for 12-15 minutes or until lightly browned. Remove to wire racks to cool.

In a mixing bowl, beat cream cheese, butter and vanilla. Gradually beat in the confectioners' sugar

1 teaspoon vanilla extract
1 cup all-purpose flour
1/4 teaspoon baking soda
1/8 teaspoon salt

In a large mixing bowl, cream the butter, peanut butter and sugars. Add egg white; beat until blended. Beat in vanilla. Combine flour, baking soda and salt; gradually add to the creamed mixture. Shape into an 8-in. roll; wrap in plastic wrap. Freeze for 2 hours or until firm.

Unwrap and cut into slices, about 1/4 in. thick. Place 2 in. apart on baking sheets coated with non-stick cooking spray. Flatten with a fork. Bake at 350° for 6-8 minutes for chewy cookies or 8-10 minutes for crisp cookies. Cool for 1-2 minutes before removing to wire racks; cool completely. **Yield:** 2 dozen.

Nutritional Analysis: One cookie equals 62 calories, 2 g fat (1 g saturated fat), 4 mg cholesterol, 64 mg sodium, 11 g carbohydrate, trace fiber, 1 g protein. **Diabetic Exchanges:** 1/2 starch, 1/2 fat.

Aniseed Biscotti

(Pictured on page 99)

My husband, Joe, is Italian, and his mother was a great cook. She made wonderful biscotti, which are popular Italian dipping cookies. She never used a recipe, but I asked her to write it down for me and I was delighted when she did. —Elizabeth Sparano, Marion, Iowa

1 cup butter, softened
1 cup sugar
3 eggs
2 teaspoons vanilla extract
3-1/2 cups all-purpose flour
1-1/2 teaspoons baking powder
3/4 cup slivered almonds
2 to 3 tablespoons aniseed
1 cup (6 ounces) semisweet chocolate chips
2 tablespoons shortening

In a mixing bowl, cream butter and sugar. Add eggs, one at a time, beating well after each addition. Beat in vanilla. Combine the flour and baking powder; add to creamed mixture. Stir in almonds and aniseed. Divide dough into thirds; shape into three 10-in. x 3-in. rectangles on a greased baking sheet. Bake at 325° for 25-30 minutes or until golden brown. Carefully remove to wire racks; cool completely.

Transfer to a cutting board; cut diagonally with a serrated knife into 3/4-in. slices. Place slices cut side down on ungreased baking sheets. Bake at

325° for 12-16 minutes or until firm and golden brown, turning once. Remove to wire racks to cool.

In a microwave, melt chocolate chips and shortening; stir until smooth. Drizzle over biscotti. Let stand until chocolate is set. Refrigerate in an airtight container with waxed paper between layers. **Yield:** about 3 dozen.

Flying W Pecan Cookies

(Pictured below)

I named these cookies after the ranch I own. They are crisp and sweet with a nice nutty crunch and a hint of almond. —Jim Wyche, Wingate, Texas

1 cup butter, softened
3/4 cup sugar
3/4 cup packed brown sugar
1 egg
2 teaspoons vanilla extract
1 teaspoon almond extract
2-1/2 cups all-purpose flour
1 teaspoon baking powder
1 teaspoon baking soda
1 teaspoon salt
2 cups chopped pecans

In a large mixing bowl, cream butter and sugars. Beat in the egg and extracts. Combine the flour, baking powder, baking soda and salt; gradually add to creamed mixture. Stir in pecans.

Roll into 1-in. balls; place 2 in. apart on ungreased baking sheets. Bake at 350° for 9-11 minutes or until set. Cool for 3 minutes before removing to wire racks. **Yield:** about 6-1/2 dozen.

Peanut Butter Christmas Mice

(Pictured below)

With their red licorice tails, candy noses and peanut ears, these chewy "mice" were always a hit at classroom parties. My children are in their teens now, but they still ask me to make these cookies for the holidays.
—Nancy Rowse, Bella Vista, Arkansas

    1 **cup creamy peanut butter**
1/2 **cup butter, softened**
1/2 **cup sugar**
1/2 **cup packed brown sugar**
    1 **egg**
    1 **teaspoon vanilla extract**
1-1/2 **cups all-purpose flour**
1/2 **teaspoon baking soda**
1/2 **cup peanut halves**
    2 **tablespoons green and red M&M miniature baking bits**
    4 **teaspoons miniature semi-sweet chocolate chips**
Cake decorator holly leaf and berry candies
  60 **to 66 pieces red shoestring licorice (2 inches *each*)**

In a large mixing bowl, cream peanut butter, butter, sugar and brown sugar. Beat in egg and vanilla. Combine the flour and baking soda; gradually add to the creamed mixture. Refrigerate for 1 hour or until easy to handle.

Roll into 1-in. balls. Place 2 in. apart on un-greased baking sheets. Pinch each ball at one end to taper. Insert two peanut halves in center of each ball for ears. Add one M&M baking bit for nose and two chocolate chips for eyes. Arrange holly and berry candies in front of one ear.

Bake at 350° for 8-10 minutes or until set. Gently insert one licorice piece into each warm cookie for tail. Remove to wire racks to cool completely. **Yield:** about 5 dozen.

Pinwheels and Checkerboards

(Pictured on page 98)

My mom used to make these cookies every Christmas, and I still love them. They are so colorful...and you can get two kinds of cookies from one dough! They're perfect for including in gift boxes.
—Jill Heatwole
Pittsville, Maryland

1-1/4 **cups butter, softened**
    1 **cup packed brown sugar**
1/2 **cup sugar**
    2 **eggs**
1/4 **teaspoon vanilla extract**
    4 **cups all-purpose flour**
    1 **teaspoon baking powder**
    1 **teaspoon salt**
1/4 **teaspoon baking soda**
Red and green gel food coloring
    1 **square (1 ounce) unsweetened chocolate, melted and cooled**

In a large mixing bowl, cream butter and sugars. Beat in eggs and vanilla. Combine flour, baking powder, salt and baking soda; gradually add to creamed mixture. Divide dough into fourths. Tint one portion red and one portion green. Stir chocolate into another portion. Wrap chocolate and plain portions in plastic wrap; chill for 1 hour or until easy to handle.

For pinwheel cookies, divide red and green portions in half. Roll out each portion between waxed paper into a 9-in. x 6-in. rectangle. Refrigerate for 30 minutes. Remove waxed paper. Place one green rectangle over a red rectangle. Roll up tightly jelly-roll style, starting with a long side; wrap in plastic wrap. Repeat. Chill for 2 hours or until firm.

For checkerboard cookies, divide plain and chocolate portions in half. Roll out each portion between waxed paper into a 6-in. x 4-in. rectangle. Cut each rectangle lengthwise into eight 1/2-in. strips. Stack the strips in groups of four, alternating plain and chocolate strips and forming eight separate stacks. Form a four-stack block by alternating chocolate-topped and plain-topped stacks. Repeat.

Press together gently. Wrap in plastic. Chill for at least 2 hours.

Unwrap and cut pinwheel and checkerboard doughs into 1/4-in. slices. Place 1 in. apart on ungreased baking sheets. Bake at 375° for 9-11 minutes or until set. Remove to wire racks to cool. **Yield:** 6 dozen pinwheel and 4 dozen checkerboard cookies.

Lemon Meltaways

Both the cookie and the frosting are sparked with lemon in these melt-in-your-mouth goodies.
—*Mary Houchin, Lebanon, Illinois*

3/4 cup butter, softened
1/3 cup confectioners' sugar
1 teaspoon lemon juice
1-1/4 cups all-purpose flour
1/2 cup cornstarch
FROSTING:
1/4 cup butter, softened
3/4 cup confectioners' sugar
1 teaspoon lemon juice
1 teaspoon grated lemon peel
1 to 3 drops yellow food coloring, optional

In a mixing bowl, cream butter and confectioners' sugar until light and fluffy; beat in lemon juice. Combine the flour and cornstarch; gradually add to the creamed mixture. Shape into two 8-in. rolls; wrap each roll in plastic wrap. Refrigerate for 2 hours or until firm.

Unwrap and cut into 1/4-in. slices. Place 2 in. apart on ungreased baking sheets. Bake at 350° for 8-12 minutes or until the cookies are firm to the touch. Remove to wire racks to cool.

For frosting, in a small mixing bowl, combine the butter, confectioners' sugar, lemon juice, lemon peel and food coloring if desired; beat until smooth. Frost cooled cookies. **Yield:** about 5 dozen.

Chocolate Caramel Thumbprints

(Pictured above right)

Covered in chopped nuts and drizzled with chocolate, these cookies are delicious and pretty, too. Everybody looks forward to munching on them during the holidays.
—*Elizabeth Marino*
San Juan Capistrano, California

1/2 cup butter, softened
2/3 cup sugar

1 egg, *separated*
2 tablespoons milk
1 teaspoon vanilla extract
1 cup all-purpose flour
1/3 cup baking cocoa
1/4 teaspoon salt
1 cup finely chopped pecans
FILLING:
12 to 14 caramels*
3 tablespoons heavy whipping cream
1/2 cup semisweet chocolate chips
1 teaspoon shortening

In a mixing bowl, cream butter and sugar. Beat in egg yolk, milk and vanilla. Combine the flour, cocoa and salt; add to the creamed mixture. Refrigerate for 1 hour or until easy to handle.

Roll into 1-in. balls. Beat egg white. Dip balls into egg white and coat with nuts. Place 2 in. apart on greased baking sheets. Using the end of a wooden spoon handle, make a 3/8- to 1/2-in. indentation in the center of each ball. Bake at 350° for 10-12 minutes or until set. Remove to wire racks to cool.

Meanwhile, in a heavy saucepan, melt caramels with cream over low heat; stir until smooth. Using about 1/2 teaspoon caramel mixture, fill each cookie. In a microwave, melt chocolate chips and shortening. Drizzle over cookies. **Yield:** about 2-1/2 dozen.

*Editor's Note: This recipe was tested with Hershey caramels.

Cakes & Pies

Top off a memorable meal with slices of mouth-watering cake or lip-smacking pie to win smiles from your family and friends.

SUBLIME SLICES. Clockwise from upper left: Fudgy Nut Coffee Pie (p. 124), Chocolate Almond Cake (p. 122), Pineapple Rhubarb Pie (p. 118), Cream-Filled Cupcakes (p. 127) and Peanut Chocolate Cake (p. 120).

Lovely Cherry Layer Cake

(Pictured above)

This delicious eye-catching cake is a variation of an Italian dessert recipe that's been in my family for years. It makes any occasion special. —Jennifer Ciccia
Hamburg, New York

  1 package (18-1/4 ounces) white cake mix
CANNOLI FILLING:
  2 packages (8 ounces *each*) cream cheese, softened
  1 carton (15 ounces) ricotta cheese
  1 cup confectioners' sugar
  1 teaspoon vanilla extract
  1/2 teaspoon almond extract
  1 jar (16 ounces) maraschino cherries
  1 cup miniature chocolate chips
FROSTING:
  1 cup shortening
  1 cup butter, softened
  1 package (2 pounds) confectioners' sugar
  3 teaspoons vanilla extract
  4 to 5 tablespoons water
Pink and green gel food coloring

Prepare and bake cake according to package directions, using two greased and floured 9-in. round baking pans. Cool for 10 minutes; remove cakes from pans to wire racks to cool completely.

In a large mixing bowl, beat cream cheese and ricotta until combined. Add confectioners' sugar and extracts. Drain cherries well, reserving 1 teaspoon cherry juice. Chop cherries. Stir chopped cherries, chocolate chips and reserved cherry juice into ricotta mixture. Refrigerate for 1 hour or until spreadable.

In another mixing bowl, cream shortening and butter until light and fluffy. Beat in confectioners' sugar and vanilla. Add enough water to achieve a spreadable consistency. Tint 3/4 cup frosting pink. Tint 1/4 cup frosting green. Set aside 1-1/2 cups white frosting.

To assemble, split each cake in half horizontally. Place one layer on a serving plate; spread with a third of the filling. Repeat layers twice. Top with remaining cake layer. Frost cake top and sides with remaining white frosting.

To decorate, place round tip #5 and reserved white frosting in a pastry bag; pipe vines on cake. Change to shell tip #21; pipe shell border along bottom and top edges. Use petal tip #103 and pink frosting to pipe the rosebuds. Use leaf tip #67 and green frosting to pipe the leaves. Store in the refrigerator. **Yield:** 14 servings.

Editor's Note: The use of a coupler will allow you to change tips easily for different designs.

Viennese Torte

I would always ask my mother to make this cake for my birthday, and now my children request it for theirs.
—Cheryl Miller, Middlebury, Indiana

  1/2 cup butter, softened
1-1/2 cups sugar, *divided*
    4 eggs, *separated*
  1/4 cup milk
    1 teaspoon vanilla extract
  3/4 cup cake flour
    1 teaspoon baking powder
  1/8 teaspoon salt
  1/8 teaspoon cream of tartar
  1/2 cup flaked coconut
  1/2 cup sliced almonds
FILLING:
    1 cup cold milk
    1 package (3.4 ounces) instant vanilla
      pudding mix
    1 cup heavy whipping cream, whipped

Line two 9-in. round baking pans with waxed paper and grease the paper; set aside. In a mixing bowl, cream butter and 1/2 cup sugar. Beat in egg yolks, milk and vanilla. Combine the flour, baking powder and salt; gradually add to creamed mixture. Pour into prepared pans.

In a mixing bowl, beat egg whites and cream of tartar on medium speed until soft peaks form. Gradually add remaining sugar, 1 tablespoon at a time, beating on high until stiff glossy peaks form and sugar is dissolved. Spread evenly over batter, sealing edges to sides of pan.

Bake at 300° for 30 minutes. Sprinkle with coconut and almonds. Bake 20-30 minutes longer or until meringue and coconut are lightly browned. Cool for 10 minutes before removing from pans to wire racks. Cool meringue side up.

In a bowl, whisk milk and pudding mix for 2 minutes. Let stand for 2 minutes or until soft-set. Fold in whipped cream. Place one cake layer on a serving plate, meringue side up; spread with pudding mixture. Top with remaining cake. Chill overnight. Refrigerate leftovers. **Yield:** 12 servings.

Almond Eggnog Pound Cake

(Pictured at right)

I love to bake pies, cookies, cakes and anything else I can think of. This pound cake recipe is one of my family's favorites, especially around the holidays.
—Rick Aynes, Oklahoma City, Oklahoma

  6 tablespoons butter, *divided*
  2/3 cup sliced almonds
    1 package (18-1/4 ounces) yellow cake mix
1-1/2 cups eggnog*
    2 eggs
    1 teaspoon rum extract
  1/8 teaspoon ground nutmeg

Grease a 10-in. fluted tube pan with 2 tablespoons butter. Press almonds onto the bottom and sides of pan; set aside. Melt remaining butter. In a large mixing bowl, beat the cake mix, eggnog, eggs, rum extract, nutmeg and melted butter on low speed for 30 seconds or just until moistened. Beat on medium for 2 minutes or until smooth. Pour into prepared pan.

Bake at 350° for 40-50 minutes or until a toothpick inserted near the center comes out clean. Cool for 15 minutes before removing from pan to a wire rack. **Yield:** 12-14 servings.

***Editor's Note:** This recipe was tested with commercially prepared eggnog.

Keeping Cakes Fresh

Keep cakes fresh by investing in a cake cover or a covered cake carrier. The more airtight a cake storage container, the longer the cake will stay moist and fresh.

If you don't have a cake cover, stick toothpicks at 4-inch intervals in the top and sides of the cake; lightly drape a large sheet of plastic wrap over the picks. Foil can also be used, but it isn't as flexible.

Cranberry Pecan Pie

(Pictured below)

I first made this pie at Thanksgiving to share with my co-workers. It was such a success! Now I freeze cranberries while they are in season so that I can make it year-round.
—*Dawn Liet Hartman*
Mifflinburg, Pennsylvania

    6 tablespoons shortening
1-1/2 teaspoons buttermilk
    2 tablespoons hot water
    1 cup all-purpose flour
  1/2 teaspoon salt
FILLING:
    3 eggs
    1 cup corn syrup
  2/3 cup sugar
  1/4 cup butter, melted
    1 teaspoon vanilla extract
    2 cups fresh cranberries
    1 cup chopped pecans

In a small mixing bowl, cream the shortening and buttermilk until smooth. Gradually add water, beating until light and fluffy. Beat in flour and salt. Wrap pastry in plastic wrap; refrigerate for 4 hours or overnight.

Roll out pastry to fit a 9-in. pie plate. Trim pastry to 1/2 in. beyond edge of plate; flute edges. In a large bowl, combine the eggs, corn syrup, sugar, butter and vanilla until blended. Stir in cranberries and pecans. Pour into crust.

Bake at 425° for 10 minutes. Reduce heat to 350°; bake 35-40 minutes longer or until filling is almost set. Cool completely on a wire rack. Cover and refrigerate overnight before slicing. **Yield:** 6-8 servings.

Coconut Blueberry Cake

My husband and I pick wild blueberries every summer and store plenty of them in the freezer. That way, we can enjoy this delicious coffee cake and other favorite blueberry treats all year long. —*Janis Plourde*
Smooth Rock Falls, Ontario

    2 cups all-purpose flour
    1 cup sugar
    3 teaspoons baking powder
  1/4 teaspoon salt
    2 eggs
    1 cup milk
  1/2 cup vegetable oil
1-1/2 cups fresh *or* frozen blueberries*
    1 cup flaked coconut
LEMON SAUCE:
  1/2 cup sugar
4-1/2 teaspoons cornstarch
    1 teaspoon grated lemon peel
    1 cup water
    1 tablespoon butter
    2 tablespoons lemon juice

In a bowl, combine the flour, sugar, baking powder and salt. Beat the eggs, milk and oil; stir into dry ingredients just until moistened. Fold in blueberries.

Transfer to a greased 13-in. x 9-in. x 2-in. baking dish. Sprinkle with coconut. Bake at 375° for 22-24 minutes or until a toothpick inserted near center of cake comes out clean. Cool on a wire rack.

In a small saucepan, combine sugar, cornstarch and lemon peel. Gradually add water until blended. Bring to a boil; cook and stir for 2 minutes or until thickened. Remove from the heat; stir in butter and lemon juice. Cut cake into squares; drizzle with the lemon sauce. **Yield:** 12-15 servings.

*Editor's Note: If using frozen blueberries, do not thaw before adding to batter.

Chocolate Cream Cake

(Pictured at right)

Whenever I take this moist chocolate cake with butter cream filling to a function, I'm asked for the recipe. My daughter-in-law, Marla, shared it with me.
— Marge Dellert, Shepherd, Michigan

- 1 package (18-1/4 ounces) devil's food cake mix
- 1/2 cup butter, softened
- 1/2 cup shortening
- 1-1/4 cups sugar
- 3/4 cup milk
- 1 teaspoon vanilla extract

GLAZE:
- 1 cup sugar
- 1/3 cup baking cocoa
- 3 tablespoons cornstarch
- 1 cup water
- 3 tablespoons butter, cubed
- 1 teaspoon vanilla extract

Prepare and bake cake according to package directions, using a greased and floured 13-in. x 9-in. x 2-in. baking pan. Cool for 10 minutes before inverting onto a wire rack. Cool completely.

For filling, in a mixing bowl, cream the butter, shortening and sugar until light and fluffy. In a small saucepan, heat milk to 140°; add to the creamed mixture. Beat until sugar is dissolved. Stir in vanilla. Split cake into two horizontal layers; spread filling over bottom cake layer. Top with remaining cake layer.

In a saucepan, combine the sugar, cocoa, cornstarch and water until smooth. Bring to a boil over medium heat, stirring constantly. Cook and stir for 1-2 minutes or until thickened. Remove from the heat; stir in butter and vanilla until glaze is smooth. Cool to lukewarm. Spread over top of cake. Let stand until set. Refrigerate leftovers. **Yield:** 16-20 servings.

Cake Cutting by Design

Puzzled about how to cut a round cake to serve a crowd? Donna Smith of Fairport, New York shares these designs that will help you cut 18 or 24 pieces of fairly equal size. Cut on dotted lines first.

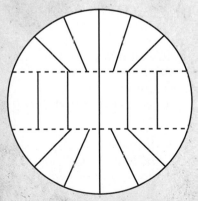

18 cake slices

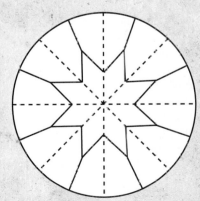

24 cake slices

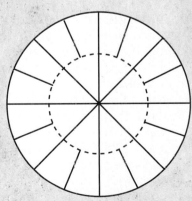

24 cake slices

Toffee-Pecan Nutmeg Cakes

A brown-sugar crust makes this nicely spiced snack cake a little different. It's especially good served with a scoop of ice cream. This is our family's most-asked-for dessert. —Roberta Ashcroft, Twin Falls, Idaho

> 3 cups all-purpose flour
> 2-1/4 cups packed brown sugar
> 1/2 teaspoon salt
> 3/4 cup cold butter
> 1-1/4 cups chopped pecans, toasted, *divided*
> 1 egg
> 1-1/2 cups (12 ounces) sour cream
> 1-1/2 teaspoons baking soda
> 1-1/2 teaspoons ground nutmeg
> 1-1/2 teaspoons vanilla extract

In a bowl, combine flour, brown sugar and salt. Cut in butter until mixture resembles coarse crumbs. Place 3 cups of mixture in a small bowl; add 1/2 cup pecans. Press gently onto the bottom of two greased 9-in. round baking pans.

In a small mixing bowl, combine the egg, sour cream, baking soda, nutmeg and vanilla; mix well. Beat in the remaining flour mixture until well blended. Pour over the crust. Sprinkle with remaining pecans.

Bake at 350° for 33-38 minutes or until a toothpick comes out clean. Cool in pans on wire racks. Cut into wedges. **Yield:** 2 cakes (12 servings each).

Blueberry Raspberry Pie

(Pictured above)

This lovely fruity dessert tastes like summer. This is one of the very best pies I have ever made.
—Earlene Ertelt, Woodburn, Oregon

> Pastry for double-crust pie (9 inches)
> 1 egg white
> 2 tablespoons water, *divided*
> 1 cup plus 1 tablespoon sugar, *divided*
> 1/4 cup cornstarch
> 1 to 2 teaspoons grated lemon peel
> 1 teaspoon vanilla extract
> 1/4 teaspoon ground cinnamon
> 3 cups fresh blueberries
> 1 cup fresh raspberries

Line a 9-in. pie plate with bottom pastry; trim pastry even with edge of plate. Beat the egg white and 1 tablespoon water; brush over crust. Set aside.

In a bowl, combine 1 cup sugar, cornstarch, lemon peel, vanilla and cinnamon. Gently stir in the berries. Pour into the crust.

Roll out the remaining pastry to fit top of pie; place over the filling. Trim, seal and flute edges. Cut slits in top. Brush with remaining water; sprinkle with remaining sugar.

Bake at 400° for 40-50 minutes or until crust is golden brown and filling is bubbly. Cool on a wire rack. Store in the refrigerator. **Yield:** 6-8 servings.

Pineapple Rhubarb Pie

(Pictured on page 113)

Fresh or frozen rhubarb works equally well in this pie. It's delicious and quick and easy to make if you use ready-made crusts.
—Lila McNamara
Dickinson, North Dakota

> 3 cups chopped fresh *or* frozen rhubarb, thawed
> 2 cans (8 ounces *each*) crushed pineapple, drained
> 1-1/2 cups sugar
> 3 tablespoons quick-cooking tapioca
> 1 tablespoon lemon juice
> 1/2 teaspoon grated lemon peel
> 1 package (15 ounces) refrigerated pie pastry

In a bowl, combine the rhubarb, pineapple, sugar, tapioca, lemon juice and lemon peel. Let stand for 15 minutes. Line a 9-in. pie plate with bottom pastry. Add the filling.

Roll out remaining pastry to fit top of pie; cut slits

or make decorative cutouts in pastry. Place over filling; trim, seal and flute edges.

Bake at 350° for 45-50 minutes or until crust is golden brown and filling is bubbly. Cool on a wire rack. Refrigerate leftovers. **Yield:** 6-8 servings.

No-Bake Apple Pie

We always have an abundance of apples in the fall, so I like to make this easy pie. My husband is diabetic, and this recipe fits into his diet...but it's delicious enough for everyone to enjoy. —Shirley Vredenburg
Ossineke, Michigan

☑ Uses less fat, sugar or salt. Includes Nutritional Analysis and Diabetic Exchanges.

   5 medium tart apples, peeled and sliced
1-3/4 cups water, *divided*
   1 package (.3 ounce) sugar-free lemon
     gelatin
  1/2 teaspoon ground cinnamon
  1/4 teaspoon ground nutmeg
   1 package (.8 ounce) sugar-free
     cook-and-serve vanilla pudding mix
  1/2 cup chopped nuts
   1 reduced-fat graham cracker crust
     (9 inches)
  1/2 cup fat-free whipped topping

In a large saucepan, combine the apples, 1-1/2 cups water, gelatin, cinnamon and nutmeg. Bring to a boil. Reduce heat; cover and simmer for 4-6 minutes or until apples are tender.

Combine the pudding mix and remaining water; add to apple mixture. Cook for 1 minute or until thickened. Remove from the heat; stir in nuts. Pour into the crust. Refrigerate for at least 2 hours before serving. Garnish with whipped topping. **Yield:** 8 servings.

Nutritional Analysis: One serving (1 piece with 1 tablespoon whipped topping) equals 218 calories, 9 g fat (2 g saturated fat), 0 cholesterol, 238 mg sodium, 32 g carbohydrate, 2 g fiber, 3 g protein. **Diabetic Exchanges:** 2 fat, 1 starch, 1 fruit.

Cranberry Zucchini Wedges

(Pictured at right)

I try to slip zucchini into as many dishes as possible. These cake wedges have wonderful flavor.
—Redawna Kalynchuk, Waskatenau, Alberta

   1 can (20 ounces) pineapple chunks
   3 cups all-purpose flour
1-3/4 cups sugar
   1 teaspoon baking powder
   1 teaspoon baking soda
   1 teaspoon salt
   3 eggs
   1 cup vegetable oil
   2 teaspoons vanilla extract
   1 cup tightly packed shredded zucchini
   1 cup fresh *or* frozen cranberries, halved
  1/2 cup chopped walnuts
Confectioners' sugar

Drain pineapple, reserving 1/3 cup juice (save remaining juice for another use). Place the pineapple and reserved juice in a blender; cover and process until smooth. Set aside.

In a mixing bowl, combine the flour, sugar, baking powder, baking soda and salt. In a bowl, whisk the eggs, oil, vanilla and pineapple mixture; beat into the dry ingredients until blended. Fold in the zucchini, cranberries and nuts.

Pour into two greased and floured 9-in. round baking pans. Bake at 350° for 30-35 minutes or until a toothpick inserted near the center comes out clean. Cool for 10 minutes before removing from pans to wire racks to cool completely. Just before serving, dust with confectioners' sugar. **Yield:** 2 cakes (8 wedges each).

Butternut Cream Pie

(Pictured below)

I enjoy making up recipes and began experimenting with squash a couple years ago. Last fall, my garden was loaded with squash, so I came up with this creamy pie. It really went over well at Thanksgiving dinner.
—*Sandra Kreuter, Burney, California*

    1 **medium butternut squash (about 2 pounds)**
1/4 **cup hot water**
    1 **package (8 ounces) cream cheese, softened**
1/4 **cup sugar**
    2 **tablespoons caramel ice cream topping**
    1 **teaspoon ground cinnamon**
1/2 **teaspoon salt**
1/2 **teaspoon ground ginger**
1/4 **teaspoon ground cloves**
    1 **package (5.1 ounces) instant vanilla pudding mix**
3/4 **cup plus 2 tablespoons milk**
    1 **pastry shell (9 inches), baked**
Whipped cream and toasted flaked coconut

Cut squash in half; discard seeds. Place squash cut side down in a microwave-safe dish; add hot water. Cover and microwave for 13-15 minutes or until tender. When cool enough to handle, scoop out pulp and mash. Set aside 1-1/2 cups squash (save remaining squash for another use).

In a mixing bowl, beat cream cheese until smooth. Stir in the squash until blended. Add the sugar, caramel topping, cinnamon, salt, ginger and cloves; beat until blended. Add pudding mix and milk; beat on low speed for 2 minutes. Spoon into pastry shell. Refrigerate for at least 3 hours. Garnish with whipped cream and coconut. **Yield:** 6-8 servings.

Peanut Chocolate Cake

(Pictured on page 112)

This is a mouth-watering layer cake with peanut butter frosting. It's luscious!
—*Iola Egle*
Bella Vista, Arkansas

1/2 **cup butter, softened**
2-1/4 **cups packed brown sugar**
    3 **eggs**
    3 **squares (1 ounce *each*) unsweetened chocolate, melted and cooled**
    2 **teaspoons vanilla extract**
2-1/4 **cups all-purpose flour**
    2 **teaspoons baking soda**
1/2 **teaspoon salt**
    1 **cup (8 ounces) sour cream**
    1 **cup water**
FROSTING:
    1 **cup butter**
    1 **cup peanut butter***
    4 **cups confectioners' sugar**
1/4 **cup milk**
    2 **teaspoons vanilla extract**
    1 **cup finely chopped peanuts**

In a large mixing bowl, combine butter and brown sugar; beat in eggs, chocolate and vanilla. Combine the flour, baking soda and salt; add to creamed mixture alternately with the sour cream.

Gradually beat in water. Pour into two greased and floured 9-in. round baking pans. Bake at 350° for 35-40 minutes or until a toothpick inserted near the center comes out clean. Cool for 10 minutes before removing from pans to wire racks to cool completely.

For frosting, cream the butter, peanut butter, confectioners' sugar, milk and vanilla in a mixing bowl until smooth; set aside. Split each cake into two layers. Place a bottom layer on a serving plate; spread with about 1/2 cup frosting.

Repeat layers twice. Top with the remaining cake. Frost top and sides of cake. Gently press peanuts into sides of cake. **Yield:** 12 servings.

*Editor's Note: Reduced-fat or generic brands of peanut butter are not recommended for this recipe.

Applesauce Cake

Cloves, cinnamon and nutmeg lend an appetizing aroma to this yummy cake made with fat-free yogurt. It's great for brunch, dessert or snacking. In fact, it's great anytime! —Tina Dierking, Skowhegan, Maine

✓ Uses less fat, sugar or salt. Includes Nutritional Analysis and Diabetic Exchanges.

1 cup all-purpose flour
3/4 cup sugar
1/4 cup cornstarch
1 teaspoon ground cinnamon
1/2 teaspoon baking powder
1/2 teaspoon baking soda
1/2 teaspoon ground nutmeg
1/2 teaspoon ground cloves
1/2 cup unsweetened applesauce
1/4 cup water
1/4 cup fat-free plain yogurt
2 egg whites, beaten
1/2 teaspoon almond extract
1/4 cup raisins
DRIZZLE:
1/4 cup confectioners' sugar
1 teaspoon water

In a large bowl, combine the first eight ingredients. Combine the applesauce, water, yogurt, egg whites and almond extract. Stir into the dry ingredients just until moistened. Fold in raisins.

Pour into a greased 8-in. square baking dish. Bake at 350° for 25-30 minutes or until a toothpick inserted near the center comes out clean. Cool on a wire rack.

For drizzle, in a bowl, whisk confectioners' sugar and water until smooth. Drizzle over cake. **Yield:** 9 servings.

Nutritional Analysis: One piece equals 167 calories, trace fat (trace saturated fat), trace cholesterol, 101 mg sodium, 39 g carbohydrate, 1 g fiber, 3 g protein. **Diabetic Exchanges:** 1-1/2 fruit, 1 starch.

Bread Pudding Pear Pie

(Pictured above right)

I've been serving this simple but elegant dessert for many years, after a friend shared the recipe. I especially enjoy baking yummy desserts. I guess it's in the genes—my grandfather came over from Norway and started a bakery in a small Minnesota town.
—Kris Bailey, Villard, Minnesota

1 can (29 ounces) pear halves, drained
4 eggs

1/3 cup sugar
1-1/2 cups milk
2 teaspoons vanilla extract
1 teaspoon grated lemon peel
1/4 teaspoon salt
3 English muffins, crumbled
BUTTERSCOTCH SAUCE:
1 cup packed brown sugar
1/2 cup butter, cubed
1 cup heavy whipping cream, *divided*
1 teaspoon vanilla extract
2 tablespoons confectioners' sugar
Fresh pear slices, optional

Coarsely chop pears; place in a greased 9-in. deep-dish pie plate. In a large mixing bowl, beat the eggs and sugar. Add the milk, vanilla, lemon peel and salt; mix well. Stir in crumbled English muffins; pour over pears. Bake, uncovered, at 350° for 30-40 minutes or until a knife inserted near the center comes out clean. Cool slightly on a wire rack.

For butterscotch sauce, combine brown sugar and butter in a saucepan. Cook over medium heat until butter is melted. Gradually add 1/2 cup cream. Bring to a slow boil over medium heat, stirring constantly. Remove from heat. Stir in vanilla; set aside.

In a small mixing bowl, beat the remaining cream until it begins to thicken. Add confectioners' sugar; beat until stiff peaks form. Cut the pie into wedges. Garnish with whipped cream and pear slices if desired. Serve with butterscotch sauce. **Yield:** 8 servings.

20 minutes or until a toothpick inserted near the center comes out clean. Cool for 10 minutes before removing from pans to wire racks to cool completely. Carefully remove waxed paper.

In a large saucepan, combine filling ingredients. Cook and stir over medium heat until mixture comes to a boil. Chill for 2 hours or until the filling reaches spreading consistency, stirring occasionally. Beat with a mixer until fluffy.

Split cakes in half horizontally; spread each layer with filling. For frosting, in a mixing bowl, beat cream, confectioners' sugar and cocoa until stiff peaks form. Spread over top and sides of cake. Garnish with chocolate curls. **Yield:** 12 servings.

Chocolate Almond Cake

(Pictured on page 112)

I love to have family over for the holidays and serve this requested dessert. —*Margaret Malinowski Oak Creek, Wisconsin*

   1/3 cup butter, softened
   1/3 cup shortening
1-3/4 cups sugar
     2 eggs
1-1/2 teaspoons vanilla extract
     2 cups all-purpose flour
   1/2 cup baking cocoa
     1 teaspoon baking powder
   1/2 teaspoon baking soda
   1/2 teaspoon salt
1-1/4 cups buttermilk
FROSTING:
     3 cups heavy whipping cream
     1 cup confectioners' sugar
     3 tablespoons baking cocoa
1-1/2 teaspoons vanilla extract
     6 tablespoons seedless raspberry jam, warmed
1-1/2 to 2 cups sliced almonds, toasted
Fresh raspberries and mint

Line two greased 9-in. round baking pans with waxed paper; set aside. In a mixing bowl, cream the butter, shortening and sugar until fluffy. Add eggs, one at a time, beating well after each addition. Add vanilla. Combine the flour, cocoa, baking powder, baking soda and salt. Add to the creamed mixture alternately with the buttermilk; mix well.

Pour into prepared pans. Bake at 350° for 25-30 minutes or until a toothpick inserted near the center comes out clean. Cool for 10 minutes before removing from pans to wire racks to cool completely.

For frosting, beat cream in a mixing bowl until

Chocolate Chiffon Torte

(Pictured above)

This is an old recipe that I made often when we were on the farm and I had lots of cream to use up. —*Iola Egle, Bella Vista, Arkansas*

     2 cups cake flour
1-1/2 cups sugar
     3 teaspoons baking powder
   1/2 teaspoon salt
   1/2 cup water
   1/2 cup vegetable oil
     6 eggs, *separated*
     2 squares (1 ounce *each*) semisweet chocolate, melted and cooled
   1/2 teaspoon cream of tartar
FILLING:
1-1/2 cups heavy whipping cream
1-1/4 cups semisweet chocolate chips
   1/4 cup butter, cubed
FROSTING:
     1 cup heavy whipping cream
   1/2 cup confectioners' sugar
     1 tablespoon baking cocoa
Chocolate curls

Line three 9-in. round baking pans with waxed paper. Grease the paper; set aside. In a large bowl, sift flour, sugar, baking powder and salt. Make a well in center; add water, oil, egg yolks and melted chocolate. Beat until smooth. In a small mixing bowl, beat egg whites and cream of tartar on high speed until stiff peaks form. Fold into the batter.

Pour into prepared pans. Bake at 350° for 15-

soft peaks form. Add sugar and cocoa, beating until stiff peaks form. Beat in vanilla. Spread about 2 tablespoons jam over each cake layer. Place one cake on a serving plate. Spread with 1-1/2 cups whipped cream mixture; drizzle with remaining jam. Top with remaining cake layer; spread the remaining whipped cream mixture over top and sides of cake. Press almonds onto sides and top of cake. Garnish with raspberries and mint. Store in the refrigerator. **Yield:** 12-14 servings.

Peach Parfait Pie

This recipe came from an old "Cooking with the Skins" cookbook. The recipes in it were sent in by players' and coaches' wives from our beloved Washington Redskins pro football team. I make this pie when our local peaches are in season. —Betsy Furin
Rockville, Maryland

3-1/2 cups sliced peeled fresh or frozen peaches, thawed
1/2 cup sugar
1 package (3 ounces) lemon gelatin
1/2 cup cold water
2 cups vanilla ice cream, softened
1 deep-dish pastry shell (9 inches), baked
1 cup heavy whipping cream, whipped

Place peaches in a bowl; sprinkle with sugar. Let stand for 15 minutes. Drain, reserving juice in a 1-cup measuring cup. Set peaches aside.

Add enough water to the juice to measure 1 cup; pour into a small saucepan. Bring to a boil. Remove from the heat.

Stir in gelatin until dissolved; add cold water. Gradually add the ice cream, 1/2 cup at a time, stirring after each addition until blended. Cover and refrigerate for 60-75 minutes or until slightly thickened, stirring occasionally (mixture may separate).

Drain peaches again; discard juice. Fold gelatin mixture into peaches. Transfer to pastry shell. Cover and refrigerate for 3 hours or until firm. Just before serving, garnish with whipped cream. **Yield:** 6-8 servings.

Light Lemon Pie

(Pictured at right)

A drizzle of spreadable fruit lends a decorative and tasty touch to this appealing dessert. One slice of the creamy and refreshing pie just won't be enough! It's great for diabetics, but even the rest of my family enjoys it. —Ruby Fleeman, Santa Ana, Texas

☑ Uses less fat, sugar or salt. Includes Nutritional Analysis and Diabetic Exchanges.

1 package (.3 ounce) sugar-free lemon gelatin
1/2 cup boiling water
3/4 cup cold water
Sugar substitute* equivalent to 3 tablespoons plus 1 teaspoon sugar
1 cup (8 ounces) reduced-fat cottage cheese
1 carton (8 ounces) frozen reduced-fat whipped topping, thawed
1 reduced-fat graham cracker crust (9 inches)
1/2 cup 100% strawberry spreadable fruit
8 large strawberries, halved

In a large bowl, dissolve gelatin in boiling water. Stir in cold water and sugar substitute; mix well. Refrigerate until partially set.

In a fine strainer, drain the cottage cheese. Place cottage cheese in a food processor or blender; cover and process until smooth. Transfer to a bowl; stir in gelatin mixture. Fold in whipped topping. Pour into crust. Refrigerate until set. Just before serving, cut into slices; garnish each with 1 tablespoon spreadable fruit and two strawberry halves. **Yield:** 8 servings.

Nutritional Analysis: One serving equals 216 calories, 7 g fat (5 g saturated fat), 4 mg cholesterol, 213 mg sodium, 31 g carbohydrate, trace fiber, 5 g protein. **Diabetic Exchanges:** 1-1/2 fat, 1 starch, 1 fruit.

*Editor's Note: This recipe was tested with Splenda No Calorie Sweetener. Look for it in the baking aisle of your grocery store.

Buttermilk Lemon Pie

(Pictured below and on back cover)

I'm proud to serve this creamy lemon pie with a light meringue topping. You'll find it's hard to resist a slice...and it cuts beautifully, too. —Helen Ordemann
Washington, Illinois

    1 cup sugar
1/2 cup all-purpose flour
    2 cups buttermilk
1/2 cup water
    3 egg yolks, lightly beaten
    6 tablespoons lemon juice
    2 tablespoons butter
MERINGUE:
    3 egg whites
    6 tablespoons sugar
    1 pastry shell (9 inches), baked

In a large saucepan, combine sugar and flour. Gradually stir in buttermilk and water until smooth. Cook and stir over medium heat until thickened and bubbly, about 4 minutes. Reduce heat; cook and stir 2 minutes longer. Remove from the heat.

Stir a small amount of hot filling into egg yolks; return all to the pan, stirring constantly. Bring to a gentle boil; cook and stir 2 minutes longer. Remove from the heat; stir in lemon juice and butter until butter is melted. Keep warm.

In a small mixing bowl, beat the egg whites on medium speed until soft peaks form. Gradually beat in sugar, 1 tablespoon at a time, on high just until stiff peaks form and sugar is dissolved.

Pour the hot filling into pastry shell. Spread meringue evenly over hot filling, sealing edges to crust. Bake at 350° for 15 minutes or until the meringue is golden brown. Cool on a wire rack for 1 hour; refrigerate for at least 5 hours before serving. Refrigerate leftovers. **Yield:** 6-8 servings.

Fudgy Nut Coffee Pie

(Pictured on page 112)

My mother served this pretty pie for my birthday dinner one year, and now it's one of my favorites. Fudge sauce, chopped pecans and coffee ice cream top the chocolate crumb crust. Sometimes I garnish the pie with dollops of whipped cream. —Amy Theis
Billings, Montana

1-1/2 cups confectioners' sugar
    1/2 cup heavy whipping cream
      6 tablespoons butter, cubed
      3 squares (1 ounce *each*) unsweetened
         chocolate
      3 tablespoons light corn syrup
Dash salt
      1 teaspoon vanilla extract
      1 chocolate crumb crust (9 inches)
    3/4 cup coarsely chopped pecans, *divided*
      3 pints coffee ice cream, softened

In a small saucepan, combine the confectioners' sugar, cream, butter, chocolate, corn syrup and salt. Cook and stir over low heat until smooth. Remove from the heat. Stir in the vanilla. Cool completely.

Spread 1/2 cup fudge sauce over the crust. Sprinkle with 1/4 cup pecans. Freeze for 20 minutes or until set. Spread with half of the ice cream. Freeze for 1 hour or until firm. Repeat layers. Cover and freeze for 4 hours or until firm.

Just before serving, drizzle remaining fudge sauce over pie and sprinkle with remaining pecans. **Yield:** 8 servings.

Strawberry Pound Cake

This beautiful bundt cake is my husband's favorite. I add chopped pecans and strawberries to the batter and brush the cake right out of the oven with a sweet strawberry glaze. Any extra glaze can be served on the side. —Sue Wesson
Springhill, Louisiana

 1 package (16 ounces) frozen sweetened
   sliced strawberries, thawed
 1 cup butter-flavored shortening
 2 cups sugar
 4 eggs
 3 cups all-purpose flour
 1 teaspoon baking soda
1/2 teaspoon baking powder
1/2 teaspoon salt
2/3 cup buttermilk
1/2 cup chopped pecans
 1 teaspoon vanilla extract
1/4 teaspoon almond *or* strawberry extract
STRAWBERRY SAUCE:
 1 cup sugar
1/2 cup sliced fresh strawberries
1/2 teaspoon vanilla extract
1/4 teaspoon almond *or* strawberry extract

Drain strawberries, reserving 1/2 cup juice. Chop the strawberries; set juice and berries aside. In a mixing bowl, cream shortening and sugar. Add eggs, one at a time, beating well after each addition. Combine the dry ingredients; add to creamed mixture alternately with buttermilk. Stir in the pecans, chopped strawberries and extracts.

Pour into a greased and floured 10-in. fluted tube pan. Bake at 325° for 1-1/4 hours or until a toothpick inserted near the center comes out clean. Cool for 10 minutes; remove from pan to a wire rack.

In a small saucepan, combine the sugar and reserved strawberry juice. Add the sliced strawberries. Bring to a boil; cook and stir for 1 minute. Remove from the heat; stir in extracts. Brush some of the sauce over the warm cake. Serve cake with remaining sauce. **Yield:** 12-16 servings.

Moist Chocolate Cake

(Pictured above right)

I work evenings in the operating room at our local hospital. Since getting away for meals can be difficult, we occasionally plan potlucks. I'm frequently asked to bring my "chocolate cake with the special icing". —Irene Peery, Charlottesville, Virginia

1-1/2 cups cake flour
 1 cup sugar
 1 teaspoon baking soda
1/2 teaspoon salt
 2 squares (1 ounce *each*) unsweetened
   chocolate
 2 tablespoons butter
 1 cup buttermilk

1/2 cup vegetable oil
 1 egg
 1 teaspoon vanilla extract
FROSTING:
1/2 cup sugar
4-1/2 teaspoons cornstarch
1/8 teaspoon salt
 1 square (1 ounce) unsweetened chocolate,
   coarsely chopped
1/2 cup hot coffee *or* water
4-1/2 teaspoons butter
1/2 teaspoon vanilla extract

In a bowl, combine the flour, sugar, baking soda and salt; set aside. In a microwave-safe bowl, combine the chocolate and butter. Cover and microwave on high for 1 minute. Stir; cook 30 seconds longer or until melted.

In a small mixing bowl, combine the buttermilk, oil and egg. Add to dry ingredients; beat just until combined. Add the chocolate mixture and vanilla. Pour into a greased 8-in. square baking dish. Bake at 350° for 30-35 minutes or until a toothpick inserted near the center comes out clean. Cool completely on a wire rack.

For frosting, in a saucepan, combine the sugar, cornstarch, salt and chocolate; stir in the coffee until blended. Bring to a boil over medium heat; cook and stir until mixture is thickened. Remove from the heat; stir in the butter and vanilla. Spread warm frosting over cake. **Yield:** 9 servings.

Nutritional Analysis: One piece (calculated without whipped cream) equals 213 calories, 5 g fat (3 g saturated fat), 14 mg cholesterol, 307 mg sodium, 40 g carbohydrate, 2 g fiber, 3 g protein. **Diabetic Exchange:** 2-1/2 starch.

Fresh Pear Pie

When I serve this to friends, they often tell me they've never heard of pear pie. It's the best when fresh pears are in season. —Marcia Severson, Hallock, Minnesota

   3/4 cup sugar
     3 tablespoons quick-cooking tapioca
     2 tablespoons lemon juice
     2 tablespoons butter, cubed
     1 teaspoon grated lemon peel
   1/2 teaspoon ground nutmeg
   1/2 teaspoon ground cinnamon
   1/4 teaspoon salt
     6 large ripe pears, peeled and sliced
     1 package (15 ounces) refrigerated pie pastry
     1 tablespoon milk

In a large bowl, combine the first eight ingredients. Add pears; toss to coat. Line a 9-in. pie plate with bottom pastry; add pear filling.

Roll remaining pastry into a 12-in. circle. With a fluted pastry wheel, pizza cutter or sharp knife, cut into eight 1/2-in. strips. Twist strips and position over filling parallel to each other, about 1/2 in. to 3/4 in. apart. Trim strips evenly with pastry edge. Seal and flute edges. Brush pastry strips with milk.

Cover pie loosely with foil to prevent over-browning. Bake at 400° for 50-60 minutes or until crust is golden brown and filling is bubbly. Cool on a wire rack. **Yield:** 6-8 servings.

Apple Snack Cake

This good-for-you dessert is packed with ingredients that remind me of fall! Chopped apples and walnuts add fun flavor to this moist snack cake that is sprinkled with cinnamon-sugar topping. —Lisa Varner
Greenville, South Carolina

✓ Uses less fat, sugar or salt. Includes Nutritional Analysis and Diabetic Exchanges.

     1 cup all-purpose flour
     1 cup plus 2 teaspoons sugar, *divided*
     2 teaspoons baking powder
     4 egg whites, beaten
     1 teaspoon vanilla extract

Pumpkin Spice Cake

(Pictured above)

Traditional gingerbread is my father's favorite. But he says that this gingerbread-like cake featuring pumpkin really hits the spot, too. It's wonderful served warm or cold. —Traci Krick, Bear, Delaware

✓ Uses less fat, sugar or salt. Includes Nutritional Analysis and Diabetic Exchanges.

   1/4 cup butter, softened
   1/2 cup packed brown sugar
     2 tablespoons sugar
 1-1/2 teaspoons grated orange peel
     3 egg whites
     1 cup canned pumpkin
   1/4 cup light corn syrup
     2 tablespoons molasses
 1-1/4 cups cake flour
     1 teaspoon baking soda
   1/2 teaspoon baking powder
   1/2 teaspoon ground cinnamon
   1/2 teaspoon ground ginger
   1/4 teaspoon salt
Whipped cream, optional

In a large mixing bowl, cream the butter, sugars and orange peel. Add egg whites, one at a time, beating well after each addition. Beat in the pumpkin, corn syrup and molasses until blended. Combine the flour, baking soda, baking powder, cinnamon, ginger and salt; add to pumpkin mixture, beating on low speed just until moistened.

Pour into a greased 8-in. baking dish. Bake at 350° for 30-35 minutes or until a toothpick inserted near the center comes out clean. Cool on a wire rack for 15 minutes. Serve warm with whipped cream if desired. **Yield:** 9 servings.

2 cups finely chopped peeled tart apples
1/4 cup chopped walnuts *or* pecans, toasted
1/2 teaspoon ground cinnamon

In a large mixing bowl, combine the flour, 1 cup sugar and baking powder. Add egg whites and vanilla; mix well. Fold in apples and nuts. Spread into a 9-in. square baking pan coated with nonstick cooking spray. Combine cinnamon and remaining sugar; sprinkle over top.

Bake at 350° for 30-35 minutes or until a toothpick inserted near the center comes out clean. Cool on a wire rack. **Yield:** 9 servings.

Nutritional Analysis: One piece equals 185 calories, 2 g fat (trace saturated fat), 0 cholesterol, 128 mg sodium, 39 g carbohydrate, 1 g fiber, 4 g protein. **Diabetic Exchanges:** 2 starch, 1/2 fruit.

Cream-Filled Cupcakes

(Pictured on page 113)

These moist chocolate cupcakes have a fun filling and shiny chocolate frosting that make them different from any other. They always disappear in a flash!
—*Kathy Kittell, Lenexa, Kansas*

1 package (18-1/4 ounces) devil's food cake mix
2 teaspoons hot water
1/4 teaspoon salt
1 jar (7 ounces) marshmallow creme
1/2 cup shortening
1/3 cup confectioners' sugar
1/2 teaspoon vanilla extract
GANACHE FROSTING:
1 cup (6 ounces) semisweet chocolate chips
3/4 cup heavy whipping cream

Prepare and bake cupcakes according to package directions, using paper-lined muffin cups. Cool for 5 minutes before removing to wire racks to cool completely.

For filling, in a small bowl, combine water and salt until salt is dissolved. Cool. In a small mixing bowl, beat the marshmallow creme, shortening, confectioners' sugar and vanilla on high until light and fluffy; add the salt mixture.

Insert a small round pastry tip into a pastry or plastic bag; fill with cream filling. Insert the tip halfway into the center of each cupcake and fill with a small amount.

In a heavy saucepan, melt the chocolate chips with cream. Cool. Dip cupcake tops into frosting; chill for 20 minutes or until set. Store in the refrigerator. **Yield:** 2 dozen.

Banana Pound Cake

(Pictured below)

I developed this recipe from a basic pound cake recipe given to me by my great-aunt. It makes a moist, rich cake that pops out of the pan perfectly every time.
—*Nancy Zimmerman*
Cape May Court House, New Jersey

3 teaspoons plus 3 cups sugar, *divided*
1 cup butter, softened
6 eggs
1 cup mashed ripe bananas (about 2 medium)
1-1/2 teaspoons vanilla extract
1/2 teaspoon lemon extract
3 cups all-purpose flour
1/4 teaspoon baking soda
1 cup (8 ounces) sour cream
GLAZE:
1-1/2 cups confectioners' sugar
1/2 teaspoon vanilla extract
3 to 4 teaspoons milk

Grease a 10-in. fluted tube pan. Sprinkle with 3 teaspoons sugar; set aside. In a large mixing bowl, cream butter and remaining sugar until light and fluffy, about 5 minutes. Add eggs, one at a time, beating well after each addition. Stir in bananas and extracts. Combine flour and baking soda; add to the creamed mixture alternately with sour cream, beating just until combined.

Pour into prepared pan (pan will be full). Bake at 325° for 75-85 minutes or until a toothpick inserted near the center comes out clean. Cool for 10 minutes before removing from pan to a wire rack to cool completely.

In a small bowl, whisk glaze ingredients until smooth; drizzle over cake. Store in the refrigerator. May be frozen for up to 1 month. **Yield:** 12-15 servings.

Just Desserts

There's nothing trifling about the tempting treats you'll find here!
Stir up something sweet to add delight to your dinner table.

🍮🍮🍮

DESERVED DESSERTS. Clockwise from upper left: Rhubarb Icebox Dessert (p. 134), Apple Streusel Ice Cream (p. 130), Peppermint Chip Cheesecake (p. 141), Chocolate Pecan Ice Cream Torte (p. 147) and Crunchy Chocolate Eggs (p. 137).

Rocky Road Ice Cream

(Pictured below)

My daughters always want to put this ice cream in cones just like the ice cream shops do. We especially like the marshmallows, chocolate chips and chopped pecans. Sometimes we even add extra chips on top.
—*Dale Langford, Atwater, California*

3 cups milk
3 cups half-and-half cream
9 squares (1 ounce *each*) semisweet chocolate
2-3/4 cups sugar
3/4 teaspoon salt
6 cups heavy whipping cream
3 cups miniature marshmallows
2-1/4 cups miniature semisweet chocolate chips
1-1/2 cups chopped pecans
6 teaspoons vanilla extract

In a large saucepan, combine milk and half-and-half; heat to 175°. Add chocolate, sugar and salt; stir until chocolate is melted and sugar is dissolved.

Remove from the heat. Cool quickly by placing pan in a bowl of ice water; stir for 2 minutes. Cool completely. Transfer to a large bowl; stir in the remaining ingredients. Cover and refrigerate for 30 minutes.

Fill cylinder of ice cream freezer two-thirds full; freeze according to the manufacturer's directions. Refrigerate remaining mixture until ready to freeze, stirring before freezing each batch.

Allow to ripen in ice cream freezer or firm up in the refrigerator freezer for 2-4 hours before serving. **Yield:** about 4-1/2 quarts.

Ladyfinger Lemon Torte

(Pictured on back cover)

Golden ladyfingers frame the luscious custard filling of this lovely frozen dessert. Everyone will enjoy the yummy combination of sweetness and lemony zest.
—*Mrs. J.H. Carroll, Ottawa, Ontario*

5 egg yolks, beaten
1-1/2 cups sugar, *divided*
3/4 cup lemon juice
2 egg whites
1 tablespoon grated lemon peel
2 cups heavy whipping cream
2 packages (3 ounces *each*) ladyfingers, split
Lemon peel and fresh mint leaves

In a heavy saucepan, combine egg yolks, 1-1/4 cups sugar, lemon juice and egg whites. Bring to a boil over medium heat; cook and stir for 8-10 minutes or until mixture is thick enough to coat a metal spoon. Remove from heat. Cool quickly by placing pan in a bowl of ice water; stir for 2 minutes. Stir in lemon peel. Transfer to a bowl; press plastic wrap onto surface of custard. Chill for 2-3 hours or until partially set.

In a mixing bowl, beat cream on medium speed until soft peaks form. Gradually beat in remaining sugar, 1 tablespoon at a time, on high until stiff peaks form. Gradually fold whipped cream into the cooled lemon mixture. Arrange 24 ladyfingers around edge of an ungreased 9-in. springform pan. Arrange 16 ladyfingers on bottom of pan. Spread with half of lemon mixture.

Arrange remaining ladyfingers over lemon mixture; top with remaining lemon mixture. Cover and freeze overnight. Remove from the freezer 5 minutes before cutting. Remove sides of the pan. Garnish with the lemon peel and mint. **Yield:** 12 servings.

Apple Streusel Ice Cream

(Pictured on page 128)

If you're a fan of apple pie, you'll be sweet on this delicious ice cream. The concoction is flavored with sauteed apple, cinnamon, caramel topping and a homemade streusel.
—*Karen Delgado,
Shawnee, Kansas*

1/3 cup packed brown sugar
1/4 cup all-purpose flour
1/2 teaspoon ground cinnamon
3 tablespoons plus 4-1/2 teaspoons cold butter, *divided*
1/2 cup chopped pecans
1 cup chopped peeled Golden Delicious apple
2 teaspoons sugar
1/4 teaspoon ground cinnamon
ICE CREAM:
1-1/4 cups milk
3/4 cup sugar
1-3/4 cups heavy whipping cream
1-1/2 teaspoons vanilla extract
1 jar (12 ounces) caramel ice cream topping

For streusel, combine the brown sugar, flour and cinnamon in a bowl; cut in 3 tablespoons butter until mixture resembles coarse crumbs. Stir in pecans. Press into a 9-in. pie plate. Bake at 350° for 10-12 minutes or until the edges are browned. Cool slightly; break into small pieces. Cool completely.

In a skillet, melt remaining butter. Stir in the apple, sugar and cinnamon. Cook for 8-10 minutes or until apple is tender; cool.

In a large saucepan, heat the milk to 175°; stir in sugar until dissolved. Cool. In a large bowl, combine the milk mixture, cream and vanilla. Refrigerate for several hours or overnight.

Fill cylinder of ice cream freezer two-thirds full; freeze according to the manufacturer's directions. Refrigerate remaining mixture until ready to freeze. Add apple mixture to each batch of ice cream; freeze 5 minutes longer.

Spoon a third of the ice cream into a freezer container. Top with a third of the streusel mixture. Drizzle with a third of the caramel topping. Repeat layers once. Top with remaining ice cream. With a spatula, cut through ice cream in several places to gently swirl layers. Cover; freeze overnight. Garnish with the remaining streusel and caramel topping. **Yield:** 1-1/2 quarts.

Caramel Flan

(Pictured above right)

Sometimes I top this popular Mexican dessert with whipped cream and toasted slivered almonds. It's popular whenever I serve it. —Anelle Mack, Midland, Texas

1/2 cup sugar
1-2/3 cups sweetened condensed milk
1 cup milk
3 eggs
3 egg yolks
1 teaspoon vanilla extract

In a large skillet over medium heat, cook sugar until melted, about 12 minutes. Do not stir. When sugar is melted, reduce heat to low and continue to cook, stirring occasionally, until syrup is golden brown, about 2 minutes. Quickly pour into an ungreased 2-qt. round souffle dish, tilting to coat the bottom; let stand for 10 minutes.

In a blender, combine the condensed milk, milk, eggs, yolks and vanilla. Cover and process for 15 seconds or until well blended. Pour over syrup.

Place the souffle dish in a larger baking pan. Add 1 in. of boiling water to baking pan. Bake at 350° for 55-60 minutes or until center is just set (mixture will jiggle). Remove souffle dish from larger pan. Place on a wire rack; cool for 1 hour. Cover and refrigerate overnight.

To unmold, run a knife around edge and invert flan onto a large rimmed serving platter. Cut into wedges or spoon onto dessert plates; spoon sauce over each serving. **Yield:** 8-10 servings.

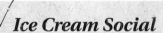

Ice Cream Social

For a fun dessert sure to impress guests, roll individually frozen balls of ice cream in fun toppings like chopped nuts, toasted coconut or chopped candy bars. Then freeze the balls until firm and arrange in a pretty serving bowl. Guests can choose whichever combination appeals to them.

DELICIOUSLY MERRY. Chocolate Mousse Cheesecake, Puff Pastry Pillows and Pecan Cherry Bark (shown above, top to bottom) are standout desserts for your holiday gatherings.

Chocolate Mousse Cheesecake

(Pictured above)

This is one of my favorite company desserts—it looks magnificent! Another easy way to decorate it is to cover the cheesecake with whipped cream, then add chocolate shavings and maraschino cherries to the top.
—Karen Grant, Tulare, California

1-1/2 cups chocolate wafer crumbs (about 24 crackers)
  1/3 cup finely chopped pecans
    2 tablespoons sugar
  1/3 cup butter, melted
FILLING:

    2 packages (8 ounces *each*) cream cheese, softened
  1/2 cup sugar
    1 tablespoon lemon juice
    1 teaspoon grated lemon peel
    1 teaspoon vanilla extract
    2 eggs, *separated*
TOPPING:
    1 cup (6 ounces) semisweet chocolate chips
    5 tablespoons butter, cubed
    4 egg yolks
  1/4 cup confectioners' sugar
    2 tablespoons strong brewed coffee
    1 teaspoon vanilla extract

1/2 cup heavy whipping cream, whipped
Chocolate dessert decorations and additional
   whipped cream

In a small bowl, combine the wafer crumbs, pecans and sugar; stir in butter. Press onto the bottom and 1-1/2 in. up the sides of a greased 9-in. spring-form pan. Place pan on a baking sheet.

Bake at 375° for 8 minutes. Cool on a wire rack. Reduce heat to 325°.

In a mixing bowl, beat cream cheese, sugar, lemon juice, lemon peel and vanilla until smooth. Add egg yolks; beat on low speed just until combined. In a small mixing bowl, beat egg whites on high until stiff peaks form; fold into cream cheese mixture. Pour into crust. Return pan to baking sheet.

Bake for 25-30 minutes or until center is almost set. Cool on a wire rack for 10 minutes. Carefully run knife around edge of pan to loosen; cool 1 hour longer. Refrigerate until completely cooled.

In a microwave, melt chocolate and butter. Cool for 10 minutes. In a small heavy saucepan, whisk egg yolks, sugar and coffee. Cook and stir over low heat until mixture reaches 160°; stir in vanilla. Whisk in chocolate mixture. Set saucepan in ice and stir until cooled, about 2 minutes. Fold in whipped cream. Spread over cheesecake and refrigerate until set. Remove sides of pan. Garnish with dessert decorations and whipped cream. Refrigerate leftovers. **Yield:** 12 servings.

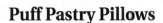

Puff Pastry Pillows

(Pictured at left)

I'm known for these sweet treats. My family and co-workers love them. —Robert Ryan, Newton, Iowa

   1 package (17.3 ounces) frozen puff pastry,
      thawed
   1 egg
1/4 cup milk
   1 to 2 tablespoons coarse *or* granulated
      sugar
FILLING:
1/4 cup all-purpose flour
   1 cup milk
   1 cup butter, softened
   1 cup sugar
   1 teaspoon vanilla extract
1/2 teaspoon almond extract
1/4 teaspoon salt

Carefully open each puff pastry sheet. Cut each sheet of pastry at creases, forming 3 strips. Cut each strip widthwise into 7 pieces. Combine egg and

milk; lightly brush egg mixture over pastry. Sprinkle with sugar. Place on lightly greased baking sheets. Bake at 400° for 10-12 minutes or until golden brown. Remove to wire racks to cool. Split into top and bottom halves.

In a saucepan, combine flour and milk until smooth. Bring to a boil over medium heat; cook and stir for 1 minute or until thickened. Cool. Transfer to a mixing bowl; beat in the butter, sugar, extracts and salt until light and fluffy, about 10 minutes. Spread 1 tablespoonful on bottom half of each pastry; replace tops. Store in refrigerator. **Yield:** about 3-1/2 dozen.

Pecan Cherry Bark

(Pictured at left)

I just love to make chocolates at Christmastime. This popular candy combines pecans, chocolate and cherries—it is crunchy, sweet and just plain yummy!
   —*Sue Kauffman, Columbia City, Indiana*

1/4 cup butter
1/2 cup brown sugar
Dash ground nutmeg
Dash ground cinnamon
1-3/4 cups chopped pecans
   1 pound semisweet chocolate candy
      coating, chopped
   3 tablespoons shortening, *divided*
   1 pound milk chocolate candy coating,
      chopped
   1 pound white chocolate candy coating,
      chopped
1-3/4 cups dried cherries *or* cranberries

In a skillet, melt butter; add brown sugar, nutmeg and cinnamon. Bring to a boil; cook and stir until sugar is dissolved, about 3 minutes. Add pecans; toss to coat. Transfer pecan mixture to a foil-lined pan. Cool completely.

In a saucepan over low heat, melt semisweet candy coating. Stir in 1 tablespoon shortening until smooth. Spread into a waxed paper-lined 15-in. x 10-in. x 1-in. baking pan. In a saucepan, melt milk chocolate candy coating; add 1 tablespoon shortening. Stir until smooth. Spread over semisweet layer. Repeat with white candy coating and remaining shortening. Spread over milk chocolate layer. Sprinkle with sugared pecans and cherries; press down gently. Let stand until set. Break into pieces. **Yield:** 4 pounds.

Editor's Note: Candy layers need not be completely set before spreading another layer over top.

Fresh Fruit Tarts

(Pictured below)

These luscious tarts are the jewels of the party whenever I serve them. I usually double this recipe. You can bake the shells ahead and freeze them, then fill and decorate the tarts the day of the gathering.
—Dona Erhart, Stockbridge, Michigan

1-1/2 **cups all-purpose flour**
  1/4 **cup sugar**
  1/4 **teaspoon salt**
  1/2 **cup cold butter**
    1 **egg, beaten**
FILLING:
    4 **ounces cream cheese, softened**
  1/4 **cup sweetened condensed milk**
    2 **tablespoons lemon juice**
Assorted fresh berries
    2 **tablespoons apricot preserves**

In a large bowl, combine the flour, sugar and salt. Cut in butter until mixture resembles coarse crumbs. Add egg; mix with a fork until blended. Shape dough into a ball. Cover and refrigerate for 1 hour or until easy to handle.

Divide dough into six portions. Press each portion into a greased 4-1/2-in. tart pan. Bake at 350° for 15-20 minutes or until the edges are lightly browned. Cool for 10 minutes before removing from pans to wire racks to cool completely.

In a small mixing bowl, beat cream cheese until smooth. Beat in sweetened condensed milk and lemon juice. Spoon 2 rounded tablespoonfuls into each cooled tart shell. Arrange berries over filling.

In a small saucepan, melt preserves over medium heat; stir until smooth. Brush over berries. **Yield:** 6 servings.

Pumpkin Rice Pudding

This pudding is the queen of comfort foods! It's creamy, spicy and smells incredible while baking. It's a great way to use up leftover rice, too. —Dee Falk
Stromsburg, Nebraska

    4 **cups milk**
    1 **can (15 ounces) solid-pack pumpkin**
  3/4 **cup sugar**
    1 **teaspoon ground cinnamon**
  1/2 **teaspoon salt**
  1/2 **teaspoon ground ginger**
  1/4 **teaspoon ground cloves**
    2 **eggs, beaten**
    3 **cups cooked rice**
  1/2 **teaspoon vanilla extract**
Vanilla ice cream, optional

In a large saucepan, combine the first seven ingredients. Bring to a boil over medium heat, stirring constantly. Gradually stir a small amount into eggs; return all to the pan. Bring to a gentle boil, stirring constantly. Remove from the heat. Stir in rice and vanilla.

Pour into a greased 13-in. x 9-in. x 2-in. baking dish. Bake, uncovered, at 375° for 25-30 minutes or until a knife inserted near the center comes out clean. Serve warm with ice cream if desired. Refrigerate leftovers. **Yield:** 8 servings.

Rhubarb Icebox Dessert

(Pictured on page 128)

A light and fluffy marshmallow layer tops the rhubarb filling in this delicious make-ahead recipe. —Renee Schwebach, Dumont, Minnesota

1-3/4 **cups crushed graham crackers**
      (about 28 squares), *divided*
    3 **tablespoons butter, melted**
    1 **cup sugar**
    2 **tablespoons cornstarch**
    4 **cups diced fresh** *or* **frozen rhubarb**
    1 **package (3 ounces) raspberry** *or*
      strawberry gelatin
    1 **carton (8 ounces) frozen whipped**
      topping, thawed
1-1/2 **cups miniature marshmallows**

2 cups cold milk
1 package (3.4 ounces) instant vanilla
pudding mix

In a bowl, combine 1-1/2 cups cracker crumbs and butter. Press mixture into a greased 13-in. x 9-in. x 2-in. baking dish. Bake at 350° for 10 minutes or until lightly browned. Cool on a wire rack.

In a large saucepan, combine the sugar, cornstarch and rhubarb. Bring to a boil; cook and stir for 2-3 minutes or until thickened and rhubarb is tender. Remove from the heat; stir in gelatin until dissolved. Cover and refrigerate for 1 hour or until partially set.

Spoon rhubarb mixture over crust. Combine whipped topping and marshmallows; spread over rhubarb mixture. In a bowl, whisk milk and pudding mix for 2 minutes. Let stand for 2 minutes or until soft-set. Carefully spread over marshmallow topping (the dish will be full). Sprinkle with remaining cracker crumbs. Refrigerate for at least 2 hours before serving. **Yield:** 15 servings.

Meringue Ice Cream Torte

(Pictured above right)

This recipe looks a little long, but it really isn't complicated. The sweet result is certainly worth the effort.
—Alice Christmas, Statesboro, Georgia

3 egg whites
1/2 teaspoon cream of tartar
1 cup sugar
RASPBERRY SAUCE:
1 package (12 ounces) frozen unsweetened
raspberries, thawed
2 tablespoons sugar
2 tablespoons cornstarch
1/3 cup maple syrup
ICE CREAM LAYERS:
1 quart coffee ice cream, softened
1-1/3 cups sliced almonds, toasted
1 quart chocolate chip ice cream, softened
2 cups heavy whipping cream
2 tablespoons sugar
1/2 teaspoon almond extract
Fresh raspberries

Let egg whites stand at room temperature for 30 minutes. In a mixing bowl, beat egg whites and cream of tartar on medium speed until soft peaks form. Gradually add sugar, 2 tablespoons at a time, beating on high until stiff peaks form and sugar is dissolved.

Line two large baking sheets with parchment paper; draw three 8-1/2-in. circles on paper. Drop meringue in mounds onto circles; spread to cover.

Bake at 250° for 1-1/4 hours or until set. Turn oven off and do not open door; let meringues dry in oven for 1 hour. Remove from the oven and cool on baking sheets. When completely cooled, remove meringues from paper.

Drain raspberries, reserving juice. Set berries aside. Add enough water to juice to measure 1/2 cup. In a small saucepan, combine sugar and cornstarch. Stir in maple syrup and juice mixture until smooth. Bring to a boil over medium heat; cook and stir for 1-2 minutes or until thickened. Remove from heat; gently stir in reserved berries. Cool.

To assemble, place one meringue in a 10-in. springform pan. Spread with coffee ice cream; sprinkle with a third of the almonds. Top with a second meringue. Spread with chocolate chip ice cream; sprinkle with a third of the almonds. Top with the remaining meringue. Cover and freeze overnight.

In a mixing bowl, beat cream until it begins to thicken. Add sugar and almond extract; beat until stiff peaks form. Remove torte from freezer; carefully run a knife around edge of pan to loosen. Remove side of pan. Frost with whipped cream.

Garnish with fresh raspberries and remaining almonds. Cover and freeze for at least 2 hours. Remove from the freezer 20 minutes before serving. Serve with raspberry sauce. **Yield:** 14-16 servings.

Two-Berry Parfaits

For variety, I use whatever fresh berries are in season for this pretty layered treat. —Mary Relyea
Canastota, New York

> 1 package (10 ounces) frozen unsweetened raspberries, thawed
> 1/4 cup sugar
> 2 tablespoons cornstarch
> 2 cups frozen sliced sweetened strawberries, thawed
> 2 teaspoons lemon juice
> 1 quart vanilla ice cream
> 1 cup (8 ounces) sour cream

Drain raspberries, reserving juice in a 1-cup measuring cup. Set raspberries aside. Add enough water to juice to measure 1 cup. In a saucepan, combine sugar and cornstarch; stir in the raspberry juice mixture until smooth.

Add the strawberries. Bring to a boil over medium heat; cook and stir for 2 minutes or until thickened. Remove from heat; stir in the lemon juice and raspberries. Cover and refrigerate for 30 minutes.

In six parfait glasses, layer 2 tablespoons berry sauce, one scoop of ice cream, 2-3 tablespoons sour cream, 3 tablespoons sauce and another scoop of ice cream. Drizzle with the remaining sauce. **Yield:** 6 servings.

Special Stuffed Strawberries

(Pictured above)

These sweet bites can be made ahead of time...and they look really colorful on a tray. I sometimes sprinkle the piped filling with finely chopped pistachio nuts.
—Marcia Orlando, Boyertown, Pennsylvania

✓ Uses less fat, sugar or salt. Includes Nutritional Analysis and Diabetic Exchanges.

> 24 large fresh strawberries
> 1/2 cup spreadable strawberry cream cheese
> 3 tablespoons sour cream

Remove stems from the strawberries. Place point side up on a cutting board. Cut a deep X in the top of each berry. Carefully spread berries apart. In a bowl, beat cream cheese and sour cream until smooth. Pipe or spoon filling into each berry. Refrigerate until serving. **Yield:** 2 dozen.

Nutritional Analysis: One strawberry (prepared with reduced-fat cream cheese and reduced-fat sour cream) equals 17 calories, 1 g fat (trace saturated fat), 2 mg cholesterol, 20 mg sodium, 2 g carbohydrate, 1 g fiber, 1 g protein. **Diabetic Exchange:** Free food.

Maple Pumpkin Cheesecake

I saw this recipe in a free booklet I got at the supermarket a few years ago and decided to try it. It is attractive and so delicious. —Elmira Trombetti
Gulfport, Florida

> 1-1/4 cups graham cracker crumbs
> 1/4 cup sugar
> 1/4 cup butter, melted
> **FILLING:**
> 3 packages (8 ounces *each*) cream cheese, softened
> 1 can (14 ounces) sweetened condensed milk
> 1 can (15 ounces) solid-pack pumpkin
> 3 eggs, lightly beaten
> 1/4 cup maple syrup
> 1-1/2 teaspoons ground cinnamon
> 1 teaspoon ground nutmeg
> **TOPPING:**
> 4 teaspoons cornstarch
> 2 tablespoons water
> 2 tablespoons butter

1/2 cup maple syrup
1/2 cup raisins
1/2 cup coarsely chopped walnuts

In a small bowl, combine cracker crumbs and sugar; stir in butter. Press onto the bottom of a greased 9-in. springform pan; set aside.

In a large mixing bowl, beat the cream cheese and milk until smooth. Beat in pumpkin. Add eggs; beat on low speed just until combined. Add syrup, cinnamon and nutmeg. Pour over crust. Place pan on a baking sheet. Bake at 325° for 70-75 minutes or until center is almost set. Cool on a wire rack for 10 minutes. Carefully run a knife around edge of pan to loosen. Cool 1 hour longer.

In a small bowl, combine cornstarch and water until smooth. In a small saucepan, melt the butter; add syrup and cornstarch mixture. Bring to a boil over medium-high heat, stirring constantly. Cook and stir for 1-2 minutes or until thickened.

Remove from the heat; stir in raisins and walnuts. Cool to lukewarm. Spoon over cheesecake. Refrigerate overnight. Remove sides of pan. **Yield:** 12 servings.

Crunchy Chocolate Eggs

(Pictured on page 128)

I've been making these candies since my children were young, and we never tire of the taste.
—Janis Plourde, Smooth Rock Falls, Ontario

1 cup packed brown sugar
1 cup light corn syrup
1 cup peanut butter*
2 cups cornflakes
2 cups crisp rice cereal
1/2 cup finely chopped peanuts
3-3/4 cups semisweet chocolate chips
1-1/2 teaspoons shortening
Candy sprinkles

In a heavy saucepan, combine brown sugar, corn syrup and peanut butter. Cook and stir over medium heat until smooth. Remove from the heat; stir in the cereals and peanuts.

When cool enough to handle, drop by tablespoonfuls onto waxed paper-lined baking sheets. Form into egg shapes. Refrigerate until firm. In a microwave, melt chocolate chips and shortening; stir until smooth. Dip eggs in chocolate; allow excess to drip off. Place on waxed paper-lined baking sheets. Decorate with sprinkles. Let stand until set. **Yield:** about 4-1/2 dozen.

*Editor's Note: Reduced-fat or generic brands of peanut butter are not recommended for this recipe.

Chocolate Peanut Freeze

(Pictured below)

This layered ice cream dessert tastes a lot like a popular candy bar. It is so easy to assemble...and both children and adults love it. The homemade chocolate-peanut topping is yummy!
—Linda Rock
Stratford, Wisconsin

2 cups confectioners' sugar
1 can (12 ounces) evaporated milk
1 cup butter, *divided*
2/3 cup semisweet chocolate chips
1 package (14 ounces) cream-filled chocolate sandwich cookies
1/2 gallon vanilla ice cream, softened
1-1/2 cups salted peanuts, coarsely chopped

In a large saucepan, combine the confectioners' sugar, milk, 1/2 cup butter and chocolate chips. Bring to a boil, stirring constantly. Cook and stir for 8 minutes or until slightly thickened. Refrigerate until cool.

Meanwhile, in a food processor or blender, cover and process cookies until finely crushed. In a large bowl, melt remaining butter; stir in crushed cookies. Press into a 13-in. x 9-in. x 2-in. dish. Refrigerate until firm.

Spread ice cream over crust; freeze. Stir peanuts into chilled chocolate mixture. Spread over ice cream. Cover and freeze for 3-4 hours or until firm. Remove from the freezer 5 minutes before serving. **Yield:** 15-18 servings.

Rhubarb Strawberry Torte

(Pictured below)

This pretty dessert has been a special favorite for years. It recently received raves from my card club.
—*Norma Wehrung, Getzville, New York*

- **6 cups chopped fresh *or* frozen rhubarb, thawed**
- **1 cup water**
- **3/4 cup sugar, *divided***
- **2 packages (3 ounces *each*) strawberry gelatin**
- **1 teaspoon vanilla extract**
- **4-1/2 teaspoons cornstarch**
- **1 tablespoon cold water**
- **4 drops red food coloring, optional**
- **2 cups heavy whipping cream, whipped**
- **24 ladyfingers, split**
- **Fresh strawberries and additional whipped cream**

In a large saucepan, bring rhubarb, water and 1/2 cup sugar to a boil. Reduce heat; simmer, uncovered, for 6-8 minutes or until rhubarb is tender. Cool slightly. Set aside 1 cup rhubarb liquid for glaze. Place rhubarb and remaining liquid in a blender or food processor; cover and process until pureed.

Return to saucepan. Bring to a boil; stir in gelatin until dissolved. Stir in vanilla. Cover and chill for 1 hour or until slightly thickened.

Meanwhile, for glaze, combine reserved rhubarb liquid and remaining sugar in a small saucepan. Bring to a boil. In a small bowl, combine cornstarch and cold water until smooth; whisk into boiling mixture. Cook and stir until thickened. Remove

RAVE REVIEWS will be forthcoming when you serve Rhubarb Strawberry Torte, Rhubarb Ice Cream or Rhubarb Angel Dessert (shown above, clockwise from left).

from the heat. Stir in food coloring if desired. Cover and refrigerate overnight.

Gradually fold whipped cream into rhubarb mixture. Arrange 17 split ladyfingers on the bottom and 26 around the edge of an ungreased 9-in. springform pan. Spread half of the rhubarb mixture into pan. Arrange remaining ladyfingers over rhubarb mixture; carefully spread with remaining rhubarb mixture. Cover and chill overnight. Carefully spread glaze over top. Remove sides of pan. Garnish with strawberries and whipped cream. **Yield:** 12 servings.

Rhubarb Ice Cream

(Pictured below left)

Always refreshing, this rich-tasting ice cream is great on a spring or summer evening. —Rachel Garcia
Honolulu, Hawaii

3 cups thinly sliced fresh *or* frozen rhubarb
2 cups sugar
1 teaspoon lemon juice
1 cup heavy whipping cream

Place rhubarb in an ungreased 13-in. x 9-in. x 2-in. baking dish; sprinkle with sugar; toss to coat. Cover and bake at 375° for 30-40 minutes or until tender, stirring occasionally. Cool slightly. Process in batches in a blender or food processor. Transfer to a bowl; cover and refrigerate until chilled.

Stir in lemon juice. In a mixing bowl, beat cream until stiff peaks form. Gradually fold into rhubarb mixture. Transfer to a shallow 2-qt. freezer container. Freeze, uncovered, for 1 hour, stirring every 15 minutes. Cover and freeze overnight. **Yield:** 2-3/4 cups.

Rhubarb Angel Dessert

(Pictured at left)

A delightfully tangy rhubarb filling tops the short-bread crust in this recipe. The tender meringue will melt in your mouth! —Patricia Staudt
Marble Rock, Iowa

1 cup all-purpose flour
1 tablespoon sugar
1/2 cup cold butter
FILLING:
1 cup sugar
2 tablespoons all-purpose flour
1/4 teaspoon salt
1/2 cup heavy whipping cream

3 egg yolks
2-1/2 cups chopped fresh *or* frozen rhubarb
MERINGUE:
3 egg whites
1 teaspoon vanilla extract
6 tablespoons sugar
1/4 cup flaked coconut, toasted

In a large bowl, combine the flour and sugar; cut in butter until mixture resembles coarse crumbs. Press mixture into an ungreased 8-in. square baking dish. Bake at 350° for 15-20 minutes or until lightly browned. Meanwhile, in a small mixing bowl, combine sugar, flour and salt. Beat in cream and egg yolks. Stir in rhubarb. Pour over hot crust. Bake, uncovered, for 40 minutes or until set.

In a mixing bowl, beat egg whites and vanilla on medium speed until soft peaks form. Gradually add sugar, 1 tablespoon at a time, beating on high until stiff peaks form. Spread over hot filling, sealing edges to baking dish.

Bake for 15 minutes or until golden brown. Sprinkle with coconut. Cool on a wire rack. Cut into squares. Refrigerate leftovers. **Yield:** 9 servings.

Three-Fruit Sundae Sauce

We brought back some rhubarb from a trip to Wisconsin, and I wanted to make something besides pie. I dreamed up this bright-red sauce that blends rhubarb with strawberries and oranges.
—Sharron Trefren, Grand Bay, Alabama

2 cups sugar
2 tablespoons cornstarch
6 cups chopped fresh *or* frozen rhubarb*
2 cups fresh *or* frozen unsweetened sliced strawberries
2 medium navel oranges, peeled and sectioned
1 teaspoon grated lemon peel
3 cups water
1 cinnamon stick (3 inches)
Vanilla ice cream

In a large saucepan, combine the sugar, cornstarch, rhubarb, strawberries, oranges and lemon peel until blended. Stir in the water and cinnamon stick. Bring to a boil; cook and stir for 2 minutes.

Reduce heat; simmer, uncovered, for 50-60 minutes or until thickened. Discard cinnamon stick. Cool. Refrigerate until chilled. Serve over the ice cream. **Yield:** 7 cups.

*Editor's Note: If using frozen rhubarb, measure rhubarb while still frozen, then thaw completely. Drain in a colander, but do not press liquid out.

la. Transfer to a large bowl. Cool to room temperature without stirring.

Meanwhile, in a saucepan, bring the rhubarb, sugar and water to a boil. Reduce heat; cook and stir for 5-8 minutes or until rhubarb is tender and mixture is thickened. Cool completely. In a mixing bowl, beat the cream until stiff peaks form. Gradually fold a fourth of the whipped cream into the custard. Fold in remaining whipped cream.

Place half of the cake cubes in a 2-1/2-qt. trifle bowl. Spread with half of the rhubarb mixture; top with 1 cup of strawberries and half of the custard. Repeat layers. Cover and chill for at least 1 hour before serving. **Yield:** 12-14 servings.

German Chocolate Cheesecake

My daughter requests this as her birthday cake, and I take it to potlucks, church dinners or any time the dessert is my responsibility. —Kathy Johnson
Lake City, South Dakota

    1 **package (18-1/4 ounces) German chocolate cake mix**
    2 **packages (8 ounces *each*) cream cheese, softened**
1-1/2 **cups sugar**
    4 **eggs, lightly beaten**
FROSTING:
    1 **cup sugar**
    1 **cup evaporated milk**
1/2 **cup butter, cubed**
    3 **egg yolks, beaten**
    1 **teaspoon vanilla extract**
1-1/2 **cups flaked coconut**
    1 **cup chopped pecans**

Prepare cake batter according to package directions; set aside. In a small mixing bowl, beat cream cheese and sugar until smooth. Add eggs; beat on low speed just until combined.

Pour half of the cake batter into a greased 13-in. x 9-in. x 2-in. baking dish. Gently pour cream cheese mixture over batter. Gently spoon remaining batter over top; spread to edge of pan.

Bake at 325° for 70-75 minutes or until a toothpick inserted near the center comes out clean. Cool on a wire rack for 1 hour.

For frosting, combine the sugar, milk, butter and egg yolks in a heavy saucepan. Cook and stir over medium-low heat until thickened and a thermometer reads 160°. Remove from the heat. Stir in vanilla; fold in the coconut and pecans. Cool until frosting reaches spreading consistency. Frost cooled cake. Refrigerate leftovers. **Yield:** 16 servings.

Strawberry Rhubarb Trifle

(Pictured above)

Guests are sure to "think spring" when they see and taste this delectable trifle. —Wendy Dowling
Port Moulton, Nova Scotia

1/2 **cup sugar**
1/4 **cup cornstarch**
    3 **cups milk**
    5 **egg yolks, beaten**
    1 **teaspoon vanilla extract**
FILLING:
    4 **cups chopped fresh *or* frozen rhubarb**
1/4 **to 1/2 cup sugar**
1/4 **cup water**
1/2 **cup heavy whipping cream**
    1 **prepared angel food cake (8 inches), cubed**
    2 **cups sliced fresh strawberries**

In a heavy saucepan, combine the sugar, cornstarch and milk until smooth. Cook and stir over medium-high heat until thickened and bubbly. Reduce heat; cook and stir 2 minutes longer. Remove from the heat. Stir a small amount of hot mixture into egg yolks; return all to the pan, stirring constantly.

Bring to a gentle boil; cook and stir 2 minutes longer. Remove from the heat. Gently stir in vanil-

Peppermint Chip Cheesecake

(Pictured on page 128)

I love to make cheesecakes and frequently give them as gifts or donate them to fund-raisers. This one is very popular. —Gretchen Ely, West Lafayette, Indiana

    1 package (10 ounces) chocolate-covered
      mint cookies*, crushed
    3 tablespoons butter, melted
    3 packages (8 ounces *each*) cream cheese,
      softened
  3/4 cup sugar
    5 teaspoons cornstarch
    3 eggs
    1 egg yolk
  1/2 cup heavy whipping cream
    2 teaspoons peppermint extract
1-1/4 teaspoons vanilla extract
    3 to 4 drops green food coloring, optional
    1 cup miniature semisweet chocolate chips

In a bowl, combine the cookie crumbs and butter. Press onto the bottom and 1 in. up the sides of a greased 9-in. springform pan.

In a large mixing bowl, beat cream cheese, sugar and cornstarch until smooth. Lightly beat eggs and egg yolk; add to cream cheese mixture. Beat on low speed just until combined. Stir in the cream, extracts and food coloring if desired. Fold in chocolate chips. Pour into crust. Place pan on a baking sheet.

Bake at 325° for 50-60 minutes or until center is almost set. Cool on a wire rack for 10 minutes. Carefully run a knife around edge of pan to loosen; cool 1 hour longer. Cover and chill overnight. Remove sides of pan. Refrigerate leftovers. **Yield:** 12 servings.

***Editor's Note:** This recipe was tested with Keebler Grasshopper Fudge Mint Cookies.*

Frozen Lemon Yogurt

(Pictured on back cover)

Wanting something with fewer calories, I tinkered with a lemon ice cream recipe until I liked what I tasted. —Carol Mead, Los Alamos, New Mexico

    1 carton (32 ounces) plain yogurt
1-2/3 cups sugar
  1/3 cup lemon juice
    1 tablespoon grated lemon peel
    4 drops yellow food coloring, optional

In a mixing bowl, combine the yogurt, sugar, lemon juice and peel; mix well. Stir in food coloring if desired. Fill cylinder of ice cream freezer two-thirds full; freeze according to the manufacturer's directions. Refrigerate remaining mixture until ready to freeze. Allow to ripen in ice cream freezer or firm up in the refrigerator freezer for at least 2-4 hours before serving. **Yield:** 5 cups.

Rich Hot Fudge Sauce

(Pictured below)

The dark chocolate flavor of this sauce, with a hint of rum extract, will satisfy a chocoholic's cravings. —Carol Hunihan, Ann Arbor, Michigan

    1 cup heavy whipping cream
  3/4 cup butter, cubed
1-1/3 cups packed brown sugar
  1/3 cup sugar
Pinch salt
    1 cup baking cocoa
  1/2 cup plus 2 tablespoons light corn syrup
    2 squares (1 ounce *each*) unsweetened
      chocolate
    3 teaspoons vanilla extract
    1 to 2 teaspoons rum extract

In a heavy saucepan, combine cream and butter. Cook and stir over medium-low heat until butter is melted. Add the sugars and salt; cook and stir until sugar is dissolved, about 4 minutes. Stir in the cocoa and corn syrup; cook and stir for 3 minutes or until cocoa is blended.

Add chocolate; cook and stir 3-4 minutes or until melted. Reduce heat to low. Simmer 12-16 minutes or until mixture reaches desired thickness, stirring constantly. Remove from heat; stir in extracts. Cool slightly. Store in the refrigerator. **Yield:** about 3-1/2 cups.

Chocolate Almond Cheesecake

(Pictured below)

After serving this once, I'm asked to make it again the next time. It has the most heavenly flavor.
—Dayna Henson, Tulsa, Oklahoma

    2 cups crushed vanilla wafers
    1 cup finely chopped almonds, toasted
  1/3 cup sugar
  1/2 cup butter, melted
FILLING:
    1 envelope unflavored gelatin
  1/2 cup milk
    2 packages (8 ounces *each*) cream cheese, softened
  1/2 cup sour cream
  1/4 to 1/2 teaspoon almond extract
    1 package (11-1/2 ounces) milk chocolate chips, melted and cooled
  1/2 cup heavy whipping cream
Milk chocolate kisses, unblanched whole almonds and additional whipped cream

In a bowl, combine the wafer crumbs, almonds and sugar; stir in butter. Press onto the bottom and 1-3/4 in. up the sides of a greased 9-in. springform pan. Cover and refrigerate for 1 hour.

In a small saucepan, soften gelatin in milk; let stand for 5 minutes. Cook and stir over medium heat until gelatin is dissolved. Cool to room temperature, about 6 minutes. In a large mixing bowl, beat the cream cheese, sour cream and extract until smooth. Beat in melted chocolate and gelatin mixture. Fold in whipped cream. Spoon into crust. Cover and chill for 6 hours or overnight.

Just before serving, run a knife around edge of pan to loosen. Remove sides of pan. Garnish with chocolate kisses, almonds and additional whipped cream. Refrigerate leftovers. **Yield:** 12 servings.

Old-Fashioned Cheesecake

(Pictured below)

For variety, I like to use fresh fruit—strawberries, kiwi, raspberries, blueberries, etc.—on top of this cheesecake.
—Marian Levin, Los Altos, California

1-1/3 cups whole almonds, toasted and ground
  3/4 cup crushed vanilla wafers
  1/3 cup butter, melted
    3 packages (8 ounces *each*) cream cheese, softened
    1 cup sugar
    3 eggs, lightly beaten
    2 teaspoons vanilla extract
  3/4 teaspoon grated lemon peel

GREAT DESSERTS include Chocolate Almond Cheesecake, Old-Fashioned Cheesecake and Layered Hazelnut Cheesecake (shown below, clockwise from top left).

TOPPING:

    2 cups (16 ounces) sour cream
    3 tablespoons sugar
    1 teaspoon vanilla extract
Assorted fresh fruit

In a bowl, combine almonds and wafer crumbs; stir in butter. Press onto the bottom and 2 in. up the sides of an ungreased 9-in. springform pan. Bake at 350° for 5 minutes. Cool on a wire rack.

In a large mixing bowl, beat cream cheese and sugar until smooth. Add eggs; beat on low speed just until combined. Beat in vanilla and lemon peel just until blended. Pour into crust. Place pan on a baking sheet. Bake at 350° for 40-45 minutes or until center is almost set.

Combine sour cream, sugar and vanilla; carefully spread over filling. Bake 10 minutes longer or until edges appear dry. Cool on a wire rack for 10 minutes. Carefully run a knife around edge of pan to loosen; cool 1 hour longer. Cover and chill overnight. Remove sides of pan. Top with fresh fruit. Refrigerate leftovers. **Yield:** 12 servings.

Layered Hazelnut Cheesecake

(Pictured below left)

A creamy topping accents each beautiful slice of this dessert. —*Leah Garnss, Spring Valley, New York*

1-1/2 cups crushed vanilla wafers
  1/4 cup butter, melted
    4 packages (8 ounces *each*) cream cheese, softened
1-3/4 cups sugar
    4 eggs, lightly beaten
    2 teaspoons vanilla extract
    4 ounces finely chopped hazelnuts, toasted
  1/3 cup semisweet chocolate chips, melted
TOPPING:
  2/3 cup vanilla *or* white chips
    3 tablespoons water
    1 teaspoon light corn syrup
  1/2 teaspoon instant coffee granules
  1/4 cup chopped hazelnuts, toasted

In a bowl, combine the wafer crumbs and butter; press onto the bottom of a greased 9-in. springform pan. In a large mixing bowl, beat the cream cheese and sugar until smooth. Add the eggs and vanilla; beat on low speed just until combined.

Divide batter into thirds. Into one portion, stir in hazelnuts. Pour over crust. Refrigerate for 20 minutes or until set. Into second portion, gradually stir in melted chocolate. Spoon over bottom layer. Refrigerate for 45 minutes or until set.

Spoon remaining batter over top. Place pan on a baking sheet. Bake at 350° for 50-60 minutes or until center is almost set. Cool on a wire rack for 10 minutes. Carefully run a knife around the edge of pan to loosen; cool 1 hour longer. Cover and refrigerate overnight.

For topping, combine vanilla chips, water, corn syrup and coffee granules in a saucepan; cook and stir over low heat until smooth. Cool to room temperature. Remove sides of springform pan. Serve cheesecake with topping; garnish with hazelnuts. Refrigerate leftovers. **Yield:** 12 servings.

Lemon Cream Puffs

(Pictured on back cover)

The fluffy filling for these light crisp shells has a delectable citrus flavor. —*Doreen Martin*
Kitimat, British Columbia

  1/2 cup water
  1/4 cup butter, cubed
  1/2 cup all-purpose flour
    2 eggs
LEMON FILLING:
    1 egg, beaten
  1/3 cup sugar
    3 tablespoons lemon juice
    2 tablespoons butter, cubed
    1 cup heavy whipping cream
    2 teaspoons sugar
Confectioners' sugar

In a saucepan, bring water and butter to a boil. Add flour all at once, stirring until a smooth ball forms. Remove from the heat; let stand for 5 minutes. Add eggs, one at a time, beating well after each addition. Continue beating until mixture is smooth.

Drop by rounded tablespoonfuls 3 in. apart onto greased baking sheets. Bake at 400° for 30-35 minutes or until golden brown. Remove to wire racks. Immediately split puffs and remove tops; discard soft dough from inside. Set puffs and tops aside to cool.

In a small heavy saucepan, combine the egg, sugar, lemon juice and butter. Bring to a boil over medium heat; cook and stir for 5-7 minutes or until mixture is thick enough to coat a metal spoon.

Remove from the heat. Cool quickly by placing pan in a bowl of ice water; stir for 2 minutes. Transfer to a bowl; press plastic wrap onto surface of filling. Chill for 1 hour or until partially set.

In a mixing bowl, beat cream and sugar until stiff peaks form; fold into lemon mixture. Fill cream puffs; replace tops. Dust with confectioners' sugar. **Yield:** 10 servings.

SWEETEN your valentine's holiday or other special occasion with creamy scrumptious Dark Chocolate Pudding or Sweetheart Custard Dessert (shown above, top to bottom). They're sure to impress!

Sweetheart Custard Dessert

(Pictured above)

Your special valentine will think you bought this gorgeous confection at a bakery! This recipe may look difficult, but it really isn't, considering that you start with premade pie crust. I'm a hairdresser with an at-home salon…and I enjoy trying out my dessert creations on customers.
—Kathy Zielicke
Fond du Lac, Wisconsin

Pastry for double-crust pie (9 inches)
Confectioners' sugar
CUSTARD:
  2/3 cup sugar
    3 tablespoons cornstarch
  1/4 teaspoon salt
1-1/3 cups milk
    2 egg yolks
  1/4 cup lemon juice
    1 tablespoon butter
    1 cup heavy whipping cream
  1/4 cup confectioners' sugar
TOPPING:
    2 to 3 cups sliced fresh strawberries
    2 tablespoons semisweet chocolate chips
    1 teaspoon shortening

Roll out each pastry between waxed paper into a 12-in. circle. Using an 11-in.-wide heart-shaped pattern, cut each pastry into a heart shape. Place on greased and floured baking sheets; prick with a fork. Bake at 450° for 7-9 minutes or until golden brown. Remove to wire racks to cool. Sprinkle with confectioners' sugar.

Meanwhile, in a saucepan, combine the sugar, cornstarch and salt; gradually stir in milk until smooth. Cook and stir over medium heat until thickened and bubbly. Reduce heat; cook and stir 2 minutes longer.

Remove from the heat. Combine the egg yolks and lemon juice. Stir a small amount of hot filling into egg yolk mixture; return all to pan, stirring constantly. Bring to a gentle boil; cook and stir for 2 minutes. Remove from heat. Stir in butter. Cover; refrigerate until cool.

In a mixing bowl, beat the cream and confectioners' sugar until stiff peaks form. Gently whisk the lemon custard, then fold in whipped cream.

Place one pastry on a serving plate; spread with half of custard. Arrange half the berries over custard. Top with remaining pastry; spread with remaining custard. Arrange remaining berries over filling. In a microwave-safe bowl, melt chocolate chips and shortening. Drizzle over the top. Refrigerate until serving. **Yield:** 8-10 servings.

Dark Chocolate Pudding

(Pictured at left)

It's not Valentine's Day without a chocolate dessert. This rich old-fashioned treat is oh-so-creamy and comforting! —_Lillian Julow, Gainesville, Florida_

- 1/4 **cup sugar**
- 3 **tablespoons cornstarch**
- 1/4 **teaspoon salt**
- 2 **cups milk**
- 3 **egg yolks, beaten**
- 1 **dark chocolate candy bar (7 ounces), melted**
- 1/2 **teaspoon vanilla extract**
- **Whipped cream, grated chocolate and Pirouette cookies**

In a large saucepan, combine the sugar, cornstarch and salt. Stir in milk until smooth. Cook and stir over medium-high heat until thickened and bubbly. Reduce heat; cook and stir 2 minutes longer. Remove from the heat.

Stir a small amount of hot mixture into egg yolks; return all to pan, stirring constantly. Bring to a gentle boil; cook and stir 2 minutes longer. Remove from the heat; gradually whisk in chocolate and vanilla until smooth.

Press plastic wrap onto surface of pudding. Refrigerate. Spoon into dessert dishes. Garnish with whipped cream, grated chocolate and cookies. Serve warm or cold. **Yield:** 4-6 servings.

Editor's Note: This recipe was tested with Hershey's Special Dark chocolate and Pepperidge Farm Pirouette cookies.

Lemon Custard Ice Cream

I found this recipe several years ago and make it whenever I have the opportunity. What I especially like about this ice cream is the pleasant lemon taste.
—_Susan Litwak, Bellevue, Nebraska_

- 2 **cups sugar**
- 1/4 **cup all-purpose flour**
- 1/4 **teaspoon salt**
- 4 **cups milk**
- 4 **eggs, lightly beaten**
- 3 **cups heavy whipping cream**
- 1 **cup lemon juice**

In a large saucepan, combine the sugar, flour and salt. Gradually add milk. Bring to a boil over medium heat; cook and stir for 2 minutes or until thickened. Remove from the heat; cool slightly.

Whisk a small amount of hot milk mixture into the eggs. Return all to the pan, whisking constantly. Cook and stir until mixture reaches 160° and coats the back of a metal spoon.

Remove from the heat. Cool quickly by placing pan in a bowl of ice water; stir for 2 minutes. Gently stir in the cream and lemon juice. Press plastic wrap onto surface of custard. Refrigerate for several hours or overnight.

Fill cylinder of ice cream freezer two-thirds full; freeze according to the manufacturer's directions. Refrigerate remaining mixture until ready to freeze. Allow to ripen in ice cream freezer or firm up in the refrigerator freezer for 2-4 hours before serving. **Yield:** 2 quarts.

Apple Cream Tart

I enjoy making desserts like this delicious tart, which is seasoned with cinnamon and nutmeg and topped with whipped cream. I don't know where I got the recipe, but I like it because it's so easy to prepare.
—_Lyle Borcherding, Johnstown, Pennsylvania_

- 1-1/2 **cups all-purpose flour**
- 3 **tablespoons sugar**
- 1/4 **teaspoon salt**
- 1/2 **cup cold butter**
- **FILLING:**
- 3 **large tart apples, peeled and sliced**
- 1/2 **cup sugar**
- 1 **teaspoon ground cinnamon**
- 1/4 **teaspoon ground nutmeg**
- 1 **cup heavy whipping cream**
- 2 **egg yolks**
- **Whipped cream, optional**

In a large bowl, combine the flour, sugar and salt; cut in the butter until mixture resembles coarse crumbs. Press onto the bottom and 1 in. up the sides of a greased 9-in. springform pan. Arrange the apple slices over the crust. Combine the sugar, cinnamon and nutmeg; sprinkle over the apples. Place pan on a baking sheet. Bake at 400° for 15 minutes.

In a small mixing bowl, beat the whipping cream and egg yolks; pour over the apples. Bake 25-30 minutes longer or until the apples are tender and the filling is almost set. Cool on a wire rack for 1 hour. Remove sides of pan. Serve with whipped cream if desired. Store in the refrigerator. **Yield:** 8-10 servings.

Butternut Apple Crisp

(Pictured below)

I had this recipe in my box for years before I finally tried it—and now we love it! It's become my son-in-law's favorite. —Barbara Ellis, Bridgewater, Massachusetts

- 1 small butternut squash (about 1 pound)
- 3 medium tart apples, peeled and sliced
- 1/4 cup corn syrup
- 2 tablespoons lemon juice
- 3/4 cup packed brown sugar
- 1 tablespoon cornstarch
- 1 teaspoon ground cinnamon
- 1/2 teaspoon salt
- OAT TOPPING:
- 1/2 cup all-purpose flour
- 1/2 cup quick-cooking oats
- 1/4 cup packed brown sugar
- 6 tablespoons cold butter
- Vanilla ice cream

Peel squash and cut in half lengthwise; discard seeds. Cut squash into thin slices. In a large bowl, toss the squash, apples, corn syrup and lemon juice. Combine the brown sugar, cornstarch, cinnamon and salt; stir into squash mixture. Transfer to a greased 13-in. x 9-in. x 2-in. baking dish. Cover and bake at 375° for 20 minutes.

In a small bowl, combine the flour, oats and brown sugar; cut in butter until mixture resembles coarse crumbs. Sprinkle over squash mixture. Bake 25 minutes longer or until squash and apples are tender and topping is lightly browned. Serve warm with ice cream. **Yield:** 6-8 servings.

Soft Chewy Caramels

One of my first experiences with cooking was helping my mother make these caramels for Christmas. We'd make up to 12 batches each year. Today, I do at least 95 percent of the cooking at home, but my wife does much of the baking. —Robert Sprenkle
Hurst, Texas

- 1 tablespoon plus 1 cup butter, *divided*
- 2-1/4 cups packed brown sugar
- 1 can (14 ounces) sweetened condensed milk
- 1 cup dark corn syrup

Line a 15-in. x 10-in. x 1-in. baking pan with foil; grease the foil with 1 tablespoon butter. In a heavy saucepan over medium heat, melt remaining butter. Add brown sugar, milk and corn syrup. Cook and stir until candy thermometer reads 250° (hardball stage). Pour into prepared pan (do not scrape saucepan). Cool completely before cutting. **Yield:** about 2-1/2 pounds.

Editor's Note: We recommend that you test your candy thermometer before each use by bringing water to a boil; the thermometer should read 212°. Adjust your recipe temperature up or down based on your test.

Lemon Pudding Cups

Love lemon? This delightful dessert is sure to satisfy. This recipe is a favorite from my mother's church cookbook. The sherbet-gelatin mixture, with little flecks of lemon peel, is light and creamy. With a dollop of reduced-fat whipped topping, the fast-to-fix cups are attractive enough to serve guests. —Dolly Jones
Highland, Indiana

✓ Uses less fat, sugar or salt. Includes Nutritional Analysis and Diabetic Exchanges.

- 1 package (.3 ounce) sugar-free lemon gelatin
- 2 cups boiling water
- 1 pint lemon sherbet, softened
- 1 tablespoon lemon juice
- 1 tablespoon grated lemon peel
- 6 tablespoons reduced-fat whipped topping

In a large bowl, dissolve gelatin in boiling water. Slowly stir in the sherbet, lemon juice and lemon

peel. Pour into six dessert cups. Cover and refrigerate overnight. Garnish with whipped topping. **Yield:** 6 servings.

Nutritional Analysis: One serving (1/2 cup pudding with 1 tablespoon whipped topping) equals 84 calories, 1 g fat (1 g saturated fat), 3 mg cholesterol, 56 mg sodium, 16 g carbohydrate, trace fiber, 1 g protein. **Diabetic Exchange:** 1 fruit.

Chocolate Pecan Ice Cream Torte

(Pictured on page 128 and on cover)

This delectable dessert layers my favorite ice cream (chocolate) and my husband's favorite (butter pecan) on a shortbread crust, along with chocolate candy pieces, toasted pecans and caramel topping. It never fails to impress our guests. —*Kelly Arvay*
Barberton, Ohio

  1 jar (12-1/4 ounces) caramel ice cream
     topping
  2 milk chocolate candy bars (1.55 ounces
     each), chopped
 12 pecan shortbread cookies, crushed
  3 tablespoons butter, melted
  1 cup pecan halves, toasted, *divided*
1/2 gallon butter pecan ice cream, slightly
     softened
1/2 gallon chocolate ice cream, slightly
     softened

In a microwave-safe bowl, combine the caramel topping and candy bars. Microwave, uncovered, on high for 1-1/2 minutes or until candy bars are melted, stirring every 30 seconds. Cool.

Combine the cookie crumbs and butter. Press onto the bottom of a greased 10-in. springform pan. Chop 1/2 cup pecans; set aside. Spoon half of the butter pecan ice cream over crust. Drizzle with 2 tablespoons caramel sauce; sprinkle with 1/4 cup chopped pecans.

Spread half of the chocolate ice cream over top. Drizzle with 2 tablespoons caramel sauce; sprinkle with remaining chopped pecans.

Spoon remaining butter pecan ice cream around the edge of pan; spread remaining chocolate ice cream in center of pan. Cover and freeze overnight.

Carefully run a knife around edge of pan to loosen; remove sides of pan. Top with remaining pecan halves; drizzle with 2 tablespoons caramel sauce. Serve with remaining caramel sauce. **Yield:** 16-20 servings.

Editor's Note: This recipe was tested in a 1,100-watt microwave.

Butter Pecan Ice Cream

(Pictured above)

This rich buttery ice cream sure beats store-bought versions. And with its pretty color and plentiful pecan crunch, it's nice to serve at a summer party.
—*Jenny White, Glen, Mississippi*

1/2 cup chopped pecans
  1 tablespoon butter
1-1/2 cups half-and-half cream
  1 cup packed brown sugar
  2 eggs, lightly beaten
1/2 cup heavy whipping cream
  1 teaspoon vanilla extract

In a small skillet, toast pecans in butter for 5-6 minutes or until lightly browned. Cool.

In a heavy saucepan, heat half-and-half to 175°; stir in the brown sugar until dissolved. Whisk a small amount of hot cream mixture into the eggs; return all to the pan, whisking constantly. Cook and stir over low heat until mixture reaches at least 160° and coats the back of a metal spoon.

Remove from the heat. Cool quickly by placing pan in a bowl of ice water; stir for 2 minutes. Stir in whipping cream and vanilla. Press plastic wrap onto surface of custard. Refrigerate for several hours or overnight. Stir in toasted pecans.

Fill cylinder of ice cream freezer two-thirds full; freeze according to the manufacturer's directions. Refrigerate remaining mixture until ready to freeze. Allow to ripen in ice cream freezer or firm up in the refrigerator freezer for 2-4 hours before serving. **Yield:** 1 quart.

New York-Style Cheesecake

(Pictured below)

My mother-in-law got this recipe from an Italian friend many years ago. I added the chocolate-nut crust. It is our very favorite dessert. —Gloria Warczak
Cedarburg, Wisconsin

1-1/4 cups crushed chocolate wafers
1/2 cup chopped walnuts
1/3 cup sugar
1/2 cup butter, melted
FILLING:
  2 packages (8 ounces *each*) cream cheese, softened
  3 tablespoons sour cream
1/3 cup sugar
  2 eggs, lightly beaten
1/2 cup evaporated milk
  1 teaspoon lemon juice
TOPPING:
  2 cups (16 ounces) sour cream
  5 tablespoons sugar
  1 teaspoon vanilla extract
Cherry pie filling

In a bowl, combine the wafer crumbs, walnuts and sugar; stir in butter. Press onto the bottom and halfway up the sides of an ungreased 10-in. spring-form pan. Freeze for 15 minutes.

In a mixing bowl, beat the cream cheese, sour cream and sugar until fluffy and smooth. Add eggs; beat on low speed just until combined. Combine milk and lemon juice; add to cream cheese mixture just until blended. Pour into crust. Place pan on a baking sheet. Bake at 350° for 35-40 minutes or until center is almost set.

Combine the sour cream, sugar and vanilla; carefully spread over cheesecake. Bake 10 minutes longer. Cool on a wire rack for 10 minutes. Carefully run a knife around edge of pan to loosen; cool 1 hour longer. Cover; chill overnight. Remove sides of pan. Top with cherry pie filling. Refrigerate leftovers. **Yield:** 12 servings.

GUESTS will say "yes" to New York-Style Cheesecake and Ginger Toffee Cheesecake (shown below, from top).

Ginger Toffee Cheesecake

(Pictured below left)

While I was spending the winter in Florida, I had my neighbors over for this creamy cheesecake. They all came back for another piece! —Jacqueline Bryson-Kapp
Landisburg, Pennsylvania

> 2 cups crushed gingersnaps (about 34 cookies)
> 1/2 cup English toffee bits *or* almond brickle chips
> 2 tablespoons butter, melted

FILLING:

> 2 packages (8 ounces *each*) cream cheese, softened
> 1 cup sugar
> 1/4 cup all-purpose flour
> 3 eggs, lightly beaten
> 1-1/2 cups (12 ounces) sour cream
> 2 teaspoons vanilla extract

TOPPING:

> 3/4 cup caramel ice cream topping
> 1/2 cup English toffee bits *or* almond brickle chips

In a bowl, combine cookie crumbs and toffee bits; stir in butter. Press onto the bottom and 2 in. up the sides of an ungreased 9-in. springform pan.

In a large mixing bowl, beat cream cheese and sugar until smooth. Beat in flour. Add eggs; beat on low speed just until combined. Beat in sour cream and vanilla just until blended. Pour into crust. Place pan on a baking sheet.

Bake at 350° for 45-50 minutes or until center is almost set. Cool on a wire rack for 10 minutes. Carefully run a knife around edge of pan to loosen; cool for 1 hour. Cover and chill overnight. Remove sides of pan. Combine topping ingredients; serve with cheesecake. Refrigerate leftovers. **Yield:** 12 servings.

Chocolate Ice Cream Sandwiches

These cute chewy cookies made with two kinds of chocolate form a perfect sandwich for vanilla ice cream...or any flavor ice cream you prefer. I really enjoy making desserts for my family, and this one hits the spot on hot Texas days. —Michelle Wolford, San Antonio, Texas

> 1/3 cup butter, softened
> 1/3 cup sugar
> 1/3 cup packed brown sugar
> 1 egg
> 1/2 teaspoon vanilla extract
> 3/4 cup plus 2 tablespoons all-purpose flour
> 1/4 cup baking cocoa
> 1/2 teaspoon baking powder
> 1/4 teaspoon baking soda
> 1/4 teaspoon salt
> 1/2 cup semisweet chocolate chips
> 1 pint vanilla ice cream

In a mixing bowl, cream butter and sugars. Beat in the egg and vanilla. Combine the flour, cocoa, baking powder, baking soda and salt; add to creamed mixture and mix well.

Drop by rounded tablespoonfuls 2 in. apart onto greased baking sheets, forming 16 cookies. Flatten slightly with a glass. Sprinkle with chocolate chips. Bake at 375° for 8-10 minutes or until set. Remove to wire racks to cool.

To assemble sandwiches, place 1/4 cup ice cream on the bottom of half the cookies. Top with remaining cookies. Wrap each in plastic wrap. Freeze overnight. **Yield:** 8 ice cream sandwiches.

Peach Ice Cream

When peaches are in season, this recipe is at the top of my list to make. The fruit lends a fresh flavor to the silky-smooth ice cream. —Toni Box, Weaver, Alabama

> 2 cups half-and-half cream
> 3-1/2 cups sugar
> 3/4 teaspoon salt
> 6 eggs, beaten
> 4 cups heavy whipping cream
> 2 teaspoons vanilla extract
> 6 to 8 medium fresh peaches, peeled and sliced *or* 4 cups frozen unsweetened peach slices

In a saucepan, heat half-and-half to 175°; stir in the sugar and salt until dissolved. Whisk a small amount of hot cream mixture into the eggs. Return all to the pan, whisking constantly. Cook and stir over low heat until the mixture reaches at least 160° and coats the back of a metal spoon.

Remove from the heat. Cool quickly by placing pan in a bowl of ice water; stir for 2 minutes. Stir in whipping cream and vanilla. Press plastic wrap onto surface of custard. Refrigerate for several hours or overnight.

In a blender or food processor, puree peaches. Stir into the custard. Fill cylinder of ice cream freezer two-thirds full; freeze according to the manufacturer's directions.

Refrigerate remaining mixture until ready to freeze, stirring before freezing each batch. Allow to ripen in ice cream freezer or firm up in refrigerator freezer for 2-4 hours before serving. **Yield:** about 3 quarts.

Black Forest Crepes

(Pictured below)

I like this recipe because it is easy to make. I often prepare the crepes and filling in advance, assembling them and adding the topping just before serving.
— *Irene Menninga, Grand Rapids, Michigan*

　　1 can (21 ounces) cherry pie filling
　　1 teaspoon almond extract
　2/3 cup milk
　　2 eggs
　　2 tablespoons butter, melted
　1/4 cup blanched almonds, ground
　1/4 cup all-purpose flour
FILLING:
　　1 cup heavy whipping cream
　　3 squares (1 ounce *each*) semisweet
　　　chocolate, melted and cooled
　1/4 cup slivered almonds, toasted

In a small bowl, combine pie filling and almond extract; cover and refrigerate until chilled. For crepes, place the milk, eggs, butter, almonds and flour in a blender; cover and process until smooth.

Heat a lightly greased 8-in. nonstick skillet; pour about 2 tablespoons batter into center of skillet. Lift and tilt pan to coat bottom evenly. Cook until top appears dry and bottom is golden brown; turn and cook 15-20 seconds longer. Remove to a wire rack. Repeat with remaining batter, greasing skillet as needed. Stack cooled crepes with waxed paper or paper towels in between.

For the filling, in a mixing bowl, beat cream and melted chocolate until soft peaks form. Spoon about 2 tablespoons over each crepe; roll up. Top

with cherry mixture and sprinkle with slivered almonds. **Yield:** 6 servings.

Cherry Nut Ice Cream

Since my husband is a cherry grower, I had our grandsons help me develop an ice cream recipe that used the fruit. This is what we came up with. Loaded with almonds, coconut, chocolate and cherries, this ice cream has become our family's all-time favorite.
— *Mary Lou Patrick, East Wenatchee, Washington*

　　6 cups heavy whipping cream
　　3 egg yolks
　　1 cup sugar
　1/8 teaspoon salt
　　3 teaspoons almond extract
　　2 cups fresh *or* frozen pitted dark sweet
　　　cherries, thawed and cut into quarters
　　1 cup flaked coconut, toasted
　　1 cup sliced almonds, toasted
　　1 milk chocolate candy bar (7 ounces),
　　　chopped

In a large saucepan, heat cream over medium heat until bubbles form around sides of saucepan. In a heavy saucepan, combine the egg yolks, sugar and salt; whisk in a small amount of hot cream. Gradually whisk in remaining cream. Cook and stir over low heat until the mixture reaches at least 160° and coats the back of a metal spoon.

Remove from the heat. Cool quickly by placing pan in a bowl of ice water; stir for 2 minutes. Stir in almond extract. Press plastic wrap onto surface of custard. Refrigerate for several hours or overnight.

Fill cylinder of ice cream freezer two-thirds full; freeze according to the manufacturer's directions. Refrigerate remaining mixture until ready to freeze.

Stir the cherries, coconut, almonds and chocolate into the ice cream just until combined. Allow to ripen in ice cream freezer or firm up in the refrigerator freezer for 2-4 hours before serving. **Yield:** 1-1/2 quarts.

Raspberry Pear Crisp

If you want a change of pace from the usual pie or cake, give this honey of a dessert a try. It's tart, crispy and just plain good.
— *Ruby Williams
Bogalusa, Louisiana*

✓ Uses less fat, sugar or salt. Includes Nutritional Analysis and Diabetic Exchanges.

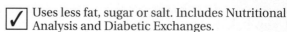

2 medium ripe pears, peeled and thinly sliced
3 cups fresh raspberries
2 tablespoons sugar
1 cup quick-cooking oats
1/4 cup honey
3 tablespoons stick margarine, melted
1 teaspoon ground cinnamon
1/2 teaspoon ground nutmeg

Place pears in an 8-in. square baking dish coated with nonstick cooking spray. Sprinkle with raspberries and sugar. Combine the remaining ingredients. Sprinkle over berries. Bake, uncovered, at 350° for 30-35 minutes or until pears are tender and mixture is bubbly. **Yield:** 8 servings.

Nutritional Analysis: One serving equals 151 calories, 3 g fat (1 g saturated fat), 0 cholesterol, 46 mg sodium, 30 g carbohydrate, 5 g fiber, 2 g protein. **Diabetic Exchange:** 2 fruit.

Strawberry Cheesecake Ice Cream

This custard-like ice cream is so rich and creamy that it tastes like you fussed for hours. —Irene Yoder
Fillmore, New York

3 cups sugar
3 tablespoons all-purpose flour
Pinch salt
8 cups milk
4 eggs, lightly beaten
1 package (8 ounces) cream cheese, cubed
1 teaspoon vanilla extract
3 cups mashed fresh *or* frozen unsweetened strawberries
2 cups heavy whipping cream

In a heavy saucepan, combine sugar, flour and salt. Gradually add milk until smooth. Bring to a boil over medium heat; cook and stir for 2 minutes or until thickened. Remove from heat; cool slightly.

Whisk a small amount of hot milk mixture into the eggs; return all to the pan, whisking constantly. Cook and stir over low heat until mixture reaches at least 160° and coats the back of a metal spoon. Stir in the cream cheese until melted.

Remove from the heat. Cool quickly by placing pan in a bowl of ice water; stir for 2 minutes. Stir in vanilla. Press plastic wrap onto surface of custard. Refrigerate for several hours or overnight.

Stir strawberries and cream into custard. Fill cylinder of ice cream freezer two-thirds full; freeze according to manufacturer's directions. Refrigerate remaining mixture until ready to freeze. Allow to ripen in ice cream freezer or firm up in refrigerator freezer for 2-4 hours before serving. **Yield:** 1 gallon.

Banana-Berry Brownie Pizza

(Pictured above)

I like to make this dessert in June and early July so I can use fresh local strawberries. The fruit lightens up the rich chocolate taste and pleases everyone.
—Tina Jacobs, Wantage, New Jersey

1 package brownie mix (13-inch x 9-inch pan size)
1/3 cup boiling water
1/4 cup vegetable oil
1 egg
TOPPING:
1 package (8 ounces) cream cheese, softened
1/4 cup sugar
1 egg
1 teaspoon vanilla extract
2 cups sliced fresh strawberries
1 to 2 medium firm bananas, sliced
1 square (1 ounce) semisweet chocolate, melted

In a bowl, combine brownie mix, water, oil and egg until well blended. Spread into a greased and floured 12-in. pizza pan. Bake at 350° for 25 minutes.

In a mixing bowl, beat the cream cheese, sugar, egg and vanilla until combined. Spread over brownie crust. Bake 15 minutes longer or until topping is set. Cool on a wire rack.

Just before serving, arrange strawberries and bananas over topping; drizzle with chocolate. Refrigerate leftovers. **Yield:** 10-12 servings.

Potluck Pleasers

Serve a small gathering or cook for a crowd with the large-quantity recipes here. Main dishes, sides and sweets are sized for 12 to 100.

FIT FOR A CROWD. Clockwise from upper left: Egg Salad for a Crowd (p. 164), Seafood Chowder (p. 155), Tenderloin Spinach Spirals (p. 154), Orange Cream Freezer Dessert (p. 158) and Cheery Cherry Compote (p. 158).

Chicken Pom-Poms

(Pictured below)

These golden baked croquettes are a fun and different way to serve chicken to a crowd. My husband and I are hosts at a mission house where we cook for groups of 30 or more each week. This recipe is a favorite with guests. —Fran Wolfley, St. Mary, Jamaica

        4 celery ribs, chopped
        1 large onion, finely chopped
        1 cup butter, cubed
        2 cups all-purpose flour
        3 teaspoons poultry seasoning
        1 teaspoon salt
        1 teaspoon pepper
        2 cartons (32 ounces *each*) chicken broth
        2 cups nonfat dry milk powder
    1/4 cup chicken bouillon granules
       16 cups cooked long grain rice
       12 cups chopped cooked chicken
        8 cups (32 ounces) shredded cheddar
            cheese
       10 cups soft bread crumbs
        3 tablespoons paprika
       10 jars (12 ounces *each*) chicken gravy

In a large Dutch oven or stockpot, saute celery and onion in butter until tender. Combine the flour, poultry seasoning, salt and pepper; stir into vegetable mixture until blended. Gradually stir in broth until blended. Add the milk powder and bouillon. Cook and stir until mixture comes to a boil; cook and stir 1-2 minutes longer or until very thick. Cool. Cover and refrigerate for at least 3 hours.

Stir the rice, chicken and cheese into sauce mixture. Combine bread crumbs and paprika in a shallow baking pan. Shape 1/4 cupfuls of chicken mixture into 2-in. balls; roll in crumb mixture. Place 3 in. apart on lightly greased baking sheets. Bake at 400° for 25-30 minutes or until heated through and golden brown. Heat the gravy; serve with pom-poms. **Yield:** 40-45 servings (2 pom-poms each).

Tenderloin Spinach Spirals

(Pictured on page 152)

Here's an elegant make-ahead dish that always gets compliments. It's nice for a summer buffet when grilling for a group just doesn't fit the bill. —Marlene Muckenhirn, Delano, Minnesota

        2 packages (10 ounces *each*) frozen
            chopped spinach, thawed and
            squeezed dry
        2 cups (8 ounces) shredded cheddar
            cheese
    1/2 cup raisins, coarsely chopped
    1/2 cup egg substitute
    1/4 cup beef broth
    1/4 cup chopped green onions
        2 teaspoons salt
        2 garlic cloves, minced
    1/4 teaspoon pepper
        2 whole beef tenderloins (2-1/2 to 3
            pounds *each*)
        2 tablespoons olive oil

In a large bowl, combine the first nine ingredients. Set aside.

Cut each tenderloin horizontally from the long side to within 1/2 in. of opposite side. Open so meat lies flat; cover with plastic wrap. Flatten to 1/2-in. thickness; remove plastic wrap. Spread the spinach mixture over each tenderloin to within 1 in. of edges. Roll up jelly-roll style, starting with a long side; tie at 1-in. intervals with kitchen string. Place seam side down on a greased rack in a shallow roasting pan; brush with oil.

Bake, uncovered, at 425° for 45-60 minutes or until meat reaches desired doneness (for rare, a meat thermometer should read 140°; medium, 160°; well-done, 170°). Let stand for 10 minutes. Cover and refrigerate until chilled. Discard kitchen string; cut into 1/2-in. slices. **Yield:** 24 servings.

Seafood Chowder

(Pictured on page 152)

My husband, Chad, is an avid fisherman. When a family party was planned and we had to bring something, we created this recipe using fish from our freezer. The chowder got rave reviews from the relatives!
—Heather Saunders
Belchertown, Massachusetts

1/2 pound sliced bacon, diced
  2 medium onions, chopped
  6 cups diced peeled potatoes
  4 cups water
  1 pound bay *or* sea scallops, quartered
  1 pound fresh *or* frozen lobster, cut into 1-inch pieces
  1 pound uncooked medium shrimp, peeled and deveined
  1 pound cod, cut into 1-inch pieces
  1 pound haddock, cut into 1-inch pieces
1/2 cup butter, melted
  4 teaspoons salt
  4 teaspoons minced fresh parsley
1/2 teaspoon curry powder
  2 quarts milk
  1 can (12 ounces) evaporated milk

In a large soup kettle or stockpot, cook bacon over medium heat until crisp. Remove with a slotted spoon to paper towels; reserve the drippings. Saute the onions in drippings until tender. Add potatoes and water; bring to a boil. Cook for 10 minutes.

Add the scallops, lobster, shrimp, cod and haddock. Cook for 10 minutes or until scallops are opaque, shrimp turn pink and fish flakes easily with a fork. Add the butter, salt, parsley and curry powder. Stir in milk and evaporated milk; heat through. Garnish with bacon. **Yield:** 32 servings (8 quarts).

Potatoes for a Crowd

(Pictured above right)

Here's a creamy, comforting potato casserole to make when you need a side dish sure to please a large group. It's so simple to assemble, and everyone likes the flavor.
—Merrill Powers, Spearville, Kansas

  5 cans (12 ounces *each*) evaporated milk
7-1/2 cups milk
  5 cans (10-3/4 ounces *each*) condensed cheddar cheese soup, undiluted
  5 cans (10-3/4 ounces *each*) condensed cream of chicken soup, undiluted

  1 pound butter, melted
  1 package (12 ounces) cornflakes, crushed
  3 medium onions, finely chopped
10 packages (2 pounds *each*) frozen cubed hash brown potatoes, thawed

In several large bowls, combine all ingredients. Transfer to 10 greased 11-in. x 7-in. x 2-in. baking dishes. Bake, uncovered, at 350° for 45-55 minutes or until potatoes are tender. **Yield:** 10 casseroles (about 10 servings each).

⌣ *Transporting Tip*

When transporting a covered casserole dish that has side handles, you can keep the lid from coming off with the help of two rubber bands. Put one over the lid knob and stretch it over one of the handles. Stretch the second rubber band from the knob over the opposite handle.

Remove the hot pad from the casserole carrier and place it under the dish to serve. It keeps the casserole hotter during serving time.

Golden Baked Chicken

(Pictured below and on cover)

This recipe makes a delicious, crispy chicken without frying. The paprika gives the chicken pieces a pleasant punch, plus pretty color. —Harriet Stichter
Milford, Indiana

      2 cups mashed potato flakes
    3/4 cup grated Parmesan cheese
      2 tablespoons dried parsley flakes
      1 tablespoon paprika
    3/4 teaspoon garlic salt
    3/4 teaspoon onion powder
    1/2 teaspoon pepper
      3 broiler/fryer chickens (3 to 4 pounds
        each), cut up and skin removed
      1 cup butter, melted

In a bowl, combine the potato flakes, Parmesan cheese, parsley, paprika, garlic salt, onion powder and pepper. Dip chicken into butter, then into potato flake mixture. Place on two greased 15-in. x 10-in. x 1-in. baking pans. Bake at 375° for 50-60 minutes or until chicken juices run clear. **Yield:** 12 servings.

Cheesy Potatoes 'n' Peppers

(Pictured below)

Roasted red sweet peppers add a dash of color to this hearty potato casserole. It has become a dinner tradition of ours at Christmastime. —Sherri Jackson
Chillicothe, Ohio

      2 cups chopped onions
      6 tablespoons butter
      6 tablespoons all-purpose flour
    1/2 to 1 teaspoon salt
    1/2 teaspoon pepper

HAPPY HOLIDAY get-togethers will be even more festive with Peanut Butter Brownies, Cheesy Potatoes 'n' Peppers, Confetti Bean Salad and Golden Baked Chicken (shown above, clockwise from top left).

4 cups milk
2 cups (8 ounces) shredded Swiss cheese
4 pounds potatoes, peeled and thinly sliced
2 jars (7 ounces *each*) roasted red peppers, drained and coarsely chopped

In a large skillet, saute onions in butter until tender. Whisk in flour, salt and pepper until blended. Gradually add milk. Bring to a boil over medium heat. Cook and stir for 2 minutes or until sauce is thickened. Remove from heat. Stir in cheese until smooth.

Place half of the potatoes in two greased 11-in. x 7-in. x 2-in. baking dishes. Pour half of sauce over potatoes. Top with half to two-thirds of peppers and remaining potatoes. Pour remaining sauce over potatoes. Sprinkle with remaining peppers.

Cover; bake at 350° for 1-1/4 hours. Uncover and bake 10-15 minutes longer or until potatoes are tender and sauce is thickened. **Yield:** 12-16 servings.

Confetti Bean Salad

(Pictured at left)

I shared this recipe with a friend a while back. Now we kid about who will make it when we're attending the same event! No matter who brings the salad, it's always a hit at get-togethers. —Doreen Storz
Bloomsburg, Pennsylvania

✓ Uses less fat, sugar or salt. Includes Nutritional Analysis and Diabetic Exchanges.

1 can (16 ounces) kidney beans, rinsed and drained
1 can (15 ounces) garbanzo beans *or* chickpeas, rinsed and drained
1 can (15 ounces) black beans, rinsed and drained
1 package (10 ounces) frozen corn, thawed
1/2 cup minced fresh cilantro
1/2 cup chopped sweet red pepper
1/2 cup chopped green pepper
1/4 cup chopped onion
1 small jalapeno pepper, seeded and finely chopped*, optional
2 garlic cloves, minced
1/2 cup balsamic vinegar
1/4 cup olive *or* canola oil
1 teaspoon chili powder
1/2 teaspoon sugar

In a large bowl, combine first 10 ingredients. In a jar with a tight-fitting lid, combine the vinegar, oil, chili powder and sugar; shake well. Pour over bean mixture; toss to coat. Cover and refrigerate overnight. Serve with a slotted spoon. **Yield:** 12 servings.

Nutritional Analysis: One 2/3-cup serving equals 179 calories, 6 g fat (1 g saturated fat), 0 cholesterol, 120 mg sodium, 27 g carbohydrate, 7 g fiber, 7 g protein. **Diabetic Exchanges:** 1-1/2 starch, 1 lean meat.

*Editor's Note: When cutting or seeding hot peppers, use rubber or plastic gloves to protect your hands. Avoid touching your face.

Peanut Butter Brownies

(Pictured below left)

A friend of mine gave me the recipe for these layered brownies, but I added my own touch—chunky peanut butter. Every time I take it to a group gathering, I get requests for the recipe. It's a real crowd-pleaser!
—Judy Sims, Weatherford, Texas

1-1/2 cups butter, *divided*
3/4 cup baking cocoa, *divided*
4 eggs
2 cups sugar
1 teaspoon vanilla extract
1-1/2 cups all-purpose flour
1/2 teaspoon salt
1 jar (18 ounces) chunky peanut butter
1/3 cup milk
10 large marshmallows
2 cups confectioners' sugar

In a saucepan, melt 1 cup butter; stir in 1/2 cup cocoa until smooth. Remove from the heat. In mixing bowl, combine the eggs, sugar and vanilla; beat for 1 minute. Combine flour and salt; gradually add to egg mixture. Beat in cocoa mixture; mix well. Transfer to a greased 15-in. x 10-in. x 1-in. baking pan. Bake at 350° for 18-22 minutes or until toothpick inserted near the center comes out clean. Place on a wire rack.

Meanwhile, place peanut butter in a microwave-safe bowl. Microwave, uncovered, at 50% power for 2 minutes, stirring once. Stir until peanut butter is blended. Spread peanut butter over warm brownies. Refrigerate for 45 minutes or until peanut butter is set.

Place the remaining cocoa in a heavy saucepan. Stir in the milk until smooth; add the marshmallows and remaining butter. Cook and stir over medium heat until butter and marshmallows are melted and mixture is smooth. Remove from the heat. Gradually stir in confectioners' sugar. Spread over peanut butter layer. Refrigerate for at least 30 minutes. Cut into squares. **Yield:** 4 dozen.

Editor's Note: This recipe was tested in an 1100-watt microwave.

pecans. Pour over crust. Bake 25-30 minutes longer or until edges are firm and center is almost set. Cool on wire racks. Cut into bars. Refrigerate until serving. **Yield:** 6-8 dozen.

Orange Cream Freezer Dessert

(Pictured on page 152)

With its bold orange taste and cool smooth texture, this appealing ice cream dessert is a crowd-pleaser. People who ask me for the recipe can't believe how easy it is to make. Plus, it serves a bunch.
—Sharon Carroll, Whittier, California

4 cups graham cracker crumbs
3/4 cup sugar
1 cup butter, melted
3-1/2 quarts vanilla ice cream, softened
2 cans (12 ounces *each*) frozen orange juice concentrate, thawed

In a bowl, combine cracker crumbs and sugar; stir in butter. Set aside 2 cups for topping. Press remaining crumb mixture into two greased 15-in. x 10-in. x 1-in. pans. Cover and freeze for at least 10 minutes.

In a large bowl, combine ice cream and orange juice concentrate until smooth. Spoon over crusts (pans will be full). Freeze for 10 minutes or until partially firm.

Sprinkle with reserved crumb mixture; gently press down. Cover and freeze for up to 2 months. Remove from the freezer 15 minutes before serving. **Yield:** 2 desserts (24 servings each).

Cheery Cherry Compote

(Pictured on page 152)

I've made this pretty gelatin salad—loaded with fruit and berries—for potluck suppers and to serve following our ladies' Bible classes. You can vary the fruit and use sugar-free gelatin, if you prefer.
—Gale Conway, Warrenton, Missouri

2 packages (3 ounces *each*) cherry gelatin
2 cups boiling water
1 package (10 ounces) frozen sweetened sliced strawberries
1 can (21 ounces) cherry pie filling
1 can (20 ounces) pineapple chunks, drained
1 can (15 ounces) pear halves, drained and cut into chunks
3 medium firm bananas, sliced

Pecan Pie Bars

(Pictured above)

I love to cook large quantities and do most of the cooking for our church functions. People seem to enjoy these scrumptious bars even more than pecan pie.
—Clara Honeyager, North Prairie, Wisconsin

6 cups all-purpose flour
1-1/2 cups sugar
1 teaspoon salt
2 cups cold butter
FILLING:
8 eggs
3 cups sugar
3 cups corn syrup
1/2 cup butter, melted
3 teaspoons vanilla extract
5 cups chopped pecans

In a large bowl, combine the flour, sugar and salt. Cut in butter until crumbly. Press onto the bottom and up the sides of two greased 15-in. x 10-in. x 1-in. baking pans. Bake at 350° for 18-22 minutes or until crust edges are beginning to brown and bottom is set.

For filling, combine the eggs, sugar, corn syrup, butter and vanilla in a large bowl; mix well. Stir in

2 medium navel oranges, peeled, sectioned and chopped
2 medium tart apples, peeled and chopped
1 cup fresh *or* frozen blackberries, thawed

In a large bowl, dissolve gelatin in boiling water. Stir in the strawberries until thawed. Stir in the remaining ingredients. Transfer to a 4-qt. serving bowl. Cover and refrigerate for 3-4 hours before serving. **Yield:** 24 servings.

Bacon-Colby Lasagna

With both bacon and ground beef, this hearty dish pleases everyone. The recipe came from my grandmother, now in her 80s. I've learned so much from helping her in the kitchen. —*Cathy McCartney Davenport, Iowa*

2 pounds ground beef
2 medium onions, chopped
2 pounds sliced bacon, cooked and crumbled
2 cans (15 ounces *each*) tomato sauce
2 cans (14-1/2 ounces *each*) diced tomatoes, undrained
2 tablespoons sugar
1 teaspoon salt
24 lasagna noodles, cooked and drained
8 cups (32 ounces) shredded Colby cheese

In a Dutch oven, cook the beef and onions over medium heat until the meat is no longer pink; drain. Stir in the bacon, tomato sauce, tomatoes, sugar and salt; cook until heated through.

Spread 1 cup meat sauce in each of two greased 13-in. x 9-in. x 2-in. baking dishes. Layer four noodles, 1-2/3 cups meat sauce and 1-1/3 cups cheese in each dish. Repeat layers twice.

Cover and bake at 350° for 40 minutes. Uncover; bake 5-10 minutes longer or until bubbly. Let stand for 15 minutes before cutting. **Yield:** 2 casseroles (12 servings each).

Colossal Caramel Apple Trifle

(Pictured at right)

As a pastor's wife and state auxiliary leader, I host many large gatherings. Whenever I make this "punch bowl cake", it makes a big impression. I return with an empty bowl every time!
—*Deborah Randall, Abbeville, Louisiana*

1 package (18-1/4 ounces) yellow cake mix
6 cups cold milk
3 packages (3.4 ounces *each*) instant vanilla pudding mix
1 teaspoon apple pie spice
1 jar (12-1/4 ounces) caramel ice cream topping
1-1/2 cups chopped pecans, toasted
2 cans (21 ounces *each*) apple pie filling
2 cartons (16 ounces *each*) frozen whipped topping, thawed

Prepare and bake cake according to package directions, using two greased 9-in. round baking pans. Cool for 10 minutes before removing to wire racks to cool completely. In a large bowl, whisk milk, pudding mixes and apple pie spice for 2 minutes. Let stand for 2 minutes or until soft-set.

Cut one cake layer if necessary to fit evenly in an 8-qt. punch bowl. Poke holes in cake with a long wooden skewer; gradually pour a third of the caramel topping over cake. Sprinkle with 1/2 cup pecans and spread with half of the pudding mixture. Spoon one can of pie filling over pudding; spread with one carton of whipped topping.

Top with remaining cake and repeat layers. Drizzle with remaining caramel topping and sprinkle with remaining pecans. Refrigerate until serving. **Yield:** 42 servings (3/4 cup each).

Pecan Salmon Casserole

(Pictured below)

Peas, pecans and pimiento complement the salmon in this potluck-perfect dish that's topped with crushed potato chips for added crunch. It's great for family dinners, too. —*Edna Coburn, Tucson, Arizona*

1 package (16 ounces) small shell pasta
2 medium onions, finely chopped
1/2 pound sliced fresh mushrooms
1/4 cup butter, cubed
2 cans (10-3/4 ounces *each*) condensed cream of mushroom soup, undiluted
1-1/2 cups milk
2 teaspoons Worcestershire sauce
1 teaspoon salt
1/2 teaspoon pepper
2 cans (14-3/4 ounces *each*) salmon, drained, bones and skin removed
2 cups frozen peas
1 cup chopped pecans, toasted
1 jar (2 ounces) diced pimientos, drained
1/2 cup crushed potato chips

YOUR FAMILY will fall for hearty Pecan Salmon Casserole, Tender Dinner Knots, Cranberry Spinach Salad and Spiced Applesauce (shown above, clockwise from bottom left).

Cook pasta according to package directions. Meanwhile, in a large skillet, saute the onions and mushrooms in butter until tender. Stir in the soup, milk, Worcestershire sauce, salt and pepper until blended; bring to a boil. Remove from the heat.

Drain pasta. Add the pasta, salmon, peas, pecans and pimientos to the skillet. Transfer to a greased shallow 3-qt. baking dish. Cover and bake at 350° for 30-35 minutes or until heated through. Sprinkle with potato chips. **Yield:** 12 servings.

Tender Dinner Knots
(Pictured at left)

These yummy yeast rolls will dress up any meal. The cute knots look like you fussed, but the dough is so easy to work with that they're a cinch to shape. Folks are bound to be asking for another. —*Renae Moncur Burley, Idaho*

    1 **package (1/4 ounce) active dry yeast**
1/4 **cup warm water (110° to 115°)**
    1 **cup warm milk (110° to 115°)**
    1 **egg**
    2 **tablespoons sugar**
    2 **tablespoons shortening**
    1 **teaspoon salt**
3-1/2 **to 4 cups all-purpose flour**

In a large mixing bowl, dissolve yeast in warm water. Add the milk, egg, sugar, shortening, salt and 2 cups flour. Beat until smooth. Stir in enough remaining flour to form a soft dough. Turn onto a floured surface; knead until smooth and elastic, about 6-8 minutes. Place in a greased bowl, turning once to grease top. Cover and let rise in a warm place until doubled, about 1 hour.

Punch dough down. Turn onto a lightly floured surface; shape into 32 pieces. To form knots, roll each piece into a 10-in. rope; tie into a knot and tuck ends under. Place 2 in. apart on greased baking sheets. Cover and let rise in a warm place until doubled, about 25 minutes. Bake at 400° for 13-16 minutes or until golden brown. Remove from pans to wire racks. **Yield:** 32 rolls.

Cranberry Spinach Salad
(Pictured at left)

*If you want something new for your Thanksgiving menu, try this salad. Fresh spinach leaves are tossed with toasted almonds and dried cranberries, then driz-*zled with poppy seed dressing. It's likely to become a holiday tradition at your house, too.*
—*Michelle Krzmarzick, Redondo Beach, California*

    1 **package (10 ounces) fresh spinach, trimmed**
3/4 **cup dried cranberries**
    2 **green onions, sliced**
1/4 **cup sugar**
    1 **teaspoon dried minced onion**
3/4 **teaspoon poppy seeds**
1/8 **teaspoon paprika**
    2 **tablespoons cider vinegar**
    2 **tablespoons white wine vinegar**
1/4 **cup vegetable oil**
3/4 **cup sliced almonds, toasted**

In a large salad bowl, toss the spinach, cranberries and green onions. In a small bowl, combine the sugar, onion, poppy seeds and paprika; whisk in the vinegars and oil. Drizzle over salad. Sprinkle with almonds; toss to coat. **Yield:** 12 servings.

Spiced Applesauce
(Pictured at left)

Cardamom and mace add a bit of unusual spicy flavor to this homemade applesauce. It's a wonderful way to make use of autumn's apple bounty.
—*Janet Thomas, McKees Rocks, Pennsylvania*

☑ Uses less fat, sugar or salt. Includes Nutritional Analysis and Diabetic Exchanges.

    6 **pounds tart apples (about 18 medium), peeled and quartered**
    1 **cup apple cider *or* juice**
3/4 **cup sugar**
    2 **tablespoons lemon juice**
    1 **cinnamon stick (3 inches)**
    1 **teaspoon ground ginger**
    1 **teaspoon vanilla extract**
1/2 **teaspoon ground nutmeg**
1/2 **teaspoon ground mace**
1/4 **to 1/2 teaspoon ground cardamom**

Place all ingredients in a Dutch oven. Cover and cook over medium-low heat for 30-40 minutes or until apples are tender, stirring occasionally.

Remove from the heat; discard the cinnamon stick. Mash the apples to desired consistency. Serve warm or cold. Store in the refrigerator. **Yield:** 9 cups.

Nutritional Analysis: One serving (1/2 cup) equals 113 calories, trace fat (trace saturated fat), 0 cholesterol, 2 mg sodium, 29 g carbohydrate, 2 g fiber, trace protein. **Diabetic Exchange:** 2 fruit.

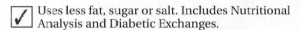

THINK SPRING for your next take-along dishes. Try out Pecan Chicken Casserole, Fruit Salad Dressing and Roasted Asparagus with Thyme (shown above, clockwise from bottom right).

Pecan Chicken Casserole

(Pictured above)

I got this recipe from a radio show years ago, and it's one of my favorites. The unusual pecan-and-cheddar-cheese crust holds a zippy egg filling flavored with chicken, cheese, dill, onion and a splash of hot pepper sauce.
—*Jackie Heyer, Cushing, Iowa*

1 cup all-purpose flour
1 cup (4 ounces) finely shredded cheddar cheese
3/4 cup finely chopped pecans
1/2 teaspoon salt
1/4 teaspoon paprika
1/3 cup vegetable oil
FILLING:
4 eggs
1 cup (8 ounces) sour cream
1 cup chicken broth
4 cups diced cooked chicken
1/2 cup finely shredded cheddar cheese
1/4 cup finely chopped onion
1/4 cup mayonnaise
1/4 teaspoon dill seed
1/8 teaspoon hot pepper sauce

In a bowl, combine the first six ingredients. Set aside 1/2 cup of crumb mixture for topping. Press remaining crumb mixture onto the bottom of a greased 13-in. x 9-in. x 2-in. baking dish. (Crust will be crumbly.) Bake at 350° for 10 minutes or until lightly browned.

In a bowl, beat eggs. Add remaining ingredients. Pour over baked crust. Sprinkle with reserved crumb mixture. Bake at 350° for 25-30 minutes or until a knife inserted near the center comes out clean. Let stand for 10 minutes before cutting. **Yield:** 12 servings.

Fruit Salad Dressing

(Pictured at left)

Served with seasonal fruit, this citrusy dressing makes a refreshing side dish or dessert for your next ladies' luncheon or breakfast buffet. It's a snap to make, too!
—Shirley Haase, Madison, Wisconsin

2/3 cup orange juice
3 tablespoons lemon juice
1 cup sugar
1 egg, lightly beaten
Assorted fresh fruit

In a small saucepan, combine juices, sugar and egg. Bring to a boil; cook and stir for 1 minute or until thickened. Strain. Cover; refrigerate until serving. Serve with fresh fruit. **Yield:** about 1 cup.

Roasted Asparagus with Thyme

(Pictured at left)

This good-for-you springtime side dish is so easy to prepare, yet the simply seasoned spears look appealing enough to serve guests or take to a carry-in dinner.
—Sharon Leno, Keansburg, New Jersey

✓ Uses less fat, sugar or salt. Includes Nutritional Analysis and Diabetic Exchanges.

3 pounds fresh asparagus, trimmed
3 tablespoons olive oil
2 teaspoons minced fresh thyme *or* 3/4
   teaspoon dried thyme
1/2 teaspoon salt
1/4 teaspoon pepper

Place asparagus in a roasting pan or baking pan lined with heavy-duty foil. Drizzle with oil and toss to coat. Sprinkle with the thyme, salt and pepper. Bake, uncovered, at 425° for 10-15 minutes or until crisp-tender. **Yield:** 12 servings.

Nutritional Analysis: One serving (7 to 8 spears) equals 55 calories, 4 g fat (trace saturated fat), 0 cholesterol, 101 mg sodium, 4 g carbohydrate, 1 g fiber, 3 g protein. **Diabetic Exchanges:** 1 vegetable, 1/2 fat.

Apricot Tea Rings

This coffee cake is a favorite of mine. It's attractive, delicious and cuts like a dream. Sometimes I use convenient canned pie filling when I want a different flavor and am pressed for time.
—Dot Christiansen
Bettendorf, Iowa

4-1/4 cups all-purpose flour
1/4 cup sugar
1 teaspoon salt
1/4 teaspoon ground nutmeg
2 packages (1/4 ounce *each*) active dry yeast
1 cup milk
1/4 cup water
1/4 cup butter, cubed
2 eggs
FILLING:
12 ounces dried apricots, diced
2 cups water
6 tablespoons brown sugar
4 teaspoons orange juice
1/2 cup chopped pecans
GLAZE:
1 cup confectioners' sugar
2 to 3 tablespoons milk

In a large mixing bowl, combine the first five ingredients. In a saucepan, heat the milk, water and butter to 120°-130°. Add to dry ingredients; beat until moistened. Beat in eggs until smooth. Cover and refrigerate overnight.

In a saucepan, combine apricots and water. Cook over medium heat for 30 minutes or until water is absorbed and apricots are tender. Remove from heat; stir in the brown sugar, juice and nuts. Cool.

Punch dough down. Turn onto a lightly floured surface; divide in half. Roll each into an 18-in. x 12-in. rectangle. Spread half of filling over each rectangle to within 1/2 in. of edges. Roll up each jelly-roll style, starting with a long side; pinch seam to seal.

Place seam side down on greased baking sheets; pinch ends of each together to form a ring. With scissors, cut each from outside edge two-thirds toward center of ring at 1-in. intervals. Separate strips slightly; twist so filling shows, slightly overlapping with previous piece. Cover; let rise in a warm place until doubled, about 1 hour. Bake at 375° for 25-28 minutes or until golden brown. Remove from pans to wire racks; cool. Combine glaze ingredients; drizzle over warm tea rings. **Yield:** 2 rings (12 servings each).

Pasta Bean Soup

(Pictured below)

This hearty Italian-style recipe proved very popular when I made it for about 90 people who attended our church's "Souper Sunday" one January. I fired up a couple of turkey deep fryers and simmered big batches of it outside! —Edward Reis, Phoenix, Arizona

       6 **large onions, chopped**
    2/3 **cup olive oil**
      18 **garlic cloves, minced**
      12 **cans (16 ounces** *each***) kidney beans, rinsed and drained**
       4 **cans (28 ounces** *each***) Italian crushed tomatoes**
       3 **cartons (32 ounces** *each***) chicken broth**
    1/4 **to 1/3 cup dried oregano**
       4 **tablespoons salt**
       1 **to 2 teaspoons pepper**
       3 **packages (1 pound** *each***) spaghetti, cut into fourths**
Grated Parmesan cheese, optional

In several soup kettles or Dutch ovens, saute onions in oil until tender. Add garlic; cook and stir about 2 minutes longer. Stir in the beans, tomatoes, broth, oregano, salt and pepper. Bring to a boil. Reduce heat; cover and simmer for at least 30 minutes. Cook spaghetti according to package directions; drain. Just before serving soup, stir in the spaghetti. Serve with Parmesan cheese if desired. **Yield:** 45-55 servings.

Egg Salad for a Crowd

(Pictured on page 152)

Black olives and vegetables add interest and texture to this big-batch egg salad I make. It's great for sandwiches and also goes a long way served on crackers as an appetizer. —Helen Lamison
Carnegie, Pennsylvania

       3 **dozen hard-cooked eggs, chopped**
       6 **celery ribs, chopped**
       3 **large carrots, finely shredded**
       3 **small green peppers, finely chopped**
       3 **small onions, finely chopped**
       3 **cans (2-1/4 ounces** *each***) sliced ripe olives, drained**
       3 **cups mayonnaise**
    3/4 **cup milk**
       1 **tablespoon ground mustard**
Salt and pepper to taste
Lettuce leaves, halved cherry tomatoes and sliced hard-cooked egg, optional
   100 bread slices (about 6 loaves)

In a large bowl, combine the first six ingredients. Whisk mayonnaise, milk, mustard, salt and pepper until smooth. Stir into egg mixture. Cover and refrigerate for at least 1 hour. Garnish with lettuce, tomatoes and sliced egg if desired.

For sandwiches, spread about 1/3 cupful egg salad on one bread slice; top with another bread slice. **Yield:** 50 sandwiches.

Cranberry Slush Punch

Its pretty color and tangy-sweet taste make this festive drink a hit at Christmastime. We also served it at my sister's wedding, where guests told us it was some of the best punch they'd ever tasted. It is an old family recipe. —Martha Artyomenko
Libby, Montana

       3 **cans (8 ounces** *each***) jellied cranberry sauce**
       2 **cans (12 ounces** *each***) lemonade concentrate**
       1 **can (12 ounces) cranberry apple juice concentrate**
       4 **cups water**

1 teaspoon ground cinnamon
1/2 teaspoon ground allspice
12 cups lemon-lime soda, chilled

In a bowl, combine the cranberry sauce, concentrates, water, cinnamon and allspice. Cover and freeze for 8 hours or overnight. Remove from the freezer 45 minutes before serving. For each serving, combine 1/2 cup slush mixture with 1/2 cup lemon-lime soda. **Yield:** 24 servings (1 cup each).

Blue Cheese Deviled Eggs

I hope you'll agree that blue cheese and a hint of hot pepper in the filling put these flavorful deviled eggs a step above the ordinary. They're always well received at a gathering. —Nina Hall
Citrus Heights, California

24 hard-cooked eggs
1 cup (4 ounces) crumbled blue cheese
2/3 cup mayonnaise
2 tablespoons minced fresh parsley
1 teaspoon hot pepper sauce
1/2 teaspoon celery seed
1/2 teaspoon pepper
Diced celery

Slice the eggs in half lengthwise; remove the yolks and set whites aside. In a bowl, mash yolks with a fork. Add the blue cheese, mayonnaise, parsley, hot pepper sauce, celery seed and pepper; stir until well blended. Evenly fill the whites. Refrigerate eggs until serving. Sprinkle with celery. **Yield:** 4 dozen.

Jambalaya Casserole

(Pictured above right)

Whenever family and friends get together, this is the dish I am asked to prepare. It's delicious, economical and easy to fix. —Evelynn Anderson Lugo
Kenner, Louisiana

3 large onions, chopped
3 large green peppers, chopped
3 celery ribs, chopped
12 garlic cloves, minced
1-1/2 cups butter
3 pounds fully cooked smoked sausage, cut into 1/2-inch slices
9 cups chicken broth
6 cups uncooked long grain rice
3 cups chopped fresh tomatoes

1-1/2 cups chopped green onions
1/2 cup minced fresh parsley
3 tablespoons Worcestershire sauce
3 tablespoons hot pepper sauce
3 tablespoons browning sauce, optional
1 tablespoon salt
1 tablespoon pepper

In a large skillet, saute onions, green peppers, celery and garlic in butter until crisp-tender. Place in a very large bowl; stir in the remaining ingredients.

Transfer to three greased shallow 3-qt. baking dishes. Cover and bake at 375° for 45-50 minutes or until rice is tender, stirring twice. **Yield:** 3 casseroles (8 servings each).

A "Gel" of an Idea

To serve gelatin at potlucks or picnics, pour it into individual plastic containers with a few small marshmallows on top. To make it more special, sprinkle with pastel marshmallows. Kids always enjoy this refreshing treat. Plus, this prevents spills that can occur when you're spooning from a larger bowl.

Sausage Pasta Sauce

(Pictured below)

Sweet peppers, onions and garlic give this red sauce its rich flavor, and a little cream gives it a smooth texture. Our toddlers love this recipe because the vegetables are "hidden" since they are pureed with the tomato sauce.
—Michelle Krzmarzick
Redondo Beach, California

 2 pounds bulk Italian sausage
 2 medium onions, chopped
 2 medium sweet red peppers, chopped
 2 medium green peppers, chopped
 6 to 8 garlic cloves, minced
 2 tablespoons olive oil
 2 cans (29 ounces *each*) tomato sauce
 2 cans (14-1/2 ounces *each*) Italian stewed
   tomatoes, drained
 2 tablespoons brown sugar
 4 teaspoons chili powder
 1 teaspoon garlic powder
 1 teaspoon dried oregano
 1 teaspoon dried basil
 1 teaspoon pepper
 1/4 to 1/2 teaspoon cayenne pepper
1-1/2 pounds uncooked bow tie pasta
 1/2 cup heavy whipping cream
Shredded Parmesan cheese

In a large skillet, cook sausage over medium heat until no longer pink; drain and set aside. In a Dutch oven, saute the onions, peppers and garlic in oil until tender. Stir in the tomato sauce, tomatoes, brown sugar and seasonings.

Cook pasta according to package directions. Meanwhile, in a blender or food processor, process tomato mixture in batches until smooth. Return to the pan. Add sausage; heat through. Gradually stir in cream. Cook and stir over low heat for 5 minutes. Drain pasta; top with sauce. Sprinkle with cheese. **Yield:** 12 servings.

FRESH-TASTING crowd-pleasing dishes like Italian Sweet Bread, Fruited Floret Salad, Sausage Pasta Sauce and Chippy Blond Brownies make any spring gathering a special event (shown above, clockwise from top).

Fruited Floret Salad

(Pictured below left)

Broccoli, cauliflower, carrots and peas are mixed together with juicy sweet grapes in this crunchy refreshing salad that always wins compliments! You can personalize the recipe by substituting your favorite vegetables and fruits. —Teresa Gunnell, Leesburg, Virginia

✓ Uses less fat, sugar or salt. Includes Nutritional Analysis and Diabetic Exchanges.

- **4 cups fresh broccoli florets (about 1 medium bunch)**
- **2 cups fresh cauliflowerets (about 1 medium head)**
- **6 large carrots, cut into 1/2-inch slices**
- **2 cups frozen peas, thawed**
- **3 celery ribs, chopped**
- **1/2 cup seedless green grapes**
- **1/2 cup seedless red grapes**
- **1/2 cup chopped onion**
- **1 cup mayonnaise**
- **1/2 cup milk**
- **2 tablespoons cider vinegar**
- **1 tablespoon sugar**
- **1/2 cup sunflower kernels _or_ mixed nuts, optional**

In a large bowl, toss broccoli, cauliflower, carrots, peas, celery, grapes and onion. In a small bowl, whisk mayonnaise, milk, vinegar and sugar; pour over broccoli mixture and toss to coat. Sprinkle with sunflower kernels if desired. **Yield:** 16 servings.

Nutritional Analysis: One 3/4-cup serving (prepared with fat-free mayonnaise, fat-free milk and without sunflower kernels) equals 62 calories, 1 g fat (trace saturated fat), 2 mg cholesterol, 172 mg sodium, 13 g carbohydrate, 3 g fiber, 3 g protein. **Diabetic Exchange:** 2 vegetable.

Italian Sweet Bread

(Pictured at left)

This golden brown bread offers satisfying sweetness in every slice. The hearty round loaves rise well and cut beautifully. With an egg wash and a sprinkling of Italian seasoning, the bread looks pretty, too.
—Kim Ooms, Cottage Grove, Minnesota

- **1 cup warm milk (70° to 80°)**
- **1 egg, lightly beaten**
- **2 tablespoons butter, softened**
- **1/4 cup sugar**
- **1 teaspoon salt**
- **3 cups all-purpose flour**

- **2 teaspoons active dry yeast**
- **EGG WASH:**
- **1 egg**
- **1 tablespoon water**
- **Italian seasoning, optional**

In bread machine pan, place the first seven ingredients in order suggested by manufacturer. Select the dough setting (check dough after 5 minutes of mixing; add 1 to 2 tablespoons of water or flour if needed).

When the cycle is completed, turn dough onto a floured surface. Divide in half. Shape each portion into a ball; flatten slightly. Place in two greased 9-in. round baking pans. Cover and let rise until doubled, about 45 minutes.

Beat egg and water; brush over the dough. Sprinkle with Italian seasoning if desired. Bake at 350° for 20-25 minutes or until golden brown. Remove from pans to wire racks to cool. **Yield:** 2 loaves (3/4 pound each).

Editor's Note: If your bread machine has a time-delay feature, we recommend you do not use it for this recipe.

Chippy Blond Brownies

(Pictured at left)

If you love chocolate and butterscotch, you won't be able to resist these chewy brownies. I often include this recipe inside a baking dish as a wedding present. Everyone, young and old, enjoys these sweet treats.
—Anna Jean Allen, West Liberty, Kentucky

- **6 tablespoons butter, softened**
- **1 cup packed brown sugar**
- **2 eggs**
- **1 teaspoon vanilla extract**
- **1-1/4 cups all-purpose flour**
- **1 teaspoon baking powder**
- **1/2 teaspoon salt**
- **1 cup (6 ounces) semisweet chocolate chips**
- **1/2 cup chopped pecans**

In a large mixing bowl, cream butter and brown sugar. Add the eggs, one at a time, beating well after each addition. Beat in vanilla. Combine the flour, baking powder and salt; gradually add to creamed mixture. Stir in the chocolate chips and pecans.

Spread into a greased 11-in. x 7-in. x 2-in. baking pan. Bake at 350° for 25-30 minutes or until a toothpick inserted near the center comes out clean. Cool on a wire rack. **Yield:** 2 dozen.

mozzarella cheese, Romano cheese, garlic powder, oregano, parsley and pepper.

Roll up each rectangle jelly-roll style, beginning with a long side. Seal seams and ends. Place seam side down on two greased baking sheets. Brush with egg yolk.

Bake at 375° for 25-30 minutes or until golden brown. Let stand for 5 minutes before slicing. Serve warm. Refrigerate leftovers. **Yield:** 4 loaves (8 slices each).

Meat Loaf for a Mob

Our small synagogue has two teams that alternate with churches of various denominations and civic organizations to provide meals at a homeless shelter. This tasty satisfying meat loaf is well liked there.
—*Niki Reese Eschen*
Santa Maria, California

> 8 **eggs, beaten**
> 1 **can (46 ounces) V8 juice**
> 2 **large onions, finely chopped**
> 4 **celery ribs, finely chopped**
> 4-1/4 **cups seasoned bread crumbs**
> 2 **envelopes onion soup mix**
> 2 **teaspoons pepper**
> 8 **pounds ground beef**
> 3/4 **cup ketchup**
> 1/3 **cup packed brown sugar**
> 1/4 **cup prepared mustard**

In a very large bowl, combine the eggs, V8 juice, onions, celery, bread crumbs, soup mix and pepper. Crumble beef over mixture; mix well. Shape into four loaves; place each loaf in a greased 13-in. x 9-in. x 2-in. baking dish. Bake, uncovered, at 350° for 45 minutes.

Meanwhile, combine the ketchup, brown sugar and mustard. Spread over loaves. Bake 15 minutes longer or until a meat thermometer reads 160°. **Yield:** 4 meat loaves (8 servings each).

Hearty Rice Dressing

At church socials and family reunions, this hearty dressing has always been well received. It's a favorite with our family, too. I cut back on the recipe to serve a smaller group.
—*Ruth Hayward*
Lake Charles, Louisiana

> 3 **pounds ground beef**
> 2 **pounds ground pork**

Three-Meat Stromboli

(Pictured above)

This hearty, spicy appetizer is a real crowd-pleaser. No one believes me when I tell them it's a simple recipe. I never have any leftovers.
—*Jude Mulvey*
East Schodack, New York

> 4 **loaves (1 pound *each*) frozen bread dough, thawed**
> 1/2 **pound thinly sliced deli salami**
> 1/2 **pound thinly sliced deli ham**
> 1/2 **pound thinly sliced pepperoni**
> 1/2 **pound thinly sliced provolone cheese**
> 2 **cups (8 ounces) shredded mozzarella cheese**
> 1/2 **cup grated Romano *or* Parmesan cheese**
> 1 **tablespoon garlic powder**
> 1 **tablespoon dried oregano**
> 1 **teaspoon dried parsley flakes**
> 1 **teaspoon pepper**
> 1 **egg yolk, beaten**

Let dough rise until doubled, according to package directions. Punch down. Roll each loaf into a 15-in. x 12-in. rectangle. Arrange a fourth of the salami, ham, pepperoni and provolone cheese over each rectangle. Sprinkle each with a fourth of the

2 large onions, chopped
3 celery ribs, chopped
1 large green pepper, chopped
1 jar (4 ounces) diced pimientos, drained
5 cups water
2 cans (10-3/4 ounces *each*) condensed cream of chicken soup, undiluted
2 cans (10-1/2 ounces *each*) condensed French onion soup, undiluted
1 can (10-3/4 ounces) condensed cream of mushroom soup, undiluted
2 tablespoons Creole seasoning
1 teaspoon salt
1 teaspoon pepper
1/2 teaspoon cayenne pepper
4 cups uncooked long grain rice

In several large Dutch ovens or stockpots, cook the beef, pork and onions over medium heat until meat is no longer pink; drain. Stir in the celery, green pepper and pimientos. Combine water and soups; stir in the Creole seasoning, salt, pepper and cayenne. Stir into meat mixture; bring to a boil. Stir in the rice.

Carefully transfer to three greased 13-in. x 9-in. x 2-in. baking dishes. Cover and bake at 350° for 30 minutes; stir. Cover and bake 30-40 minutes longer or until rice is tender. **Yield:** 45-50 servings.

Kiwi Dessert Squares

(Pictured at right)

Be ready to share the recipe for this do-ahead dessert for a large group. It's a real eye-catcher with taste to match!
—*Marlene Muckenhirn*
Delano, Minnesota

2 cups all-purpose flour
1/2 cup confectioners' sugar
1 cup cold butter
CITRUS GLAZE:
6 tablespoons sugar
2 teaspoons cornstarch
1/2 cup cold water
1/4 teaspoon orange extract
TOPPING:
2 packages (8 ounces *each*) cream cheese, softened
2/3 cup sugar
1-1/2 teaspoons orange extract
4 kiwifruit, peeled
14 fresh strawberries, halved

In a large bowl, combine flour and confectioners' sugar. Cut in the butter until crumbly.

Press into a greased 15-in. x 10-in. x 1-in. baking pan. Bake at 350° for 16-19 minutes or until golden brown. Cool on a wire rack.

In a small saucepan, combine the sugar and cornstarch. Stir in water until smooth. Bring to a boil over medium heat; cook and stir for 2 minutes or until thickened. Remove from the heat; stir in orange extract. Cool completely.

In a mixing bowl, beat the cream cheese, sugar and orange extract until smooth. Spread over crust. Cover and refrigerate for 45 minutes. Cut into 28 squares.

Cut each kiwi into seven slices. Place a kiwi slice in the middle of each square; top each with a strawberry half. Brush with glaze; refrigerate until set. **Yield:** 28 servings.

Meat Loaf Makeover

Place a slice of leftover meat loaf between two cheese slices and two slices of bread. Then coat both sides of the sandwich with butter spray and fry it in a pan until golden brown. For a Mexican flavor, add chili or taco seasoning to the meat loaf mix.

You can also crumble leftover meat loaf and use it in chili. Or combine it with a sauce and serve it over rice or noodles.

Pigskin Barbecue

(Pictured below)

I've taken these saucy sandwiches to potlucks and tailgate parties with our polo club...and served them at our own backyard picnics. They're simple to make and always draw rave reviews.
—Bobbie Love
Kapaa, Hawaii

1 bone-in pork blade roast (about 5 pounds), cut in half
1 tablespoon vegetable oil
1 cup water
1 can (8 ounces) tomato sauce
1/4 cup packed brown sugar
1/4 cup cider vinegar
1/4 cup Worcestershire sauce
2 to 3 tablespoons hot pepper sauce
1 tablespoon chili powder
1-1/2 teaspoons celery seed
1 to 2 teaspoons salt
1 medium onion, halved and thinly sliced
1 cup chopped sweet red *or* green pepper
1 to 2 tablespoons cornstarch
3 tablespoons cold water
14 to 16 kaiser rolls, split

In a large kettle or Dutch oven, brown pork in oil on all sides; drain. Combine the water, tomato sauce, brown sugar, vinegar, Worcestershire sauce, hot pepper sauce, chili powder, celery seed and salt; pour over roast. Bring to a boil. Reduce heat; cover and simmer for 1-3/4 hours.

Stir in onion and sweet pepper. Cover and simmer 30-45 minutes longer or until the meat is tender. Remove roast. When cool enough to handle, shred meat with two forks; set aside.

Skim fat from pan juices. Combine cornstarch and cold water until smooth; gradually add to pan juices. Bring to a boil; cook and stir for 2 minutes or

EVERYONE will be dishing out compliments when they taste this crowd-pleasing menu of Pigskin Barbecue, Sweet Macaroni Salad and Peanut Pudding Dessert (shown above, clockwise from bottom).

until slightly thickened. Return pork to pan and heat through. Serve on rolls. **Yield:** 14-16 servings.

Sweet Macaroni Salad

(Pictured below left)

A sweet out-of-the-ordinary dressing makes this macaroni salad special. My aunt gave me the recipe and it has become one of my favorites. I occasionally leave out the green pepper if I know that people don't like it...and it still tastes great. —Idalee Scholz
Cocoa Beach, Florida

  1 package (16 ounces) elbow macaroni
  4 medium carrots, shredded
  1 large green pepper, chopped
  1 medium red onion, chopped
  2 cups mayonnaise
  1 can (14 ounces) sweetened condensed milk
  1 cup sugar
  1 cup cider vinegar
  1 teaspoon salt
1/2 teaspoon pepper

Cook macaroni according to package directions; drain and rinse in cold water. In a large serving bowl, combine the macaroni, carrots, green pepper and onion.

In a small bowl, whisk the mayonnaise, milk, sugar, vinegar, salt and pepper until smooth. Pour over macaroni mixture and toss to coat. Cover and refrigerate overnight. **Yield:** 14 servings.

Peanut Pudding Dessert

(Pictured at left)

I prepared this rich yummy dessert recently, and our guests wanted seconds. The crunchy chopped peanut crust is such a nice complement to the creamy chocolate and peanut butter layers. You're sure to be asking for seconds, too! —Patricia Senkow
Dickson City, Pennsylvania

1/2 cup cold butter
  1 cup all-purpose flour
2/3 cup chopped dry-roasted peanuts
  1 package (8 ounces) cream cheese, softened
  1 cup confectioners' sugar
1/3 cup peanut butter
  1 carton (8 ounces) frozen whipped topping, thawed, *divided*

2-3/4 cups cold milk
  1 package (3.9 ounces) instant chocolate pudding mix
  1 package (3.4 ounces) instant vanilla pudding mix
Chocolate curls and additional chopped peanuts, optional

In a bowl, cut butter into flour until crumbly. Stir in peanuts. Press into an ungreased 13-in. x 9-in. x 2-in. baking dish. Bake at 350° for 16-20 minutes or until lightly browned. Cool on a wire rack.

In a mixing bowl, beat the cream cheese, confectioners' sugar and peanut butter until smooth. Fold in 1-1/2 cups whipped topping. Carefully spread over crust.

In a bowl, whisk the milk and pudding mixes for 2 minutes. Let stand for 2 minutes or until soft-set. Carefully spread over cream cheese layer. Top with remaining whipped topping. Garnish with chocolate curls and additional peanuts if desired. Refrigerate until serving. **Yield:** 15-18 servings.

Hearty Bean Bake

Because it makes such a big batch, this popular four-bean bake is perfect for potlucks...but I like to serve it with rolls and a salad at home, too. We take the leftovers for lunch during the week. —Barb Wilkin
Coshocton, Ohio

  1 pound ground beef
  1 medium onion, chopped
1/2 pound sliced bacon, cooked and crumbled
  1 can (28 ounces) baked beans
  1 can (16 ounces) kidney beans, rinsed and drained
  1 can (14-1/2 ounces) wax beans, drained
  1 can (14-1/2 ounces) cut green beans, drained
1/2 cup packed brown sugar
1/2 cup ketchup
  3 tablespoons honey
  2 tablespoons cider vinegar

In a large skillet, cook beef and onion over medium heat until meat is no longer pink; drain. Add the bacon and beans; mix well. Transfer to a greased 2-1/2-qt. baking dish.

In a small bowl, combine the brown sugar, ketchup, honey and vinegar. Pour over the bean mixture. Bake, uncovered, at 325° for 45-50 minutes or until heated through and bubbly. Let stand for 10 minutes; stir and serve. **Yield:** 12 servings.

END SUMMER on an appetizing note with this potluck-perfect menu featuring Apple-Feta Tossed Salad, Garden Herb Braid and Italian Spaghetti Bake (shown above, clockwise from top left).

Italian Spaghetti Bake

(Pictured above)

This casserole recipe makes two large baking dishes. The layers of meat sauce, spaghetti and gooey cheese are sure to appeal to pizza-loving kids and adults.
—Janice Fredrickson, Elgin, Texas

   2 **packages (one 16 ounces, one 8 ounces) spaghetti**
1-1/2 **pounds ground beef**
   1 **large green pepper, chopped**
   1 **medium onion, chopped**
   2 **cans (15 ounces *each*) tomato sauce**
   1 **package (8 ounces) sliced pepperoni**
   1 **can (8 ounces) mushroom stems and pieces, drained**
   1 **can (3.8 ounces) sliced ripe olives, drained**
1/2 **teaspoon dried basil**
1/2 **teaspoon dried oregano**
1/4 **teaspoon garlic salt**
1/4 **teaspoon pepper**
   3 **cups (12 ounces) shredded mozzarella cheese**
1/2 **cup grated Parmesan cheese**

Cook spaghetti according to package directions. Meanwhile, in a large saucepan, cook the beef, green pepper and onion over medium heat until meat is no longer pink; drain. Stir in the tomato sauce, pepperoni, mushrooms, olives and seasonings. Drain spaghetti.

Spoon 1 cup meat sauce into each of two greased 13-in. x 9-in. x 2-in. baking dishes. Top each with about 2-1/2 cups spaghetti, 1-1/2 cups meat sauce, and remaining spaghetti and meat sauce. Sprinkle with cheeses. Bake, uncovered, at 350° for 20-25 minutes or until heated through.
Yield: 2 casseroles (8-10 servings each).

Garden Herb Braid

(Pictured at left)

In the summer, I like to use fresh herbs from my mom's garden for this bread. —Martha Smith, Orient, Ohio

    4 to 4-1/2 cups all-purpose flour
    3 tablespoons sugar
    2 packages (1/4 ounce *each*) quick-rise yeast
1-1/2 teaspoons salt
    3/4 teaspoon *each* dried marjoram, thyme, parsley flakes, basil and oregano
    3/4 teaspoon dried rosemary, crushed
    3/4 teaspoon rubbed sage
    3/4 cup milk
    1/2 cup water
    1/4 cup butter, cubed
    1 egg
TOPPING:
    1 tablespoon butter, melted
    1/8 teaspoon *each* dried marjoram, thyme, parsley flakes, basil and oregano
    1/8 teaspoon dried rosemary, crushed
    1/8 teaspoon rubbed sage

In a large mixing bowl, combine 1-1/2 cups flour, sugar, yeast, salt and herbs. In a saucepan, heat the milk, water and butter to 120°-130°. Add to dry ingredients; beat just until moistened. Add egg; beat until smooth. Stir in enough remaining flour to form a soft dough. Turn onto a floured surface; knead until smooth and elastic, about 4-6 minutes. Cover and let rest for 10 minutes.

Divide dough into thirds. Shape each portion into a 15-in. rope. Place ropes on a greased baking sheet and braid; pinch ends to seal and tuck under. Cover; let rise until doubled, about 20 minutes.

Bake at 375° for 25-30 minutes or until golden brown. Brush with melted butter. Combine herbs; sprinkle over bread. Remove from pan to a wire rack to cool. **Yield:** 1 loaf (16 slices).

Apple-Feta Tossed Salad

(Pictured above left)

A friend of mine shared this recipe with me after I raved about it. —Marlene Clark, Apple Valley, California

    2 tablespoons butter
    1 cup walnut halves
    1 tablespoon sugar
    1/8 teaspoon pepper
    5 cups torn romaine
    5 cups torn red leaf lettuce
    1 *each* medium red and green apple, chopped
    1/2 to 1 cup crumbled feta cheese

DRESSING:
    6 tablespoons olive oil
    2 tablespoons white wine vinegar
    2 tablespoons finely chopped onion
1-1/2 teaspoons Dijon mustard
    2 garlic cloves, minced
    1/2 teaspoon sugar
    1/4 teaspoon dried oregano
    1/8 teaspoon *each* salt and pepper
    1/8 teaspoon dried parsley flakes

In a small skillet, melt the butter over medium heat. Add the walnuts; sprinkle with sugar and pepper. Stir until well coated. Spread onto a baking sheet. Bake at 350° for 15 minutes or until lightly browned, stirring every 5 minutes. Cool on a wire rack.

In a large bowl, combine romaine, red lettuce, apples and feta cheese; set aside. In a blender, combine the dressing ingredients; cover and process until blended. Drizzle over salad; toss to coat. Sprinkle with sugared walnuts. **Yield:** 12 servings.

Peppermint Brownies

I think these minty-tasting brownies are the best around. —Tami Samorajski, New Berlin, Wisconsin

    1 tablespoon plus 1 cup butter, *divided*
    8 squares (1 ounce *each*) unsweetened chocolate, chopped
    4 teaspoons instant coffee granules
    1 tablespoon boiling water
    5 eggs
3-3/4 cups sugar
    2 teaspoons vanilla extract
    1/2 teaspoon salt
    1/2 teaspoon almond extract
1-2/3 cups all-purpose flour
    2 cups coarsely chopped walnuts
    44 chocolate-covered peppermint patties

Line a 13-in. x 9-in. x 2-in. baking pan with foil. Melt 1 tablespoon butter; brush over foil. In a microwave, melt chocolate and remaining butter; cool slightly. Dissolve granules in water.

In a mixing bowl, beat the eggs, sugar, coffee mixture, vanilla, salt and almond extract on high for 3-4 minutes or until fluffy. Beat in chocolate mixture and flour until blended. Stir in walnuts.

Pour half of the batter into prepared pan. Top with a layer of peppermint patties, filling in the gaps with peppermint patty pieces. Top with remaining batter. Bake at 425° for 23-27 minutes or until top is set. Cool on a wire rack. Using foil, remove brownies from pan. Chill for 6 hours or overnight before cutting. **Yield:** 3 dozen.

Cooking for One or Two

Don't let the small sizes fool you—these dishes are all big on flavor!
Each recipe makes just enough for you or you and a loved one.

TREATS FOR TWO. Clockwise from upper left: Hash Brown Reubens (p. 195), Traditional Stuffed Peppers (p. 177), Ham Salad Pineapple Boats (p. 192), Solo Chicken Stroganoff (p. 178) and Grilled Jumbo Shrimp (p. 192).

Turkey with Apple Slices

(Pictured below)

*Any day can be "Turkey Day" when you make this
smaller-scale main course. These moist tasty tenderloins and tangy apple glaze offer the goodness of turkey
in a hurry without a fridge-filling surplus.*
—*Mary Lou Wayman, Salt Lake City, Utah*

2 **turkey breast tenderloins (about 4 ounces
  each)**
1 **tablespoon butter**
2 **tablespoons maple syrup**
1 **tablespoon cider vinegar**
1 **teaspoon Dijon mustard**
1/2 **teaspoon chicken bouillon granules**
1 **medium tart apple, sliced**

SEASONAL SUPPER for two features tasty Turkey with Apple Slices, Honey-Mustard Sprouts and Chocolate Layer
Cake (shown above).

In a large skillet, cook turkey in butter over medium heat for 4-5 minutes on each side or until the juices run clear. Remove from skillet; cover and keep warm. In same skillet, combine syrup, vinegar, mustard and bouillon. Add the apple; cook and stir over medium heat for 2-3 minutes or until apple is tender. Spoon over turkey. **Yield:** 2 servings.

Honey-Mustard Sprouts

(Pictured at left)

I like to make these special brussels sprouts when I need a fast dressed-up vegetable side dish. The recipe is sized perfectly for a dinner for my husband, Gene, and me. And it's easy to triple when we're expecting guests. —Karen Haen, Sturgeon Bay, Wisconsin

☑ Uses less fat, sugar or salt. Includes Nutritional Analysis and Diabetic Exchanges.

10 fresh *or* frozen brussels sprouts, halved
1-1/2 teaspoons butter, melted
1-1/2 teaspoons honey
1/2 teaspoon Dijon mustard
Dash *each* onion powder and dill weed

Place brussels sprouts in a steamer basket. Place in a saucepan over 1 in. of water; bring to a boil. Cover and cook for 8-12 minutes or until crisp-tender; drain. In a bowl, combine the butter, honey, mustard, onion powder and dill. Drizzle over the sprouts and toss to coat. **Yield:** 2 servings.

Nutritional Analysis: One 3/4-cup serving equals 125 calories, 4 g fat (2 g saturated fat), 8 mg cholesterol, 109 mg sodium, 22 g carbohydrate, 7 g fiber, 7 g protein. **Diabetic Exchanges:** 2 vegetable, 1/2 fat, 1/2 starch.

Chocolate Layer Cake

(Pictured at left)

You can "halve" your cake and eat it, too, when you make this chocolaty classic for two. My mother came up with this delicious dessert after we kids left the nest. Today, I split this tempting two-layer treat with my husband. —Verna Mae Floyd, Highlands, Texas

1/4 cup shortening
1 cup sugar
1 egg
1/2 teaspoon vanilla extract
1 cup all-purpose flour
1/4 cup baking cocoa
1 teaspoon baking powder

1/4 teaspoon baking soda
1/4 teaspoon salt
3/4 cup milk
FROSTING:
1/2 cup butter, softened
2-1/2 cups confectioners' sugar
1/2 cup baking cocoa
1 teaspoon vanilla extract
2 to 3 tablespoons hot water

In a mixing bowl, beat shortening and sugar. Beat in egg and vanilla. Combine the flour, cocoa, baking powder, baking soda and salt; add to creamed mixture alternately with milk. Pour into a greased and floured 9-in. round baking pan.

Bake at 350° for 30-35 minutes or until a toothpick inserted near the center comes out clean. Cool in pan for 10 minutes before removing to a wire rack to cool completely.

In a small mixing bowl, cream butter. Gradually beat in confectioners' sugar, cocoa, vanilla and enough water to achieve spreading consistency.

To assemble, cut cake in half. Place one half on a serving plate. Spread with 1/2 cup frosting. Top with remaining cake. Spread remaining frosting over top and rounded edge of cake. **Yield:** 4 servings.

Traditional Stuffed Peppers

(Pictured on page 174)

My husband, Steve, loves these stuffed peppers. They're so filling and easy to prepare. I like to serve them with mashed potatoes and coleslaw for a no-fuss supper. —Karen Gentry, Somerset, Kentucky

2 large green peppers
1/2 pound ground beef
1/4 cup chopped onion
1 can (15 ounces) tomato sauce, *divided*
1 cup cooked rice
1/8 teaspoon salt
1/8 teaspoon garlic powder
1/8 teaspoon pepper

Cut tops off peppers and remove seeds. Place peppers in a large saucepan and cover with water. Bring to a boil; cook for 3 minutes. Drain and rinse in cold water; invert on paper towels.

In a skillet, cook beef and onion over medium heat until meat is no longer pink; drain. Remove from the heat. Stir in 1 cup tomato sauce, rice, salt, garlic powder and pepper. Spoon into peppers. Place in an ungreased shallow 2-qt. baking dish. Drizzle with remaining tomato sauce. Cover and bake at 350° for 25-30 minutes or until peppers are tender. **Yield:** 2 servings.

and bake at 350° for 20-25 minutes or until a knife inserted near the center comes out clean. **Yield:** 2 servings.

Stuffed Squash for Two

My husband and I loved this recipe as newlyweds, and now that our children are grown, we are enjoying it again. As soon as the weather turns cool, we get hungry for this squash dish, filled with savory ground beef and topped with a sprinkling of cheese.
—Barbara Rohlck
Sioux Falls, South Dakota

> 1 medium acorn squash
> 1 tablespoon butter, melted
> 2 tablespoons brown sugar
> 3/4 teaspoon salt, *divided*
> 1/8 teaspoon pepper
> 1/2 pound ground beef
> 3 tablespoons chopped celery
> 3 tablespoons chopped onion
> 2 tablespoons all-purpose flour
> 1/2 teaspoon rubbed sage
> 3/4 cup milk
> 1 cup salad croutons
> 1/4 cup shredded cheddar cheese

Cut squash in half; discard seeds. Place squash cut side down in an 11-in. x 7-in. x 2-in. baking pan; add 1/2 in. of hot water. Bake, uncovered, at 350° for 30 minutes. Drain water from pan; turn squash cut side up. Brush with butter; sprinkle with brown sugar, 1/4 teaspoon salt and pepper. Bake 30-40 minutes longer or until squash is tender.

Meanwhile, in a skillet, cook the beef, celery and onion over medium heat until the meat is no longer pink; drain. Stir in the flour, sage and remaining salt. Gradually stir in milk. Bring to a boil; cook and stir for 2 minutes or until thickened.

Remove from the heat; stir in croutons. Spoon into squash halves. Bake, uncovered, for 25 minutes. Sprinkle with cheese. Bake 5 minutes longer or until cheese is melted. **Yield:** 2 servings.

Solo Chicken Stroganoff

(Pictured on page 174)

I use chicken breasts as a base for building a variety of interesting meals. This quick meal requires only one skillet plus a pan for the rice or pasta. Sometimes I like to make the dish as a pilaf, adding a half cup of un-

Raspberry-Pecan Dressing

(Pictured above)

Stuffing isn't just for company, as this deliciously downsized recipe for dressing proves. With its sweet raspberry flavor and pecan-packed crunch, this dish is perfect for pairing up with pork or poultry.
—Beverly Coyde, Gasport, New York

> 4 slices day-old bread, cubed
> 1/2 cup chopped pecans, toasted
> 1/2 cup chopped green onions
> 1 egg, beaten
> 2 tablespoons butter, melted
> 1 teaspoon raspberry *or* cider vinegar
> Salt and pepper to taste
> 1 cup fresh raspberries

Place the bread cubes, pecans and onions in a large bowl. Combine the egg, butter, vinegar, salt and pepper. Pour over bread mixture; toss to combine. Gently fold in raspberries.

Transfer to a greased 1-qt. baking dish. Cover

cooked rice after the meat and peppers have been sauteed. —Bill Hilbrich, St. Cloud, Minnesota

    1 boneless skinless chicken breast half, cut
      into 2-inch strips
    1 cup sliced fresh mushrooms
1/3 cup chopped onion
1/3 cup chopped green pepper
    2 tablespoons butter
    2 tablespoons all-purpose flour
1/2 cup chicken broth
    2 tablespoons sour cream
1/4 teaspoon salt
1/8 to 1/4 teaspoon pepper
1/8 teaspoon ground nutmeg
Hot cooked pasta

In a large skillet, saute the chicken, mushrooms, onion and green pepper in butter until chicken is no longer pink. Combine the flour and broth until smooth; gradually add to skillet. Bring to a boil; cook and stir for 2 minutes or until thickened. Reduce heat. Add the sour cream, salt, pepper and nutmeg; cook and stir until heated through (do not boil). Serve over pasta. **Yield:** 1 serving.

Buckwheat Brunch Crepes

(Pictured below right)

My husband and I enjoy these delicious crepes with sweet berry sauce and cream on Saturday mornings or even at supper time with sausage and eggs. They're considered a delicacy here, especially with a drizzle of maple syrup. —Sharon Dyck Roxton Falls, Quebec

    5 tablespoons heavy whipping cream
1/2 cup sour cream
    2 eggs
1/2 cup milk
1/3 cup all-purpose flour
    3 tablespoons buckwheat flour *or* whole
      wheat flour
1/2 teaspoon salt
BERRY SAUCE:
1/2 cup sugar
    1 tablespoon cornstarch
Dash salt
1/2 cup water
    1 teaspoon lemon juice
1/3 cup fresh blueberries
1/3 cup fresh raspberries
4-1/2 teaspoons butter, *divided*

In a small mixing bowl, beat whipping cream until stiff peaks form; fold into sour cream. Cov-

er and refrigerate until serving.

In a bowl, whisk the eggs and milk. Add flours and salt; beat until smooth. Let stand for 30 minutes.

Meanwhile, combine the sugar, cornstarch and salt in a saucepan; stir in water and lemon juice until smooth. Bring to a boil. Cook and stir for 1-2 minutes or until thickened and bubbly. Add berries; cook over medium-low heat until berries burst. Stir in 1-1/2 teaspoons butter until melted; set aside and keep warm.

Melt 1 teaspoon butter in an 8-in. skillet. Pour about 2 tablespoons batter into the center of skillet; lift and tilt skillet to coat bottom evenly. Cook until top appears dry; turn and cook bottom until lightly browned. Remove to a wire rack.

Repeat with remaining batter, adding butter to skillet as needed. Stack crepes with paper towels in between and keep warm. Serve crepes warm with berry sauce and cream mixture. **Yield:** about 6 crepes.

Plan Ahead

If you're hungry for a tender roast, but don't want to buy one because of leftovers, try this. Purchase the smallest roast you can find (some are available as small as 2 pounds). Invite guests over for dinner or plan to use the leftover meat for another meal in a salad, casserole, potpie or sandwich. Also keep a portion for a quick and easy roast dinner later in the week.

Chicken Parmigiana

(Pictured below)

These tender crumb-coated chicken breasts are topped with a savory homemade spaghetti sauce and served over pasta. You can adjust the seasonings in this dish to your taste. My husband and I like lots of garlic, onion and herbs in everything.
—Heather Powers Sauter, Silver Spring, Maryland

1 small onion, chopped
4 garlic cloves, minced
1 tablespoon olive oil
1 can (15 ounces) tomato sauce
1 can (14-1/2 ounces) stewed tomatoes, cut up
1 teaspoon *each* dried basil, thyme and oregano
1/4 teaspoon pepper

SET YOUR TABLE for two with scrumptious Chicken Parmigiana and Lemony Cucumber Salad (shown below).

1/4 cup milk
1/2 cup all-purpose flour
  1 egg, lightly beaten
1/4 cup seasoned bread crumbs
1/4 cup grated Parmesan cheese
  1 teaspoon salt-free garlic and herb
    seasoning
  2 boneless skinless chicken breast halves
  2 tablespoons butter
1/2 cup shredded mozzarella cheese
Hot cooked spaghetti

In a saucepan, saute onion and garlic in oil until tender; add the tomato sauce, tomatoes, herbs and pepper. Bring to a boil. Reduce heat; cover and simmer for 20 minutes.

Meanwhile, place the milk, flour and egg in separate shallow bowls. In another bowl, combine the bread crumbs, Parmesan cheese and herb seasoning. Dip chicken in milk; roll in flour. Dip in egg, then coat with crumb mixture.

In a skillet, brown chicken in butter over medium heat until golden brown and juices run clear. Sprinkle with mozzarella cheese. Cover and cook 3-4 minutes longer or until cheese is melted. Serve over spaghetti; top with tomato sauce. **Yield:** 2 servings.

Lemony Cucumber Salad

(Pictured at left)

In the summer, we use fresh cucumber and tomatoes from my husband's prolific garden for this colorful salad. It's one of our favorite light suppers.
—*Marcia Severson, Hallock, Minnesota*

  1 medium cucumber, diced
  2 medium plum tomatoes, seeded and diced
1/2 cup minced fresh parsley
1/2 cup minced fresh cilantro
1/4 cup finely chopped onion
1/4 cup lemon juice
1/4 cup olive oil
  1 tablespoon grated lemon peel
  1 garlic clove, minced
1/2 teaspoon seasoned salt
1/4 teaspoon coarsely ground pepper
  1 whole pita bread, cut into small pieces
1/4 cup whole unblanched almonds, toasted

In a serving bowl, combine the cucumber, tomatoes, parsley, cilantro and onion. In a small bowl, whisk the lemon juice, oil, lemon peel, garlic, seasoned salt and pepper. Pour over vegetables. Add the pita bread and almonds; toss to coat. Serve immediately. **Yield:** 2 servings.

Tomato 'n' Cheese Pasta

(Pictured above)

Garlic, basil and oregano add pizzazz to this savory side dish. The pasta is tender and moist, and there's plenty of cheese flavor. I like to serve it alongside steaks or chicken.
—*Dawn Dhooghe
Concord, North Carolina*

  1 cup uncooked small tube pasta
  1 small onion, chopped
  2 garlic cloves, minced
  1 tablespoon olive oil
  1 can (14-1/2 ounces) Italian diced
    tomatoes
1/2 teaspoon dried basil
1/2 teaspoon dried oregano
1/4 teaspoon sugar
1/4 teaspoon pepper
1/4 cup shredded mozzarella cheese
1/4 cup grated Parmesan cheese

Cook pasta according to package directions. In a small saucepan, saute onion and garlic in oil until tender. Stir in the tomatoes, basil, oregano, sugar and pepper. Bring to a boil. Reduce heat; simmer, uncovered, for 15 minutes. Drain pasta; stir into saucepan.

Transfer to a greased 1-qt. baking dish. Top with cheeses. Bake, uncovered, at 375° for 10-15 minutes or until cheese is melted. **Yield:** 2 servings.

oil, pepper and remaining salt; shake well. Drizzle over salad. **Yield:** 2 servings.

Pineapple-Stuffed Cornish Hens

My mother brought this recipe back with her from Hawaii about 25 years ago. The tender meat, pineapple-coconut stuffing and sweet-sour sauce make it a favorite of my family and friends. I keep copies of the recipe on hand to share.
—*Vicki Corners, Rock Island, Illinois*

    2 Cornish game hens (20 ounces *each*)
1/2 teaspoon salt, *divided*
    1 can (8 ounces) crushed pineapple
    3 cups cubed day-old bread (1/2-inch cubes), crusts removed
    1 celery rib, chopped
1/2 cup flaked coconut
2/3 cup butter, melted, *divided*
1/4 teaspoon poultry seasoning
    2 tablespoons steak sauce
    2 tablespoons cornstarch
    2 tablespoons brown sugar
    1 cup water
    1 tablespoon lemon juice

Sprinkle inside of hens with 1/4 teaspoon salt; set aside. Drain pineapple, reserving the juice.

In a bowl, combine the pineapple, bread cubes, celery and coconut. Add 6 tablespoons butter; toss to coat.

Loosely stuff hens; tie legs together with kitchen string. Place on a rack in a greased shallow roasting pan. Place remaining stuffing in a greased 1-1/2-cup baking dish; cover and set aside. Add poultry seasoning and remaining salt to remaining butter. Spoon some butter mixture over hens. Bake, uncovered, at 350° for 40 minutes, basting twice with butter mixture.

Stir steak sauce and reserved pineapple juice into remaining butter mixture; baste hens. Bake reserved stuffing with hens for 30 minutes; baste hens twice.

Uncover stuffing; baste hens with remaining butter mixture. Bake 15-20 minutes longer or until a meat thermometer reads 185° for hens and 165° for stuffing in hens. Remove hens from pan; keep warm.

Pour drippings into a saucepan; skim fat. Combine cornstarch, brown sugar, water and lemon juice until smooth; add to the drippings. Bring to a boil; cook and stir for 1-2 minutes or until thickened. Serve with hens and stuffing. **Yield:** 2 servings.

Pecan-Pear Green Salad

(Pictured above)

This lovely salad adds a special touch to any meal. The juicy pear slices, toasted pecans and mixed greens are coated in a tangy vinaigrette dressing that's a pleasant complement to the sweet and crunchy combination.
—*Katie Nicklas, Ridgway, Pennsylvania*

    1 large ripe red pear, sliced
    2 tablespoons butter, *divided*
1/2 cup coarsely chopped pecans
1/4 teaspoon salt, *divided*
    2 cups mixed salad greens
    2 tablespoons balsamic vinegar
    2 tablespoons olive oil
Pepper to taste

In a large skillet, saute pear in 1 tablespoon butter until lightly browned, about 7 minutes. In another skillet, saute pecans in remaining butter until lightly browned, about 5 minutes; sprinkle with 1/8 teaspoon salt.

Divide salad greens between two salad plates; arrange pears over greens. Sprinkle with pecans. In a jar with a tight-fitting lid, combine the vinegar,

Rustic Fruit Tart

(Pictured below)

Husband Don and I love pie, but we can't eat a whole 9-inch pie by ourselves. So I make these easy tarts using rhubarb and fruit from our red raspberry bushes. Sometimes I substitute apples, peaches or our home-grown blueberries for the rhubarb. —Naomi Olson
Hamilton, Michigan

    1 cup all-purpose flour
1/2 teaspoon salt
1/4 cup vegetable oil
    2 tablespoons milk
    1 cup diced fresh *or* frozen rhubarb*, thawed
    1 cup fresh *or* frozen raspberries, thawed
1/2 cup sugar
    2 tablespoons quick-cooking tapioca
GLAZE:
    6 tablespoons confectioners' sugar
    1 teaspoon water
1/8 teaspoon almond extract

In a bowl, combine the flour and salt. Add oil and milk, tossing with a fork until mixture forms a ball.

Shape dough into a disk; wrap in plastic wrap. Refrigerate for at least 1 hour.

In another bowl, combine the rhubarb, raspberries, sugar and tapioca; let stand for 15 minutes. Unwrap dough and place on a parchment-lined baking sheet. Cover with waxed paper and roll the dough into an 11-in. circle. Discard waxed paper.

Spoon fruit mixture into the center of dough to within 2 in. of the edges. Fold edges of dough over fruit, leaving center uncovered. Bake at 400° for 25-30 minutes or until crust is golden brown and filling is bubbly. Remove to a wire rack. Combine the glaze ingredients until smooth. Drizzle over warm tart. **Yield:** 2 servings.

*Editor's Note: If using frozen rhubarb, measure it while still frozen, then thaw completely. Drain in colander, but do not press liquid out.

Black Bean Soup for Two

I'm a stay-at-home mom with a toddler and appreciate small-scale recipes. I like to serve this zesty soup with tortillas topped with melted cheese.
—Wendy Anderson, Santa Rosa, California

✓ Uses less fat, sugar or salt. Includes Nutritional Analysis and Diabetic Exchanges.

1/4 cup chopped onion
2 garlic cloves, minced
1 tablespoon olive oil
1 teaspoon ground cumin
1 teaspoon dried oregano
1/2 teaspoon chili powder
1 can (15 ounces) tomato sauce
1 can (15 ounces) black beans, rinsed and drained
1 can (14 ounces) vegetable *or* beef broth
1 bay leaf
1 to 2 tablespoons lime juice
1/8 teaspoon hot pepper sauce
Pepper to taste

In a large saucepan, saute onion and garlic in oil until tender. Stir in the cumin, oregano and chili powder; saute 2 minutes longer. Add tomato sauce, beans, broth and bay leaf.

Bring to a boil. Reduce heat; cover and simmer for 45 minutes. Stir in lime juice; simmer 10-15 minutes longer. Discard bay leaf. Add pepper sauce and pepper. **Yield:** 2 servings.

Nutritional Analysis: One 2-cup serving (prepared with reduced-sodium beef broth) equals 314 calories, 8 g fat (1 g saturated fat), 0 cholesterol, 1,419 mg sodium, 43 g carbohydrate, 10 g fiber, 17 g protein. **Diabetic Exchanges:** 2 starch, 2 vegetable, 1 lean meat, 1 fat.

Chicken with Lemon Sauce

(Pictured at right)

This delicious Italian dish is easy to prepare, but it looks like you fussed.
—Brenda Hoffman
Stanton, Michigan

2 boneless skinless chicken breast halves
5 tablespoons all-purpose flour, *divided*
1/4 cup grated Parmesan cheese
3/4 teaspoon salt, *divided*
1/2 teaspoon pepper, *divided*
2 eggs
2 tablespoons butter, *divided*
1 tablespoon olive oil
3/4 cup chicken broth
1/2 cup apple juice

1 tablespoon lemon juice
1 tablespoon minced fresh parsley

Flatten chicken to 1/4-in. thickness. In a shallow bowl, combine 4 tablespoons flour, Parmesan cheese, 1/2 teaspoon salt and 1/4 teaspoon pepper. In another bowl, beat the eggs. Dip chicken into eggs; coat with flour mixture.

In a skillet, cook chicken in 1 tablespoon butter and oil over medium heat for 3-5 minutes on each side or until juices run clear. Remove; keep warm.

In a small bowl, combine the remaining flour, salt and pepper; stir in broth until smooth. Add apple juice to the skillet, stirring to loosen any browned bits. Stir broth mixture and add to the pan. Bring to a boil; cook and stir for 1-2 minutes or until thickened and bubbly.

Stir in lemon juice; cook for 1 minute. Add parsley and remaining butter; cook and stir until butter is melted. Serve over chicken. **Yield:** 2 servings.

Pea Pods with Onion

(Pictured at right)

This simple side is a welcome alternative to green beans, and the pea pods look so pretty tossed with chopped onion.
—Heather Sauter
Silver Spring, Maryland

1/2 pound fresh pea pods
2 tablespoons water
1/4 cup chopped onion
3 tablespoons butter, *divided*
Salt and pepper to taste

Place the pea pods and water in a microwave-safe bowl; cover and cook on high for 3-5 minutes or until crisp-tender. Meanwhile, in a small skillet, cook onion in 2 tablespoons butter over medium heat until crisp-tender.

Drain peas; add to onion mixture. Add salt, pepper and remaining butter; toss to coat. Cook and stir until heated through. **Yield:** 2 servings.

Editor's Note: This recipe was tested in a 1,100-watt microwave.

Coffee Cream Tortilla Cups

(Pictured above right)

Here's a special dessert for two. Crispy tortilla bowls hold creamy coffee-flavored pudding topped with a mix of colorful fresh berries.
—Amber Zurbrugg
Alliance, Ohio

PERFECT FOR A PAIR is this delicious springtime dinner featuring Chicken with Lemon Sauce, Pea Pods with Onion and Coffee Cream Tortilla Cups (shown above).

   2 flour tortillas (8 inches), warmed
   1 tablespoon butter, melted
   1 tablespoon sugar
 1/2 teaspoon ground cinnamon
 1/2 cup half-and-half cream
   2 teaspoons instant coffee granules
   5 tablespoons instant French vanilla
     pudding mix
   1 cup whipped topping
1-1/2 cups fresh blueberries, raspberries and
     sliced strawberries

Brush one side of tortillas with butter. Gently press each into a 10-oz. custard cup, buttered side up; pleat edges. Combine sugar and cinnamon; sprinkle over tortillas. Bake at 400° for 8-10 minutes or until crisp and lightly browned. Cool on a wire rack.

In a small bowl, combine the cream and coffee granules until dissolved. Add pudding mix; whisk for 2 minutes. Let stand for 2 minutes or until soft-set. Fold in whipped topping. Cover and refrigerate for 1 hour. Spoon into tortilla cups. Top with berries. **Yield:** 2 servings.

Butterflied Pork Chop Dinner

(Pictured below)

The sliced apple and sweet potatoes that complement these tender pork chops remind me of a crisp fall day, but I enjoy this hearty main dish any time of year. I serve it with salad and dinner rolls.
—Angela Leinenbach, Mechanicsville, Virginia

    2 butterflied pork chops (3/4 inch thick)
    1 tablespoon butter
    1 cup apple juice *or* cider, *divided*
    1 teaspoon rubbed sage
  3/4 teaspoon salt
  1/2 teaspoon pepper
    2 medium sweet potatoes, peeled and cut
      into 1/2-inch slices
    1 green onion, thinly sliced
    1 medium tart apple, peeled, cored and cut
      into 1/4-inch rings
    2 teaspoons cornstarch

In a skillet, brown pork chops in butter; drain. Remove from skillet and keep warm. In same skillet, combine 3/4 cup apple juice, sage, salt and pepper. Add sweet potatoes and green onion. Bring to a boil. Reduce heat.

Cover and simmer for 10 minutes; add apple rings and pork chops. Cover and simmer for 13-15 minutes or until apple rings and sweet potatoes are tender and meat juices run clear.

With a slotted spoon, remove pork chops, sweet potatoes and apple to serving plates; keep warm. Combine cornstarch and remaining apple juice until smooth. Gradually stir into pan juices. Bring to a boil; cook and stir for 1-2 minutes or until thickened. Serve over pork chops, sweet potatoes and apple. **Yield:** 2 servings.

Oriental Skillet Supper

When I'm too busy to spend much time in the kitchen, I make a personalized serving of steak. This colorful combination of cube steak, vegetables and rice is a quick and simple meal.
—Dona Shroyer
Titonka, Iowa

  1/4 pound beef cube steaks, cut into strips
    2 teaspoons vegetable oil
  1/4 cup julienned green pepper
    2 tablespoons chopped celery
    2 teaspoons cornstarch
  1/4 cup water
    4 teaspoons soy sauce
  1/2 teaspoon sugar
  1/8 teaspoon salt
    1 small tomato, cut into wedges
Hot cooked rice

In a small skillet, stir-fry the steak in oil for 4 minutes or until no longer pink. Remove steak and keep warm. Stir-fry green pepper and celery until crisp-tender. Combine cornstarch, water, soy sauce, sugar and salt until smooth; add to the skillet.

Bring to a boil. Cook and stir for 1 minute or until thickened. Add steak and tomato to skillet; heat through. Serve over rice. **Yield:** 1 serving.

Shrimp Pasta Primavera

They say the way to a man's heart is through his stomach. So when I invite that special guy to dinner, I like to prepare something equally special. This well-seasoned pasta dish has lots of flavor...and it won't hurt your budget! *—Shari Neff*
Silver Spring, Maryland

4 ounces uncooked angel hair pasta
8 jumbo shrimp, peeled and deveined
6 fresh asparagus spears, trimmed and cut into 2-inch pieces
12 garlic cloves, minced
1/4 cup olive oil
1/2 cup sliced fresh mushrooms
1/2 cup chicken broth
1 small plum tomato, peeled, seeded and diced
1/4 teaspoon salt
1/8 teaspoon crushed red pepper flakes
1 tablespoon *each* minced fresh basil, oregano, thyme and parsley
1/4 cup grated Parmesan cheese

Cook pasta according to package directions. Meanwhile, in a large skillet, saute the shrimp, asparagus and garlic in oil for 3-4 minutes or until shrimp turn pink.

Add the mushrooms, broth, tomato, salt and pepper flakes; simmer, uncovered, for 2 minutes. Drain pasta. Add the pasta and seasonings to skillet; toss to coat. Sprinkle with Parmesan cheese. **Yield:** 2 servings.

Strawberry Pretzel Dessert

(Pictured at right)

I love the sweet-salty flavor of this pretty layered dessert. Sliced strawberries and gelatin top a smooth cream cheese filling and crispy pretzel crust. I think it's best when eaten within a day of being made.
—Wendy Weaver, Leetonia, Ohio

1/3 cup crushed pretzels
2 tablespoons butter, softened
2 ounces cream cheese, softened
1/4 cup sugar
3/4 cup whipped topping
2 tablespoons plus 1-1/2 teaspoons strawberry gelatin powder
1/2 cup boiling water
1 cup sliced fresh strawberries

In a bowl, combine pretzels and butter. Press onto the bottom of two 10-oz. greased custard cups. Bake at 375° for 6-8 minutes or until set. Cool on a wire rack.

In a small mixing bowl, combine the cream cheese and sugar. Fold in the whipped topping. Spoon over crust. Refrigerate for 30 minutes.

Meanwhile, in a bowl, dissolve gelatin in boiling water. Cover and refrigerate for 20 minutes or until slightly thickened. Fold in strawberries.

Carefully spoon over filling. Cover and refrigerate for at least 3 hours. **Yield:** 2 servings.

Downsizing Recipes

Select recipes with yields between 4 and 6 servings. Recipes often can be divided proportionally by 2, 3 or 4. Entrees, side dishes, soups, salads, sandwiches, chili and stews usually lend themselves to proportional downsizing. Desserts and breads can be more challenging.

Recipes that start with small measures of ingredients, such as 1/8 teaspoon, dashes and pinches, can be difficult to adjust for smaller yields. When scaling down seasonings such as herbs, salt, pepper or spices, it's best to round off to the next smallest measure. You can always add more seasonings during cooking or just before serving.

Cooking and baking times may need to be adjusted, too. A good instant-read thermometer is the ideal way to determine the doneness of certain items.

HUNGRY for some tasty twosomes? Try this meal of Citrus-Ginger Tuna Steaks, Fruited Caesar Salad and Raspberry Cream Dessert (shown above) on for size.

Citrus-Ginger Tuna Steaks

(Pictured above)

We had tuna steaks similar to this in Hawaii. I tried mixing different ingredients before coming up with this recipe. Now that I am retired, I have lots of time to plan, experiment and prepare meals...but this tuna, with its well-seasoned marinade, takes only a few minutes to make. —Fran Roff, Rochester, New York

1/2 **cup olive oil**
1/4 **cup white wine vinegar**
  2 **tablespoons soy sauce**

1 tablespoon lemon juice
1 tablespoon lime juice
2 garlic cloves, minced
1 tablespoon minced fresh gingerroot
2 tuna steaks (8 ounces *each*)

In a bowl, combine the first seven ingredients. Pour 1/2 cup marinade into a large resealable plastic bag; add tuna steaks. Seal bag and turn to coat; refrigerate for 2-4 hours. Cover and refrigerate remaining marinade.

Drain and discard marinade from tuna. Coat grill rack with nonstick cooking spray before starting grill. Grill tuna, uncovered, for 5-7 minutes on each side or until fish flakes easily with a fork. Serve with the reserved marinade. **Yield:** 2 servings.

Fruited Caesar Salad

(Pictured at left)

I couldn't find a single Caesar salad recipe I liked, so I came up with this one. The addition of fruit gives this salad such a wonderful flavor. —*Kathy Keleher Oak Creek, Wisconsin*

  4 tablespoons olive oil, *divided*
  2 garlic cloves, peeled, *divided*
1/4 teaspoon salt, *divided*
  2 cups cubed French bread
  4 teaspoons lemon juice
1-1/2 teaspoons Dijon mustard
1/2 teaspoon Worcestershire sauce
1/8 teaspoon pepper
  4 cups torn romaine
  2 tablespoons shredded Parmesan cheese
  1 medium apple *or* ripe pear, diced

For croutons, combine 2 tablespoons oil, one garlic clove and 1/8 teaspoon salt in a bowl; let stand for 1 hour. Strain oil and discard the garlic. Toss bread cubes in the oil; place on a baking sheet. Bake at 400° for 6-7 minutes or until golden brown, stirring occasionally. Cool.

In a small bowl, combine the lemon juice, mustard, Worcestershire sauce, pepper and remaining oil and salt. Mince remaining garlic; stir into dressing. Place romaine in a salad bowl; drizzle with dressing. Add the croutons, Parmesan cheese and apple; toss to coat. **Yield:** 2 servings.

Raspberry Cream Dessert

(Pictured above left)

This creamy and elegant dessert turns any meal for two into something special. It's rich and light, with a sweet raspberry sauce and a sprinkling of berries. —*Marie Guthmiller, Mobridge, South Dakota*

  1 package (8 ounces) cream cheese, softened
1/4 cup sugar
1/2 cup heavy whipping cream, whipped
  1 package (10 ounces) frozen sweetened raspberries, thawed
  1 tablespoon cornstarch

In a small mixing bowl, beat the cream cheese and sugar until smooth. Gradually fold in whipped cream. Pipe mixture into two dessert dishes or spoon into two 4-in. springform pans coated with nonstick cooking spray. Refrigerate for 4 hours or until set.

Drain raspberries, reserving juice; set berries aside. Add enough water to the juice to measure 3/4 cup. In a small saucepan, combine cornstarch and juice mixture until smooth. Bring to a boil over medium heat; cook and stir for 1-2 minutes or until thickened. Cool slightly.

Stir in reserved raspberries. Cover and refrigerate until chilled. Serve with cream dessert. **Yield:** 2 servings.

Veggie Chicken Packet

Cooking doesn't get much easier than this tasty recipe. An aluminum foil "boat" holds a chicken breast, rice, veggies and seasonings for baking. There's little cleanup and no leftovers. —*Teresa Stough Augusta, Georgia*

  2 tablespoons uncooked instant rice
  1 bone-in chicken breast half
1/4 cup sliced carrot
  2 onion slices, separated into rings
1/4 cup julienned green and sweet red pepper
  1 tablespoon water
  1 tablespoon Worcestershire sauce
  2 to 3 teaspoons soy sauce
  1 tablespoon butter

Place rice in the center of a piece of heavy-duty foil (about 14 in. square); top with chicken and vegetables. Combine the water, Worcestershire sauce and soy sauce; pour over vegetables.

Dot with butter. Fold foil around the chicken and vegetables and seal tightly. Place in a baking pan. Bake at 350° for 65-75 minutes or until chicken juices run clear. Open foil carefully to allow steam to escape. **Yield:** 1 serving.

for 2 minutes or until thickened. Stir in the chicken, peas and potato mixture and heat through. Serve over biscuits. **Yield:** 2 servings.

Pickled Poached Salmon

(Pictured at right)

This flaky, moist salmon is topped with a delightful homemade tartar sauce and chopped sweet peppers. This entree goes well with rice pilaf, seasoned rice or scalloped potatoes. Add a colorful vegetable, a green salad, rolls and dessert, and you have a gourmet meal for two.
—*Fred Richard Day, St. George, Utah*

1-1/2 cups water
  1/4 cup dill pickle juice
    1 teaspoon salt
  1/2 teaspoon seasoned salt
    2 salmon steaks (1 inch thick)
SAUCE:
  1/4 cup mayonnaise
    2 teaspoons dill *or* sweet pickle relish
    1 teaspoon dill pickle juice
    1 teaspoon Catalina salad dressing
Chopped sweet red and green pepper,
  optional

In a large skillet, combine the water, pickle juice, salt and seasoned salt. Add salmon; bring to a boil. Reduce heat; cover and simmer for 12-16 minutes or until fish flakes easily with a fork.

In a small bowl, combine the mayonnaise, relish, pickle juice and salad dressing. Serve over salmon. Garnish with red and green pepper if desired. **Yield:** 2 servings.

Touch of Honey Biscuits

(Pictured at right)

Honey lends just a hint of sweetness to these light and tender dinner biscuits. Our friend Joan gave us this recipe, so when my husband or I make them, we always call them Joan's Biscuits.   —*Donna Jeffers*
Petersburg, West Virginia

    1 cup all-purpose flour
1-1/2 teaspoons baking powder
  1/4 teaspoon salt
  1/4 teaspoon cream of tartar
  1/4 cup cold butter
  1/3 cup milk
    1 teaspoon honey

Creamed Chicken over Biscuits

(Pictured above)

A friend of mine prepared this homey dish for my husband and me after our first son was born. I've made just a few minor modifications over the years.
—*Pam Kelley, Uniontown, Ohio*

    1 cup cubed peeled potato
  1/2 cup diced carrot
    2 tablespoons butter
    2 tablespoons all-purpose flour
    1 cup milk
2-1/2 teaspoons chicken bouillon granules
  1/8 teaspoon pepper
  1/2 pound boneless skinless chicken breasts,
      cooked and cubed
  1/2 cup frozen peas, thawed
    4 warm buttermilk biscuits

Place the potato and carrot in a small saucepan. Cover with water. Bring to a boil. Reduce heat; cover and simmer for 8-10 minutes or until vegetables are tender. Drain and set aside.

In a large skillet, melt butter. Stir in flour until smooth. Gradually whisk in the milk. Add the bouillon and pepper. Bring to a boil; cook and stir

In a bowl, combine flour, baking powder, salt and cream of tartar; cut in butter until crumbly. Stir in milk and honey just until moistened. Turn onto a floured surface; knead gently 8-10 times.

Roll out to 3/4-in. thickness; cut with a floured 2-1/2-in. biscuit cutter. Place 1 in. apart on a greased baking sheet. Bake at 450° for 10-15 minutes or until golden brown. **Yield:** 4 biscuits.

TREAT YOURSELF and a companion to Pickled Poached Salmon and Touch of Honey Biscuits (shown above).

Blackberry Crisp

(Pictured below)

I adapted this comforting dessert from a recipe my mother-in-law gave to me. Hers fed a family with nine growing kids who were never full, so there was never any left. When I make my downsized version, there are never any leftovers either! —Marliss Lee
Independence, Missouri

        2 cups fresh *or* frozen blackberries
        2 tablespoons sugar
        1 teaspoon cornstarch
    1-1/2 teaspoons water
      1/2 teaspoon lemon juice
      1/2 cup quick-cooking oats
      1/4 cup all-purpose flour
      1/4 cup packed brown sugar
      1/2 teaspoon ground cinnamon
      1/4 cup cold butter
Vanilla ice cream

Place blackberries in a greased 1-qt. baking dish. In a small bowl, combine the sugar, cornstarch, water and lemon juice until smooth. Pour over berries. Combine the oats, flour, brown sugar and cinnamon; cut in butter until crumbly. Sprinkle over berries.

Bake, uncovered, at 375° for 20-25 minutes or until filling is bubbly. Serve warm with ice cream. **Yield:** 2 servings.

Ham Salad Pineapple Boats

(Pictured on page 174)

These bountiful "boats" hold a chunky mixture of ham, pineapple, celery and green pepper dressed with a blend of mayonnaise and mustard. We love this light meal, especially during the summer. —Carol Shafer
Manhattan Beach, California

        1 medium fresh pineapple
      1/4 cup mayonnaise
      1/2 teaspoon prepared mustard
        1 cup cubed fully cooked ham
      1/2 cup chopped celery
        1 tablespoon chopped green pepper

Stand pineapple upright and cut in half, leaving the top attached. Remove fruit, leaving a 1-in. shell. Dice fruit; set aside 1 cup for salad and refrigerate the remaining fruit for another use.

In a bowl, combine mayonnaise and mustard. Stir in the ham, celery, green pepper and reserved pineapple. Spoon into pineapple halves. **Yield:** 2 servings.

Grilled Jumbo Shrimp

(Pictured on page 174)

At your next barbecue, skip the burgers and toss these zippy marinated shrimp on the grill. I dress up their great grilled flavor with a hint of orange and dashes of ginger and red pepper.
—Grace Yaskovic, Lake Hiawatha, New Jersey

✓ Uses less fat, sugar or salt. Includes Nutritional Analysis and Diabetic Exchanges.

        2 tablespoons soy sauce
        1 tablespoon orange juice
        1 tablespoon olive oil
      1/2 teaspoon sugar
        1 garlic clove, minced
Dash crushed red pepper flakes
Dash ground ginger
      2/3 pound jumbo shrimp, peeled and
            deveined
       12 cherry tomatoes
Hot cooked rice, optional

In a bowl, combine first seven ingredients. Cover and refrigerate 2 tablespoons for basting. Pour remaining marinade into a large resealable plastic bag; add shrimp. Seal bag and turn to coat; refrigerate for at least 1 hour.

Drain and discard marinade from shrimp. Alternately thread shrimp and tomatoes onto metal or soaked wooden skewers. Coat grill

rack with nonstick cooking spray before starting the grill. Grill kabobs, uncovered, over medium heat for 3 minutes on each side or until shrimp turn pink, basting occasionally with reserved marinade. Serve over rice if desired. **Yield:** 2 servings.

Nutritional Analysis: One serving (prepared with reduced-sodium soy sauce; calculated without rice) equals 262 calories, 10 g fat (1 g saturated fat), 230 mg cholesterol, 838 mg sodium, 10 g carbohydrate, 1 g fiber, 33 g protein. **Diabetic Exchanges:** 4 lean meat, 1/2 starch.

Ole Omelet

My teenage stepsons are hearty eaters, so I like to make them a big breakfast when they visit. With its zesty filling, this Southwestern-style omelet is one of their favorites. I serve it with fresh-baked corn muffins. —LuAnn Edele, Brewster, New York

  2 eggs
  3 tablespoons water
1/2 teaspoon minced chives
1/4 teaspoon hot pepper sauce
1/8 teaspoon salt
1/8 teaspoon pepper
1/8 teaspoon dill weed
  1 tablespoon butter
1/4 cup shredded cheddar cheese
1/4 cup salsa
Sour cream and additional salsa, optional

In a bowl, beat the eggs, water, chives, hot pepper sauce, salt, pepper and dill until blended. In an 8-in. skillet, melt butter over medium-low heat; add the egg mixture.

As eggs set, lift edges, letting uncooked portion flow underneath. Top with cheese and salsa. Fold omelet in half. Cover and cook for 1-2 minutes or until the cheese is melted. Serve with sour cream and additional salsa if desired. **Yield:** 1 serving.

Summer Squash Casserole

(Pictured above right)

Onion and cheddar cheese perk up the rich flavor of summer squash in this comforting casserole. A crispy cornflake-crumb topping adds a little crunch.
—Katherine Metz, Jacksonville, Florida

  2 small yellow summer squash, sliced
1/4 cup chopped onion

1/2 teaspoon salt, *divided*
  1 egg
1/4 cup mayonnaise*
  2 teaspoons sugar
Pepper to taste
1/4 cup shredded cheddar cheese
  2 tablespoons crushed cornflakes
1-1/2 teaspoons butter, melted

In a small saucepan, combine squash, onion and 1/4 teaspoon salt. Cover with water. Bring to a boil. Reduce heat; simmer, uncovered, for 2 minutes or until squash is crisp-tender. Drain.

In a bowl, beat the egg, mayonnaise, sugar, pepper and remaining salt until blended. Stir in cheese and squash mixture. Transfer to a greased 2-cup baking dish. Toss the cornflakes and butter; sprinkle over top. Bake, uncovered, at 350° for 25-30 minutes or until golden brown and bubbly. **Yield:** 2 servings.

*Editor's Note: Reduced-fat or fat-free mayonnaise is not recommended for this recipe.

Bread in Brief

Do you love home-baked bread but you never eat a whole loaf? Prepare the recipe as directed, but bake the dough in miniature loaf pans. After the bread cools, wrap them individually and freeze to be eaten at a later time.

Bacon-Egg English Muffin
(Pictured below)

I stack cheese, Canadian bacon and poached eggs on an English muffin to make this appealing eye-opener. Perfect for one, this delicious open-faced sandwich is special enough for guests, too. —*Terry Kuehn*
Waunakee, Wisconsin

2 eggs
1 tablespoon cream cheese, softened
1 English muffin, split and toasted
2 slices process American cheese
2 slices Canadian bacon

In a skillet, saucepan or omelet pan with high sides, bring 2-3 in. water to a boil. Reduce the heat;

WAKE UP your taste buds with this delightful breakfast menu featuring Fruity French Toast, Berry Banana Smoothies and Bacon-Egg English Muffin (shown below).

simmer gently. Break cold eggs, one at a time, into a custard cup or saucer. Holding the dish close to the surface of the water, slip eggs, one at a time, into the water. Cook, uncovered, until whites are completely set and yolks begin to thicken, about 3 minutes.

Meanwhile, spread cream cheese over muffin halves. Top with cheese slices. In a small skillet, cook Canadian bacon until heated through; place over cheese. Using a slotted spoon, place eggs over bacon. **Yield:** 1-2 servings.

Berry Banana Smoothies

(Pictured at left)

This quick-to-fix nutritious drink is thick and frothy with a refreshing fruit taste. My mother gave me this recipe. It tastes fabulous. I fix it for breakfast or a bedtime snack. —Linda Barker, Mohawk, Michigan

1-1/2 cups vanilla _or_ plain yogurt
  2/3 cup orange juice
    2 medium ripe bananas, cut into chunks
    1 cup halved fresh strawberries
    2 teaspoons honey

In a blender, combine all ingredients; cover and process until smooth. Pour into chilled glasses; serve immediately. **Yield:** 2 servings.

Fruity French Toast

(Pictured at left)

My son begged me to try making the stuffed French toast we enjoyed when our family visited Walt Disney World. His encouragement resulted in this easy delicious breakfast that's a favorite on Saturday mornings.
—Nancy Hawthorne, Gettysburg, Pennsylvania

    1 medium firm banana, sliced
    4 slices Texas toast
    2 teaspoons confectioners' sugar, _divided_
    2 large strawberries, sliced
    1 egg
  1/2 cup milk
  1/2 teaspoon vanilla extract
  1/4 teaspoon ground cinnamon
    2 teaspoons butter
Maple syrup

Place banana slices on two slices of toast. Sprinkle each with 1/2 teaspoon confectioners' sugar. Top with strawberries and remaining toast. In a

shallow bowl, whisk the egg, milk, vanilla and cinnamon. Dip toast in egg mixture, coating both sides.

In a large skillet, melt the butter over medium heat; cook toast for 2-4 minutes on each side or until golden brown. Sprinkle with the remaining confectioners' sugar. Serve with maple syrup. **Yield:** 2 servings.

Hash Brown Reubens

(Pictured on page 174)

If you love Reubens, you'll enjoy this twist on the classic sandwich made with frozen hash brown patties. I came up with the recipe because a member of our family has a sensitivity to bread. Now I wouldn't think of making a Reuben any other way! —Alice Stanwix
Honeoye, New York

    2 frozen hash brown patties
    1 tablespoon butter, softened
    2 thick slices corned beef
  1/2 cup sauerkraut, rinsed and drained
    2 tablespoons brown sugar
    2 tablespoons cinnamon applesauce
  1/4 cup Thousand Island salad dressing
  1/2 cup finely shredded Swiss cheese

Place hash brown patties in a greased 11-in. x 7-in. x 2-in. baking pan. Spread each with butter; top with corned beef. In a bowl, combine the sauerkraut, brown sugar and applesauce; spoon over corned beef. Top with salad dressing and Swiss cheese. Bake, uncovered, at 400° for 15-20 minutes or until heated through. **Yield:** 2 servings.

Shopping Savvy

Buy frozen vegetables and fruits in bags so that the amount needed can be easily poured out of the bag.

Buy fresh fruit and vegetables by the piece rather than by the bag. Even though the bag might be a better price per unit, it's not a bargain if half the bag spoils before it can be used. Or buy the bag and share it with a couple of friends or neighbors.

For small amounts of fresh vegetables, look in the produce section for prepackaged stir-fry vegetable combinations. For example, coleslaw mix makes a good substitution for shredded cabbage.

Asparagus Crab Omelets

(Pictured below)

These satisfying omelets are filled with a savory blend of crab, asparagus, tomatoes and provolone cheese...and they're attractive enough to serve guests. Sometimes I top the omelets with hollandaise sauce.
—*Mae Jean Damron, Sandy, Utah*

    6 **fresh asparagus spears, trimmed**
    4 **eggs**
Dash salt and pepper
  1/2 **cup diced plum tomatoes**
    2 **tablespoons butter,** *divided*
    1 **can (6 ounces) crabmeat, drained, flaked and cartilage removed**
  1/2 **cup shredded provolone cheese**

Place asparagus in a steamer basket. Place in a saucepan over 1 in. water; bring to a boil. Cover and steam for 4-6 minutes or until crisp-tender; set aside. In a bowl, whisk together the eggs, salt and pepper. Stir in tomatoes.

Melt 1 tablespoon butter in a skillet over medium heat; add half of the egg mixture. As eggs set, lift edges, letting uncooked portion flow underneath. When the eggs are set, spoon half of the crab, asparagus and provolone cheese over one side; fold omelet over filling. Cover and let stand for 1-2 minutes or until cheese is melted. Repeat for second omelet. **Yield:** 2 servings.

Orange-Glazed Pork Chops

(Pictured at right)

I came across the recipe for this glaze in a grilling manual but wasn't satisfied with it. I kept the combination of orange marmalade and lime juice and adapted the seasonings to my liking. It's also great on spare ribs and chicken.
—*Helen Faddis*
Gloucester, Massachusetts

    1 **teaspoon cornstarch**
  1/8 **teaspoon ground ginger**
    1 **tablespoon soy sauce**
    1 **teaspoon water**
  1/4 **cup orange marmalade**
    1 **tablespoon lime juice**
1-1/2 **teaspoons olive oil**
    1 **garlic clove, minced**
    2 **bone-in pork chops (3/4 inch thick)**
    1 **small lime, thinly sliced**

In a small saucepan, combine the cornstarch, ginger, soy sauce and water until smooth. Stir in the marmalade, lime juice, oil and garlic until blended. Bring to a boil; cook and stir for 1-2 minutes or until thickened.

Place pork chops in a greased 8-in. baking dish. Spoon glaze over pork; turn to coat. Top with lime slices. Bake, uncovered, at 400° for 30-40 minutes or until pork juices run clear. **Yield:** 2 servings.

Bacon Scalloped Potatoes

(Pictured at right)

I dress up my pared-down potato dish with a layer of sliced onions and a sprinkling of crumbled bacon. It makes the potatoes seem more special. The recipe can easily be doubled for company, too. —*Valerie Belley*
St. Louis, Missouri

    2 **teaspoons butter**
    2 **tablespoons all-purpose flour**
  1/4 **teaspoon salt**
  3/4 **cup milk**
    2 **medium potatoes, peeled and sliced**
    2 **small onions, sliced**
    3 **bacon strips, cooked and crumbled**

In a saucepan, melt butter. Stir in flour and salt until smooth. Gradually add milk. Bring to a boil; cook and stir for 2 minutes or until thickened.

In a greased 1-qt. baking dish, layer the potatoes and onions. Pour white sauce over the top. Cover and bake at 350° for 65-75 minutes or until potatoes are tender. Sprinkle with bacon. **Yield:** 2 servings.

A DOWN-HOME DINNER featuring Orange-Glazed Pork Chops, Bacon Scalloped Potatoes and Red Cabbage Apple Slaw (shown above) is perfect for a crisp fall day.

Red Cabbage Apple Slaw

(Pictured above)

A pleasing celery seed dressing coats this colorful cabbage and apple concoction. —Dorothy Pritchett
Wills Point, Texas

3/4 **cup cubed peeled tart apple**
1 **tablespoon lemon juice**
1-3/4 **cups shredded red cabbage**
2 **tablespoons mayonnaise**
2 **tablespoons plain yogurt**
Dash *each* **onion salt, celery seed and white pepper**

In a bowl, toss apple cubes with lemon juice. Add the remaining ingredients and toss to coat. Serve immediately. **Yield:** 2 servings.

'My Mom's Best Meal'

Six cooks share meals and memories made Mom's way in these straight-from-the-kitchen, home-cooked dinners.

HEART-WARMING MEALS. Clockwise from upper left: Special Sunday Dinner (p. 208), Contest-Winning Cuisine (p. 212), Down-Home Cooking (p. 216) and Fresh Catch of the Day (p. 204).

Her mom's German heritage flavored many memorable family Christmas dinners over the years.

By Rosemarie Forcum, White Stone, Virginia

SOME of my happiest memories as a child involve holidays spent with family and wonderful foods.

Although my parents, Katherine (above) and Tobias Ress, met in New Jersey, they were both German immigrants. Some of their siblings also came to America and settled nearby…so our Christmas gatherings were large, with all the aunts, uncles and cousins. What feasts we had!

To me, the ultimate Yuletide menu included Roast Christmas Goose, greens with Mixed Herb Salad Dressing, Creamed Fresh Spinach and Apple Plum Streusel Dessert.

I'll never forget the wonderful aroma of my mother's Roast Christmas Goose, stuffed with apple, orange and lemon. She served this dish with greens topped with Mixed Herb Salad Dressing and flavorful Creamed Fresh Spinach.

The festive meal, which also included mashed potatoes and homemade rolls, would end with yummy Apple Plum Streusel Dessert, a coffee cake-like pastry drizzled with icing. Usually, we served it with fresh whipped cream or vanilla ice cream.

My sister and I loved watching our mother in the kitchen and learned how to cook from her. She always fixed wonderful meals for our family.

I inherited my love of cooking from my mom and aunts and still prepare many of Mom's recipes, mostly in winter, since German foods are rich and hearty. Family favorites include goulash, sauerbraten and Wiener schnitzel. At Christmas, Mom's roast goose is often on the menu.

Although it is difficult to get my own children and grandchildren together, when we are, good food like my mom's helps make it a happy and memorable occasion!

PICTURED AT LEFT: Roast Christmas Goose, Mixed Herb Salad Dressing, Creamed Fresh Spinach and Apple Plum Streusel Dessert (recipes are on the next page).

Mixed Herb Salad Dressing

This oil and vinegar dressing, seasoned with onion and a handful of lively herbs, will perk up any combination of greens you choose. Mom liked to mix salad and field greens together.

> 6 tablespoons white wine vinegar
> 6 tablespoons vegetable oil
> 2 tablespoons finely chopped onion
> 1 teaspoon salt
> 1/2 teaspoon *each* dried chives, chervil and tarragon
> 1/2 teaspoon dill weed

Assorted salad greens

In a small bowl, whisk the vinegar, oil, onion and seasonings until blended. Serve with salad greens. **Yield:** 2/3 cup.

Creamed Fresh Spinach

This flavorful no-frills side dish is a great way to incorporate the nutritious leafy greens into a meal. My mom always included creamed spinach or carrots on our holiday menu.

Roast Christmas Goose

I have such fond childhood memories of Christmas dinner and my mother serving a golden brown Christmas goose. To flavor the meat, Mom stuffed the bird with peeled and quartered fruit that's discarded after baking.

> 1 goose (10 to 12 pounds)

Salt and pepper

> 1 medium apple, peeled and quartered
> 1 medium navel orange, peeled and quartered
> 1 medium lemon, peeled and quartered
> 1 cup hot water

Sprinkle the goose cavity with salt and pepper. Place apple, orange and lemon in the cavity. Place breast side up on a rack in a large shallow roasting pan. Prick skin well with a fork. Pour water into pan. Bake, uncovered, at 350° for 2-1/4 to 2-3/4 hours or until a meat thermometer reads 185°. If necessary, drain fat from pan as it accumulates. Discard fruit. **Yield:** 6-8 servings.

1 teaspoon vanilla extract
3 cups all-purpose flour
1/2 teaspoon baking powder
6 to 7 medium unpeeled plums, thinly sliced
5 to 6 medium unpeeled Golden Delicious apples, thinly sliced

STREUSEL TOPPING:
1/3 cup all-purpose flour
1/4 cup packed brown sugar
1/4 cup cold butter
1/4 cup chopped pecans

GLAZE:
1 cup confectioners' sugar
1 to 2 tablespoons milk

In a large mixing bowl, cream butter, shortening and sugar. Beat in eggs and extracts until blended. Beat mixture on high speed for 3 minutes. Combine the flour and baking powder; gradually add to creamed mixture. Spread the batter into a greased 15-in. x 10-in. x 1-in. baking pan. Arrange plum and apple slices over batter.

For streusel, combine the flour and brown sugar. Cut in butter until mixture resembles coarse crumbs; stir in pecans. Sprinkle over fruit. Bake at 350° for 40-45 minutes or until lightly browned. Cool on a wire rack. For glaze, whisk confectioners' sugar and milk until smooth. Drizzle over streusel. **Yield:** 16-20 servings.

6 packages (6 ounces *each*) baby spinach
1/4 cup butter, cubed
1/4 cup all-purpose flour
1 cup heavy whipping cream
1 cup milk
2 tablespoons finely chopped onion
Salt and white pepper to taste

Wash and trim spinach, leaving the water that clings to the leaves. Place in a Dutch oven. Bring to a boil. Reduce heat and steam just until wilted, about 4 minutes. Drain and chop; set aside.

Melt butter in a large saucepan over medium heat. Whisk in the flour until smooth. Gradually add cream and milk. Bring to a boil; cook and stir for 2 minutes or until thickened. Stir in the onion, salt and pepper. Fold in spinach; heat through. **Yield:** 8 servings.

Apple Plum Streusel Dessert

Mom would make this German delicacy and other sweets a day ahead to keep the oven free for the roast goose. Similar to coffee cake, this attractive dessert is filled with sweet fruit and topped with chopped nuts and a drizzle of icing.

1/2 cup butter, softened
1/2 cup shortening
1-1/2 cups sugar
4 eggs
1 teaspoon almond extract

This mom puts her heart in to her cooking, whether it's a casual family dinner or a lavish wedding buffet.

By Susan Emery, Everett, Washington

EVERYONE who knows my mother, Sarah Ringstad (above) of Lynnwood, Washington, would agree that she has a passion for cooking.

As a teenager, Mom enjoyed cooking so much that she took 3 years of home economics. As a wife and mother, she has always enjoyed cooking from scratch. And for the past 15 years, she has been decorating cakes and catering events for friends and family.

A native Alaskan, Mom grew up near the gold-rush town of Nome. Fresh fish, especially salmon, was plentiful. So it's no surprise that her best meal features Salmon with Creamy Dill Sauce, along with Fried Rice with Bacon, Bean Sprout Spinach Salad and Rhubarb Strawberry Cobbler.

It's always a treat to be invited to my parents' home for dinner after Mom and my dad, Gerald, come back from a successful fishing trip.

Her Salmon with Creamy Dill Sauce is tender perfection. We hang around in the kitchen eagerly awaiting the first taste, and our patience is always rewarded.

Sauteed leeks add flavor to Mom's tasty Fried Rice with Bacon. Her Bean Sprout Spinach Salad, drizzled with a tangy vinaigrette, gets its delightful crunch from crumbled cooked bacon and sunflower kernels.

When everyone feels they can't eat another bite, Mom marches to the table with Rhubarb Strawberry Cobbler. No one can resist this sweet-tart dessert, topped with a scoop of vanilla ice cream.

Over the years, I've phoned my mom numerous times with cooking questions. She's always eager to share her helpful tips and new recipes.

Some of Mom's recipes are among my family's favorites. I hope you'll find her recipes among your family's favorites, too.

PICTURED AT LEFT: Salmon with Creamy Dill Sauce, Fried Rice with Bacon, Bean Sprout Spinach Salad and Rhubarb Strawberry Cobbler (recipes are on the next page).

Salmon with Creamy Dill Sauce

My family agrees there's nothing like fresh salmon, and my mom bakes it just right so it nearly melts in your mouth. The sour cream sauce is subtly seasoned with dill and horseradish so that it doesn't overpower the delicate salmon flavor.

    1 salmon fillet (about 2 pounds)
    1 to 1-1/2 teaspoons lemon-pepper seasoning
    1 teaspoon onion salt
    1 small onion, sliced and separated into
        rings
    6 lemon slices
    1/4 cup butter
DILL SAUCE:
    1/3 cup sour cream
    1/3 cup mayonnaise
    1 tablespoon finely chopped onion
    1 teaspoon lemon juice
    1 teaspoon prepared horseradish
    3/4 teaspoon dill weed
    1/4 teaspoon garlic salt
Pepper to taste

Line a 15-in. x 10-in. x 1-in. baking pan with heavy-duty foil; grease lightly. Place salmon skin side down on foil. Sprinkle with lemon-pepper and onion salt. Top with onion and lemon. Dot with butter. Fold foil around salmon; seal tightly.

Bake at 350° for 20 minutes. Open foil. Broil 4-6 in. from the heat for 8-12 minutes or until the fish flakes easily with a fork.

Combine the sauce ingredients until smooth. Serve with salmon. **Yield:** 6 servings.

Fried Rice with Bacon

Crispy bacon gives this fried rice recipe a delicious difference. The sauteed leeks and onion season the rice nicely and give it an appealing look. It goes great with my mom's baked salmon.

    2 medium leeks (white portion only),
        chopped
    1 medium onion, chopped
    2 tablespoons olive oil
4-1/2 cups cooked rice
    1/2 teaspoon salt
    1 egg, lightly beaten
    5 bacon strips, cooked and crumbled
Pepper to taste

In a large skillet, saute leeks and onion in oil until tender, about 10 minutes. Add the rice and salt; cook until lightly browned, stirring frequently. Quickly stir in the egg until blended; cook and stir until egg is completely cooked. Sprinkle with the bacon and pepper. **Yield:** 6 servings.

Bean Sprout Spinach Salad

Bean sprouts, bacon crumbles and sunflower kernels lend a pleasant crunch to my mom's refreshing version of spinach salad. The tangy oil- and-vinegar dressing coats the mixture well. Mom will sometimes add a few radish slices for color.

1 cup olive oil
1/4 cup sugar
1/4 cup cider vinegar
2 tablespoons finely chopped onion
1 egg
2 tablespoons Worcestershire sauce
1 package (10 ounces) fresh spinach, torn
1 cup canned bean sprouts
4 bacon strips, cooked and crumbled
4 green onions, sliced
2 hard-cooked eggs, sliced
2 tablespoons sunflower kernels

In a small saucepan, whisk together the first six ingredients. Cook and stir over low heat until the mixture reaches 160°. Remove from the heat; cool.

In a serving bowl, toss the spinach, bean sprouts, bacon and green onions. Drizzle with 1/2 cup salad dressing; toss to coat. Garnish with egg slices and sunflower kernels. Serve immediately. Refrigerate remaining dressing. **Yield:** 6-8 servings.

Rhubarb Strawberry Cobbler

Mom's yummy fruit cobbler is a truly wonderful finale to any meal. This sweet-tart family favorite is chock-full of strawberries and rhubarb and has a thick easy-to-make crust.

1-1/3 cups sugar
1/3 cup all-purpose flour

4 cups diced fresh *or* frozen rhubarb*
    (1/2-inch pieces)
2 cups halved fresh strawberries
2 tablespoons butter, cubed
CRUST:
2 cups all-purpose flour
1/2 teaspoon salt
2/3 cup vegetable oil
1/3 cup warm water
1 tablespoon milk
1 tablespoon sugar
Vanilla ice cream, optional

In a bowl, combine the sugar and flour; stir in rhubarb and strawberries. Transfer to a greased 11-in. x 7-in. x 2-in. baking dish. Dot with butter.

For crust, combine the flour and salt; add oil and water. Stir with a fork until mixture forms a ball. Roll out between two pieces of waxed paper to an 11-in. x 7-in. rectangle.

Discard top sheet of waxed paper. Invert dough over filling and gently peel off waxed paper. Brush dough with milk; sprinkle with sugar. Bake at 425° for 40-50 minutes or until golden brown. Serve with ice cream if desired. **Yield:** 6-8 servings.

*Editor's Note: If using frozen rhubarb, measure rhubarb while frozen, then thaw completely. Drain in a colander, but do not press liquid out.

Appetizing aromas and attractive foods flavor the memories of her mom's old-fashioned cooking.

By Mari Anne Warren, Milton, Wisconsin

BY THE TIME that my mom, Irene Voss (above), was 8 years old, she was responsible for much of her family's cooking. The oldest girl in a family of eight children, Mom learned to cook alongside her mother and often took over the meal preparation.

Mom cooked from scratch like her mother did ...never using a recipe, just adding a pinch of this and a teacup of that. I think she started using cookbooks only after she married my dad, Irving.

When my sister, June, and I were young, our family of four sat down together every day for breakfast, lunch and dinner. My favorite meal was Sunday Pork Loin, Lemon Parsley Potatoes, Green Beans with Bacon and yummy Raspberry Cherry Pie.

I remember helping Mom prepare this meal for Sunday dinner. She'd have me take off a strip of peel around the center of each little potato to make the Lemon Parsley Potatoes attractive.

Everything had to look pretty on the plate—the reddish barbecue sauce on the tender Sunday Pork Loin, the bright green beans with bits of onion and bacon, and her Raspberry Cherry Pie, with its golden crust and sweet-tart red berries. We even requested that pie for our birthdays instead of birthday cake.

When Mom served this menu, we knew something special was happening. She made this meal the first time I brought my husband, Jim, to dinner.

I've inherited my mom's love of cooking. In fact, my passion for cooking, baking and trying new recipes has never been greater.

When Jim and I built our "retirement home" 7 years ago, Mom moved in with us and lived in an attached apartment. She did her own cooking until she was 92. Now her recipes inspire my sister and me. We hope you'll try them soon.

PICTURED AT LEFT: Sunday Pork Loin, Lemon Parsley Potatoes, Green Beans with Bacon and Raspberry Cherry Pie (recipes are on the next page).

Lemon Parsley Potatoes

Seasoned with lemon and butter, these potatoes are a perfect complement to Mom's pork loin. She often made the potatoes on Saturday, then heated them in the oven on Sunday while the pork was roasting.

    3 pounds small red potatoes
    1/2 cup butter
    1/3 cup minced fresh parsley
    1 tablespoon lemon juice

Place potatoes in a large saucepan and cover with water. Bring to a boil. Reduce heat; cover and cook for 15-20 minutes or until tender. Drain. In a small saucepan, melt the butter; stir in parsley and lemon juice. Pour over potatoes; toss to coat. **Yield:** 8 servings.

Green Beans with Bacon

Bits of bacon and onion dress up the green beans in this easy-to-prepare side dish. These beans lend a crisp fresh flavor to any meal. They're best when served hot.

    4 bacon strips, diced
    1/2 cup chopped onion
    8 cups fresh green beans, trimmed

Sunday Pork Loin

My mom often made this moist roast, covered with a thick homemade barbecue sauce, for our Sunday dinner. When this pork dish was in the oven, you could smell the appetizing aroma all through the house.

    1 boneless whole pork loin roast (4 to 5
      pounds)
    1/3 cup chopped onion
    1/3 cup chopped celery
    1 garlic clove, minced
    1 teaspoon vegetable oil
    1 can (10-3/4 ounces) condensed tomato
      soup, undiluted
    1/3 cup water
    2 tablespoons brown sugar
    2 tablespoons lemon juice
    2 tablespoons Worcestershire sauce
    2 tablespoons Dijon mustard
    1/8 to 1/4 teaspoon hot pepper sauce

Place roast on a rack in a shallow roasting pan. Bake, uncovered, at 325° for 1-1/2 hours. In a skillet, saute the onion, celery and garlic in oil until tender. Stir in the remaining ingredients.

Spoon 1 cup sauce over roast. Bake 45-55 minutes longer or until a meat thermometer reads 160°. Let stand for 10-15 minutes before slicing. Serve with the remaining sauce. **Yield:** 8 servings.

1/2 teaspoon baking powder
1 cup shortening
1 egg
5 to 6 tablespoons cold water
1 teaspoon white vinegar
1 tablespoon butter

For filling, in a bowl, combine sugar and tapioca. Add the raspberries, cherries and lemon juice; toss to coat. Let stand for 15 minutes. Meanwhile, in a bowl, combine the flour, sugar, salt and baking powder; cut in shortening until crumbly. Combine the egg, water and vinegar. Gradually add to flour mixture, tossing with a fork until dough forms a ball.

Divide the dough in half. On a lightly floured surface, roll out one portion to fit a 9-in. pie plate. Place pastry in plate; trim even with edge.

Spoon filling into pastry. Dot with butter. Roll out remaining pastry to fit top of pie; make decorative cutouts from scraps if desired. Place top crust over filling. Trim, seal and flute edges.

Cut slits in pastry. Brush cutouts with water; place on top of pie. Cover edges loosely with foil. Bake at 350° for 60-70 minutes or until golden brown. Cool on a wire rack. Store in the refrigerator. **Yield:** 8 servings.

1/4 teaspoon salt
1/8 teaspoon pepper

In a large skillet, cook bacon and onion over medium heat until bacon is crisp and onion is tender.

Meanwhile, place beans in a large saucepan and cover with water. Bring to a boil. Cook, uncovered, for 8-10 minutes or until crisp-tender; drain well. Add to bacon mixture. Sprinkle with salt and pepper; toss to coat. Serve immediately. **Yield:** 8 servings.

Raspberry Cherry Pie

No one can resist a slice (or two!) of this tart "cherry-berry" pie. Growing up, my sister and I requested this pie for our birthdays instead of cake. Now it's a favorite of my own family.

1-1/2 cups sugar
3 tablespoons quick-cooking tapioca
2 cups fresh *or* frozen unsweetened raspberries
1 cup pitted fresh, frozen *or* canned tart cherries
1 teaspoon lemon juice
PASTRY:
3 cups all-purpose flour
2 teaspoons sugar
1-1/2 teaspoons salt

His mom's tasty experiments in cooking created some winning recipes...and a spoiled, well-fed son!

By Kevin Weeks, North Palm Beach, Florida

MY MOM, Marie Weeks (above) of Valdosta, Georgia, has a recipe for every occasion, whether she's competing in a cooking contest, organizing a meal at church or feeding family and friends.

Of course, everyone has their favorite "Marie recipe", but there are some things universally considered "the best you've ever tasted"...like her famous Buttery Crescents.

No meal is complete without these yeast rolls. When Mom serves them, there's always a fight for the leftovers. The crescents go great with her Spicy Seafood Bisque, Chicken Romaine Salad and Lemon Baked Alaska, which, I think, together make up Mom's "best meal you've ever tasted".

Spicy Seafood Bisque, loaded with shrimp and crab, is a definite crowd-pleaser and earned Mom an award in a local cooking contest. Chicken Romaine Salad is an interesting blend of flavors and textures. Its fruits and nuts make it special.

Lemon Baked Alaska, another award-winner, is Mom's signature dish. This ice cream creation in a flaky pie crust is baked just long enough to brown the meringue. A friend of mine declared this the best dessert he's ever had, and I'd have to agree!

My parents love to entertain and invite people to their home. Some of my fondest memories are of parties they threw and of all the good food Mom served. Most of that food she makes from scratch, and the results have created a spoiled son!

I visit with my parents several times a year at each of our homes and while traveling together. No matter what the location, Mom finds a way to cook at least one meal for our family. I hope you'll try this meal of hers and enjoy it as much as I do!

PICTURED AT LEFT: Buttery Crescents, Spicy Seafood Bisque, Chicken Romaine Salad and Lemon Baked Alaska (recipes are on the next page).

Buttery Crescents

These golden brown rolls are my mother's bread of choice for holiday meals. No one in our extended family can imagine a celebratory meal without them.

   1 package (1/4 ounce) active dry yeast
1/2 cup warm water (110° to 115°)
1/2 cup warm milk (110° to 115°)
1/2 cup butter, softened
1/3 cup sugar
   1 egg
3/4 teaspoon salt
   4 to 4-1/2 cups all-purpose flour
Additional butter, melted

In a large mixing bowl, dissolve yeast in warm water. Add the milk, butter, sugar, egg, salt and 2 cups flour. Beat on medium speed for 2 minutes. Stir in enough remaining flour to form a soft dough.

Turn onto a floured surface; knead until smooth and elastic, about 6-8 minutes. Place in a greased bowl, turning once to grease top. Cover and let rise in a warm place until doubled, about 1 hour.

Punch the dough down. Turn onto a floured surface; divide in half. Roll each portion into a 12-in. circle; cut each circle into 12 wedges. Roll up wedges from the wide end and place pointed end down 2 in. apart on greased baking sheets. Curve ends to form crescents. Cover and let rise in a warm place until doubled, about 30 minutes.

Bake at 375° for 12-14 minutes or until golden brown. Brush with melted butter. Remove from pans to wire racks to cool. **Yield:** 2 dozen.

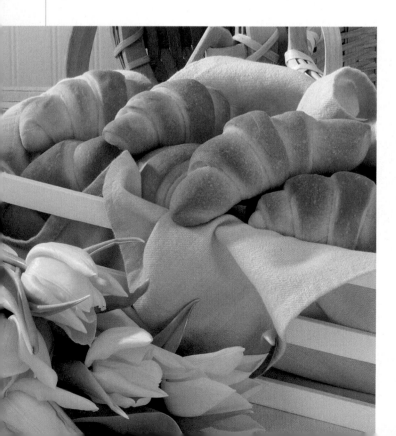

Spicy Seafood Bisque

This spicy soup, featuring shrimp, crabmeat and tomatoes, gets its zip from hot pepper sauce and cayenne pepper.

1/2 cup chopped onion
1/2 cup chopped celery
  2 tablespoons butter
  4 cups chicken broth
  3 cups tomato juice
  1 can (14-1/2 ounces) diced tomatoes, undrained
  1 tablespoon Worcestershire sauce
  1 teaspoon seafood seasoning
  1 teaspoon dried oregano
1/2 teaspoon garlic powder
1/2 teaspoon hot pepper sauce
1/4 teaspoon cayenne pepper
  1 bay leaf
1/2 cup uncooked small shell pasta *or* elbow macaroni
  1 pound uncooked medium shrimp, peeled and deveined
  1 can (6 ounces) crabmeat, drained, flaked and cartilage removed

In a large saucepan, saute onion and celery in butter until tender. Add broth, tomato juice, tomatoes, Worcestershire sauce and seasonings; bring to a boil. Reduce heat; cover and simmer for 20 minutes.

Discard bay leaf. Add pasta to the soup; cook,

uncovered, until tender. Add shrimp and crab; simmer 5 minutes longer or until the shrimp turn pink. **Yield:** 10-12 servings (about 3 quarts).

Chicken Romaine Salad

Mom invented this colorful salad by combining romaine lettuce with toasted pecans, chicken strips, grapes, dried cranberries and cheddar cheese. I think she's particularly proud of this recipe.

>   3 tablespoons butter, melted
>   1 cup chopped pecans
>   1/2 teaspoon salt
>   1/2 cup all-purpose flour
>   1/2 pound boneless skinless chicken breasts,
>   cut into 1-inch strips
>   1/2 cup vegetable oil
>   7 cups torn romaine
>   1 cup seedless red grapes
>   1/2 cup dried cranberries
>   1/2 cup shredded sharp cheddar cheese
>   1 bottle (8 ounces) Vidalia onion *or* honey
>   mustard salad dressing

Pour butter into a 15-in. x 10-in. x 1-in. baking pan; stir in pecans and salt. Bake at 350° for 10 minutes, stirring twice. Set aside.

Place flour in a large resealable plastic bag; add chicken, a few pieces at a time, and shake to coat. In an electric skillet, heat oil to 375°. Fry chicken for 2-3 minutes or until golden brown on all sides and juices run clear. Drain on paper towels.

In a large salad bowl, toss the romaine, pecans, chicken, grapes, cranberries and cheese. Serve with dressing. **Yield:** 10-12 servings.

Lemon Baked Alaska

This impressive dessert, piled high with vanilla ice cream, lemon sauce and meringue, won my mother the grand prize in a local cooking contest.

>   6 tablespoons butter
>   1 cup sugar
>   1/3 cup lemon juice
>   1 teaspoon grated lemon peel
>   1/8 teaspoon salt
>   2 eggs
>   2 egg yolks, lightly beaten
> 1-1/2 quarts vanilla ice cream, softened
>   1 pastry shell (9 inches), baked
> **MERINGUE:**
>   5 egg whites
>   1/2 cup plus 2 tablespoons sugar
>   1/2 teaspoon cream of tartar
>   1 teaspoon vanilla extract

In a heavy saucepan, melt butter; add sugar, lemon juice, lemon peel and salt. Stir in eggs and yolks; cook and stir for 10-12 minutes or until mixture is thickened and a thermometer reads 160°. Cool completely. Refrigerate until chilled. Spread half of ice cream into pastry shell. Top with lemon mixture and remaining ice cream. Cover; freeze overnight.

In a heavy saucepan over low heat, combine the egg whites, sugar and cream of tartar. With a portable mixer, beat on low speed for 1 minute. Continue beating over low heat until mixture reaches 160°, about 12 minutes.

Remove from heat. Add vanilla; beat until stiff peaks form. Immediately spread over frozen pie. Bake at 450° for 3-5 minutes or until lightly browned. Serve immediately. **Yield:** 8-10 servings.

From baking pies to making sausage, her mom's homey cooking is a major ingredient in her daily life.

By Brenda Beachy, Belvidere, Tennessee

LIKE most Amish and Mennonite women, my mom, Orpha Beachy (above), learned to cook from her mother.

Mom makes most everything from scratch, including pie crusts, breads and rolls. We even mix our own sausage. She fixes foods for church carry-ins, picnics and "widows' luncheons", in addition to feeding our family of eight.

My sister Rosanna teaches in Missouri and comes home during the summers. My brother Philip is finishing up 2 years of teaching at a mission school in Belize. The rest of us—Samuel, Kenneth, Esther and I—live at home. At age 16, I'm the youngest. We work in our family's woodworking business.

After a busy day in the shop, we can't wait to sit down for one of Mom's delicious suppers. We think her best menu consists of Grilled Thighs and Drumsticks, Grated Potato Salad, Frozen Fruit Slush and Mom's Molasses Cookies.

Ever since my mom got the Grilled Thighs and Drumsticks recipe a few years ago from a friend, it's been our favorite way to enjoy chicken.

My aunt's recipe for Grated Potato Salad can be made the day before and refrigerated. The grated potatoes have a texture that we really like.

Frozen Fruit Slush hits the spot on a hot summer day. It keeps very well in the freezer, so we often make a large batch to have on hand.

Mom's Molasses Cookies is one of our favorite recipes. A neighbor lady gave us the recipe when we made sorghum several years ago.

Although my mom has taught me to cook, I don't often get the chance since I work in the shop 5 days a week. Mom's scrumptious meals are always something to look forward to, though!

PICTURED AT LEFT: Grilled Thighs and Drumsticks, Grated Potato Salad, Frozen Fruit Slush and Mom's Molasses Cookies (recipes are on the next page).

card marinade. Sprinkle chicken with seasoned salt. Grill chicken skin side down, covered, over indirect medium heat for 15 minutes. Turn; grill 15-20 minutes longer or until juices run clear. **Yield:** 12-14 servings.

Grated Potato Salad

Mom's creamy combination of chopped hard-cooked eggs and grated potatoes is both smooth and chunky. The dressing coats the salad nicely.

> 6 cups grated peeled cooked potatoes
> 6 hard-cooked eggs, chopped
> 1 celery rib, chopped
> 1 cup mayonnaise
> 3/4 cup sugar
> 1/4 cup milk
> 2 tablespoons cider vinegar
> 2 teaspoons salt
> 2 teaspoons prepared mustard

In a large bowl, combine potatoes, eggs and celery. In a small bowl, whisk the mayonnaise, sugar, milk, vinegar, salt and mustard. Pour over the potato mixture; stir until combined. Cover and refrigerate for 4 hours. **Yield:** 8-10 servings.

Grilled Thighs and Drumsticks

When Mom makes chicken, this is the way we like it prepared. It's juicy, has great barbecue flavor and makes a big batch, so it's perfect for summer picnics and family reunions.

> 2-1/2 cups packed brown sugar
> 2 cups water
> 2 cups cider vinegar
> 2 cups ketchup
> 1 cup vegetable oil
> 4 tablespoons salt
> 3 tablespoons prepared mustard
> 4-1/2 teaspoons Worcestershire sauce
> 1 tablespoon soy sauce
> 1 teaspoon pepper
> 1 teaspoon Liquid Smoke, optional
> 10 pounds chicken thighs and drumsticks
> 1/2 teaspoon seasoned salt

In a large bowl, combine the first 10 ingredients; add Liquid Smoke if desired. Pour into two large resealable plastic bags; add chicken. Seal bags and turn to coat; refrigerate overnight.

Prepare grill for indirect heat. Drain and dis-

They're chewy and tender, with a sugary coating. It's hard to eat just one!

3/4 cup shortening
1-1/4 cups sugar, *divided*
1 egg
1/4 cup molasses *or* sorghum
2 tablespoons milk
1 teaspoon vanilla extract
2-1/2 cups all-purpose flour
1-1/2 teaspoons baking soda
1 teaspoon ground cinnamon
3/4 teaspoon salt
3/4 teaspoon ground nutmeg

In a large mixing bowl, cream shortening and 1 cup sugar. Beat in the egg, molasses, milk and vanilla. Combine the flour, baking soda, cinnamon, salt and nutmeg; gradually add to creamed mixture. Cover and refrigerate for 1 hour.

Roll into 1-1/4-in. balls; roll in remaining sugar. Place 2 in. apart on greased baking sheets. Bake at 350° for 10-14 minutes or until tops crack and edges are slightly firm. Remove to wire racks to cool. **Yield:** 5 dozen.

Frozen Fruit Slush

Our family loves this refreshing fruit-filled salad, but it's pretty enough to serve company, too. The salad combines pineapple, bananas, grapes and peaches along with lemonade and orange juice concentrates. It is so good, you'll want seconds.

3 medium firm bananas, sliced
1/2 cup lemonade concentrate
6 medium ripe peaches, peeled and cubed
3 cups water
1 can (20 ounces) crushed pineapple, undrained
2 cups sugar
1-1/3 cups seedless red grapes, halved
1 cup orange juice concentrate

In a large bowl, stir the bananas and lemonade concentrate until coated. Stir in the remaining ingredients. Cover and freeze for 8 hours or until firm. Remove from the freezer 1 to 1-1/4 hours before serving so mixture becomes slushy. **Yield:** 12 servings.

Mom's Molasses Cookies

The kitchen smells so good when Mom is baking these yummy cookies, which we like to make with sorghum.

Her mom always cooks from the heart, bringing comfort and joy to both family and friends.

By Jody Fisher, Stewartstown, Pennsylvania

MY MOM, Anita Bowman (above), was an accomplished cook at a young age. She grew up in West Virginia, where both of her parents worked full-time, which was unusual in the 1950s. So Mom would have dinner ready every evening when they came home.

She spent summers with her grandmother, learning to make Southern specialties and family favorites from scratch. Mom also learned to can and preserve fruits and vegetables.

My parents raised my brother, Dean, and me outside Baltimore, so Mom's cooking became a blend of her Southern roots, Maryland seafood dishes and regional favorites of our new home state, Pennsylvania. Her best meal is a combination of old and new recipes—Shrimp Fettuccine, Roasted Asparagus, Mixed Green Salad and Apple Dumplings.

Mom's Shrimp Fettuccine is elegant but surprisingly simple to prepare. And the aroma is out of this world! Dean, who's a chef, has used this recipe as a daily special at the restaurant where he works.

Roasted Asparagus is a fairly recent addition of Mom's…and now we don't want asparagus any other way. I've been guilty of sampling it from the pan before it reaches the table.

With its light zippy wine vinegar dressing, her Mixed Green Salad makes a delightful accompaniment to the fettuccine.

And comforting Apple Dumplings, a recipe from my great-grandmother, has a deliciously spicy aroma that always reminds me of family and fall. We live near four orchards, so Mom always has apples ready and waiting in the freezer.

I'm glad I was able to share some of her recipes with you…and hope you'll pass them down in your family as they have been passed down in ours.

PICTURED AT LEFT: Shrimp Fettuccine, Roasted Asparagus, Mixed Green Salad and Apple Dumplings (recipes are on the next page).

Shrimp Fettuccine

The combination of shrimp, fresh garlic and lemon juice make this one of my mom's most memorable dishes. Instead of fettuccine, the shrimp can also be served over toast points.

    1 package (12 ounces) fettuccine
1-1/2 pounds uncooked medium shrimp, peeled
      and deveined
    1/2 cup butter
    1/4 cup minced fresh parsley
      2 garlic cloves, minced
      2 tablespoons lemon juice
      2 tablespoons chicken broth
    1/2 teaspoon salt
    1/8 teaspoon pepper

Cook fettuccine according to package directions. Meanwhile, in a large skillet, saute shrimp in butter for 4 minutes or until shrimp turn pink. Add the parsley, garlic, lemon juice, broth, salt and pepper. Cook and stir for 2 minutes or until garlic is tender. Drain fettuccine; top with shrimp mixture. **Yield:** 6 servings.

Roasted Asparagus

Asparagus never tasted so good! Simply seasoned with butter and green onions, the roasted spears have a fresh flavor and keep their bright color, too. You might want to make extra.

      2 pounds fresh asparagus, trimmed
    1/2 cup butter, melted

      2 to 4 green onions, chopped
    1/2 teaspoon salt

Place asparagus in a shallow baking dish coated with nonstick cooking spray. Combine the butter and green onions; spoon over asparagus. Sprinkle with salt. Bake, uncovered, at 425° for 10-15 minutes or until lightly browned. **Yield:** 6 servings.

Mixed Green Salad

I add garlic, basil and crushed red pepper flakes to the light vinaigrette that dresses this refreshing salad. A sprinkling of Parmesan cheese on top gives it even more flavor.

    1/4 cup olive oil
      1 tablespoon plus 1-1/2 teaspoons red wine
        vinegar
      1 garlic clove, minced
    1/2 teaspoon dried basil
    1/8 teaspoon crushed red pepper flakes
      6 cups torn salad greens
      2 medium tomatoes, cut into thin wedges
      1 medium cucumber, sliced
      2 tablespoons shredded Parmesan cheese

In a jar with a tight-fitting lid, combine the oil, vinegar, garlic, basil and pepper flakes; shake well. In a salad bowl, combine the greens, tomatoes and cucumber. Drizzle with dressing and sprinkle with the Parmesan cheese; toss to coat. **Yield:** 6 servings.

Apple Dumplings

This dessert always reminds me of my great-grand-mother, who gave my mom her love of good, whole-some food. The crispy golden dumplings are filled with apples and topped with a sweet caramel sauce. A scoop of ice cream is the perfect finishing touch.

- 2 cups all-purpose flour
- 1 teaspoon salt
- 2/3 cup shortening
- 4 to 5 tablespoons cold water
- 2 cups chopped peeled tart apples (about 5 medium)
- 2 cups packed brown sugar
- 1 cup water
- 1/4 cup butter, cubed

Vanilla ice cream

In a bowl, combine the flour and salt; cut in short-ening until crumbly. Gradually add water, tossing with a fork until dough forms a ball. On a lightly floured surface, roll out dough to a 12-in. x 18-in. rectangle. Cut into six squares.

Place 1/3 cup chopped apples in the center of

each square. Brush edges of dough with water; fold up corners to center and pinch to seal. Place in a greased 13-in. x 9-in. x 2-in. baking dish. Bake at 350° for 30 minutes.

In a saucepan, combine the brown sugar, water and butter; bring to a boil, stirring constantly. Re-move from the heat. Pour over dumplings. Bake 25-30 minutes longer or until apples are tender. Serve warm with ice cream. **Yield:** 6 servings.

Apple Extras

Looking for ways to use up apples? Turn them into one of these "a-peeling" desserts.

To make baked apples, core each apple and stuff with brown sugar, cinnamon and butter. Place in a baking dish with a little water and bake until apples are tender.

Fry apple slices in a greased skillet until ten-der. Sprinkle with cinnamon-sugar. Serve warm with vanilla ice cream.

Blend a package of cream cheese with brown sugar and vanilla to taste. Serve as a dip with apple slices. Or serve apple slices with a store-bought caramel dip.

Editors' Meals

Taste of Home is edited by 1,000 cooks across North America. Here, you'll "meet" some of those cooks who share a family-favorite meal.

DELIGHTFUL DINING. Clockwise from upper left: Supper Says "Spring" (p. 234), Family Favorite Fare (p. 246), Feast on Easter Favorites (p. 230) and Ham for the Holidays (p. 226).

Ham for the Holidays

It wouldn't be Christmas at this busy cook's home without her festive ham dinner.

By Christine Eilerts, Tulsa, Oklahoma

I LOVE to cook and bake for the holidays. During this busy season, because I have a full-time job, I get up an hour earlier each morning so I can prepare foods ahead of time for the upcoming celebrations.

It starts with baking our pies 3 weeks before Thanksgiving—I triple-wrap them with aluminum foil and freeze them. For Christmas, I get an early start making treats to fill several pretty holiday plates of goodies I give out.

Also, I plan ahead for our family's festive dinner. While the menu may vary a bit from year to year, there are some "must-haves".

It just would not be Christmas—or Easter—at our house if we did not have Ham with Peach Glaze. With the ham, I'll serve Home-Style Scalloped Potatoes, Beans with Celery Bacon Sauce and Cherry Cheesecake Dessert. In addition to this traditional fare, I'll add another side dish or two and at least one more dessert.

We like the peach glaze for the ham so much that I always double, if not triple, the recipe. I have found that the leftover ham, pineapple and glaze taste wonderful served with scrambled eggs and fresh fruit the next morning for breakfast.

Potatoes Can't Be Beat

Over the years, I've tried many extra-nice potato recipes, but I always keep going back to the Home-Style Scalloped Potatoes recipe that was in my high school economics class cookbook. It's so good and simple to prepare, which I appreciate when I'm working against the clock. I assemble this dish the day before and refrigerate it.

Beans with Celery Bacon Sauce is a tasty side dish—and pretty, too! I found the recipe in a farm magazine. The first time I made it was many years ago, when my grandmother gave me fresh beans from her garden. The recipe can easily be doubled for a crowd.

My mother made Cherry Cheesecake Dessert for as long as I can remember, and it is my sons' absolute favorite treat. I serve it for each holiday. It is also requested for every birthday celebration…and our oldest son even wanted it for his college graduation party.

Mom taught me how to cook while I was growing up on the family wheat farm near McPherson, Kansas. She was a wonderful cook but didn't enjoy it. So, cooking became my chore while she worked with my father in the fields.

Dad "Dressed" for Dinner

I took pride in the meals I prepared and often set the dining room table with Mom's china and a white tablecloth for the evening meal. I can still vividly recall the night my dad came to the table—after he had cleaned up from a hot day of harvesting wheat—wearing a tie and no shirt!

My husband, Gene, and I celebrated our 35th wedding anniversary in 2003. Gene is in industrial sales, and we were transferred to Tulsa from Wichita, Kansas over 15 years ago. We have two sons. Jeff and his wife, Tiffany, live in Oklahoma and have busy sales careers. Joel works for an oil company in Texas.

Homemade, great-tasting food is very important to our family. I am an assistant in a commercial real estate office. Although I have worked full-time for over 35 years, I still manage to cook a lot. I try to prepare several new recipes each week. Baking cookies, pies, bars and cobblers and making candy are my specialties. But I also enjoy working with fresh seasonal produce.

I have lots and lots of cookbooks. My library includes every issue of *Taste of Home* magazine and its "sister" publication *Quick Cooking*, as well as their annual recipe books.

As for other interests, Gene and I travel every chance we get. I look forward to retirement, when I will have time to entertain large groups in our home. We are planning to retire somewhere out in the country.

In the meantime, it is such a pleasure to be a *Taste of Home* field editor and to be asked to share one of our favorite meals with you. From our family to yours, have a blessed and most joyous holiday season!

PICTURED AT LEFT: Ham with Peach Glaze, Home-Style Scalloped Potatoes, Beans with Celery Bacon Sauce and Cherry Cheesecake Dessert (recipes are on the next page).

has. My husband and sons rate this simply delicious potato casserole the "best ever" and request it often.

> 1/3 cup chopped onion
> 5 tablespoons butter
> 5 tablespoons all-purpose flour
> 1-1/4 teaspoons salt
> 1/2 teaspoon pepper
> 5 cups milk
> 6 cups thinly sliced potatoes

In a large saucepan, saute onion in butter until tender. Stir in flour, salt and pepper until blended. Gradually add milk. Bring to a boil; cook and stir for 2 minutes or until sauce is thickened.

Place half of potatoes in a greased 3-qt. baking dish. Pour half of sauce over potatoes. Repeat layers. Bake, uncovered, at 350° for 60-70 minutes or until potatoes are tender and top is lightly browned. Serve immediately. **Yield:** 8 servings.

Ham with Peach Glaze

Tender slices of this fruit-glazed ham are on our family's Christmas menu every year. Topping the meat with pineapple slices, cherries and cloves makes it look festive and adds to the flavor of this easy holiday entree.

> 1 bone-in fully cooked ham (5 to 7 pounds)
> Whole cloves
> 2 cans (8 ounces *each*) sliced pineapple, drained
> Maraschino cherries with stems
> 1-1/2 cups packed brown sugar
> 1/3 cup peach *or* apricot nectar
> 3 tablespoons cider vinegar
> 1/8 teaspoon ground cloves

Place ham on a rack in a roasting pan. Score the surface with shallow diagonal cuts, making diamond shapes; insert whole cloves into diamonds. Secure pineapple slices and cherries on ham with toothpicks. In a small bowl, combine the brown sugar, peach nectar, vinegar and ground cloves. Spoon half of glaze over ham.

Cover and bake at 350° for 2 hours. Uncover; bake 20-30 minutes longer or until a meat thermometer reads 140°, basting twice with remaining glaze. **Yield:** 8-10 servings.

Home-Style Scalloped Potatoes

The secret to a good scalloped potato dish is to make sure it has plenty of creamy sauce, which this recipe

Beans with Celery Bacon Sauce

Bacon adds nice crunch and flavor to the sauce for the dressed-up green beans I serve for our Christmas ham dinner. Since this pretty side dish goes well with many other foods, too, it's a recipe I like to use often throughout the year.

FILLING:

 2 packages (one 8 ounces, one 3 ounces)
 cream cheese, softened
1/2 cup sugar
 2 eggs
 1 teaspoon vanilla extract
 1 can (21 ounces) cherry pie filling

In small bowl, combine cracker crumbs and sugar; stir in butter. Press into a greased 8-in. square baking dish; set aside.

In a mixing bowl, beat cream cheese and sugar until smooth. Beat in eggs and vanilla just until blended; pour over crust. Bake at 350° for 15-20 minutes or until almost set. Cool for 1 hour on a wire rack. Refrigerate for 8 hours or overnight. Spoon pie filling over top. **Yield:** 9 servings.

♪ Ham Hints

Choose firm, plump hams that are rosy pink and finely grained. Check the label before using a ham. Most are fully cooked and may be eaten immediately or heated until hot (140°). Some hams, however, are labeled "cook before eating", requiring them to be heated to an internal temperature of 160°.

Never throw out a ham bone. Freeze it for later to use to flavor soups, stews, beans or broth.

6 cups fresh green beans
4 bacon strips, diced
1 cup finely chopped onion
1 can (10-3/4 ounces) condensed cream of
 celery soup, undiluted
1/2 cup milk

Place beans in a large saucepan and cover with water; bring to a boil. Cook, uncovered, for 8-10 minutes or until crisp-tender; drain and set aside.

In a skillet, cook bacon over medium heat until crisp. Remove to paper towels; drain, reserving 2 tablespoons drippings. Saute onion in drippings until tender. Stir in soup and milk until blended; heat through. Spoon over beans. Sprinkle bacon over top. **Yield:** 8 servings.

Cherry Cheesecake Dessert

My mother often made this lovely fruit-topped cheese-cake. Now our grown sons consider it my "signature dessert". Sometimes, I bake and freeze the cheesecake ahead of time. On the day I serve it, I thaw it and then add the fruit.

1-1/4 cups graham cracker crumbs (about 20
 squares)
 2 tablespoons sugar
1/3 cup butter, melted

Feast on Easter Favorites

Her savory feast makes a memorable menu for Easter or other springtime suppers.

By Marie Hattrup, The Dalles, Oregon

EASTER DINNER is a wonderful time to serve leg of lamb. It has always been my favorite treat! Often, one or more of our four children and their families will join my husband, Kenny, and me for a holiday celebration.

Along with my Rosemary Leg of Lamb, I like to serve Romaine Caesar Salad, Sour Cream Yogurt Braid, Cran-Orange Coconut Cake and Ginger Ale Citrus Cooler.

Although there are some people who prefer lamb rare, I love its distinctive flavor when it's cooked a little more well done. Garlic and rosemary complement the flavorful meat, and the pan drippings make a delicious gravy.

Daughter's Tangy Dressing

We have enjoyed zesty Romaine Caesar Salad for years. Everyone who tastes it is impressed. My daughter Ann was first in the family to make this salad after getting the recipe from a dear old German friend.

Ann cut down on the amount of anchovies in the original recipe and added more lemon and garlic. She has a talent for knowing how to improve any dish.

I'm proud that all three of my daughters are good cooks. They have inherited my love of cooking, which rubbed off on me from my mother. I grew up on a wheat ranch in north central Oregon, about 63 miles from where we now live.

Mom sent for every offer of recipes that came her way. We had a woodstove, which actually made food taste better, as I remember.

My Sour Cream Yogurt Braid is a twist on a bread recipe I found in a 1960s cookbook. Wanting to try for a "San Francisco flavor", I substituted yogurt for half of the sour cream called for in the recipe. The bread turned out very well. Later, when I decided to enter it in a fair, I braided the dough—and loved the look!

Lifelong Love of Fairs

I was the youngest of six in a very competitive family. Everything went to the fair, and I've been entering ever since! My main interest has always been baking.

I never learned the knack of knowing when the woodstove felt right for baking. But electricity came to our area in 1940, when I was 9.

Our Easter dessert of Cran-Orange Coconut Cake is a lovely bundt cake with complementary flavors of cranberries, nuts and coconut. Brown sugar and grated orange peel add to this cake's appeal.

We usually call Ginger Ale Citrus Cooler "mock champagne" because it's fizzy and fruity but not overly sweet. This pretty pink-orange punch is one that we often enjoy with company.

Through the years, I taught 4-H sewing and cooking, and I have been judging fair entries for about 40 years. I've written a pictorial history for the local high school, put together pictorial family histories of both sides of our families and authored two cookbooks.

I like trying all kinds of new dishes. I'm finding easier ways to do things these days, but I still like the challenge of a dish made from scratch.

Happy Easter to you! If you have a chance to try my recipes, I know you'll have delicious results.

Ginger Ale Citrus Cooler

2/3 cup sugar
2/3 cup water
1 cup grapefruit juice
1/2 cup orange juice
3-1/2 cups ginger ale, chilled
3 tablespoons maraschino cherry juice

In a large saucepan, cook and stir the sugar and water over low heat until sugar is dissolved. Bring to a boil; boil for 5 minutes. Cool.

Stir in grapefruit and orange juices. Cover and refrigerate until chilled. Just before serving, stir in the ginger ale and cherry juice. **Yield:** 6 cups.

PICTURED AT LEFT: Rosemary Leg of Lamb, Romaine Caesar Salad, Sour Cream Yogurt Braid, Cran-Orange Coconut Cake and Ginger Ale Citrus Cooler (recipes are on the next page and at right).

Rosemary Leg of Lamb

Roast lamb is a treat for our family at Eastertime and on other special occasions. Before putting the meat in the oven, I rub on a mixture of garlic, rosemary, salt and pepper, which enhances the flavor.

- 4 garlic cloves, minced
- 1 to 2 tablespoons minced fresh rosemary *or* 1 teaspoon dried rosemary, crushed
- 1 teaspoon salt
- 1/2 teaspoon pepper
- 1 bone-in leg of lamb (7 to 9 pounds), trimmed
- 1 teaspoon cornstarch
- 1/4 cup beef broth

In a bowl, combine the garlic, rosemary, salt and pepper; rub over meat. Place on a rack in a large roasting pan. Bake, uncovered, at 350° for 1-1/2 to 2-1/2 hours or until the meat reaches desired doneness (for rare, a meat thermometer should read 140°; medium, 160°; well-done, 170°). Let stand for 10 minutes before slicing.

Meanwhile, pour pan drippings into a small saucepan, scraping browned bits. Skim fat. Combine cornstarch and broth until smooth. Whisk into saucepan. Bring to a boil; cook and stir for 1 minute or until thickened. Serve with lamb. **Yield:** 10-12 servings.

Romaine Caesar Salad

After tasting this terrific salad my daughter made, I was eager to get the recipe and try it myself. The dressing is easy to mix up in the blender.

- 2 hard-cooked eggs
- 1/4 cup lemon juice
- 2 tablespoons balsamic vinegar
- 1 anchovy fillet
- 1 tablespoon Dijon mustard
- 2 garlic cloves, peeled
- 1 teaspoon Worcestershire sauce
- 1 teaspoon pepper
- 3/4 teaspoon salt
- 1/2 cup olive oil
- 1 bunch romaine, torn
- 1 cup (4 ounces) shredded Parmesan cheese
- 1 cup Caesar salad croutons

Slice eggs in half; remove yolks. Refrigerate whites for another use. In a blender or food processor, combine the lemon juice, vinegar, anchovy, mustard, garlic, Worcestershire sauce, pepper, salt and egg yolks; cover and process until blended. While processing, gradually add oil in a steady stream. Cover and refrigerate for 1 hour.

In a salad bowl, combine romaine, Parmesan cheese and croutons. Drizzle with dressing; toss to coat. Serve immediately. **Yield:** 8 servings.

Sour Cream Yogurt Braid

I won best of show at the county fair with this favorite yeast bread. I like to shape the dough into an attractive braid. It smells wonderful coming out of the oven, and everyone likes the texture and flavor.

- 2 packages (1/4 ounce *each*) active dry yeast
- 1/3 cup plus 1/2 cup warm water (110° to 115°), *divided*

1/2 cup sour cream
1/2 cup plain yogurt
  4 tablespoons butter, softened, *divided*
  2 tablespoons sugar
  1 teaspoon salt
3-1/2 to 4-1/2 cups bread flour
Cornmeal

In a small bowl, dissolve yeast in 1/3 cup warm water. In a large mixing bowl, beat sour cream, yogurt, 2 tablespoons butter, sugar, salt and remaining water. Add yeast mixture and 2 cups flour; beat until smooth. Stir in enough remaning flour to form a soft dough.

Turn onto a floured surface; knead until smooth and elastic, about 6-8 minutes. Place in a greased bowl, turning once to grease top. Cover and let rise in a warm place until doubled, about 1 hour.

Punch dough down. Turn onto a lightly floured surface. Divide into thirds. Shape each into a 16-in. rope. Grease a baking sheet and sprinkle with cornmeal. Place three ropes on prepared baking sheet and braid; pinch seams to seal and tuck ends under.

Cover and let rise in a warm place until doubled, about 30 minutes. Bake at 400° for 20-25 minutes or until golden brown. Melt remaining butter; brush over braid. **Yield:** 1 loaf (12 slices).

Cran-Orange Coconut Cake

This popular dessert is part of my Easter menu, but it's a recipe I use throughout the year.

1/2 cup dried cranberries
1/4 cup orange juice
1/2 cup chopped pecans
  2 tablespoons grated orange peel
  2 tablespoons brown sugar
3/4 cup butter, softened
  1 cup sugar
  4 eggs
  1 teaspoon vanilla extract
2-2/3 cups all-purpose flour
  1 teaspoon baking powder
  1 teaspoon baking soda
1/4 teaspoon salt
  1 cup plus 2 tablespoons sour cream
1-1/2 cups flaked coconut
Confectioners' sugar

In a saucepan, combine cranberries and orange juice. Cook over medium-high heat for 2-3 minutes or until juice is absorbed. Remove from heat. When cool, finely chop cranberries. Place in a bowl; add pecans, orange peel and brown sugar. Set aside.

In a mixing bowl, cream butter and sugar. Beat in eggs, one at a time, beating well after each addition. Stir in vanilla. Combine the dry ingredients; add to creamed mixture alternately with sour cream, beating just until smooth. Fold in coconut.

Spoon a third of batter into a greased and floured 10-in. fluted tube pan. Spoon half of the cranberry mixture over batter. Repeat layers. Carefully spread remaining batter over cranberry mixture.

Bake at 325° for 50-60 minutes or until toothpick comes out clean. Cool for 10 minutes before removing from pan to a wire rack to cool completely. Dust with confectioners' sugar. **Yield:** 12-16 servings.

Supper Says 'Spring'

Garden-fresh rhubarb brings a touch of springtime to her produce-packed supper.

By Edie DeSpain, Logan, Utah

WHILE it is exquisite and elegant enough to serve on Sundays for special dinner guests, my favorite meal is also suitable for a week-night supper.

The menu includes Rhubarb Pork Chop Bake, Broccoli with Orange Sauce, Poppy Seed Fruit Salad, Macadamia Lemon Bars and Citrus Punch. Grouped together, these recipes make a pretty presentation on the dinner table.

I'll concede that rhubarb is a unique ingredient for dressing up pork chops. My mother, who was born and raised in Germany, had an abundance of rhubarb in our family's backyard garden and came up with this creative use for it.

My family has grown to love the deliciously tangy taste of the chops and dressing. As a single mother, I raised three children and now also have seven wonderful grandchildren.

I've also served this dish to many dinner guests. There are few people who don't like pork chops, so this recipe seems to work well every time.

Few Ingredients, Fine Flavor

Since I've worked away from home all my life, I try to find recipes I can whip up in a hurry on busy weeknights. Broccoli with Orange Sauce has only five ingredients and is very tasty. The orange juice adds a distinctive citrus accent to this versatile veggie side dish.

For interest and variety, you can use any kind of fresh fruit that you like in my Poppy Seed Fruit Salad. Cantaloupe, honeydew melon, raspberries, kiwifruit, grapes and orange sections are good choices to substitute for the fruits listed in my recipe. In a pinch, I've picked up 4 cups of cut-up fruit from the supermarket to save time.

PICTURED AT LEFT: Rhubarb Pork Chop Bake, Broccoli with Orange Sauce, Poppy Seed Fruit Salad, Macadamia Lemon Bars and Citrus Punch (recipes are on the next page).

Whenever I am asked to supply a salad for a picnic or potluck event, I take it along in an oversized glass jar—it's so pretty and tastes so good, it always gets compliments.

I make Macadamia Lemon Bars often for dessert. I love macadamias, so I substituted them for walnuts in a bar recipe I got from a dear friend a number of years ago. I keep copies on hand since I get so many requests for this recipe.

People always come back for seconds of refreshing Citrus Punch. It has added the crowning touch to many of our holiday meals. The ample recipe fills two big pitchers or a punch bowl. I like to garnish the punch bowl with an ice ring as well as fresh berries or sprigs of mint.

Gifts from Her Kitchen

After a busy workweek, I enjoy entertaining small groups on the weekend. I also do a lot of baking for friends and relatives during the holidays.

It's a great time to fuss a little on fancy cookies and desserts. But the kids always say I can never go wrong with my well-liked banana nut bread and chocolate chip cookies.

I like to experiment with new recipes to suit my tastes (I have 300 cookbooks) and especially like to make casseroles, soups, quick breads, cookies and some of the German dishes my mom passed down to me. My favorites include her sauerbraten, Wiener schnitzel and roast pork.

As her only daughter, I helped Mom a lot in the kitchen while I was growing up. My five brothers were voracious eaters! Mother canned everything from our huge garden, such as beans, corn and other vegetables, as well as apples and peaches.

I will admit that at first I didn't have a burning desire to learn how to cook, but it grew on me. As a 4-H member, I learned basic food skills. With that, along with my experience at home, I began to really enjoy preparing meals.

Nowadays, spending time with my children and grandchildren is my greatest pleasure. I try to do as much with them as possible. Often that includes gathering for a meal, such as the one I'm sharing with you here. I hope you decide to try it soon…and that it's as popular at your house as it is at mine!

Broccoli with Orange Sauce

As a busy working mother, I was looking for a good broccoli recipe that didn't take very long to make. This one, adapted from an old cookbook, can be whipped up in a hurry. I think you'll find it complements the rest of my favorite meal.

> 2 packages (10 ounces *each*) frozen broccoli spears
> 1/4 cup butter, cubed
> 1 teaspoon cornstarch
> 1/2 cup orange juice
> 1 tablespoon grated orange peel

Cook broccoli according to package directions. Meanwhile, in a saucepan, melt butter. Whisk in cornstarch until smooth. Gradually stir in orange juice; add orange peel. Bring to a boil; cook and stir for 2 minutes or until thickened. Drain broccoli; drizzle with sauce. **Yield:** 4 servings.

Poppy Seed Fruit Salad

Almonds add a nice crunch to this pretty salad which is always a hit when I serve it. It's refreshing and goes with just about anything. The sweet-tart dressing can be used with any combination of fruits.

> 1/4 cup honey
> 1/4 cup limeade concentrate
> 2 teaspoons poppy seeds
> 1 cup halved fresh strawberries

Rhubarb Pork Chop Bake

True, it's a little unusual to combine rhubarb with meat in an entree, but my family loves this recipe! It was created by my mother in an effort to use abundant rhubarb from our farm garden. I'm sure you'll enjoy it, too!

> 4 bone-in pork loin chops (1/2 inch thick)
> 2 tablespoons vegetable oil
> 1-1/2 teaspoons minced fresh rosemary *or* 1/2 teaspoon dried rosemary, crushed
> 1/4 teaspoon salt
> 1/8 teaspoon pepper
> 2-1/2 cups chopped fresh *or* frozen rhubarb (1/2-inch pieces)
> 4 slices day-old bread, crusts removed and cubed
> 3/4 cup packed brown sugar
> 2 tablespoons all-purpose flour
> 1/2 teaspoon ground cinnamon
> 1/4 teaspoon ground allspice

In a large skillet, brown pork chops in oil. Sprinkle with rosemary, salt and pepper. In a bowl, combine the rhubarb, bread cubes, brown sugar, flour, cinnamon and allspice.

Place half of the rhubarb mixture in a greased 11-in. x 7-in. x 2-in. baking dish. Top with chops and remaining rhubarb mixture. Cover and bake at 350° for 30-35 minutes. Uncover; bake 10 minutes longer or until meat juices run clear. **Yield:** 4 servings.

In a bowl, combine the flour, confectioners' sugar and butter; stir in nuts. Press onto the bottom and 1/2 in. up the sides of a greased 8-in. square baking dish. Bake at 350° for 15-20 minutes or until lightly browned.

In a small mixing bowl, combine the sugar, flour, baking powder and salt. Beat in the eggs, lemon juice and lemon peel until light and fluffy. Pour over hot crust. Sprinkle with nuts. Bake for 10-15 minutes or until lightly browned. Cool completely on a wire rack. Cut into bars. Sprinkle with the confectioners' sugar. **Yield:** 1 dozen.

Citrus Punch

(Pictured on page 234)

- 1 can (12 ounces) frozen lemonade concentrate, thawed
- 1 can (12 ounces) frozen orange juice concentrate, thawed
- 1 cup sugar
- 1 teaspoon vanilla extract
- 1 teaspoon almond extract, optional
- 8 cups cold water
- 2 liters lemon-lime soda, chilled

In two large pitchers or a large punch bowl, combine the first six ingredients. Gently stir in soda. Serve immediately. **Yield:** 4 quarts.

- 1 cup cubed fresh pineapple
- 1 cup fresh blueberries
- 1 cup cubed seedless watermelon
- 1/4 cup slivered almonds, toasted

In a bowl, combine the honey, limeade concentrate and poppy seeds. In a serving bowl, combine the fruit. Drizzle with dressing; toss gently to coat. Sprinkle with the almonds. Serve with a slotted spoon. **Yield:** 4-6 servings.

Macadamia Lemon Bars

"These bars melt in your mouth" and "They're out of this world" are compliments I receive frequently when people taste these treats. They are excellent for showers and other get-togethers.

- 1 cup all-purpose flour
- 1/4 cup confectioners' sugar
- 1/2 cup butter, melted
- 1/4 cup chopped macadamia nuts

FILLING:
- 1 cup sugar
- 2 tablespoons all-purpose flour
- 1/2 teaspoon baking powder
- 1/4 teaspoon salt
- 2 eggs
- 2 tablespoons lemon juice
- 2 teaspoons grated lemon peel
- 2 tablespoons chopped macadamia nuts

Confectioners' sugar

Entertain with Italian Entrees

This creative cook spices up her company-worthy dinner with an Italian flair!

By Barbara McCalley, Allison Park, Pennsylvania

WHEN I'm preparing a meal, I enjoy thinking about how certain recipes came to be among my personal favorites. So many of mine are all tied up in decades of delicious memories as well as my family background.

That is certainly true of Tomato Basil Bruschetta, Baked Mushroom Chicken, Berry Vinaigrette and Cheesecake Praline Squares.

Tomato Basil Bruschetta definitely reflects my heritage. I'm part of a large Italian family that celebrates every possible occasion with great food. Bruschetta is traditional Italian garlic bread that is delightful when it's served as an appetizer or an accompaniment to any meal.

I came up with this variation several summers ago, when I had a surplus of ripe garden tomatoes. My husband, Bruce, and I were expecting guests for dinner one evening, and we put together this combination. They loved the fresh-tasting topping of tomatoes, herbs and cheese.

She Dresses Up Chicken

A delightful entree that goes together quickly, Baked Mushroom Chicken is elegant enough to be company worthy. I found the recipe in a church cookbook in my collection, then made some changes. The result was wonderful!

A quick word about my cookbook collection—I stopped counting my books at 1,500! Among them are three cookbooks I have published. These contain recipes I have created myself or received from friends and relatives.

Although I like to prepare long, involved recipes when time allows, I also enjoy producing relatively simple meals like this one. I feel comfortable with it,

and it is very popular.

As unbelievable as it may sound, I started cooking when I was 5. My maternal grandfather owned three Italian restaurants and kept me perched at his side in the kitchens of his businesses.

Grandpa's Salad Girl

My first job was to tear salad greens at one of my grandfather's restaurants. Early on, I learned that a good salad adds much to a meal and that it's easy to mix up homemade dressings.

Berry Vinaigrette was created in honor of one of my college professors, who has become a wonderful friend and loves everything raspberry. It has a fruity flavor and ruby red color.

I am a retired high school honors English teacher. Plus, I have taught sign language and speed reading. After my retirement, I taught culinary classes at a local college, with my 83-year-old mother as my sous (assistant) instructor. What a great experience!

She and my father gave me free rein as a child in our family kitchen. They always ate whatever I cooked, whether it tasted good or not, and helped to clean up afterward.

Every time I serve Cheesecake Praline Squares, I get requests for the recipe. It began as a recipe I clipped from a magazine and has evolved into a fabulous dessert. The creamy texture of the filling as well as the praline flavors of the crust and topping are sure winners.

I love to entertain in any fashion—from casual gatherings to multicourse dinners. Casual for me usually means a dozen or more appetizers served with various beverages, or a soup-and-bread party where I prepare three or four from-scratch soups and several homemade breads.

When I have free time, I garden, make fancy hand-dipped chocolates and paint sweatshirts to sell at craft shows and fairs.

Our home is the favorite "eating place" for many of our friends and family members. That's a wonderful compliment! So I always have enthusiastic tasters for new recipes or tried-and-true ones like those that make up my favorite meal featured here. I hope you'll enjoy it soon.

PICTURED AT LEFT: Tomato Basil Bruschetta, Baked Mushroom Chicken, Berry Vinaigrette and Cheesecake Praline Squares (recipes are on the next page).

Tomato Basil Bruschetta

This is one of the appetizers my friends request most. There is rarely any left over when I serve it. The red pepper flakes and basil add a nice little kick to the taste.

☑ Uses less fat, sugar or salt. Includes Nutritional Analysis and Diabetic Exchanges.

   3 tablespoons olive oil, *divided*
   1 loaf (1 pound) Italian bread, cut into 1/2-inch slices
1-1/2 cups chopped seeded plum tomatoes
   1 jar (4 ounces) diced pimientos, rinsed and drained
   2 tablespoons chopped fresh basil
   1 teaspoon red wine vinegar
   1 teaspoon minced fresh parsley
   1 garlic clove, minced
 1/4 teaspoon salt
 1/4 teaspoon crushed red pepper flakes
 1/8 teaspoon pepper
   1 tablespoon grated Romano cheese
Fresh basil leaves

Using 2 tablespoons oil, lightly brush one side of bread slices. Place bread oil side up on an ungreased baking sheet. Bake at 350° for 15 minutes or until lightly browned.

In a bowl, combine the tomatoes, pimientos, chopped basil, vinegar, parsley, garlic, salt, pepper flakes and pepper; stir in Romano cheese. Place a whole basil leaf on each slice of toasted bread. Top with the tomato mixture. Drizzle with remaining

olive oil. Serve immediately. **Yield:** 20 appetizers.

Nutritional Analysis: One piece equals 85 calories, 3 g fat (1 g saturated fat), trace cholesterol, 168 mg sodium, 12 g carbohydrate, 1 g fiber, 2 g protein. **Diabetic Exchanges:** 1 vegetable, 1/2 starch.

Baked Mushroom Chicken

Here's a way to dress up chicken breasts for a family dinner or party, using fresh mushrooms, green onions and two kinds of cheese. It's a recipe I can count on to yield tender flavorful chicken every time.

   4 boneless skinless chicken breast halves (1 pound)
 1/4 cup all-purpose flour
   3 tablespoons butter, *divided*
   1 cup sliced fresh mushrooms
 1/2 cup chicken broth
 1/4 teaspoon salt
 1/8 teaspoon pepper
 1/3 cup shredded mozzarella cheese
 1/3 cup grated Parmesan cheese
 1/4 cup sliced green onions

Flatten each chicken breast half to 1/4-in. thickness. Place flour in a resealable plastic bag; add chicken, a few pieces at a time. Seal and shake to coat.

In a large skillet, brown chicken in 2 tablespoons butter on both sides. Transfer to a greased 11-in. x 7-in. x 2-in. baking dish. In the same skillet, saute mushrooms in the remaining butter until tender. Add the broth, salt and pepper. Bring to a boil; cook

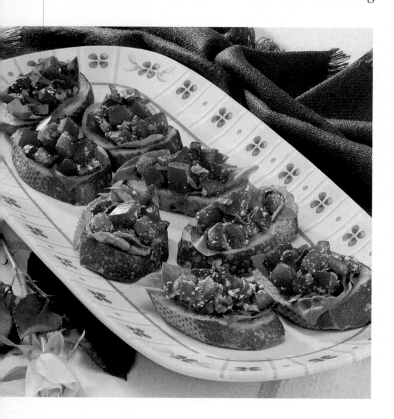

for 5 minutes or until liquid is reduced to 1/2 cup. Spoon over chicken.

Bake, uncovered, at 375° for 15 minutes. Sprinkle with the cheeses and green onions. Bake 5 minutes longer or until the chicken juices run clear. **Yield:** 4 servings.

Berry Vinaigrette

This dressing is wonderful on tossed fresh salad greens and your favorite salad ingredients. Because the raspberry flavor comes from jam, this versatile vinaigrette is convenient to make year-round.

    3 tablespoons seedless raspberry jam
    2/3 cup vegetable oil
    1/3 cup red wine vinegar
    1/4 teaspoon salt
    1/4 teaspoon pepper
Torn salad greens

Place jam in a small microwave-safe bowl. Microwave, uncovered, on high for 10-15 seconds or until melted. Pour into a jar with a tight-fitting lid. Add the oil, vinegar, salt and pepper; shake well. Serve with salad greens. Refrigerate any remaining vinaigrette. **Yield:** 3/4 cup.

Cheesecake Praline Squares

A smooth cheesecake layer, a nutty crust and praline-like topping make this dessert extra special. I fix these

squares often for friends or when my big Italian family gets together.

    2-1/2 cups all-purpose flour
      1 cup butter, melted
    2/3 cup finely chopped pecans
      2 tablespoons confectioners' sugar
FILLING:
      3 packages (8 ounces *each*) cream cheese, softened
    2/3 cup sugar
      1 can (14 ounces) sweetened condensed milk
      2 teaspoons vanilla extract
    1/2 teaspoon grated lemon peel
      4 eggs, lightly beaten
TOPPING:
      1 cup packed brown sugar
      1 cup heavy whipping cream
      1 cup chopped pecans
1-1/2 teaspoons vanilla extract

In a bowl, combine the flour, butter, pecans and confectioners' sugar. Press into an ungreased 13-in. x 9-in. x 2-in. baking dish. Bake at 350° for 20-24 minutes or until lightly browned. Cool on a wire rack.

In a large mixing bowl, beat cream cheese and sugar until smooth. Add the milk, vanilla and lemon peel. Add eggs; beat on low speed just until combined. Pour over crust. Bake at 350° for 35-40 minutes or until edges are lightly browned. Cool on a wire rack.

In a saucepan, combine brown sugar and cream. Cook and stir over medium heat until mixture comes to a boil. Reduce heat; simmer, uncovered, for 10 minutes. Remove from heat; stir in pecans and vanilla. Pour over cheesecake. Refrigerate for 4 hours or overnight. Cut into squares. **Yield:** 15 servings.

Mealtime Is Sizzling

Her zesty cheeseburger meal is perfect to serve for a patio picnic on a warm summer evening!

By Cheryl Maczko, Arthurdale, West Virginia

FIRE UP the grill! My most popular casual summer meal means hamburgers will be sizzling and served alongside side dishes that provide a combination of great flavors.

Our family and friends, young and old alike, anticipate my meal of Provolone Burgers, Greek Macaroni Salad, Fried Dill Pickle Coins and Lemonade Icebox Pie when the weather turns warm.

Whether they're prepared on the backyard patio, at a picnic, at the lake or at a campground, Provolone Burgers get an overwhelming thumbs-up from everyone who tastes them. Neither my son, Ricky—who is always hungry—nor his dad, Rick, ever tire of these burgers.

Garlic, onion, basil and oregano give a savory spark to the beef patties. A slice of provolone cheese is the perfect topping for these well-seasoned burgers... and it's a nice change from the usual cheddar or American. Of course, you can substitute whatever cheese you like best.

When daughter Heather comes over for this meal, she usually goes back for seconds of Greek Macaroni Salad. I've had many compliments on the combination of ingredients and the salad's pleasant oil and lemon dressing.

Lunch Bunch

It's a great dish to take to potluck events, like the luncheons we often plan at my office. I have worked in the business services office at West Virginia University for 25 years.

Our staff looks for any excuse for a party. One of us will bring in a covered dish or slow-cooked main dish, and the rest will sign up to contribute other foods and beverages for the meal.

PICTURED AT LEFT: Provolone Burgers, Greek Macaroni Salad, Fried Dill Pickle Coins and Lemonade Icebox Pie (recipes are on the next page).

On any given day, someone in the department may bring in something new that they've cooked or baked for the rest of us to sample. These goodies are always devoured, and we are constantly exchanging good recipes.

Trying new dishes and fixing foods that are a little different keeps cooking interesting. That's why I hope you'll try Fried Dill Pickle Coins. New to many folks, fried pickles are featured at several restaurants in our county. They're fun and make a nice accompaniment to a burger or sandwich. So I tried making them at home and have found they're quite easy.

I tell doubters not to turn up their nose until they taste this unusual condiment. Usually one puffy golden fried pickle slice leads to another!

To top off a meal on a warm day, Lemonade Icebox Pie looks and tastes refreshing. It's hard for anyone to turn down a slice of this high, fluffy, creamy dessert.

I love lemon. So when I'm perusing the many cookbooks in my big collection, recipes with lemon as a main ingredient always catch my eye. Homemade lemonade has long been a treat for me on a hot day, and this pie has a lemonade personality.

Moms Were Mentors

I've been interested in cooking since I was in junior high. Helping my mother make and decorate molasses cookies at Christmastime was something I particularly enjoyed.

My mother-in-law, Jennie Maczko, has also influenced my cooking in so many delicious ways. She's given me great cooking pointers and has taught me how to prepare many of her Polish specialties. We've shared lots of recipes over the years.

Besides my full-time job, I'm a part-time student in a regent's program of general studies at the university. Plus, I try to keep up with Ricky's busy school schedule and other activities.

Keeping my growing son filled up around the clock is always a challenge. With our busy schedule, I need quick-to-fix meals and recipes that can be made ahead. That's why this favorite summer meal suits us so well.

Next time you're up for grilling, I hope you'll give my menu a try. If your gang is like mine, they'll be asking for a repeat performance soon.

Greek Macaroni Salad

I've found that I can't go wrong taking this colorful bean and pasta salad to a potluck, patio party or picnic. It is easy to put together ahead of time...and the flavors blend as the salad chills.

  1 cup uncooked elbow macaroni
  4 medium plum tomatoes, chopped
  1 can (15 ounces) garbanzo beans *or*
    chickpeas, rinsed and drained
  1 medium onion, chopped
  1 can (6 ounces) pitted ripe olives, drained
  1 package (4 ounces) crumbled feta cheese
  1 teaspoon salt
1/2 teaspoon pepper
  1 garlic clove, minced
1/2 cup olive oil
1/4 cup lemon juice

Cook macaroni according to package directions; drain and rinse in cold water. In a large bowl, combine the macaroni, tomatoes, beans, onion, olives, feta cheese, salt, pepper and garlic.

In a small bowl, whisk the oil and lemon juice. Pour over the salad and toss to coat. Cover and refrigerate until chilled. Stir before serving. **Yield:** 8 servings.

Provolone Burgers

Grilled hamburgers that are seasoned with garlic, onion and herbs and topped with melted cheese are a summertime staple for us. A nice change of pace from the usual American or cheddar, mild provolone cheese is great on these beef patties.

  2 eggs, beaten
  1 medium onion, finely chopped
  3 teaspoons dried basil
  1 teaspoon dried oregano
  2 garlic cloves, minced
1/2 teaspoon salt
1/4 teaspoon pepper
  3 pounds ground beef
  8 slices provolone cheese
  8 sandwich rolls, split
Lettuce leaves

In a bowl, combine the first seven ingredients. Crumble beef over mixture; mix well. Shape into eight patties. Grill, uncovered, over medium-hot heat for 5-7 minutes on each side or until juices run clear.

Top each patty with a cheese slice; grill 1 minute longer or until cheese is melted. Grill rolls cut side down for 1-2 minutes or until toasted. Top with lettuce and burgers. **Yield:** 8 servings.

Fried Dill Pickle Coins

If you've never tried fried pickles, step up to the plate and try these puffy golden bites. They're a delicious ac-

1 package (8 ounces) cream cheese,
   softened
1 can (14 ounces) sweetened condensed
   milk
3/4 cup lemonade concentrate
1 carton (8 ounces) frozen whipped
   topping, thawed
Yellow food coloring, optional
1 graham cracker crust (9 inches)

In a large mixing bowl, beat the cream cheese until smooth. Gradually beat in milk until blended.
Beat in lemonade concentrate. Fold in whipped topping and food coloring if desired. Pour into crust.
Cover and refrigerate until set. **Yield:** 8 servings.

Cheryl's Helpful Hints

For a simple side dish to go with meat, stuff a
whole onion with one clove of garlic and bake
until tender. Serve with sour cream and chopped
chives.

Deep-fry curly parsley sprigs for a few seconds
to make a deliciously different garnish.

For crunchy coleslaw, cut a cabbage in half and
soak in salted water for 1 hour. Drain and pro-
ceed with the recipe.

To test the freshness of dried herbs, rub them between your hands. If there is no aroma, they have
lost their potency.

Add a tablespoon of butter to an inexpensive
cake mix for a richer flavor.

Soups and stews too salty? Add a raw potato to
absorb the salt.

*companiment to a burger or a sandwich. For a fun and
different appetizer, serve fried pickle slices with ranch
dressing for a dip.*

2 cups all-purpose flour
1/2 teaspoon salt
1/4 teaspoon pepper
2 eggs
1 cup milk
3 cups thin dill pickle slices, drained
Oil for deep-fat frying
Ranch salad dressing, optional

In a shallow bowl, combine the flour, salt and pepper. In another bowl, beat eggs and milk. Blot pickles with paper towels to remove moisture. Coat
pickles with flour mixture, then dip in egg mixture;
coat again with flour mixture.

   In an electric skillet or deep-fat fryer, heat oil to
375°. Fry pickles, about 10 at a time, for 3 minutes or until golden brown, turning once. Drain
on paper towels. Serve warm with ranch dressing
if desired. **Yield:** 8 servings.

Lemonade Icebox Pie

*You will detect a definite lemonade flavor in this
refreshing pie. High and fluffy, this dessert has a
creamy smooth consistency that we really appreciate.
It's the dessert that came to mind immediately when I
put together my favorite summer meal for Taste of
Home magazine.*

Family Favorite Fare

A palate-pleasing pasta dinner rates high with her family, friends and company, too.

By Elaine Anderson, Aliquippa, Pennsylvania

MY FAMILY gets excited when delicious aromas fill the house, especially when the meal is going to include Baked Ziti, Pretty Layered Salad, Breadsticks with Parmesan Butter and Chocolate Chunk Cookies.

We spend a lot of time in the kitchen and dining room. Daughters Elizabeth, Emily, Isabelle and Olivia all love stirring, rolling, mixing and measuring. My husband, Dave, enjoys the results after a busy day. He works at the airport as an air traffic controller.

Dave really likes my Baked Ziti, and the kids say it is the best meal ever. I first had ziti at my sister-in-law's when I was younger and liked it very much. After trying quite a few different recipes with this tube-shaped pasta and adding other ingredients, I've settled on this hearty version.

Often, I double the recipe and freeze half for later. Or, I may give one dish to a family in need of a meal because of illness or a new baby. I really enjoy sharing the dishes I prepare…and the recipients seem to enjoy eating them, too!

Leeway with Salad Layers

Although I'm giving you a specific recipe for Pretty Layered Salad, we seldom make it the same way twice. Our oldest, Elizabeth, loves to make this salad and think up new layers.

I've used so many variations that I can't even remember them all. But here are a few: Use lettuce instead of spinach. Vary the type of cheese. Add a layer of chopped tomatoes, red pepper rings on top or enough cubed chicken to make it a main-dish salad.

Breadsticks with Parmesan Butter are tender and tasty. They are also excellent with other casseroles or soups. When we have them with pizza, we like to dip breadsticks in pizza sauce instead of Parmesan Butter.

Baking for the family was a job I loved while growing up in Erie, Pennsylvania. Mother taught me to bake and cook. She canned everything she could from our gardens and froze some, too. We picked berries and made jams and other preserves.

My dad raised chickens (and still does), so I learned a lot about cooking chicken for Sunday dinner. I have five older brothers and a younger sister, so we had plenty of people to eat everything. We all helped out with meals. Now there are 20 grandchildren, and Mom often cooks for the whole bunch of us!

Best Cookie in the Jar

Cookies are our favorite treat to make and eat. Of the many kinds we bake, Chocolate Chunk Cookies are right at the top of the list. If we're in a hurry, we might not add the drizzle. But it makes the cookies look fancy when they are served on a tray.

They also make a fun gift. I often make a batch of the cookies and freeze them to have on hand when we need them.

It was hard for me to cut down on baking large quantities when Dave and I were first married. So I often took cakes and cookies to neighbors and family. A few years ago, we started selling cookies at a nearby farmers market in the summer and fall as an outlet for my baking surplus. Through this venture, we have made some nice new friends. And now, my daughters are baking and delivering and learning to manage money. People call us "the cookie ladies"!

I taught elementary school in Erie and in Virginia before Dave and I moved here and started our family. We homeschool our daughters and do a variety of activities together. Dave's schedule at the airport means he's often home during the day.

Things around here are busy but joyful. I often rely on *Taste of Home* recipes to decide my menus. The magazine really simplifies things for me when it comes to meal planning. My issues are so worn out! But I keep taping them back together and plan to pass them on to my children one day.

We also enjoy having guests in our home for dinner. I've found that the family-favorite meal I'm sharing here is also fine for company. I hope these recipes will be popular at your house, too!

PICTURED AT LEFT: Baked Ziti, Pretty Layered Salad, Breadsticks with Parmesan Butter and Chocolate Chunk Cookies (recipes are on the next page).

Baked Ziti

I enjoy making this dish for family and friends. It's easy to prepare, and I like to get creative with the sauce. For example, I might add my home-canned tomatoes, mushrooms or other extra vegetables.

12 ounces uncooked ziti *or* small tube pasta
2 pounds ground beef
1 jar (28 ounces) spaghetti sauce
2 eggs
1 carton (15 ounces) ricotta cheese
2-1/2 cups (10 ounces) shredded mozzarella cheese, *divided*
1/2 cup grated Parmesan cheese

Cook pasta according to package directions. Meanwhile, in a skillet, cook beef over medium heat until no longer pink; drain. Stir in spaghetti sauce. In a bowl, combine the eggs, ricotta cheese, 1-1/2 cups mozzarella cheese and Parmesan cheese.

Drain pasta; add to cheese mixture and toss to coat. Spoon a third of the meat sauce into a greased 13-in. x 9-in. x 2-in. baking dish; top with half of the pasta mixture. Repeat layers. Top with remaining meat sauce.

Cover and bake at 350° for 40 minutes. Uncover; sprinkle with remaining cheese. Bake 5-10 minutes longer or until cheese is melted. Let stand for 15 minutes before serving. **Yield:** 6-8 servings.

Pretty Layered Salad

A salad like this one is a pretty accompaniment to almost any dinner. You can change the mix of ingredients to include layers of your favorites. I like the tangy vinaigrette dressing with it, but ranch and other types are also very good.

5 cups torn fresh spinach
1/2 pound sliced bacon, cooked and crumbled
1/2 cup grated carrot
3 hard-cooked eggs, chopped
5 cups torn romaine
1 medium sweet red pepper, cut into rings
1/2 cup salad croutons
1/4 cup shredded Parmesan cheese
DRESSING:
6 tablespoons red wine vinegar
1/4 cup water
1/4 cup vegetable oil
2 tablespoons sugar
1/2 teaspoon celery salt
1/4 teaspoon salt
1/8 teaspoon pepper

In a large bowl, layer the spinach, bacon, carrot, eggs, romaine, red pepper, croutons and Parmesan cheese. In a jar with a tight-fitting lid, combine the dressing ingredients; shake until sugar is dissolved. Serve with salad. **Yield:** 8 servings.

Breadsticks with Parmesan Butter

My kids love these nice, tender breadsticks and so does anyone else who has tasted them. Any leftovers are great with butter and honey for breakfast the next day.

> 2 packages (1/4 ounce _each_) active dry yeast
> 1/2 cup sugar, _divided_
> 2 cups warm water (110° to 115°), _divided_
> 3 tablespoons vegetable oil
> 1 egg
> 1 teaspoon salt
> 4-1/2 to 5 cups all-purpose flour
> 1/2 cup butter, softened
> 2 tablespoons grated Parmesan cheese
> 1/4 to 1/2 teaspoon garlic powder

In a large mixing bowl, dissolve yeast and 1 tablespoon sugar in 1 cup warm water. Add the oil, egg, salt, 2 cups flour, and remaining sugar and water. Beat until smooth. Stir in enough remaining flour to form a soft dough. Turn onto a floured surface; knead until smooth and elastic, about 6-8 minutes. Place in a greased bowl, turning once to grease top. Cover and let rise in a warm place until doubled, about 40 minutes.

Punch dough down. Turn onto a floured surface; divide into 36 pieces. Shape each piece into a 6-in. rope. Place 2 in. apart on greased baking sheets. Cover and let rise until doubled, about 25 minutes.

Bake at 400° for 10-12 minutes or until golden brown. Meanwhile, in a small mixing bowl, cream the butter, Parmesan cheese and garlic powder. Serve with breadsticks. **Yield:** 3 dozen breadsticks and about 2/3 cup butter.

Chocolate Chunk Cookies

It's such a pleasure to serve delicious cookies like these to neighbors and family. I love to bake cookies more than anything else. My four daughters are eager to help with the mixing, measuring and stirring!

> 6 squares (1 ounce _each_) white baking chocolate, _divided_
> 1 cup butter, softened
> 1/2 cup sugar
> 1/2 cup packed brown sugar
> 2 eggs
> 2 teaspoons vanilla extract
> 2-1/2 cups all-purpose flour
> 1 teaspoon baking soda
> 1/4 teaspoon salt
> 1 package (11-1/2 ounces) semisweet chocolate chunks _or_ 2 cups semisweet chocolate chips

Melt three squares of white chocolate; cool. In a large mixing bowl, cream butter and sugars. Add eggs, one at a time, beating well after each addition. Beat in melted chocolate and vanilla. Combine the flour, baking soda and salt; gradually add to the creamed mixture. Stir in semisweet chocolate chunks.

Drop by tablespoonfuls onto ungreased baking sheets. Bake at 375° for 10-12 minutes or until golden brown. Cool for 1 minute before removing to wire racks. Melt remaining white chocolate; drizzle over cookies. May be frozen for up to 3 months. **Yield:** 3 dozen.

Meals in Minutes

Time is on your side with these speedy meal solutions that can be on the dinner table in just 30 minutes or less.

GREAT ON THE GO. Clockwise from upper left: Speedy Soup and Sandwich Duo Is Always a Delight (p. 262), Packed with Produce (p. 274), Timely Meal Tastes Like You Spent Hours in the Kitchen (p. 256) and A Special Meal Just for Mom (p. 272).

Reel in Compliments with This Speedy Seafood Supper

FINDING an excellent meal to prepare in just 30 minutes is a necessity some days for the busy cook. This one combines recipes from three such cooks.

Crumb-Coated Salmon, shared by Kathy Peltier of Kalispell, Montana, is pleasantly seasoned with lemon-pepper and dill.

Kathy also shared the recipe for Parsleyed Rice Pilaf, noting, "While the salmon bakes in the oven, I dress up instant rice with bouillon, minced onion and parsley."

Snow Pea Stir-Fry is a family favorite from Pam Rahmer in Phillips, Wisconsin. "When my children were growing up, they requested this often."

The yummy recipe for Pears with Raspberry Sauce comes from Constance Rak of Westlake, Ohio. "This dish came about when I was expecting company and wanted to make a light pretty dessert with items that I already had on hand," she recalls.

Crumb-Coated Salmon

2 eggs
1/2 cup milk
1 cup dry bread crumbs
2 teaspoons lemon-pepper seasoning
1/2 teaspoon dill weed
1/4 teaspoon garlic powder
4 salmon fillets (6 ounces *each*)

In a shallow dish, beat the eggs and milk. In another shallow dish, combine the bread crumbs, lemon-pepper seasoning, dill and garlic powder. Dip salmon in egg mixture, then coat with crumb mixture. Place on a greased baking sheet. Bake at 350° for 14-18 minutes or until fish flakes easily with a fork. **Yield:** 4 servings.

Parsleyed Rice Pilaf

2 cups water
1/4 cup dried minced onion
4 teaspoons butter
2 teaspoons chicken bouillon granules
2 cups instant rice
1/4 cup minced fresh parsley

In a small saucepan, bring water, onion, butter and bouillon to a boil. Stir in rice and parsley. Remove from the heat. Cover and let stand for 5 minutes. Fluff with a fork. **Yield:** 4 servings.

Snow Pea Stir-Fry

2 tablespoons slivered almonds
2 tablespoons butter
1 package (6 ounces) fresh *or* frozen snow peas, thawed
1-1/2 cups sliced mushrooms
1-1/2 teaspoons cornstarch
1/4 teaspoon chicken bouillon granules
1/2 cup water
1 tablespoon soy sauce

In a large skillet, stir-fry almonds in butter for 2 minutes or until lightly toasted. Add snow peas and mushrooms; stir-fry 2 minutes longer.

In a small bowl, combine the cornstarch, bouillon, water and soy sauce until smooth. Add to skillet; bring to a boil. Cook and stir for 1-2 minutes or until thickened. **Yield:** 4 servings.

Pears with Raspberry Sauce

1 package (10 ounces) frozen sweetened raspberries, thawed
4 medium firm pears
2 cups white grape juice
1 cup sugar
2 tablespoons lemon juice
Whipped cream

Place raspberries in a blender or food processor; cover and process until pureed. Strain, reserving juice; set aside. Discard seeds. Core pears from bottom, leaving stems intact. Peel pears; set aside.

In a large saucepan, bring grape juice, sugar and lemon juice to a boil; add pears. Reduce heat; cover and simmer for 5-7 minutes or until tender; drain. For each serving, spoon raspberry sauce on plate, then top with a pear. Garnish with whipped cream. **Yield:** 4 servings.

Spice Up Dinnertime with These Well-Seasoned Dishes

SPENDING TIME preparing an elaborate meal is no big deal for those who like to cook. But some days, speed is the key ingredient in what you whip up for your hungry clan.

The complete-meal menu here is comprised of family favorites from three super cooks. You can have it all ready to serve in just 30 minutes.

"Chicken with Paprika Cream is quick to make when you buy boned and skinned chicken breasts," notes Marilou Robinson of Portland, Oregon. "Serving it over rice lets you get every last bit of the tasty paprika cream."

Steamed Broccoli Florets, with a tart mustard vinaigrette, is a delightful fast-to-fix recipe from Peggy Van Arsdale of Crosswicks, New Jersey. "My Aunt Marion was a wonderful cook. I have many recipes from her, including this one," Peggy says.

Tender sliced mushrooms and a sprinkling of Parmesan cheese dot crisp Mushroom Bread Wedges, made with convenient refrigerated crescent rolls. You can also serve them with soup, chili or a salad. Patricia Mele of Apollo, Pennsylvania contributed the recipe.

Chicken with Paprika Cream

- **6 boneless skinless chicken breast halves**
- **6 tablespoons butter, *divided***
- **1 tablespoon vegetable oil**
- **6 green onions, chopped**
- **1 to 2 tablespoons paprika**
- **2 cups heavy whipping cream**
- **1 teaspoon salt**
- **1/4 teaspoon pepper**
- **Hot cooked rice**
- **Additional chopped green onions, optional**

In a large skillet, brown chicken in 1 tablespoon butter and oil over medium heat. Cover and cook for 5-7 minutes or until juices run clear. Remove chicken; keep warm.

In the same skillet, saute onions until tender. Reduce heat to medium. Add paprika and remaining butter; heat until butter is melted. Stir in the cream, salt and pepper; cook and stir until sauce is thickened, about 4 minutes. Serve with chicken over rice. Garnish with onions if desired. **Yield:** 6 servings.

Steamed Broccoli Florets

- **1/4 cup sugar**
- **3 tablespoons cider vinegar**
- **2 tablespoons vegetable oil**
- **2 tablespoons water**
- **1/2 teaspoon prepared mustard**
- **Dash *each* of salt, pepper and ground mustard**
- **1 pound fresh broccoli florets**

In a jar with a tight-fitting lid, combine the sugar, vinegar, oil, water, prepared mustard, salt, pepper and ground mustard; shake well. Set aside. Place broccoli in a steamer basket. Place in a saucepan over 1 in. of water; bring to a boil.

Cover and steam for 5-8 minutes or until crisp-tender. Place in a serving bowl. Shake dressing; drizzle over broccoli and toss to coat. **Yield:** 6 servings.

Mushroom Bread Wedges

- **1 tube (8 ounces) refrigerated crescent rolls**
- **1/2 pound fresh mushrooms, sliced**
- **3 tablespoons butter, melted**
- **1/4 cup grated Parmesan cheese**
- **1/4 teaspoon Italian seasoning**

Separate crescent dough into eight triangles and place on a greased 12-in. round pizza pan with points toward the center; seal perforations. In a bowl, combine the mushrooms and butter; toss to coat. Spoon mushroom mixture over dough. Sprinkle with Parmesan cheese and Italian seasoning.

Bake at 375° for 15-20 minutes or until crust is golden brown and mushrooms are tender. **Yield:** 8 servings.

♪ *Paprika Particulars*

Paprika is a powder made by grinding dried sweet red peppers. Its flavor can range from mild to hot. Hot paprika is always labeled such; sweet paprika is often just labeled "paprika". Hot paprika is indeed hot—if it's all you have, use it sparingly.

Timely Meal Tastes Like You Spent Hours in the Kitchen

FIXING a balanced meal for your family doesn't have to be a chore. But when extra minutes are in short supply, you can whip up a meal that's both time-easing and appetite-pleasing.

This menu, made up of favorites from three fellow busy cooks, is ready in just 30 minutes.

Apricot slices give a burst of fruit flavor to Apricot Beef Stir-Fry from Susan Payne of Corner Brook, Newfoundland. "This is a delicious blend with broccoli, onion, cherry tomatoes and strips of beef," Susan says.

Mini Pepper Corn Muffins, from Lucy Fouts of Jacksonville, Texas, make a cute accompaniment to almost any meal. These golden bite-size gems are enhanced by flecks of red and green pepper.

Miriam Christophel of Goshen, Indiana shares Microwave Apple Cobbler, a quick-to-fix dessert that's yummy served warm with ice cream or whipped cream. Says Miriam, "I make it quite often, sometimes with blackberries…and oh, my, is that good!"

Apricot Beef Stir Fry

   1 can (15 ounces) apricot halves
   2 tablespoons cornstarch
3/4 cup beef broth
   2 tablespoons soy sauce
1-1/2 pounds boneless beef round *or* sirloin
     steak, cut into thin strips
   1 tablespoon canola oil
   2 cups fresh broccoli florets
1/2 cup chopped onion
   1 cup cherry tomatoes
Hot cooked rice

Drain apricots, reserving 1/4 cup juice. Cut apricots into quarters and set aside. In a small bowl, combine the cornstarch, broth, soy sauce and reserved apricot juice until smooth; set aside.

In a large skillet or wok, stir-fry beef in oil for 3 minutes. Add broccoli and onion; stir-fry 2-3 minutes longer or until vegetables are crisp-tender. Stir sauce and add to the pan. Bring to a boil; cook and stir for 2 minutes or until thickened. Add tomatoes and reserved apricots; heat through. Serve over rice. **Yield:** 6 servings.

Mini Pepper Corn Muffins

   2 tablespoons *each* diced sweet red and
     green pepper
1-1/2 teaspoons olive oil
1/2 cup plus 2 tablespoons cornmeal
   6 tablespoons all-purpose flour
1-1/2 teaspoons sugar
1/2 teaspoon baking powder
1/4 teaspoon baking soda
1/4 teaspoon salt
   1 egg
1/2 cup buttermilk
   3 tablespoons butter, melted

In a skillet, saute peppers in oil for 5 minutes or until tender; cool slightly. In a bowl, combine the next six ingredients. Whisk the egg, buttermilk, butter and peppers until blended. Stir into dry ingredients just until moistened.

Fill paper-lined miniature muffin cups three-fourths full. Bake at 425° for 6-9 minutes or until a toothpick comes out clean. Cool 5 minutes. Remove to wire racks. **Yield:** about 2 dozen.

Microwave Apple Cobbler

   5 cups sliced peeled tart apples
1/2 cup sugar
   2 tablespoons all-purpose flour
1/2 teaspoon ground cinnamon *or* cloves
TOPPING:
3/4 cup biscuit/baking mix
   3 tablespoons sugar, *divided*
1/3 cup milk
1/2 teaspoon ground cinnamon *or* cloves

Place apples in a 1-1/2-qt. microwave-safe dish. Combine the sugar, flour and cinnamon; sprinkle over apples and toss to coat. Cover and microwave on high for 3-4 minutes or until apples are tender.

Combine biscuit mix, 2 tablespoons sugar and milk. Drop by tablespoonfuls over apples. Combine cinnamon and remaining sugar; sprinkle over top. Microwave, uncovered, for 4-6 minutes or until a toothpick comes out clean. **Yield:** 6 servings.

Editor's Note: This recipe was tested in a 1,100-watt microwave.

Quick and Colorful Cuisine Ideal for Summer Cookouts

WHEN warm summer breezes beckon, even folks who love to cook want to spend less time in the kitchen and more time on the patio or porch. Since fresh air builds appetites, a filling fast-to-fix meal is the order of the day.

The complete-meal menu here consists of favorites from three great cooks and was combined by our Test Kitchen staff. You can have everything ready to serve in just half an hour!

"I created French Onion Burgers one day when I needed to stretch a pound of hamburger," recalls Beth Johnson of Dalton, Ohio. "When we have high school boys help with baling hay, this is one of their favorite foods to enjoy after the work is done."

With its pretty pink blush and tart refreshing flavor, Cranberry Lemonade is sure to satisfy, glass after glass after glass. Darlene Brenden of Salem, Oregon shared this summer thirst-quencher.

Old Glory Angel Food makes a glorious dessert for your Fourth of July celebration. It's easy to assemble, but the triple layers and stars-and-stripes topping look like you fussed.

"One July, we invited a couple over for a backyard barbecue," relates Anne Nabbefeld from Greenville, Wisconsin. "The woman had recently become a United States citizen, so I created this cake for her. It was a big hit."

French Onion Burgers

    1 can (4 ounces) mushroom stems and
      pieces, drained and diced
    1 can (2.8 ounces) french-fried onions
    1 tablespoon Worcestershire sauce
  1/2 teaspoon salt
    1 pound ground beef
    4 hamburger buns, split
Lettuce leaves and tomato slices

In a bowl, combine the mushrooms, onions, Worcestershire sauce and salt. Crumble beef over mixture and mix well. Shape into four patties. Grill, uncovered, over medium heat or broil 4 in. from the heat for 6-9 minutes on each side or until no longer pink. Serve on buns with lettuce and tomato. **Yield:** 4 servings.

Cranberry Lemonade

  3/4 cup sugar
  2/3 cup lemon juice
    3 cups cold water
    1 cup cranberry juice

In a small saucepan, combine sugar and lemon juice. Cook and stir over medium heat until sugar is dissolved. Stir in the water and cranberry juice. Cool; pour into a pitcher. Refrigerate until chilled. Serve over ice. **Yield:** 4 servings.

Old Glory Angel Food

    1 loaf (10-1/2 ounces) angel food cake
    1 carton (8 ounces) frozen whipped
      topping, thawed
    1 cup quartered fresh strawberries
    1 cup fresh blueberries
Additional blueberries and strawberries

Split cake horizontally into thirds. Place bottom layer on a serving platter. Combine 1 cup whipped topping and strawberries; spread over bottom layer. Top with second cake layer. Combine 1 cup topping and blueberries; spread over second layer. Top with remaining cake layer. Spread with remaining topping. Arrange additional berries over top of cake to form a flag. **Yield:** 8 servings.

⌇ Patriotic Party Pizzazz

It's a snap to give your Fourth of July picnic some festive flair with these fun (and fast!) ideas:

Turn strawberry shortcake into a red, white and blue dessert by adding blueberries and topping with whipped cream.

Enhance a bowl of fruit punch with strawberries and blueberries. Or freeze the berries in ice cubes and add the cubes to the punch.

Poke American flag picks into cupcakes spread with red, white or blue frosting or top sugar cookies with red and blue sprinkles.

Serve Fish Kabobs for a Fast but Fun Supper

BUSY LIFESTYLES often don't leave time for preparing mouth-watering meals on a daily basis. And when the weather's warm and inviting, even less-hurried cooks don't want to spend all their time in the kitchen.

Our Test Kitchen home economists combined the three recipes here to make up a delicious dinner that you'll have on the table in no time. The fast-to-fix trio here will be ready to serve in just 30 minutes.

"My grandmother used to prepare Broiled Halibut Kabobs for special occasions," relates Tiffany O'Neill from Rossville, Kansas. "The orange-flavored barbecue sauce complements the fish nicely, whether it is broiled or grilled."

Tangy Salad Dressing, with bits of green olives, onion and celery, will perk up any bowl of mixed greens. Mildred Spinn from Cameron, Texas shares the recipe.

Says Connie Jurjevich of Atmore, Alabama, "While Lemon Dessert Sauce makes a wonderful topping for angel food cake, it's also great as a glaze for roasted chicken with some thyme or rosemary…or swirled into a homemade cheesecake."

Broiled Halibut Kabobs

1-1/4 pounds halibut fillets
  1 medium green pepper, cut into 1-inch pieces
  1 medium onion, cut into 1-inch wedges
  1 can (20 ounces) pineapple chunks, drained
  8 to 10 cherry tomatoes
BARBECUE SAUCE:
  1/2 cup ketchup
  1/4 cup vegetable oil
  3 tablespoons orange juice
  2 to 3 green onions, finely chopped
  2 garlic cloves, minced
  1 teaspoon grated orange peel
  1/4 teaspoon salt

Cut fish into 1-in. pieces. Alternately thread the fish, green pepper, onion, pineapple and tomatoes onto metal or soaked wooden skewers. Place on a greased broiler pan.

In a small bowl, whisk the sauce ingredients until blended. Spoon some sauce over the kabobs.

Broil 5-6 in. from the heat for 5-7 minutes. Turn; broil 5-7 minutes longer or until fish flakes easily with a fork, basting occasionally with sauce. **Yield:** 4 servings.

Tangy Salad Dressing

✓ Uses less fat, sugar or salt. Includes Nutritional Analysis and Diabetic Exchanges.

  1/2 cup mayonnaise
  2 tablespoons lemon juice
  2 tablespoons white wine vinegar
  1 tablespoon Dijon mustard
  2 tablespoons minced fresh parsley
  2 tablespoons finely chopped stuffed olives
  1 tablespoon finely chopped onion
  1 tablespoon finely chopped celery
  1/2 teaspoon sugar
  1/4 teaspoon pepper
Salad greens

In a small bowl, whisk the mayonnaise, lemon juice, vinegar and mustard until blended. Stir in the parsley, olives, onion, celery, sugar and pepper. Serve with salad greens. **Yield:** 1 cup.

Nutritional Analysis: One 2-tablespoon serving (prepared with reduced-fat mayonnaise; calculated without greens) equals 59 calories, 5 g fat (1 g saturated fat), 5 mg cholesterol, 249 mg sodium, 2 g carbohydrate, trace fiber, trace protein. **Diabetic Exchange:** 1 fat.

Lemon Dessert Sauce

  2 eggs
  3/4 cup sugar
  2 tablespoons butter
  1/2 cup lemon juice
  1 tablespoon grated lemon peel
Angel food _or_ pound cake

In the top of a double boiler, beat eggs and sugar. Stir in butter, lemon juice and lemon peel. Cook over simmering water for 10-12 minutes or until mixture reaches 160° and is thick enough to coat the back of a metal spoon. Refrigerate for up to 1 week. Serve chilled over the cake. **Yield:** 1 cup.

Speedy Soup and Sandwich Duo Is Always a Delight

WITH the hustle and bustle that begins as the holidays draw near, even dedicated cooks can't always find as much time as they'd like for making everyday meals. That's when filling, fast-to-fix menus like the one on this page come in handy.

Our Test Kitchen home economists combined tried-and-true recipes from three *Taste of Home* readers for this super-speedy meal, which is ready to serve in just 30 minutes.

"I got the idea for Veggie Chicken Wraps from a wrap I tried at a little cafe here," says Jolene Britten of Gig Harbor, Washington.

"During warmer months, I make them for a picnic in the park," adds Jolene, "I also like to prepare a large batch, cut them into slices and serve on a platter. They disappear every time!"

"My family and friends are always ready to dig right in when I serve my Quick Corn Chowder," Dorothy Faulkner shares from Benton, Arkansas. "It's thick and rich…and pairs well with a favorite salad or sandwich. They never guess it gets its start with a can of condensed soup!"

Chai (pronounced "Chi")is the word for tea in some parts of the world…but in India, it's a spiced milk tea that's becoming more popular in North America.

Terese Block of Waukesha, Wisconsin shares her version of this winter warm-up. The cinnamon, clove, cardamom and ginger make this cup of tea something special enough to serve guests.

Veggie Chicken Wraps

1 carton (8 ounces) spreadable garden
  vegetable cream cheese
4 flour tortillas (8 inches)
2 cups shredded romaine
2 small tomatoes, thinly sliced
8 slices provolone cheese
1 small red onion, thinly sliced
2 cups diced cooked chicken

Spread cream cheese evenly over each tortilla. Layer with romaine, tomatoes, cheese, onion and chicken. Roll up tightly. Cut in half to serve. **Yield:** 4 servings.

Quick Corn Chowder

1/4 cup chopped green pepper
  2 tablespoons chopped onion
  2 garlic cloves, minced
  2 tablespoons butter
  2 cans (10-3/4 ounces *each*) condensed
    cream of potato soup, undiluted
  1 can (14-3/4 ounces) cream-style corn
  2 cups milk
  1 package (3 ounces) cream cheese, cubed
Pepper to taste

In a large saucepan, saute the green pepper, onion and garlic in butter until tender. Stir in the soup, corn, milk, cream cheese and pepper. Bring to a boil, stirring frequently. Reduce heat; simmer, uncovered, for 5 minutes or until cream cheese is melted. **Yield:** 4-6 servings.

Chai

2 cups water
2 individual tea bags
1 cinnamon stick (3 inches)
6 cardamom seeds, crushed
1 whole clove
1/4 teaspoon ground ginger
2-1/2 cups milk
1/3 cup sugar
Sweetened whipped cream, ground cinnamon
  and additional cinnamon sticks, optional

In a small saucepan, combine the first six ingredients. Bring to a boil. Reduce heat; cover and simmer for 5 minutes. Stir in milk; return to a boil for 1 minute. Strain; discard tea bags and spices. Stir in sugar until dissolved. Ladle into mugs. Garnish if desired. **Yield:** 4 servings.

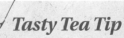

Tasty Tea Tip

Like the combination of chocolate and mint? Heat a cup of milk with a mint tea bag, then stir in a little hot cocoa mix.

Pass the Pasta, Please!

IF you have a lot to do but not a lot of time, you'll appreciate this quick and easy stovetop supper from our Test Kitchen staff. Serve Creamy Tortellini and Sausage with oven-fresh Italian Garlic Breadsticks alongside. Then for the finale, offer Pound Cake with Cherry Chocolate Topping.

Creamy Tortellini and Sausage

You don't need to spend loads of time in the kitchen creating an irresistible pasta dish. Simply jazz up a jar of store-bought Alfredo sauce with Italian sausage, vegetables, pasta and seasonings.

      1 pound bulk Italian sausage
      1 medium onion, chopped
      2 garlic cloves, minced
      1 package (19 ounces) frozen cheese tortellini
      3 cups frozen mixed vegetables
      1 jar (17 ounces) Alfredo sauce
  1/4 cup minced fresh basil *or* 3 teaspoons
         dried basil

In a large skillet, cook sausage, onion and garlic over medium heat until meat is no longer pink; drain. Meanwhile, in a Dutch oven, cook pasta and vegetables in boiling water for 3-5 minutes or until pasta is floating and vegetables are tender; drain.
   Add to skillet; mix well. Pour sauce over top. Bring to a boil, stirring occasionally. Sprinkle with basil; toss to coat. **Yield:** 6 servings.

Italian Garlic Breadsticks

A seasoned Parmesan cheese coating gives refrigerated breadsticks a terrific taste twist.

  1/2 cup grated Parmesan cheese
      2 teaspoons Italian seasoning
      1 teaspoon garlic powder
  1/4 cup butter, melted
      1 tube (11 ounces) refrigerated breadsticks

In a shallow bowl, combine the cheese, Italian seasoning and garlic powder. Place butter in another shallow bowl. Separate dough into individual breadsticks. Dip in butter, then in cheese mixture.

Twist 2-3 times and place on an ungreased baking sheet. Bake at 375° for 12-14 minutes or until golden brown. Serve immediately. **Yield:** 1 dozen.

Pound Cake with Cherry Chocolate Topping

Chocolate and cherries are a classic combination. For this recipe they come together in a succulent sauce

that's draped over generous slices of convenient frozen pound cake that's been thawed.

    1 can (14-1/2 ounces) pitted tart cherries,
      undrained
  1/2 cup sugar
    2 tablespoons cornstarch
    2 tablespoons water
  1/4 teaspoon vanilla extract
    3 to 4 drops red food coloring, optional
    1 package (16 ounces) frozen pound cake,
      thawed

6 tablespoons chocolate syrup

In a small saucepan, combine the cherries and sugar. Bring to a boil, stirring occasionally. Combine the cornstarch and water until smooth; add to the cherries. Bring to a boil; cook and stir for 1-2 minutes or until thickened. Remove from the heat; stir in vanilla and red food coloring if desired.

Cut pound cake into 12 slices. For each serving, place 2 slices on an individual plate. Top with 1 tablespoon chocolate sauce and about 1/4 cup of cherry sauce. **Yield:** 6 servings.

For Your Valentine

THE VIBRANT red color of Mediterranean Chicken Stew makes it perfect for this special Valentine's dinner dreamed up by our Test Kitchen. Best of all, this meal can be prepared in no time. First, pop Double Chocolate Biscotti into the oven, then start simmering the stew and preparing Herbed Rice.

Mediterranean Chicken Stew

Tomatoes and peppers lend to the eye-catching color of this fast-to-fix stew. The mild seasonings will appeal to everyone's tastes.

       1 medium onion, chopped
       2 garlic cloves, minced
       2 tablespoons vegetable oil
  1-1/2 pounds boneless skinless chicken breast, cut into 1-inch pieces
       2 cans (14-1/2 ounces *each*) stewed tomatoes
       1 medium green pepper, julienned
       1 medium sweet red pepper, julienned
       1 cup pitted ripe olives
       1 teaspoon salt
       1 teaspoon dried oregano
       2 tablespoons cornstarch
       3 tablespoons cold water
Hot cooked rice

In a large skillet, saute onion and garlic in oil for 3-4 minutes or until tender. Add chicken and cook for 6-8 minutes or until meat juices run clear. Stir in the tomatoes, peppers, olives, salt and oregano; bring to a boil. Reduce heat; cover and simmer for 10-12 minutes, stirring occasionally.

Combine cornstarch and water until smooth; stir into chicken mixture. Bring to a boil; cook and stir for 1 minute or until thickened. Serve with rice. **Yield:** 6 servings.

Herbed Rice

Ordinary rice is spiced up with zesty poultry seasoning. This pairs well with the Mediterranean Chicken Stew but would also be a nice stand-alone side dish with any entree.

       2 tablespoons butter
       3 cups uncooked instant rice
       3 cups water
       3 teaspoons chicken bouillon granules
  1/2 to 1 teaspoon poultry seasoning

Heat butter in a saucepan over medium heat until golden brown for about 2 minutes, stirring occasionally. Stir in the rice, water, bouillon and poultry seasoning. Bring to a boil. Remove from heat; cover and let stand for 5 minutes. Fluff with a fork. **Yield:** 6 servings.

Double Chocolate Biscotti

In Italian, biscotti means twice-baked. Here, refrigerated chocolate chip cookie dough gives you a head start on making these perfect-for-dunking cookies from scratch. For true chocolate lovers, substitute chocolate chips for the vanilla.

  1 tube (18 ounces) refrigerated chocolate chip cookie dough
1/2 cup vanilla *or* white chips
1/2 cup coarsely chopped macadamia nuts

In a medium bowl, combine the refrigerated cookie dough, vanilla chips and nuts; knead until well combined. Divide the dough in half. On greased baking sheets, shape each piece into a 13-in. x 2-1/2-in. log. Bake at 375° for 12-14 minutes or until golden brown.

Remove from oven; cut diagonally with a serrated knife into 1-in. slices, separating each piece about 1/4 in. after cutting. Bake 5-6 minutes longer or until firm. Cool for 2 minutes before removing to wire racks. **Yield:** about 2 dozen.

Success with Savory Soup

LOOKING for a nourishing meal that adds more fruits and vegetables to your day? Then turn to hearty Black Bean Soup and refreshing Peachy Fruit Smoothies. Both recipes are packed with vitamins as well as flavor. Savory Drop Biscuits nicely round out the meal put together by our Test Kitchen staff.

Black Bean Soup

Blending some of the beans gives this soup just the right consistency. (After rinsing your blender container, remember to leave it out for the Peachy Fruit Smoothies!)

        1 medium onion, chopped
        2 garlic cloves, minced
        1 tablespoon vegetable oil
        2 cups chicken broth, *divided*
        3 cans (15 ounces *each*) black beans, rinsed and drained, *divided*
        1 can (10 ounces) diced tomatoes and green chilies, undrained
        1 teaspoon ground cumin
    1/2 teaspoon garlic salt
Minced fresh cilantro, sour cream and tortilla chips, optional

In a saucepan, saute onion and garlic in oil for 2-3 minutes or until tender. In a blender or food processor, place 1/2 cup chicken broth and 1 can beans; cover and process until smooth. Add to onion mixture.

Stir in the tomatoes, cumin, garlic salt and remaining broth and beans. Bring to a boil. Reduce heat; cover and simmer for 10 minutes. Garnish with cilantro, sour cream and tortilla chips if desired. **Yield:** 6 servings.

Savory Drop Biscuits

The addition of cheese and green chilies makes these mouth-watering biscuits wonderfully moist. They're a fabulous accompaniment to soup and stew.

2-1/2 cups biscuit/baking mix
        1 cup (4 ounces) shredded cheddar cheese

        1 can (4 ounces) chopped green chilies, drained
        1 teaspoon chili powder
    1/2 teaspoon garlic powder
    1/2 teaspoon onion powder
    2/3 cup milk

In a medium bowl, combine the first six ingredients; mix well. Stir in milk just until moistened. Drop by tablespoonfuls 2 in. apart onto ungreased baking sheets. Bake at 450° for 10-12 minutes or until golden brown. Serve warm. **Yield:** 2 dozen.

Peachy Fruit Smoothies

The color of this refreshing beverage just says "spring!" Smoothies are great for breakfast, dessert or a midday snack.

1-1/4 **cups milk**
   1 **cup (8 ounces) lemon yogurt**
   1 **cup orange juice**
   3 **tablespoons sugar**
 1/2 **teaspoon vanilla extract**
   1 **package (16 ounces) frozen unsweetened peach slices**

In a blender or food processor, combine all the ingredients; cover and process until blended and smooth. Serve immediately. **Yield:** 6 servings.

A Berry Good Idea

Try substituting frozen raspberries or blueberries for the peaches called for in the smoothie recipe.

Scrambling For Supper

YOU'D be hard-pressed to find a food that cooks faster than eggs. So next time you have a busy day, team up Veggie Ham 'n' Eggs and Mock Caesar Salad for a lovely light lunch or dinner. A sweet ending is just minutes away with Triple Chocolate Bundles. Our Test Kitchen staff whipped up all three speedy dishes.

Veggie Ham 'n' Eggs

This versatile recipe works well with a number of alternate ingredients. Instead of ham, try cooked and crumbled bacon. Or use different vegetables and cheese to suit your family's tastes.

> 1 cup cubed fully cooked ham
> 1 cup sliced fresh mushrooms
> 1/2 cup chopped sweet red pepper
> 1/4 cup sliced green onions
> 2 tablespoons butter
> 8 eggs
> 1/4 cup milk
> 1/4 teaspoon salt
> 1 cup (4 ounces) shredded cheddar cheese

In a skillet, saute the ham, mushrooms, pepper and onions in butter for 6 minutes or until vegetables are tender. In a bowl, combine the eggs, milk and salt. Remove ham mixture from skillet; keep warm.

In same skillet, add egg mixture; cook and stir until eggs are slightly set. Add ham mixture. Cook and stir until eggs are completely set. Sprinkle with cheese. **Yield:** 4 servings.

Mock Caesar Salad

This salad has the flavor of an authentic Caesar salad but without the fuss. You can keep the dressing on hand to quickly and deliciously top a variety of greens and vegetables.

> 3 tablespoons mayonnaise
> 2 teaspoons grated Parmesan cheese
> 1-1/2 teaspoons red wine vinegar
> 1/2 teaspoon garlic powder
> 1/2 teaspoon lemon juice
> 4 cups torn romaine lettuce

> 1/4 cup Caesar salad croutons
> 2 tablespoons shredded Parmesan cheese

In a bowl, combine the first five ingredients; mix well. In a large bowl, combine lettuce and dressing; toss to coat. Sprinkle with croutons and shredded cheese. **Yield:** 4 servings.

Triple Chocolate Bundles

No one will be able to resist three kinds of chocolate in a fuss-free flaky dough. Instead of sprinkling the bundles with sugar, try drizzling with melted chocolate.

3 tablespoons semisweet chocolate chips
3 tablespoons vanilla *or* white chips
3 tablespoons milk chocolate chips
1 tube (8 ounces) refrigerated crescent rolls
Confectioners' sugar, optional

In a small bowl, combine the semisweet chocolate, vanilla and milk chocolate chips. Separate crescent dough into eight triangles. Place triangles on a work surface with the short edge toward you.

For each bundle, place 1 tablespoon of chips in the center of each triangle. Bring top point over chips and tuck underneath dough. Fold side points over top, pressing to seal.

Place on an ungreased baking sheet. Bake at 375° for 10-12 minutes or until the bundles are golden brown. Cool on a wire rack until serving. Sprinkle each with confectioners' sugar if desired. **Yield:** 8 bundles.

A Special Meal Just for Mom

ANYONE can make this meal from our Test Kitchen for Mom on Mother's Day. Tomato Bisque conveniently uses canned broth, tomato paste and cream. For Broiled Shrimp Toast, a quick-to-mix topping is simply spread on bread and broiled. And just six ingredients are needed for Melon with Sweet Lime Dressing.

Tomato Bisque

A bowl brimming with this creamy soup is sure to impress Mom. She'll think you fussed for hours!

- 2 garlic cloves, minced
- 2 tablespoons butter
- 2 tablespoons all-purpose flour
- 4 cups chicken broth
- 1 can (6 ounces) tomato paste
- 1/8 to 1/4 teaspoon cayenne pepper
- 1 cup half-and-half cream

Chopped fresh tomatoes

In a saucepan, saute garlic in butter. Stir in flour until blended; gradually add broth. Stir in tomato paste and cayenne until well blended. Bring to a boil; cook and stir for 2 minutes or until thickened. Reduce heat; gradually stir in cream. (Do not boil.) Serve immediately. Garnish with chopped tomatoes. **Yield:** 6 servings.

Broiled Shrimp Toast

This open-faced sandwich has pretty flecks of pink shrimp, red tomatoes and green parsley. To save time, blend the spread the night before and refrigerate.

- 2 cups frozen cooked salad shrimp, thawed
- 2 cups (8 ounces) shredded cheddar cheese
- 1 cup mayonnaise
- 3/4 cup chopped fresh tomatoes
- 1/3 cup minced fresh parsley
- 2 tablespoons grated onion
- 1/4 teaspoon cayenne pepper
- 6 slices English muffin bread *or* bread of your choice, toasted

In a large bowl, combine first seven ingredients; mix well. Place 1/4 cup mixture on top of each

slice of bread. Broil 3-4 in. from heat for 6-7 minutes or until top is lightly browned and cheese is melted. Serve immediately. **Yield:** 6 servings.

Melon with Sweet Lime Dressing

Not all desserts need to be decadent in order to be delicious. A simple lime dressing coats cubed cantaloupe and honeydew for a refreshing finale.

3 cups cubed cantaloupe
3 cups cubed honeydew
2 tablespoons orange marmalade
2 tablespoons lime juice
1 tablespoon honey
1 teaspoon chopped fresh mint

In a large bowl, combine cantaloupe and honeydew. In a small bowl, combine the orange marmalade, lime juice, honey and mint; mix well. Pour over the fruit and toss gently to coat. Serve immediately. **Yield:** 6 servings.

Fresh Fruit Finesse

Here are two more simple ways to present fruit in a special way:

Combine strawberries, blueberries, bananas and other favorite fruits with a can of peach pie filling. Chill.

Fold your favorite fruits into a mixture of softened cream cheese and marshmallow creme. You can also add coconut or chopped nuts.

Packed with Produce

LET summer's produce shine with help from our Test Kitchen staff! Strawberries, kiwi and pineapple star in Chicken Breasts with Fruit Salsa, while Asparagus with Orange Butter features citrus-topped spears. In Raspberry-Lemon Cheese Tarts, berries are topped with a cool cream cheese mixture.

Chicken Breasts with Fruit Salsa

Preparing this tropical-tasting dish in a skillet keeps your kitchen cool, which is especially nice on a summer day.

      1 tablespoon vegetable oil
  1/4 teaspoon *each* salt and pepper
      1 garlic clove, minced
      4 boneless skinless chicken breast halves
      2 tablespoons butter
      1 can (8 ounces) pineapple tidbits, drained
  1/2 cup quartered fresh strawberries
      1 kiwifruit, peeled, quartered and sliced
  1/4 cup chopped red onion
      1 jalapeno pepper, seeded and chopped*
      1 teaspoon cornstarch
  1/4 cup orange juice

In a small bowl, combine the oil, salt, pepper and garlic. Spread over one side of each chicken breast. In a skillet, saute chicken seasoned side down in butter for 4-6 minutes; turn and cook 4-6 minutes longer until chicken juices run clear.

For salsa, in a bowl, combine fruit, onion and pepper. Combine cornstarch and juice until smooth. Remove chicken to serving platter; keep warm. Stir juice mixture into skillet. Bring to a boil; cook and stir for 1-2 minutes or until thickened. Remove from heat; pour over fruit mixture. Gently toss to coat. Serve over chicken. **Yield:** 4 servings.

***Editor's Note:** When chopping or seeding hot peppers, use rubber or plastic gloves to protect your hands. Avoid touching your face.

Asparagus with Orange Butter

A simple orange butter is all that's needed to enhance the naturally great taste of asparagus.

      3 tablespoons butter, softened
      1 tablespoon orange juice concentrate
  1/2 teaspoon grated orange peel
  1/8 teaspoon onion powder
  1/8 teaspoon Dijon mustard
  1/2 cup water
      1 pound fresh asparagus, trimmed
  Salt to taste

In a small bowl, combine the first five ingredients until blended. In a large skillet, bring water to a boil. Add asparagus; cover and boil for 3-4 minutes or until tender. Drain and set aside. In the same

skillet, melt butter mixture, then add asparagus and toss to coat. Sprinkle with salt. **Yield:** 4 servings.

Raspberry-Lemon Cheese Tarts

These no-bake tarts blend cream cheese and lemon pie filling for a cool end to the meal.

  1 cup prepared lemon pie filling, *divided*
  1 package (3 ounces) cream cheese, softened
  1/2 cup whipped topping
  1/2 cup confectioners' sugar
    1 teaspoon lemon juice
  1/2 cup fresh raspberries
    4 individual graham cracker shells
Additional fresh raspberries and mint leaves

In a mixing bowl, combine 3/4 cup pie filling, cream cheese, whipped topping, sugar and lemon juice. Beat until smooth. Place 3-4 berries in each shell, pressing down slightly. Divide cream cheese mixture among shells. Top with remaining pie filling. Garnish with berries and mint. **Yield:** 4 servings.

Meals on a Budget

Eating big doesn't have to mean paying big. These economical meals fully satisfy the palate and please the wallet.

NIFTY AND THRIFTY. Clockwise from upper left: French Toast Sandwiches, Spiced Fruit Cup and Orange Juice Spritzer (p. 278); Vegetable Noodle Bake, Green Bean Salad and Chocolate Ribbon Bars (p. 284); Honey Barbecued Chicken, Party Potatoes and Sweet-Sour Beans and Carrots (p. 280) and Tuna Cheese Melts, Radish Potato Salad and Cinnamon-Sugar Crisps (p. 286).

Feed Your Family for $1.58 a Plate!

BUDGET-CONSCIOUS cooks will love this easy-to-make holiday breakfast or brunch. Your family members and guests will be impressed with this satisfying meal, and they'll never know how inexpensive it is to prepare.

Our Test Kitchen staff estimates you can serve this meal for just $1.58 per serving. The recipes come from three thrifty cooks.

Deborah Fagan of Lancaster, Pennsylvania dips her French Toast Sandwiches in eggnog to give them distinctive flavor. "I serve these on Christmas while we sit around the table opening our stocking gifts," she says. "They've become a tasty tradition for the family."

Spiced Fruit Cup from Barbara Kole of Holland, Michigan is a colorful medley with a little fizz. "Cream soda is the secret ingredient in this dish," she reveals. "You can vary the fruits to your taste. I often add a mango for special occasions. I entered this in a recipe contest sponsored by a soft-drink company...and it was chosen as runner-up among side dishes."

Refreshing and pretty, Orange Juice Spritzer was submitted by Michelle Krzmarzick from Redondo Beach, California. "It's a nice light wake-me-up drink and an easy way to give a twist to an ordinary glass of orange juice," she suggests. "Most people appreciate that it is not overly sweet."

French Toast Sandwiches

    12 slices Canadian bacon
     6 slices Monterey Jack cheese
    12 slices French bread (1/2 inch thick)
    3/4 cup eggnog*
     3 tablespoons butter
     6 tablespoons strawberry preserves

Place two slices of Canadian bacon and one slice of cheese on each of six slices of bread. Top with remaining bread. Place eggnog in a shallow dish. Dip sandwiches in eggnog.

In a large skillet or griddle, melt butter. Cook sandwiches on both sides for 2-3 minutes or until bread is golden brown. Serve with strawberry pre-

serves. **Yield:** 6 servings.

*Editor's Note: This recipe was tested with commercially prepared eggnog.

Spiced Fruit Cup

✓ Uses less fat, sugar or salt. Includes Nutritional Analysis and Diabetic Exchanges.

     1 can (20 ounces) unsweetened pineapple
       chunks, drained
     1 can (15-1/4 ounces) sliced peaches,
       drained
     1 cup sliced fresh strawberries

1 cup cubed honeydew *or* cantaloupe
1 cup cream soda, chilled
1 tablespoon sugar
1 teaspoon ground cinnamon
1/2 teaspoon ground coriander
1 medium firm banana, sliced

In large bowl, combine pineapple, peaches, strawberries, melon and cream soda. Combine the sugar, cinnamon and coriander; stir into fruit mixture. Cover and refrigerate for 2-4 hours. Just before serving, add banana. Serve with a slotted spoon. **Yield:** 6 servings.

   Nutritional Analysis: One 1-cup serving (prepared with diet soda) equals 116 calories, trace fat (trace saturated fat), 0 cholesterol, 14 mg sodium, 30 g carbohydrate, 3 g fiber, 1 g protein. **Diabetic Exchange:** 2 fruit.

Orange Juice Spritzer

1 quart orange juice
1 liter ginger ale, chilled
1/4 cup maraschino cherry juice
Orange wedges and maraschino cherries

In a 2-qt. container, combine the orange juice, ginger ale and cherry juice; stir well. Serve over ice. Garnish each glass with an orange wedge and cherry. **Yield:** 2 quarts.

Feed Your Family for $1.42 a Plate!

IT'S POSSIBLE to save on your grocery bill without scrimping on good flavor when feeding your family.

The recipes here are suggested by three budget-minded cooks and combined by our Test Kitchen staff into a delicious meal you can serve for just $1.42 per person.

Honey Barbecued Chicken from Debbi Smith of Crossett, Arkansas has plenty of taste and eye appeal. It's baked to perfection in an onion tomato sauce that's both sweet and spunky.

Flavored with garlic salt and chives, Party Potatoes are rich, creamy and oh, so yummy. A sprinkling of paprika gives this dish a festive look. Cyneli Fynaardt of Oskaloosa, Iowa submitted the recipe. "We prefer them to plain mashed potatoes," she says.

"I love German food, so I tried out the recipe for Sweet-Sour Beans and Carrots on my family and they really liked it," says Sherry DeHaan of Hays, Kansas. "I like to serve this side dish with German noodles and pork cutlets or a roast."

Honey Barbecued Chicken

    2 broiler/fryer chickens (3 pounds *each*),
        cut up
1/2 teaspoon salt
1/2 teaspoon pepper
    2 large onions, chopped
    2 cans (8 ounces *each*) tomato sauce
1/2 cup cider vinegar
1/2 cup honey
1/4 cup Worcestershire sauce
    2 teaspoons paprika
1/2 teaspoon hot pepper sauce

Place chicken skin side down in an ungreased 13-in. x 9-in. x 2-in. baking dish. Sprinkle with salt and pepper. Combine the remaining ingredients; pour over chicken.

Bake, uncovered, at 375° for 30 minutes. Turn chicken and bake 20 minutes longer or until chicken juices run clear, basting occasionally with sauce. **Yield:** 8 servings.

Party Potatoes

    6 large potatoes, peeled and cubed
    1 package (8 ounces) cream cheese, cubed
    1 cup (8 ounces) sour cream
1/2 cup milk
    1 teaspoon garlic salt
    2 teaspoons minced chives
    2 tablespoons butter, melted
1/2 teaspoon paprika

Place potatoes in a large saucepan and cover with water. Bring to a boil. Reduce heat; cover and cook for 15-20 minutes or until tender. Drain; mash potatoes. Beat in the cream cheese, sour cream, milk, garlic salt and chives; beat until well blended.

Transfer to a greased shallow 3-qt. baking dish. Drizzle potatoes with butter and sprinkle with paprika. Bake, uncovered, at 350° for 30-35 minutes or until edges are bubbly and potatoes are heated through. **Yield:** 8 servings.

Sweet-Sour Beans and Carrots

2 cups sliced carrots
4 cups frozen cut green beans
4 bacon strips, diced
2 medium onions, finely chopped
2 medium tart apples, peeled and diced
1/4 cup cider vinegar
2 tablespoons sugar
1 teaspoon salt

Place carrots in a large saucepan and cover with water. Bring to a boil. Cook, uncovered, for 4 minutes. Stir in beans. Return to a boil. Cook mixture 5-6 minutes longer or until the beans and carrots are tender. Drain.

In a large skillet, cook bacon over medium heat until crisp. Remove to paper towels to drain. Saute onions in drippings until tender. Add the apples, vinegar, sugar and salt; mix well. Cover and cook until apples are tender, about 2 minutes. Stir in the bean mixture; heat through. Sprinkle with bacon. **Yield:** 8 servings.

Feed Your Family for $1.73 a Plate!

GROCERY BUDGET a little tight? Don't worry! You can still enjoy foods that are satisfying and full of flavor.

Three frugal cooks prove it with this mouth-watering meal that's perfect for a springtime luncheon or a light supper. Our Test Kitchen home economists estimate the total cost of this meal at just $1.73 per setting.

Canned salmon and frozen peas streamline the preparation of hearty Salmon Chowder from Pat Waymire of Yellow Springs, Ohio. Shredded Swiss and cheddar cheeses, along with cauliflower and dill weed, add flavor to this appealing dish.

"I love my bread machine and am always trying new recipes in it," says Joy McMillan from The Woodlands, Texas. "Cracked Pepper Bread is one of my successes. When it's baking, the whole kitchen smells wonderful." Basil, garlic, chives and Parmesan cheese give this tall tender loaf a real Italian flavor.

Bernice Morris from Marshfield, Missouri dresses up her Garden Lettuce Salad with tomatoes, radishes, green onions, crisp bacon, hard-cooked eggs and a creamy homemade dressing. "It's a nice change from our usual wilted lettuce salad," she says. "This salad's also good with fried chicken and mashed potatoes or with a barbecue dinner."

Salmon Chowder

✓ Uses less fat, sugar or salt. Includes Nutritional Analysis and Diabetic Exchanges.

    1 cup thinly sliced green onions
    2 celery ribs, thinly sliced
    2 tablespoons butter
    2 tablespoons all-purpose flour
  1/2 teaspoon salt
  1/2 teaspoon dill weed
    4 cups milk
    2 cups cauliflowerets, cooked
    1 can (14-3/4 ounces) salmon, drained, skin and bones removed
    1 package (10 ounces) frozen peas, thawed
  1/2 cup shredded Swiss cheese
  1/2 cup shredded cheddar cheese

In a large saucepan, saute onions and celery in butter until tender. Stir in the flour, salt and dill until blended. Gradually add milk. Bring to a boil; cook and stir for 2 minutes or until thickened. Add the cauliflower, salmon and peas; heat through. Stir in the cheeses until melted. Serve immediately. **Yield:** 8 servings.

Nutritional Analysis: One 1-cup serving (prepared with fat-free milk and reduced-fat cheeses) equals 230 calories, 9 g fat (5 g saturated fat), 41 mg cholesterol, 558 mg sodium, 15 g carbohydrate, 3 g fiber, 22 g protein. **Diabetic Exchanges:** 2-1/2 lean meat, 1 starch.

Cracked Pepper Bread

1-1/2 cups water (70° to 80°)
    3 tablespoons olive oil

3 tablespoons sugar
2 teaspoons salt
3 tablespoons minced chives
2 garlic cloves, minced
1 teaspoon garlic powder
1 teaspoon dried basil
1 teaspoon cracked black pepper
1/4 cup grated Parmesan cheese
4 cups bread flour
2-1/2 teaspoons active dry yeast

In bread machine pan, place all ingredients in order suggested by manufacturer. Select basic bread setting. Choose crust color and loaf size if available. Bake according to bread machine directions (check the dough after 5 minutes of mixing; add 1 to 2 tablespoons of water or flour if needed). **Yield:** 1 loaf (2 pounds).

Editor's Note: If your bread machine has a time-delay feature, we recommend you do not use it for this recipe.

Garden Lettuce Salad

5 cups torn leaf lettuce
2 medium tomatoes, chopped
3 hard-cooked eggs, sliced
3/4 cup sliced radishes
4 bacon strips, cooked and crumbled
3 green onions, sliced
DRESSING:
3/4 cup mayonnaise
1 tablespoon red wine vinegar
1 teaspoon lemon-lime soda
1/2 teaspoon salt
1/2 teaspoon sugar

In a salad bowl, toss the lettuce, tomatoes, eggs, radishes, bacon and onions. In a small bowl, whisk the dressing ingredients. Serve with salad. **Yield:** 6 servings.

Feed Your Family for $1.56 a Plate!

EATING WELL at today's prices isn't impossible. The frugal yet flavorful meal here combines recipes from three creative cooks. Our Test Kitchen staff estimates the total cost at just $1.56 per serving.

Traditional lasagna fixin's (minus the meat) make up Vegetable Noodle Bake, a satisfying casserole shared by Dixie Terry of Goreville, Illinois. The egg noodles are a great substitute for the usual lasagna noodles. "If you're out of hamburger, serve this dish and no one will even notice it's meatless because it's so tasty," Dixie assures.

Potato, tomato and onion complement the fresh green beans in colorful Green Bean Salad. A subtle oil-and-vinegar dressing lends fresh herb flavor to the mix. The recipe comes from the kitchen of Sarah Maranto of Bakersfield, California.

No one will be able to eat just one of Gail Wiese's yummy Chocolate Ribbon Bars, full of butterscotch, peanut butter and chocolate flavor. "Over the years I've accumulated quite a few recipes from my co-workers, and this one is so easy to prepare," says Gail from her home in Athens, Wisconsin.

Vegetable Noodle Bake

  1 **can (14-1/2 ounces) whole tomatoes, drained and cut up**
3/4 **cup canned tomato puree**
1/3 **cup chopped onion**
1-1/4 **teaspoons dried oregano**
1/4 **teaspoon garlic powder**
1/4 **teaspoon salt**
1/8 **teaspoon pepper**
2-1/2 **cups uncooked medium egg noodles**
1/2 **cup small-curd cottage cheese**
  1 **package (10 ounces) frozen chopped spinach, thawed and squeezed dry**
1/3 **cup shredded American cheese**

In a large saucepan, combine the tomatoes, tomato puree, onion, oregano, garlic powder, salt and pepper. Bring to a boil. Reduce heat; simmer, uncovered, for 15 minutes. Meanwhile, cook noodles according to package directions; drain.

Spread 1/3 cup tomato mixture in a greased shallow 2-qt. baking dish. Top with half of the noodles. Spread with cottage cheese; top with spinach. Drizzle with 1/2 cup tomato mixture; top with remaining noodles and tomato mixture. Sprinkle with American cheese. Cover; bake at 350° for 20-25 minutes until cheese is melted. **Yield:** 4 servings.

Green Bean Salad

✓ Uses less fat, sugar or salt. Includes Nutritional Analysis and Diabetic Exchanges.

  1 **medium potato, peeled**
1/2 **pound fresh green beans, cut into 2-inch pieces**
  1 **medium tomato, cubed**
1/2 **small red onion, sliced and separated into rings**

2 tablespoons red wine vinegar
2 tablespoons canola oil
2 tablespoons minced fresh oregano
2 tablespoons minced fresh parsley
1/8 teaspoon salt

Place potato in a saucepan and cover with water. Bring to a boil; cook for 15 minutes or until tender. Drain and cool; cut into cubes. Place green beans in a saucepan and cover with water. Bring to a boil; cook, uncovered, for 6-8 minutes or until crisp-tender. Drain and cool.

In a serving bowl, combine beans, potato, tomato and onion. In a jar with a tight-fitting lid, combine the remaining ingredients; shake well. Pour over the bean mixture and toss to coat. **Yield:** 4 servings.

Nutritional Analysis: One serving (1 cup) equals 120 calories, 7 g fat (1 g saturated fat), 0 cholesterol, 81 mg sodium, 14 g carbohydrate, 3 g fiber, 3 g protein. **Diabetic Exchanges:** 1 vegetable, 1 fat, 1/2 starch.

Chocolate Ribbon Bars

1 package (10 to 11 ounces) butterscotch chips
1 cup peanut butter*
8 cups crisp rice cereal
2 cups (12 ounces) semisweet chocolate chips
1/4 cup butter, cubed
2 tablespoons water
3/4 cup confectioners' sugar

Microwave butterscotch chips with peanut butter until melted; stir until smooth. Stir in cereal until coated. Press half the mixture into a greased 13-in. x 9-in. x 2-in. pan; set remaining mixture aside.

Microwave semisweet chips with butter until melted; stir until smooth. Stir in water. Gradually add confectioners' sugar; stir until smooth.

Spread over cereal layer. Chill for 10 minutes or until chocolate layer is set. Spread remaining cereal mixture over top. Chill. **Yield:** 2 dozen.

*Editor's Note: Reduced-fat or generic brands of peanut butter are not recommended for this recipe.

Feed Your Family for 99¢ a Plate!

LOOKING for ways to save on your grocery bill while still serving your family delicious and nutritious meals? Leave it to our readers to come up with some taste-tempting solutions!

Our Test Kitchen home economists have put together this satisfying meal with recipes from three great cooks. It makes a filling lunch or a light summer supper...at just 99¢ per person.

For her Tuna Cheese Melts, Bernadine Dirmeyer of Harpster, Ohio dresses up a typical tuna sandwich with American cheese and rye bread spread with a mixture of sour cream and garlic salt. Cooked in a skillet, this sandwich oozes with flavor.

Radish Potato Salad from Lydia Garcia of Hanover, Pennsylvania is well coated with a creamy dill dressing. This summery salad, made with radish slices and chopped eggs, is not only pretty but easy to prepare, too.

"Cinnamon-Sugar Crisps are a favorite with children...and adults, too," says Kim Marie Van Rheenen of Mendota, Illinois. These sweet and spicy refrigerator cookies go great with a cup of coffee or a glass of milk. You won't be able to eat just one!

Tuna Cheese Melts

1/2 **cup sour cream**
1/2 **teaspoon garlic salt**
  8 **slices light rye bread**
  1 **can (6 ounces) tuna, drained**
  2 **tablespoons mayonnaise**
  4 **slices process American cheese**
  4 **tablespoons butter,** *divided*

Combine sour cream and garlic salt; spread on one side of each slice of bread. In a small bowl, combine tuna and mayonnaise; spread on four slices of bread. Top with cheese and remaining bread; gently press together.

Melt 2 tablespoons butter in a large skillet over medium heat. Add two sandwiches; cook until both sides are golden brown and cheese is melted. Repeat with remaining butter and sandwiches. **Yield:** 4 servings.

Radish Potato Salad

  5 **medium red potatoes (about 1-1/2 pounds)**
  1 **cup sliced radishes**
  2 **hard-cooked eggs, chopped**
3/4 **cup mayonnaise**
  3 **tablespoons minced fresh dill** *or* 2 **teaspoons dill weed**
  2 **tablespoons cider vinegar**
  1 **tablespoon sugar**
1/4 **teaspoon salt**
Dash pepper

Place potatoes in a saucepan and cover with water. Bring to a boil. Reduce heat; cover and cook for 15-20 minutes or until tender. Drain and cool.

Peel and cube the potatoes; place in a large bowl. Add the radishes and eggs. In a small bowl, combine the mayonnaise, dill, vinegar, sugar, salt and pepper. Gently fold into potato mixture. Cover and refrigerate for at least 1 hour. **Yield:** 4 servings.

Cinnamon-Sugar Crisps

3/4 cup butter, softened
1/3 cup sugar
1/3 cup packed brown sugar
1 egg
1 teaspoon vanilla extract
1-3/4 cups all-purpose flour
1 teaspoon ground cinnamon
1/4 teaspoon salt
2 tablespoons colored sprinkles

In a mixing bowl, cream butter and sugars. Beat in egg and vanilla. Combine the flour, cinnamon and salt; gradually add to creamed mixture. Shape into a 12-in. roll; wrap in plastic wrap. Refrigerate for 2 hours or until firm.

Unwrap and cut into 1/4-in. slices. Place 2 in. apart on ungreased baking sheets. Decorate with sprinkles. Bake at 350° for 10-12 minutes or until lightly browned. Remove to wire racks to cool. **Yield:** 3-1/2 dozen.

Feed Your Family for $1.11 a Plate!

WE'RE HERE to tell you that you can be frugal and satisfy hearty appetites at dinner. Three budget-conscious cooks prove it with these penny-pinching dishes compiled by our Test Kitchen, who estimate the total cost for this meal at just $1.11 a serving!

Thick and hearty Great Northern Bean Stew is guaranteed to chase the winter chills away, assures Mildred Sherrer of Bay City, Texas.

"We love Herbed Popovers with a roast beef dinner," says Lorraine Caland of Thunder Bay, Ontario.

Hoosier Cream Pie, from Edna Hoffman of Hebron, Indiana, ends a meal on a cozy, comforting note.

Great Northern Bean Stew

- 1 **pound bulk pork sausage**
- 1 **cup chopped onion**
- 1 **can (28 ounces) diced tomatoes, undrained**
- 1 **can (15-1/2 ounces) great northern beans, rinsed and drained**
- 2 **cups chopped cabbage**
- 1 **cup sliced carrots**
- 1 **tablespoon white vinegar**
- 1 **tablespoon brown sugar**
- 1/2 **teaspoon salt**
- 1/2 **teaspoon dried thyme**
- 1/2 **teaspoon paprika**
- 1/2 **teaspoon pepper**
- 1/4 **teaspoon hot pepper sauce**
- 2 **tablespoons minced fresh parsley**

In a large saucepan, cook sausage and onion over medium heat until meat is no longer pink; drain. Add the next 11 ingredients. Bring to a boil. Reduce heat; cover and simmer for 50-60 minutes or until vegetables are tender. Stir in parsley; cook 5 minutes longer. **Yield:** 6 servings.

Herbed Popovers

- 1 **cup all-purpose flour**
- 1 **teaspoon dried thyme**
- 1 **teaspoon dried basil**
- 1 **teaspoon rubbed sage**
- 1/4 **teaspoon celery salt**
- 3 **eggs**
- 1 **cup milk**
- 1 **tablespoon vegetable oil**

In a bowl, combine the flour, thyme, basil, sage and celery salt. Combine the eggs, milk and oil; whisk into dry ingredients just until blended (batter will be lumpy). Refrigerate for 30 minutes.

Fill eight greased and floured 6-oz. custard cups half full. Place on a baking sheet. Bake at 450° for 15 minutes. Reduce heat to 350° (do not open oven door). Bake 15-20 minutes longer or until deep golden brown (do not underbake). Serve immediately. **Yield:** 8 popovers.

Hoosier Cream Pie

- 3/4 cup sugar
- 1/4 cup cornstarch
- 1/4 teaspoon salt
- 2-1/2 cups milk
- 3 egg yolks, lightly beaten
- 2 tablespoons butter
- 1-1/2 teaspoons vanilla extract
- 3 medium firm bananas
- 1 pastry shell (9 inches), baked

MERINGUE:
- 3 egg whites
- 1/4 teaspoon cream of tartar
- 6 tablespoons sugar

In a saucepan, combine the sugar, cornstarch and salt. Stir in milk until smooth. Cook and stir over medium-high heat until thickened and bubbly. Reduce heat; cook and stir for 2 minutes. Remove from the heat. Stir a small amount of hot filling into egg yolks; return all to the pan. Bring to a gentle boil; cook and stir for 2 minutes. Stir in butter and vanilla until butter is melted; keep warm. Slice bananas into the pastry shell.

In a mixing bowl, beat egg whites and cream of tartar on medium speed until soft peaks form. Gradually beat in sugar, 1 tablespoon at a time, on high until stiff glossy peaks form and sugar is dissolved. Pour hot filling over bananas. Spread meringue evenly over filling, sealing edges to crust.

Bake at 350° for 15 minutes or until meringue is golden brown. Cool on a wire rack for 1 hour. Refrigerate for at least 3 hours before serving. Store leftovers in the refrigerator. **Yield:** 6-8 servings.

Getting in the Theme of Things

Any day can taste like a holiday when you liven it up with the creative treats in this recipe-packed chapter.

MAKE IT MARVELOUS. Clockwise from upper left: Baby Shower Buffet Feeds a Bunch (p. 296), Bugs Buzz In for Summer Supper (p. 298), Bonnets Top Off Easter Brunch (p. 294) and Christmas Tea Steeped In Tradition (p. 292).

Christmas Tea Steeped In Tradition

By Linda Ault, Newberry, Indiana

TWO FRIENDS and I were hostesses for our study club's December meeting, which was to include a program about England. So the three of us decided to make the gathering a Christmas Tea.

We set tables for four with white linen cloths, Christmas china, a teapot and quilted tea cozies in holiday prints.

Egg 'n' Cress Tea Sandwiches, Date-Nut Fruitcake, Christmas Petits Fours and Hot Spiced Tea were all inspired by the types of treats that were traditionally served at Victorian tea parties.

The Egg 'n' Cress Tea Sandwiches looked very festive when we cut them out with a holly leaf cookie cutter. We used both white and wheat bread to vary the color and flavor.

Unlike traditional fruitcake, with its dark color and dense texture, our Date-Nut Fruitcake was light-colored and light-textured, flavored with orange, coconut, dates, raisins and nuts. It was baked in a fluted cake pan to give it a different shape.

The pretty, dainty Christmas Petits Fours were attractive and fun to make. You can trim them simply with sprinkles or more elegantly, as time allows.

The Hot Spiced Tea we served was delightful.

Everyone enjoyed its spicy cranberry flavor and wonderful aroma!

Wreath-shaped candy canes made cute easy napkin rings. And we found booklets titled *Christmas Tea Time*, with holiday stories, poems and recipes, to give as favors.

The afternoon was a huge success! All of us agreed this holiday theme would work for other groups. So, in the spirit on Christmas, I'm happy to share it!

Egg 'n' Cress Tea Sandwiches

- 4 hard-cooked eggs, finely chopped
- 1/4 cup snipped watercress, chives *or* parsley
- 2 tablespoons chopped stuffed olives
- 2 tablespoons mayonnaise
- 1/4 teaspoon salt
- 1/4 teaspoon white pepper
- 2 tablespoons butter, softened
- 8 thin slices whole wheat *and/or* white bread

In a small bowl, combine the eggs, watercress, olives, mayonnaise, salt and pepper; mix well. Spread butter over one side of each slice of bread.

Spread egg mixture over buttered side of four bread slices. Top with remaining bread, buttered side down. Using a 3-in. holly-leaf-shaped cookie cutter, cut out two tea sandwiches from each sandwich. **Yield:** 8 tea sandwiches.

Date-Nut Fruitcake

   1 cup butter, softened
   2 cups sugar
   4 eggs
3-1/2 cups all-purpose flour
   1 teaspoon baking soda
   1/2 cup buttermilk
   1 cup flaked coconut
   1 cup golden raisins
   1 cup chopped dates
   1 cup chopped pecans
   2 tablespoons grated orange peel
GLAZE:
   1/3 cup sugar
   3 tablespoons orange juice
   1 tablespoon grated orange peel

In large mixing bowl, cream butter and sugar. Add eggs; mix well. Combine flour and baking soda. Add to creamed mixture alternately with buttermilk; mix well. Stir in the coconut, raisins, dates, pecans and orange peel. Spoon into a greased and floured 10-in. fluted tube pan. Bake at 300° for 85-95 minutes or until a toothpick inserted near the center comes out clean.

Cool for 10 minutes before removing from pan to a wire rack. Place a piece of waxed paper under rack. In a small saucepan, bring the sugar and orange juice to a boil; boil for 1 minute. Stir in orange peel. Poke holes in cake with a long wooden skewer; gradually spoon glaze over fruitcake. Cool completely. **Yield:** 16 servings.

Christmas Petits Fours

   2 eggs
   2 egg yolks
   1 cup sugar
   2 cups all-purpose flour
   2 teaspoons baking powder
   1/2 cup milk
   5 tablespoons butter, melted
GLAZE:
   4 cups sugar
   2 cups water

   1/4 teaspoon cream of tartar
   3 cups confectioners' sugar
   1 tube *each* red and green decorating
     frosting
Holiday sprinkles

In a large mixing bowl, beat the eggs and egg yolks until slightly thickened. Gradually add sugar, beating until thick and lemon-colored. Combine flour and baking powder. Add to egg mixture gradually with milk and butter; mix well (batter will be thick).

Spead evenly into a greased and floured 15-in. x 10-in. x 1-in. baking pan. Bake at 350° for 12-15 minutes or until a toothpick inserted near the center comes out clean.

Cool for 10 minutes; invert onto a wire rack to cool completely. Cut a thin slice off each side of cake. Cut cake into 1-1/4-in. squares. Freeze cakes.

In a large saucepan, combine the sugar, water and cream of tartar. Bring to a boil, without stirring, until a candy thermometer reaches 226°. Cool to 100°; beat in confectioners' sugar until smooth. Keeping glaze warm, dip cake squares into glaze with a two-tine fork, allowing excess to drip off. Place on wire racks over waxed paper. Add hot water, 1 teaspoon at a time, if glaze becomes too thick. Let dry completely. Decorate with frosting and sprinkles. **Yield:** 35 servings.

Editor's Note: We recommend that you test your candy thermometer before each use by bringing water to a boil; the thermometer should read 212°. Adjust your recipe temperature up or down based on your test.

Hot Spiced Tea

   2 cinnamon sticks
   6 to 12 whole allspice
   1 teaspoon whole cloves
   12 cups water
   12 individual tea bags
   1 cup packed brown sugar
   1 cup cranberry juice
   1/2 cup orange juice
   1/4 cup lemon juice

Place cinnamon sticks, allspice and cloves on a double thickness of cheesecloth. Bring up corners of cloth; tie with a string to form a bag. Place water and spice bag in large saucepan; bring to a boil.

Remove from the heat. Add tea bags; cover and steep for 5 minutes. Discard tea bags and spice bag. Stir in brown sugar until dissolved. Add juices; heat through. Serve warm. **Yield:** 3 quarts.

Bonnets Top Off Easter Brunch

By Lois Jacobsen, Dallas, Wisconsin

"IN YOUR Easter Bonnet, with all the frills upon it…"

That classic yet familiar song came to mind when my sister, Laurie Neverman, and I put our heads together to come up with an Easter theme meal. The "bonnets" we made for our family's brunch would've been the envy of any Easter parade-goer!

My fashionable creation was Pink Bonnet Gelatin, shaped like a fancy hat with fruit-scallop brim. Laurie's Bavarian Cream Bonnet was also an eye-catcher. She decorated the top of her lovely dessert with fruit arranged in a flower design.

Our main course was Spring-Ahead Brunch Bake, an enchilada-style dish that can be made ahead.

We asked our mom, Irene Zmrazek, to bake her famous Caramel-Pecan Cinnamon Rolls in a cross-shaped pan for the gathering. They're irresistible!

It was a joyful day, with plenty of good food. Our delicious hats were such a hit. Hopefully, they will inspire you to plan a delicious parade of your own.

Pink Bonnet Gelatin

- 1 cup ginger ale
- 1 package (3 ounces) strawberry *or* cherry gelatin
- 1 can (15 ounces) fruit cocktail, drained
- 1-1/2 cups cooked rice, chilled
- 1 carton (12 ounces) whipped topping
- 2 red Fruit by the Foot fruit rolls
- 1 cup sliced fresh strawberries
- Silk flowers, optional

In a small saucepan, bring ginger ale to a boil. Remove from the heat; stir in gelatin until dissolved. Cover and refrigerate for 1 hour or until partially set. Stir in fruit cocktail and rice. Fold in whipped topping. Spoon 2 cups mixture into a 9-in. pie plate lined with plastic wrap.

Spoon remaining mixture into a 1-qt. round-bottomed bowl lined with plastic wrap. Cover and refrigerate for 4 hours or until set. Invert gelatin in pie plate onto a serving platter. Invert gelatin from bowl on top. Wrap fruit rolls around the hat and tie into a bow. Garnish with strawberries and silk flowers if desired. **Yield:** 12 servings.

Bavarian Cream Bonnet

1/2 cup sugar
1 envelope unflavored gelatin
1/4 teaspoon salt
2-1/4 cups milk
4 egg yolks, beaten
1 teaspoon vanilla extract
1 cup heavy whipping cream, whipped
1 green fruit roll-up
Blueberries, strawberry halves, peach slices and kiwifruit wedges

In a large saucepan, combine the sugar, gelatin and salt. Whisk in milk and egg yolks. Let stand for 1 minute. Bring to a boil over medium heat; cook and stir for 12 minutes or until mixture is thick enough to coat a metal spoon.

Remove from heat. Place pan in a bowl of ice water; stir for 2 minutes. Stir in vanilla. Transfer to a bowl; press plastic wrap onto surface. Refrigerate for 1 to 1-1/2 hours or until thickened, but not set.

Fold in whipped cream. Transfer to a 9-in. round pan lined with plastic wrap and coated with nonstick cooking spray. Cover; refrigerate until firm. Invert onto a serving platter; remove plastic. Cut fruit roll-up into strips with a width equal to the height of the Bavarian cream. Wrap strips around bonnet; tie into a bow. Garnish with fruit **Yield:** 8 servings.

Spring-Ahead Brunch Bake

2 cups sliced fresh mushrooms
1/2 cup sliced green onions
1/2 cup chopped green pepper
2 tablespoons butter
8 slices deli ham
8 flour tortillas (7 inches)
1-1/2 cups (6 ounces) shredded Swiss cheese
1/2 cup shredded cheddar cheese
1 tablespoon all-purpose flour
4 eggs
2 cups milk
1/4 teaspoon garlic powder
1/4 teaspoon salt
1/8 teaspoon hot pepper sauce

In a large skillet, saute mushrooms, onions and green pepper in butter until tender; set aside. Place one slice of ham on each tortilla. Top each with

about 1/4 cup mushroom mixture. Combine cheeses; set aside 1/4 cup. Sprinkle remaining cheese over tortillas.

Roll up tortillas. Place seam side down in a greased 11-in. x 7-in. x 2-in. baking dish. In a large bowl, beat the flour, eggs, milk, garlic powder, salt and hot pepper sauce until blended. Pour over tortillas. Sprinkle with reserved cheese. Cover and refrigerate for at least 30 minutes. Bake, uncovered, at 350° for 35-45 minutes or until set. Cut into slices. **Yield:** 8 servings.

Caramel-Pecan Cinnamon Rolls

2 packages (1/4 ounce *each*) active dry yeast
1 cup warm milk (110° to 115°)
2 eggs
5 tablespoons butter, softened
1/2 cup sugar
1 teaspoon salt
4-1/2 to 5 cups all-purpose flour
CARAMEL SAUCE:
1 cup butter, cubed
2 cups packed brown sugar
1/4 cup corn syrup
1/2 to 3/4 cup chopped pecans
FILLING:
2 tablespoons butter, melted
1/2 cup sugar
1 teaspoon ground cinnamon

In a large mixing bowl, dissolve yeast in warm milk. Add the eggs, butter, sugar, salt and 3 cups flour. Beat until smooth. Stir in enough remaining flour to form a soft dough. Turn onto a lightly floured surface; knead until smooth and elastic, about 6-8 minutes. Place in a greased bowl, turning once to grease top. Cover and let rise in a warm place until doubled, about 1 hour.

Meanwhile, for sauce, melt butter in a large saucepan. Stir in the brown sugar and corn syrup. Bring to a boil over medium heat for 2 minutes, stirring constantly. Pour into a greased 13-in. x 9-in. x 2-in. baking dish. Sprinkle with pecans; set aside.

Punch dough down. Turn onto a floured surface. Roll into a 17-in. x 15-in. rectangle. Spread butter to within 1/2 in. of edges. Combine sugar and cinnamon; sprinkle over dough. Roll up jelly-roll style, starting with a long side; pinch seams to seal.

Cut into 15 slices. Place cut side down over caramel sauce. Cover; let rise until doubled, about 30 minutes. Bake at 350° for 30-35 minutes or until golden brown. Let stand 5 minutes; invert onto a serving platter. **Yield:** 15 rolls.

Baby Shower Buffet Feeds a Bunch

By Betty Otten, Tea, South Dakota

WHEN I was planning a shower for our first grandbaby, our son suggested a couples' shower instead of the traditional "women only" party.

What a wonderful idea, I thought to myself. But that would mean double the number of guests and at least twice the amount of food. I quickly came up with some of my favorite crowd recipes and renamed them for the occasion.

I planned a menu to serve 50-some people, choosing easy tried-and-true recipes. Many of the dishes could be made ahead, which saved me time the day of the party.

A hearty sloppy joe sandwich always goes over well with our bunch, so my saucy, slightly sweet version became Baby-ques for the shower.

Sweet Pea Salad is a popular accompaniment I usually make with elbow macaroni. But to better fit the theme, I substituted bow tie pasta in my recipe.

Another side dish with broad appeal, Cabbage Patch Coleslaw is nice and crispy. Sour cream blends well with the cider vinegar, oil and seasonings in the dressing.

The recipe for Rock-a-Bye Baby Punch couldn't be much simpler, but both men and women enjoy its refreshing frothy taste. It's not too sweet and is such a pretty color.

The happy couple chose not to know the baby's gender ahead of time, but I had both bases covered! I found paper goods and candy available in the perfect pastel colors for both Easter and spring—pink, blue, yellow and green. Balloon bouquets added to the festivity as we decorated the church hall for the shower.

Men and women alike commented on how nice it was to include the guys for the baby shower. And my easy menu for a crowd worked out so well that I'm happy to share it. I hope you can use it to welcome someone new into the world, too.

Baby-ques

14 pounds ground beef
1 can (50 ounces) condensed tomato soup, undiluted
2 cans (14-1/2 ounces *each*) diced tomatoes, drained
2-1/2 cups barbecue sauce
3/4 cup grape jelly
2 tablespoons *each* garlic powder, onion powder and chili powder
2 teaspoons pepper
1/2 teaspoon ground mustard
4-1/2 to 5-1/2 dozen sandwich buns, split

In two large Dutch ovens or soup kettles, cook beef over medium heat until no longer pink; drain. Combine the tomato soup, tomatoes, barbecue sauce, jelly, garlic powder, on on powder, chili powder, pepper and mustard; stir half into each pan. Cook over medium heat for 15 minutes or until thickened and heated through. Serve on buns. **Yield:** 54-66 servings.

Sweet Pea Salad

5 pounds uncooked bow tie pasta
1 pound carrots, shredded
1 package (16 ounces) frozen peas, thawed
10 celery ribs, diced
1 small onion, finely chopped
5 cups mayonnaise
4 cups sweetened condensed milk
2-1/2 cups sugar
3/4 cup cider vinegar
3/4 cup buttermilk
2 teaspoons salt
1 teaspoon pepper

Cook pasta according to package directions; drain. In three large bowls, combine the pasta, carrots, peas, celery and onion. In a large bowl, combine the remaining ingredients. Stir a third of the dressing into each bowl of pasta mixture. Cover and refrigerate until chilled. **Yield:** 58 (3/4-cup) servings.

Cabbage Patch Coleslaw

4 cups sugar
2 cups cider vinegar
2 cups vegetable oil
1 teaspoon celery seed
4 large heads cabbage, shredded
8 medium carrots, shredded
2 large onions, finely chopped
2 cups (16 ounces) sour cream
2 teaspoons salt
1 teaspoon pepper
1 teaspoon ground mustard

In a large saucepan, combine sugar, vinegar and oil. Bring to a boil, stirring occasionally. Remove from heat; stir in celery seed. Cool completely.

In two large bowls, combine the cabbage, carrots and onions. Add the celery seed mixture, sour cream, salt, pepper and mustard; mix well. Cover and refrigerate until chilled. **Yield:** 48-55 (3/4-cup) servings.

Rock-a-Bye Baby Punch

3 quarts raspberry sherbet, softened
6 liters ginger ale, chilled

Just before serving, place the sherbet in punch bowls. Add the ginger ale; stir until sherbet is almost melted. **Yield:** about 2 gallons (about 64 half-cup servings).

✑ Quantities for a Crowd

When planning a buffet, use this guide to estimate how much you'll need per person. Keep in mind, if you offer more than one item from each category, the less you'll need per serving.

Beverages
3/4 cup of coffee or tea
24 ounces of soft drinks, juices, lemonade or bottled water
1 cup of milk

Breads
1 to 2 slices of bread
1 biscuit, roll or muffin

Salads
1 cup of green salads
1/2 cup of fruit, potato or pasta salads

Condiments
3 to 4 pickle slices or 1 pickle spear
3 olives
1 ounce of ketchup, mustard and pickle relish

Meats
4 to 6 ounces of meat, fish or poultry
1 to 2 ounces of sliced luncheon meat

Dairy
1 teaspoon (1 pat) of butter for bread
1 ounce of sliced cheese for sandwiches
2 tablespoons of cream for coffee

Miscellaneous
1 ounce of potato or corn chips
3 to 4 ounces of ice for beverages

Desserts
1/2 cup of ice cream or frozen yogurt
1 portion of cake or pie

Bugs Buzz In for Summer Supper

By Lenore Walters, Oklahoma City, Oklahoma

IT REALLY bugged me that I was unable to have a birthday party when our son Adam turned 8 because I wasn't feeling well. So I decided that we'd have a gathering for him in the summertime...and I let my feelings inspire the theme.

I served a supper of "way cool bugs", including Fly Burgers, Butterfly Cheese Sandwiches, Cheese Worms with Grasshopper Dip and a Ladybug Cake...plus "swamp" punch with gummy worms hanging off each glass.

I used a cookie cutter to shape the Butterfly Cheese Sandwiches, then decorated them using olives and piped cream cheese. I made "wings" for the Fly Burgers by cutting a narrow V shape in the tops of the buns. Green onion "eyes" peered out from the patties.

Turning string cheese snacks into wiggly worms was simply a matter of poking in whole cloves for the eyes. (We reminded the kids to be sure to remove these before eating the worms.)

For serving the dip, I halved and seeded a green pepper, then added olives for eyes and green onion "legs".

A bright Ladybug Cake for dessert stole the show. It was really easy to make. I baked the batter in a bowl, colored the frosting a vivid red with paste food coloring and used licorice and gumdrop trims.

The buffet table was swarming with flies, ants and other plastic bugs I found at a novelty shop. I also cut out a few large bugs from construction paper and laminated them...and used them as decorative accents around the house.

The amusing invasion of insects—both edible and otherwise—made the party very special. Since it turned out so well, I wanted to share the idea. Some of you might be game for this infestation of fun, too!

Fly Burgers

- **8 frozen bread dough dinner rolls, thawed**
- **1 pound ground beef**
- **1 egg**
- **1/4 cup ketchup**
- **32 thin green onion slices**

Cut each roll in half; shape each into a ball. Place on an ungreased baking sheet; flatten slightly. Cover and let rise until doubled, about 30 minutes. Bake at 350° for 10-12 minutes or until lightly browned. Cool on a wire rack.

In a bowl, combine beef and egg; mix well. Shape into 16 patties, 2 in. each. In a large skillet, cook patties over medium heat until no longer pink. Drain on paper towels.

Split rolls; place a beef patty on each bottom. For wings, cut a narrow V shape from each roll top; position on each patty (discard removed sections). Secure with toothpicks. For eyes, pipe two dots of ketchup near the edge of each patty opposite the V; top with onion slices. **Yield:** 16 sandwiches.

Butterfly Cheese Sandwiches

    1 package (8 ounces) cream cheese, softened
    2 tablespoons milk
  1/2 teaspoon garlic powder
  1/2 teaspoon onion powder
   12 slices white bread
   12 slices American cheese
   22 pitted ripe olives

In a small mixing bowl, beat the cream cheese, milk, garlic powder and onion powder until smooth; set aside 1/4 cup mixture. Spread 1 tablespoon of the remaining cream cheese mixture over each slice of bread. Top each with a cheese slice. Cut out each sandwich with a butterfly-shaped cookie cutter. Discard trimmings.

Cut 12 olives in half lengthwise; place two halves, cut side down, in the center of each sandwich for butterfly body. Cut remaining whole olives into slices; place two on each wing. Set olive ends aside.

Cut a small hole in the corner of a pastry or plastic bag; insert a small star tip. Fill bag with reserved cream cheese mixture. Pipe a star on each olive slice; pipe two stars on front of each butterfly body for eyes. Cut olive ends into small pieces; place on eyes. **Yield:** 1 dozen.

Cheese Worms with Grasshopper Dip

Flaked coconut
Green liquid food coloring
   24 whole cloves
    6 plain mozzarella string cheese sticks
    6 twirled mozzarella cheese sticks*
DIP BOWLS:
    1 medium green pepper
   12 green onions
    2 pitted ripe olives
Dip of your choice

Place coconut in a resealable plastic bag; add food coloring and shake until color is evenly distributed. Sprinkle coconut onto a serving plate. Press two cloves into one end of each cheese stick for worm eyes. As cheese sticks reach room temperature, they can be positioned to appear more worm-like.

Cut green pepper in half lengthwise. Remove and discard stem and seeds. Cut the white portion from green onions; save for another use. Bend the green portion of onions in half for legs. Attach six legs to each pepper half with toothpicks. For eyes, cut olives widthwise in half; attach to grasshoppers with toothpicks. Fill pepper halves with dip. Remove cloves from worms before eating. **Yield:** 12 cheese worms and 2 grasshopper bowls.

*Editor's Note: This recipe was tested with Sargento Twirls. Look for them in the dairy aisle of your grocery store.

Ladybug Cake

    1 package (18-1/4 ounces) chocolate cake mix
1-1/4 cups water
  1/3 cup vegetable oil
    3 eggs
    1 tablespoon mayonnaise
1-1/3 cups vanilla frosting
Red paste food coloring
    2 large white gumdrops
    3 large black gumdrops
    1 strip black rope licorice
    1 piece black shoestring licorice

In a large mixing bowl, beat the cake mix, water, oil, eggs and mayonnaise on low speed for 30 seconds. Beat on medium for 2 minutes. Pour into a greased and floured 2-qt. ovenproof bowl.

Bake at 350° for 60-70 minutes or until a toothpick inserted near the center comes out clean. Cool for 10 minutes before removing from bowl to a wire rack to cool completely. Place on a serving plate.

In a small mixing bowl, combine the frosting and food coloring. Spread over cake. For eyes, flatten white gumdrops and shape into ovals; place on ladybug. Cut black gumdrops horizontally into three slices; discard tops. Slightly flatten slices; place two on white gumdrops for pupils, securing with a toothpick if necessary. Arrange remaining slices on body for spots, pressing down gently.

Cut rope licorice into six pieces; insert into cake for legs. Cut a small piece from the shoestring licorice; add for mouth. **Yield:** 12-16 servings.

Have Fun with a Fiesta Party!

By Terri Newton, Marshall, Texas

WHEN my friend Cynthia turned 40, another friend and I decided a fiesta was in order! Rather than plan a meal, we decided on a buffet of appetizers and desserts. Three of the most popular foods were Tex-Mex Dip, Chili Pepper Cookies and Cactus Cake.

Perfect for a party, Tex-Mex Dip is a real crowd-pleaser. Ingredients in the recipe blend very well, and it makes a large platterful.

Cut out to look like their namesake, Chili Pepper Cookies were sweet treats at the celebration. We used a favorite recipe that makes a tender, slightly soft sugar cookie. By tinting the frosting and adding some colored sugar sprinkles, these can be decorated without a lot of fuss. They really say "fiesta".

The birthday cake was succulent—a Cactus Cake! I "doctored up" two white cake mixes and baked them in 13- by 9-inch pans. When the cakes had cooled, I cut them into several pieces to put together a cactus shape.

Colorful pottery serving pieces, chili pepper paper plates, and brightly colored napkins and tablecloths lent a festive look to the buffet tables. Cynthia had a memorable 40th birthday, and everyone had a *tiempo bueno*—a good time!

Tex-Mex Dip

      1 can (16 ounces) refried beans
    1/4 cup picante sauce
  1-1/2 cups prepared guacamole
    1/2 cup *each* sour cream and mayonnaise
  4-1/2 teaspoons taco seasoning
      1 cup (4 ounces) shredded cheddar cheese
      1 can (2-1/4 ounces) sliced ripe olives, drained
Chopped green onions, shredded lettuce and chopped tomatoes
Tortilla chips

Combine beans and picante sauce. Spread onto a serving platter. Spread with guacamole. Combine sour cream, mayonnaise and taco seasoning; spread over guacamole. Sprinkle with cheese, olives, onions, lettuce and tomatoes. Refrigerate until serving with tortilla chips. **Yield:** 12-14 servings.

Chili Pepper Cookies

  3/4 cup butter-flavored shortening
    1 cup packed brown sugar

1/4 **cup sugar**
1 **egg**
2 **tablespoons milk**
1 **tablespoon vanilla extract**
2-1/4 **cups all-purpose flour**
3/4 **teaspoon baking soda**
1/8 **teaspoon salt**
BUTTERCREAM FROSTING:
1/2 **cup butter, softened**
4-1/2 **cups confectioners' sugar**
2 **teaspoons vanilla extract**
3 **to 5 tablespoons milk**
Green and red gel food coloring
Green and red colored sugar

In a small mixing bowl, cream shortening and sugars. Beat in the egg, milk and vanilla. Combine the flour, baking soda and salt; gradually add to creamed mixture. Cover and refrigerate for 2 hours or until easy to handle.

On a lightly floured surface, roll and pat out dough to 1/4-in. thickness. Cut with a floured 3-1/2-in. chili pepper-shaped cookie cutter. Place 1 in. apart on ungreased baking sheets. Bake at 325° for 6-8 minutes or until edges are lightly browned. Remove to wire racks to cool.

In a mixing bowl, beat the butter, confectioners' sugar, vanilla and enough milk until frosting reaches spreading consistency. Tint 1/3 cup green; set aside. Tint remaining frosting red. Frost "peppers" red and "stems" green; sprinkle with matching sugar. **Yield:** about 4 dozen.

Cactus Cake

2 **packages (18-1/4 ounces *each*) white cake mix**
2 **envelopes whipped topping mix**
2-1/2 **cups milk**
6 **eggs**
2/3 **cup vegetable oil**
4 **teaspoons vanilla extract**
BUTTERCREAM FROSTING:
1 **cup butter, softened**
9 **cups confectioners' sugar**
4 **teaspoons vanilla extract**
6 **to 10 tablespoons milk**
Red and green gel food coloring
Chocolate sprinkles and M&M's miniature baking bits

In a large mixing bowl, combine the first six ingredients; beat on low speed for 30 seconds. Beat on medium for 2 minutes.

Pour into two greased and floured 13-in. x 9-in.

x 2-in. baking pans. Bake at 350° for 30-35 minutes or until a toothpick inserted near the center comes out clean. Cool for 10 minutes before removing from pans to wire racks. Cool completely.

Level cake tops. Referring to Fig. 1 (below), cut a 12-in. x 3-1/2-in. strip from one long side of one cake. Place larger rectangle on a 20-in. x 18-in. covered board for cactus stem; place strip below it for the base. Round top corners of cactus stem.

Referring to Fig. 2, cut two 5-1/2-in. squares from second cake for branches. Cut a 3-in. square from one corner of each 5-1/2-in. square. (Save remaining cake for another use.) Position one branch on each side of stem. Round top corners of branches.

In a mixing bowl, cream butter. Gradually add confectioners' sugar, beating well. Add vanilla and enough milk to achieve spreading consistency. Frost base with 1 cup frosting. Tint 1/4 cup frosting red; set aside. Tint remaining frosting green; frost cactus.

Cut a small hole in the corner of a pastry or plastic bag; insert round tip #3. Fill with red frosting. Pipe "Fiesta" and wavy designs on top and sides of base. Decorate cactus with sprinkles; decorate base with baking bits. **Yield:** 24-30 servings.

Fig. 1: **13" x 9" Cake**

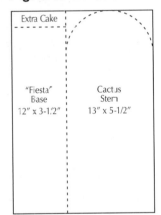

Extra Cake

"Fiesta" Base
12" x 3-1/2"

Cactus Stem
13" x 5-1/2"

Fig. 2: **13" x 9" Cake**

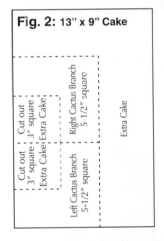

Cut out 3" square
Extra Cake

Cut out 3" square
Extra Cake

Right Cactus Branch 5-1/2" square

Left Cactus Branch 5-1/2" square

Extra Cake

Family Enjoys Pumpkin Pickin' Potluck

By Barb Schlafer, Appleton, Wisconsin

OUR FAMILY'S annual Pumpkin Patch Party, held at my sister's country place, is a wonderful way to celebrate fall. Molly and her husband, Bob Tews, built a home on 5 acres near Dale, Wisconsin several years ago. The "farmer" in Bob surfaced when he purchased a tractor and began planting sweet corn, sunflowers, gourds and lots of pumpkins.

When the produce is ripe, our relatives from all over the state gather for the party. Bob dons bib overalls and hauls us out to the pumpkin patch in a wagon behind his tractor. After we take our pick of the patch, we have a potluck meal at the edge of the field.

Most everyone's dish-to-pass is a pumpkin or Halloween theme. Scarecrow Chili, Pumpkin Patch Bread, Spooky Chocolate Cupcakes and Peter Peter Pumpkin Bars were a few of the choices on last year's buffet.

The hungry bunch enthusiastically ladled up my thick Scarecrow Chili. It has a hearty flavor but isn't too spicy, so even the younger kids like it.

Our mom makes the best Pumpkin Patch Bread! She knows it's a "must bring" each year.

Spooky Chocolate Cupcakes, decorated with bats, black cats, webs and ghosts, disappeared fast!

The sweet tooths also polished off Peter Peter Pumpkin Bars. They have a delicious orange frosting and can be decorated with candy pumpkins.

All of the "city kids" in our family love coming to the country for this special day. We have such a good time!

Scarecrow Chili

1-1/2 pounds ground beef
    2 celery ribs, chopped
    1 medium onion, chopped
    1 can (46 ounces) tomato juice
    1 can (28 ounces) diced tomatoes, undrained
    1 can (16 ounces) kidney beans, rinsed and drained
    1 can (10-3/4 ounces) condensed tomato soup, undiluted
1/2 cup water
    2 tablespoons chili powder

1 to 2 tablespoons brown sugar
3 bay leaves
Salt and pepper to taste
2 cups elbow macaroni, cooked and drained

In a Dutch oven, cook beef, celery and onion over medium heat until meat is no longer pink; drain. Add tomato juice, tomatoes, beans, soup, water, chili powder, brown sugar, bay leaves, salt and pepper. Bring to a boil. Reduce heat; cover and simmer for 30 minutes. Stir in macaroni. Cook, uncovered, 5 minutes or until heated through. Discard bay leaves. **Yield:** 16 servings (4 quarts).

Pumpkin Patch Bread

1-1/2 cups sugar
1 cup canned pumpkin
1/2 cup vegetable oil
1/2 cup water
2 eggs
1-2/3 cups all-purpose flour
1 teaspoon baking soda
3/4 teaspoon salt
1/2 teaspoon *each* ground cloves, cinnamon
 and nutmeg
1/4 teaspoon baking powder
1/2 cup chopped pecans

In a mixing bowl, combine first five ingredients. Combine flour, baking soda, salt, spices and baking powder; gradually add to pumpkin mixture. Fold in pecans. Pour into a greased 9-in. x 5-in. x 3-in. loaf pan. Bake at 350° for 70-80 minutes or until a toothpick comes out clean. Cool for 10 minutes; remove from pan to a wire rack to cool completely. **Yield:** 1 loaf.

Spooky Chocolate Cupcakes

3 cups all-purpose flour
2 cups sugar
1/2 cup baking cocoa
2 teaspoons baking soda
1 teaspoon salt
2 cups water
1 cup vegetable oil
2 teaspoons white vinegar
2 teaspoons vanilla extract
FROSTING:
1/2 cup shortening
1/2 cup butter, softened
4-1/4 cups confectioners' sugar

3 tablespoons water
1/2 teaspoon vanilla extract
1/8 teaspoon almond extract
Black paste food coloring
Orange and black M&M's
Tart-N-Tiny candies

In a bowl, combine dry ingredients. Combine water, oil, vinegar and vanilla; stir into dry ingredients just until moistened. Fill greased or paper-lined muffin cups two-thirds full. Bake at 350° for 15-18 minutes or until a toothpick comes out clean. Cool for 5 minutes; remove from pans to wire racks.

In a mixing bowl, cream shortening, butter and confectioners' sugar. Stir in water and extracts. Remove 1/2 cup frosting to a small bowl; tint with black food coloring. Frost cupcakes with remaining white frosting. Cut a small hole in corner of a pastry or plastic bag. Insert a small round #5 tip; fill bag with black frosting. Decorate cupcakes with black frosting and candies. **Yield:** 2 dozen.

Peter Peter Pumpkin Bars

1/2 cup shortening
1 cup packed brown sugar
2 eggs
2/3 cup canned pumpkin
1 teaspoon vanilla extract
1 cup all-purpose flour
1 teaspoon ground cinnamon
1/2 teaspoon baking powder
1/2 teaspoon baking soda
1/4 teaspoon *each* ground ginger and nutmeg
1/2 cup chopped walnuts
ORANGE FROSTING:
3 tablespoons shortening
2-1/4 cups confectioners' sugar
3 tablespoons orange juice
1 tablespoon grated orange peel
Candy pumpkins

In a large mixing bowl, cream shortening and brown sugar. Add eggs, one at a time, beating well after each addition. Beat in pumpkin and vanilla. Combine the flour, cinnamon, baking powder, baking soda, ginger and nutmeg; add to creamed mixture and mix well. Stir in nuts.

Spread into a greased 13-in. x 9-in. x 2-in. baking dish. Bake at 350° for 20-25 minutes or until a toothpick comes out clean. Cool on a wire rack.

In a mixing bowl, beat the shortening, confectioners' sugar, orange juice and peel until blended. Frost bars; cut into squares. Top with candy pumpkins. **Yield:** 2 dozen.

Substitutions & Equivalents

Equivalent Measures

3 teaspoons	=	1 tablespoon	16 tablespoons	=	1 cup
4 tablespoons	=	1/4 cup	2 cups	=	1 pint
5-1/3 tablespoons	=	1/3 cup	4 cups	=	1 quart
8 tablespoons	=	1/2 cup	4 quarts	=	1 gallon

Food Equivalents

Grains

Macaroni	1 cup (3-1/2 ounces) uncooked	= 2-1/2 cups cooked
Noodles, Medium	3 cups (4 ounces) uncooked	= 4 cups cooked
Popcorn	1/3 to 1/2 cup unpopped	= 8 cups popped
Rice, Long Grain	1 cup uncooked	= 3 cups cooked
Rice, Quick-Cooking	1 cup uncooked	= 2 cups cooked
Spaghetti	8 ounces uncooked	= 4 cups cooked

Crumbs

Bread	1 slice	= 3/4 cup soft crumbs, 1/4 cup fine dry crumbs
Graham Crackers	7 squares	= 1/2 cup finely crushed
Buttery Round Crackers	12 crackers	= 1/2 cup finely crushed
Saltine Crackers	14 crackers	= 1/2 cup finely crushed

Fruits

Bananas	1 medium	= 1/3 cup mashed
Lemons	1 medium	= 3 tablespoons juice, 2 teaspoons grated peel
Limes	1 medium	= 2 tablespoons juice, 1-1/2 teaspoons grated peel
Oranges	1 medium	= 1/4 to 1/3 cup juice, 4 teaspoons grated peel

Vegetables

Cabbage	1 head	= 5 cups shredded	**Green Pepper**	1 large	=	1 cup chopped
Carrots	1 pound	= 3 cups shredded	**Mushrooms**	1/2 pound	=	3 cups sliced
Celery	1 rib	= 1/2 cup chopped	**Onions**	1 medium	=	1/2 cup chopped
Corn	1 ear fresh	= 2/3 cup kernels	**Potatoes**	3 medium	=	2 cups cubed

Nuts

Almonds	1 pound	= 3 cups chopped	**Pecan Halves**	1 pound	=	4-1/2 cups chopped
Ground Nuts	3-3/4 ounces	= 1 cup	**Walnuts**	1 pound	=	3-3/4 cups chopped

Easy Substitutions

When you need...		Use...
Baking Powder	1 teaspoon	1/2 teaspoon cream of tartar + 1/4 teaspoon baking soda
Buttermilk	1 cup	1 tablespoon lemon juice *or* vinegar + enough milk to measure 1 cup (let stand 5 minutes before using)
Cornstarch	1 tablespoon	2 tablespoons all-purpose flour
Honey	1 cup	1-1/4 cups sugar + 1/4 cup water
Half-and-Half Cream	1 cup	1 tablespoon melted butter + enough whole milk to measure 1 cup
Onion	1 small, chopped (1/3 cup)	1 teaspoon onion powder *or* 1 tablespoon dried minced onion
Tomato Juice	1 cup	1/2 cup tomato sauce + 1/2 cup water
Tomato Sauce	2 cups	3/4 cup tomato paste + 1 cup water
Unsweetened Chocolate	1 square (1 ounce)	3 tablespoons baking cocoa + 1 tablespoon shortening *or* oil
Whole Milk	1 cup	1/2 cup evaporated milk + 1/2 cup water

Cooking Terms

HERE'S a quick reference for some of the cooking terms used in *Taste of Home* recipes:

Baste—To moisten food with melted butter, pan drippings, marinades or other liquid to add more flavor and juiciness.

Beat—A rapid movement to combine ingredients using a fork, spoon, wire whisk or electric mixer.

Blend—To combine ingredients until *just* mixed.

Boil—To heat liquids until bubbles form that cannot be "stirred down". In the case of water, the temperature will reach 212°.

Bone—To remove all meat from the bone before cooking.

Cream—To beat ingredients together to a smooth consistency, usually in the case of butter and sugar for baking.

Dash—A small amount of seasoning, less than 1/8 teaspoon. If using a shaker, a dash would comprise a quick flip of the container.

Dredge—To coat foods with flour or other dry ingredients. Most often done with pot roasts and stew meat before browning.

Fold—To incorporate several ingredients by careful and gentle turning with a spatula. Used generally with beaten egg whites or whipped cream when mixing into the rest of the ingredients to keep the batter light.

Julienne—To cut foods into long thin strips much like matchsticks. Used most often for salads and stir-fry dishes.

Mince—To cut into very fine pieces. Used often for garlic or fresh herbs.

Parboil—To cook partially, usually used in the case of chicken, sausages and vegetables.

Partially set—Describes the consistency of gelatin after it has been chilled for a small amount of time. Mixture should resemble the consistency of egg whites.

Puree—To process foods to a smooth mixture. Can be prepared in an electric blender, food processor, food mill or sieve.

Saute—To fry quickly in a small amount of fat, stirring almost constantly. Most often done with onions, mushrooms and other chopped vegetables.

Score—To cut slits partway through the outer surface of foods. Often used with ham or flank steak.

Stir-Fry—To cook meats and/or vegetables with a constant stirring motion in a small amount of oil in a wok or skillet over high heat.

Guide to Cooking with Popular Herbs

HERB	APPETIZERS SALADS	BREADS/EGGS SAUCES/CHEESE	VEGETABLES PASTA	MEAT POULTRY	FISH SHELLFISH
BASIL	Green, Potato & Tomato Salads, Salad Dressings, Stewed Fruit	Breads, Fondue & Egg Dishes, Dips, Marinades, Sauces	Mushrooms, Tomatoes, Squash, Pasta, Bland Vegetables	Broiled, Roast Meat & Poultry Pies, Stews, Stuffing	Baked, Broiled & Poached Fish, Shellfish
BAY LEAF	Seafood Cocktail, Seafood Salad, Tomato Aspic, Stewed Fruit	Egg Dishes, Gravies, Marinades, Sauces	Dried Bean Dishes, Beets, Carrots, Onions, Potatoes, Rice, Squash	Corned Beef, Tongue Meat & Poultry Stews	Poached Fish, Shellfish, Fish Stews
CHIVES	Mixed Vegetable, Green, Potato & Tomato Salads, Salad Dressings	Egg & Cheese Dishes, Cream Cheese, Cottage Cheese, Gravies, Sauces	Hot Vegetables, Potatoes	Broiled Poultry, Poultry & Meat Pies, Stews, Casseroles	Baked Fish, Fish Casseroles, Fish Stews, Shellfish
DILL	Seafood Cocktail, Green, Potato & Tomato Salads, Salad Dressings	Breads, Egg & Cheese Dishes, Cream Cheese, Fish & Meat Sauces	Beans, Beets, Cabbage, Carrots, Cauliflower, Peas, Squash, Tomatoes	Beef, Veal Roasts, Lamb, Steaks, Chops, Stews, Roast & Creamed Poultry	Baked, Broiled, Poached & Stuffed Fish, Shellfish
GARLIC	All Salads, Salad Dressings	Fondue, Poultry Sauces, Fish & Meat Marinades	Beans, Eggplant, Potatoes, Rice, Tomatoes	Roast Meats, Meat & Poultry Pies, Hamburgers, Casseroles, Stews	Broiled Fish, Shellfish, Fish Stews, Casseroles
MARJORAM	Seafood Cocktail, Green, Poultry & Seafood Salads	Breads, Cheese Spreads, Egg & Cheese Dishes, Gravies, Sauces	Carrots, Eggplant, Peas, Onions, Potatoes, Dried Bean Dishes, Spinach	Roast Meats & Poultry, Meat & Poultry Pies, Stews & Casseroles	Baked, Broiled & Stuffed Fish, Shellfish
MUSTARD	Fresh Green Salads, Prepared Meat, Macaroni & Potato Salads, Salad Dressings	Biscuits, Egg & Cheese Dishes, Sauces	Baked Beans, Cabbage, Eggplant, Squash, Dried Beans, Mushrooms, Pasta	Chops, Steaks, Ham, Pork, Poultry, Cold Meats	Shellfish
OREGANO	Green, Poultry & Seafood Salads	Breads, Egg & Cheese Dishes, Meat, Poultry & Vegetable Sauces	Artichokes, Cabbage, Eggplant, Squash, Dried Beans, Mushrooms, Pasta	Broiled, Roast Meats, Meat & Poultry Pies, Stews, Casseroles	Baked, Broiled & Poached Fish, Shellfish
PARSLEY	Green, Potato, Seafood & Vegetable Salads	Biscuits, Breads, Egg & Cheese Dishes, Gravies, Sauces	Asparagus, Beets, Eggplant, Squash, Dried Beans, Mushrooms, Pasta	Meat Loaf, Meat & Poultry Pies, Stews & Casseroles, Stuffing	Fish Stews, Stuffed Fish
ROSEMARY	Fruit Cocktail, Fruit & Green Salads	Biscuits, Egg Dishes, Herb Butter, Cream Cheese, Marinades, Sauces	Beans, Broccoli, Peas, Cauliflower, Mushrooms, Baked Potatoes, Parsnips	Roast Meat, Poultry & Meat Pies, Stews & Casseroles, Stuffing	Stuffed Fish, Shellfish
SAGE		Breads, Fondue, Egg & Cheese Dishes, Spreads, Gravies, Sauces	Beans, Beets, Onions, Peas, Spinach, Squash, Tomatoes	Roast Meat, Poultry, Meat Loaf, Stews, Stuffing	Baked, Poached & Stuffed Fish
TARRAGON	Seafood Cocktail, Avocado Salads, Salad Dressings	Cheese Spreads, Marinades, Sauces, Egg Dishes	Asparagus, Beans, Beets, Carrots, Mushrooms, Peas, Squash, Spinach	Steaks, Poultry, Roast Meats, Casseroles & Stews	Baked, Broiled & Poached Fish, Shellfish
THYME	Seafood Cocktail, Green, Poultry, Seafood & Vegetable Salads	Biscuits, Breads, Egg & Cheese Dishes, Sauces, Spreads	Beets, Carrots, Mushrooms, Onions, Peas, Eggplant, Spinach, Potatoes	Roast Meat, Poultry & Meat Loaf, Meat & Poultry Pies, Stews & Casseroles	Baked, Broiled & Stuffed Fish, Shellfish, Fish Stews

General Recipe Index

This handy index lists every recipe by food category, major ingredient and/or cooking method, so you can easily locate recipes to suit your needs.

✓ Recipe includes Nutritional Analysis and Diabetic Exchanges.

✓ *Recipe includes Nutritional Analysis and Diabetic Exchanges.*

✓ Recipe includes Nutritional Analysis and Diabetic Exchanges.

✓ *Recipe includes Nutritional Analysis and Diabetic Exchanges.*

✓ Recipe includes Nutritional Analysis and Diabetic Exchanges.

✓ Recipe includes Nutritional Analysis and Diabetic Exchanges.

✓ *Recipe includes Nutritional Analysis and Diabetic Exchanges.*

✓ Recipe includes Nutritional Analysis and Diabetic Exchanges.

✓ Recipe includes Nutritional Analysis and Diabetic Exchanges.

✓ *Recipe includes Nutritional Analysis and Diabetic Exchanges.*

Alphabetical Recipe Index

*This handy index lists every recipe in alphabetical
order so you can easily find your favorite recipes.*

A

Acorn Cookies, 108
Almond Eggnog Pound Cake, 115
Almond Sugar Cookies, 100
Aniseed Biscotti, 109
✓Apple-Cranberry Wild Rice, 53
Apple Cream Tart, 145
Apple Dumplings, 223
Apple-Feta Tossed Salad, 173
Apple Plum Streusel Dessert, 203
✓Apple Snack Cake, 126
Apple Streusel Ice Cream, 130
✓Applesauce Cake, 121
Apricot Beef Stir-Fry, 257
Apricot Tea Rings, 163
Artichoke Nibbles, 12
Asparagus Crab Omelets, 196
Asparagus Ham Spirals, 9
Asparagus Ham Tartlets, 25
Asparagus Leek Chowder, 47
Asparagus Pasta Primavera, 88
✓Asparagus Salsa, 21
Asparagus Sausage Crepes, 87
Asparagus with Mustard Sauce, 54
Asparagus with Orange Butter, 274

B

Baby-ques, 297
Bacon-Colby Lasagna, 159
Bacon-Egg English Muffin, 194
Bacon Scalloped Potatoes, 196
Baked Mushroom Chicken, 240
✓Baked Pork Chimichangas, 70
Baked Trout Fillets, 67
Baked Venison Burgers, 40
Baked Ziti, 248
Banana-Berry Brownie Pizza, 151
Banana Pound Cake, 127
Barbecue Chicken Wings, 22
Barbecue Turkey Wings, 63
Barbecued Beef Short Ribs, 83
Bavarian Cream Bonnet, 295
Bean 'n' Beef Quesadillas, 78

Bean Sprout Spinach Salad, 206
Beans with Celery Bacon Sauce, 228
Beef 'n' Eggplant Pie, 75
Beefy Corn Bread Casserole, 66
Berry Banana Smoothies, 195
Berry Vinaigrette, 241
Best Baby-Back Ribs, 82
Big Batch Bismarks, 96
Black Bean Soup, 268
✓Black Bean Soup for Two, 184
Black Forest Crepes, 150
Blackberry Crisp, 192
Blue Cheese Deviled Eggs, 165
Blueberry Raspberry Pie, 113
✓Bob's Crab Cakes, 74
Braised Rabbit, 77
Braised Short Ribs, 81
Bread Pudding Pear Pie, 121
✓Breaded Orange Roughy, 68
Breaded Rack of Lamb, 73
Breadsticks with Parmesan
  Butter, 249
Brie in Puff Pastry, 24
Broccoli with Orange Sauce, 236
Broiled Halibut Kabobs, 261
✓Broiled Orange Roughy, 60
Broiled Shrimp Toast, 272
Buckwheat Brunch Crepes, 179
Butter Pecan Ice Cream, 147
Butterflied Pork Chop Dinner, 186
Butterfly Cheese Sandwiches, 299
Buttermilk Lemon Pie, 124
Butternut Apple Crisp, 146
Butternut Cream Pie, 120
Butterscotch Eggnog Stars, 107
Buttery Crescents, 214

C

Cabbage Patch Coleslaw, 297
Cactus Cake, 301
Candy Cane Snowballs, 101
Candy-Topped Bars, 100
Caramel Flan, 131
Caramel-Pecan Cinnamon Rolls, 295
✓Caramelized-Onion Pork, 85
Carrot Zucchini Fritters, 24

Celery Seed Potato Salad, 30
Chai, 263
Cheery Cherry Compote, 158
Cheese Worms with Grasshopper
  Dip, 299
Cheesecake Praline Squares, 241
Cheesy Potatoes 'n' Peppers, 156
Cherry Cheesecake Dessert, 229
Cherry Kolaches, 93
Cherry Nut Ice Cream, 150
Chewy Granola Bars, 24
Chicken Breasts with Fruit
  Salsa, 274
Chicken Parmigiana, 180
Chicken Patties, 80
Chicken Pesto Pizza, 84
Chicken Pom-Poms, 154
Chicken Romaine Salad, 215
Chicken Vegetable Soup, 43
Chicken with Lemon Sauce, 184
Chicken with Paprika Cream, 255
Chili Cheddar Biscuits, 96
Chili Pepper Cookies, 300
✓Chili Stew, 81
Chinese Turkey Pasta Salad, 35
Chippy Blond Brownies, 167
Chocolate Almond Cake, 122
Chocolate Almond Cheesecake, 142
Chocolate Caramel
  Thumbprints, 111
Chocolate Chiffon Torte, 122
Chocolate Chunk Cookies, 249
Chocolate Cream Cake, 117
Chocolate Ice Cream
  Sandwiches, 149
Chocolate Layer Cake, 177
Chocolate Mint Dreams, 101
Chocolate Mousse Cheesecake, 132
Chocolate Peanut Freeze, 137
Chocolate Pecan Ice Cream
  Torte, 147
Chocolate Ribbon Bars, 285
Christmas Petits Fours, 293
Chunky Taco Soup, 40
Cinnamon-Basil Fruit Salad, 36
Cinnamon-Sugar Crisps, 287
Citrus-Ginger Tuna Steaks, 188
Citrus Punch, 237
Coconut Blueberry Cake, 116

✓ Recipe includes Nutritional Analysis and Diabetic Exchanges.

✓ *Recipe includes Nutritional Analysis and Diabetic Exchanges.*

✓ Recipe includes Nutritional Analysis and Diabetic Exchanges.

✓ Recipe includes Nutritional Analysis and Diabetic Exchanges.